Robert Wuthnow is the Gerhard R. Andlinger '52 Professor of Social Sciences at Princeton University and author of numerous books, including *American Mythos: Why Our Best Efforts to Be a Better Nation Fall Short* and *America and the Challenges of Religious Diversity* (both Princeton).

Remaking the Heartland

Remaking the Heartland

Middle America since the 1950s

Robert Wuthnow

PRINCETON UNIVERSITY PRESS

PRINCETON AND OXFORD

Copyright © 2011 by Princeton University Press
Published by Princeton University Press, 41 William Street, Princeton, New Jersey 08540
In the United Kingdom: Princeton University Press, 6 Oxford Street, Woodstock, Oxfordshire
OX20 1TW
press.princeton.edu

Library of Congress Cataloging-in-Publication Data

Wuthnow, Robert.
    Remaking the heartland : Middle America since the 1950s / Robert Wuthnow.
        p. cm.
    Includes bibliographical references and index.
    ISBN 978-0-691-14611-9 (hardback : alk. paper) 1. Middle West—Economic conditions.
2. Middle West—Social conditions. 3. Agriculture—Middle West. 4. Social change—Middle
West. 5. Community development—Middle West. 6. Agriculture—Economic aspects—
Middle West. I. Title.
    HC107.A14W88 2011
    330.977—dc22

                                                                        2010021518

British Library Cataloging-in-Publication Data is available

This book has been composed in ITC Century Std
Printed on acid-free paper. ∞
Printed in the United States of America

10 9 8 7 6 5 4 3 2 1

Contents

Tables

Preface

It may have been that cold windy morning in central Nebraska when I pulled off the highway to watch the sun rise, golden red, across the open fields. That may have been the day I decided to write this book. Or it may have been another day, when I was driving through small towns in eastern Iowa. That moment, perhaps, when a highway marker reminded me of my childhood home. Or it may have been only the slow realization that something there in the nation's heartland was calling me to write about it. Who knows?

What I do recall as vividly as if it were yesterday is listening to a public lecture by a visiting speaker at my university, my mind wandering as it often does, and realizing that I had it all wrong. Well into the research at that point, I was working on the assumption that the heartland was a place of withering decline, like the soil itself gradually eroding away. I thought that was the story that needed to be told. It made sense of small towns with empty storefronts. Large fields with no farmsteads. Reports of joblessness. But it did not square with other evidence. New technology. A surprisingly robust economy. Strong schools. An upbeat feeling among residents about the future. Clearly I needed to think harder about what was happening. By the time I finished with the research, I had a much different story in mind than when I started.

My central claim is that the American Middle West has undergone a strong, positive transformation since the 1950s. The reshaping that occurred in this period is striking because the region was worse off in the years immediately following World War II than has commonly been assumed. The transformation is surprising because it took place in the nation's heartland. Most accounts of dramatic social change have focused on other parts of the country—especially the Sunbelt and coastal cities—not on the Middle West, a region of small towns and farms, wheat fields and prairies. The transformation that occurred here was largely beneficial, notwithstanding the fact that millions of people were displaced from their communities, because this displacement resulted in new opportunities for employment and a healthier relationship between the region and the rest of the nation. By the first decade of the twenty-first century, the Middle West was a more vibrant contributor to the national economy than it had been a half century earlier.

This argument, I confess, is counterintuitive. The typical approach is to regard the American Middle West as a kind of throwback to earlier times, a vast museum of dwindling farms and small towns to be visited by folks who live elsewhere and would not want to stay for very long. The view that things were better in the past fits neatly with a nostalgic image of an America that was in fact rural and less complicated than it is today. A related view popularized in news magazines and schoolbooks showed a heartland in the 1950s prospering from good crops, with happy housewives preparing luscious meals on modern kitchen appliances for grateful husbands and children—a time followed by disappointment and decline. That image of the 1950s may have been true for the few but not for the many. A better sense of how the Middle West has changed over the past five or six decades is gained by thinking of the 1950s as a time when many families were still recovering from the Great Depression. Farmers were again suffering from dust storms, uncertain crops, and wildly fluctuating prices. Farm communities often lacked paved roads, electricity, or dependable telephone service. Millions of people were leaving the farms and rural communities in search of meager employment opportunities elsewhere.

It is also counterintuitive to argue that the Middle West is vibrant economically and culturally. Most depictions of the region's recent history view it as a sad tale of rural people clinging to outmoded lives, of dying communities, and of old-fashioned values tinged with bigotry and ignorance. When writers who pass briefly through the region find other stories to tell, the stories are usually about food the writers romantically wished was still grown in the family garden, smelly feedlots, or undocumented workers being exploited by rich agribusiness owners who reap unjustified millions in government subsidies. But these accounts miss the fact that the region has upgraded itself even as it has downsized. The technology, the new industries, and the cultural diversity of the heartland could hardly have been imagined a half century ago.

The transformation that has occurred in the American Middle West cannot be attributed to any single cause, tempting as it may be to seek answers in the magic of, say, rugged individualism. I break the narrative into several parts. The first is about the struggles of Middle Western farmers in the 1950s. Difficult as those struggles were, they enabled farming to become more efficient and capital intensive. The second is a saga of cultural redefinition. As the Middle West modernized, it rediscovered its legends of hardy pioneers, adventuresome cowboys, and Dust Bowl survivors. It reshaped these legends into a less spatially confined image of congeniality and can-do inventiveness. These new understandings improved the region's self-image and contributed to its ability to transform itself. A third story is about public education. The region invested heavily in schools, administered them well, and encouraged children to regard school achievement as their best hope for occupational success. Higher education became the source of both upward and outward mobility. A fourth story tells of small communities that are dying by the hundreds and yet are not doing so very quickly or completely. Community downsizing has been a matter of great concern to the residents of these communities, but it has worked remarkably well for the region as a whole. Small communities remain attractive for low-income families needing inexpensive housing. Many of these communities are within commuting distance of larger towns where work can be found in construction, manufacturing, and human services. High fuel prices are making it harder for these commuters, but electronic technology and decentralization are opening new opportunities. A fifth story examines the growth of large-scale agribusiness and its effects on the ethnic composition of the region. Contrary to tales about extreme ethnic conflicts, the picture that comes into focus from closer inspection is one of greater diversity over a longer period, continuing difficulties for immigrants and undocumented workers, and yet shows a striking degree of communitywide accommodation to new realities. A final story is about the phenomenon least expected in this part of the county—rapidly expanding edge cities. The growth of these communities has been nothing short of spectacular. And yet the sources of this growth lie in more than simply the availability of land and the decline of smaller towns.

My approach treads the line between history and social science. Change in the heartland is a big topic that can only be grasped by delving deeply into the lives of particular communities, looking at their past, learning from their current residents, and situating these communities in wider comparisons. Much of the change resides in small details that can only be seen in the trajectories of children leaving, stores closing, citizens remembering dust storms and taking pride in their ancestors, neighbors watching out for one another, schools consolidating, residents looking for new jobs, and planners planning. The Middle West is enormously diverse in both its geography and its people. The diversity makes for interesting comparisons. Missouri and Arkansas developed schools quite differently than Iowa and Minnesota. Farming diverged sharply between the grasslands of western Nebraska and the wheat fields of western Kansas. The evidence for these comparisons comes from data on population, crops, schools, and economic conditions; information about the growth and decline of towns and about their business conditions; records of town meetings and planning boards; diaries and newspaper stories; and interviews with more than two hundred residents about farming, school administration, town and county government, agribusiness, and regional planning.

Although no single factor can explain the region's transformation, several preconditions for the social change that has taken place loom large. One is the fact that the region largely comprised rich land with vast potential for crops and livestock and often mineral wealth as well. The region was essentially taken from its native inhabitants and used by the United States for colonization by white settlers, who in turn raised crops and livestock, created a demand for towns and railroads, and for years existed as debtors to eastern banks. During the last half of the twentieth century, the land continued to be a crucial aspect of the region's social life, shaping the location and livelihood of towns, influencing the establishment of agribusiness, providing funds for public schools, and encouraging the development of military and transportation industries. Another precondition may have been less obvious. That was the extensive geographic mobility of the region's first several generations of white settlers. Settlement implied people coming to stay, and those who did were often hailed as community founders. But they were the exception rather than the rule. Settlers were people who had lived elsewhere before, often in several places, and although they may have wished to stay in one place, they moved on in hopes of something better. They seldom objected when their children packed up to attend college or to marry and find jobs in other towns or states. That adaptability made it possible for the region's population to disperse as economic conditions warranted. A third precondition was the institution building carried out by the region's first century of settlers. They came as merchants and schoolteachers, with skills in business and law and with knowledge of shops and offices. The region benefited from carefully crafted laws, town and county governments, school districts, and state constitutions that had been worked out previously in other parts of the country. The smallest towns soon had churches, Masonic lodges, opera houses, and schools. Despite an ethic of self-sufficiency, residents worked out programs to care for the needy and established asylums for the blind and the insane. All of these institutional precedents served as resources when the time came to consider new schools, new jobs, and new programs of government assistance.

For anyone interested, an afterword tells of my own connections with the Middle West. The danger in writing about a place in which one lived as a child is the possibility of either romanticizing it or viewing it too harshly. To guard against these tendencies, I tried to employ the same mind-set an academic writer would adopt for any other topic. I read countless memoirs to see how other writers have dealt with the issue. Unlike some, I am not so glad to have escaped the Middle West that I hold it in disdain; and unlike others, I have never been much tempted by pangs of regret. As the research progressed, I was surprised to find myself telling an upbeat story. That focus, however, in no way diminishes the difficulties communities face when their populations decline.

Acknowledgments to the many people whose ideas, information, and publications proved useful are amply given in notes, references, and the appendix. My appreciation to the hundreds of people who spent time being interviewed runs especially deep. They gave me a rich sense of the Middle West that I could have acquired in no other way. I was able to do the research, to travel, to hire assistants, and to spend time writing through the generous support of Princeton University. I am extraordinarily grateful to the many librarians and archivists there and around the country who assisted me in locating information about the small details of community life. My greatest debt is to my wife and children.

Remaking the Heartland

Introduction

During the half century that began in the 1950s, the American Middle West—Iowa, Kansas, Nebraska, Minnesota, Missouri, North and South Dakota, Arkansas, and Oklahoma—underwent a dramatic social transformation. The region's population grew at only half the national rate. More than three thousand towns declined. Agriculture suffered from adverse weather and wild market fluctuations in the 1950s, experienced worse conditions in the 1980s, and became far less significant to the region's economy. At the start of the period, analysts wondered if the Middle West would ever fully recover from the devastation of the Dust Bowl era. Large numbers of rural families lived in houses without electricity, telephone service, or indoor plumbing. By the early 1960s, the number of farm youth going to college was startlingly low. Social scientists administered IQ tests to determine if these youngsters were intellectually inferior. Journalists wrote of country hicks lacking refinement. Big-city newspaper editors complained that many of these yokels were on the government dole. The region, analysts wrote, was a huge scar on the national psyche that needed somehow to be fixed—or turned back to grassland and buffalo.

But the heartland was far different in the early twenty-first century than predictions of its demise had suggested. The region's economy fared surprisingly well. While its population declined relative to the nation, its economic productivity grew as rapidly as the rest of the nation, and its contribution to the nation's economic strength remained undiminished. Agribusiness was flourishing. Stereotypes of a benighted hinterland had been replaced by images of hospitality and ingenuity. The region's elementary and secondary schools were among the best in the nation. Its commitment to public higher education consistently ranked high. Without any of the nation's largest cities, the region was known for innovative medical research and bioscience technology. It hosted some of the nation's largest businesses and had become a magnet for sprawling exurban commercial districts and housing developments.

A transformation of such magnitude is not without costs. Millions of Americans were displaced. They lost the farms their parents and grandparents had worked hard to create and maintain. They said goodbye to neighbors who moved on and to children who left, never to pursue the lifestyles their parents anticipated. Country schools closed by the thousands and were replaced by large consolidated districts with fleets of yellow school buses. Retailers in small towns lost business to franchise outlets in regional centers. People who moved to cities in other states where employment opportunities were better experienced in-between lives still tethered in their home communities. Those who stayed sensed acutely that much of the action was elsewhere and composed accounts of why staying was a sensible choice. The region was not devoid of tensions roiling into political, moral, and religious conflicts.

The Middle West nevertheless remade itself without the extreme ill effects that often accompany such economic restructurings. Hardly any strikes, work stoppages, or protests took place. Families who found it necessary to move on did so. They did not hunker down and opt for poverty but sought opportunities wherever they could be found. Unemployment and the numbers of people receiving public assistance remained markedly low. People may have regretted school closings, but they seldom resisted. They found ways to improve the weakest schools and equalize educational opportunities. Racial divisions gradually eroded. The influx of new immigrants that came with agribusiness expansion resulted in fewer conflicts than might have been anticipated.

How did communities adapt to—and indeed facilitate—the kind of transition that middle America experienced during the last half of the twentieth century? Adaptation depends on the resources at communities' disposal and the habits residents have developed for making use of these resources. For the Middle West, land was a key resource. In 1803, Thomas Jefferson purchased the territory that became America's heartland for its water, chiefly the port of New Orleans and access to the Mississippi River, and for security against invasion from the rear that these assets provided. But it was the land that proved far more valuable to the nation's development. Public land, purchased from the French and taken from the native peoples who occupied it, became a vast resource affecting nearly everything the nation did in the nineteenth century. Public land paid for the founding of the Middle West's common schools and subsidized its colleges and universities. It served as an inducement for Northern farmers to join the Union army during the Civil War, it persuaded native peoples to relocate farther west, and it provided the incentive to railroad companies that brought transportation to every corner of the Middle West. Nothing about it was left to chance. Surveyors laid out section boundaries and townships prior to settlers arriving. The Middle West was a planned community if ever there was one.

Land remained the region's principal resource in the second half of the twentieth century. Its productivity increased even as mechanization required fewer people to labor on it. Transporting goods from it and across it kept the region's rail and trucking industry strong. Property taxes ensured revenue for schools and local government services even when the population dwindled. The land—what crops the soil would sustain, how the terrain was configured, where streams and rivers were located, and who would prosper from railways and roads—dictated the spatial dispersion of communities from the start and continued to shape their dispersal as inhabitants moved away.

Habits reflect the surroundings in which they emerge. Settlers in the Middle West learned quickly that the land necessitated both persistence and flexibility. One year's bounty was followed by next year's drought, and a good harvest could be destroyed in an instant by hail or grasshoppers. Midwesterners took pride in staying through hard times, but they also knew when they were licked. For all the talk about farms having been in the family for generations, residents of the Middle West were an itinerant people. One reason they moved so readily during the second half of the twentieth century was that they had done it before. To have descended from settlers was to have hailed from migrants. Communities forged bonds among neighbors and kin, but those bonds could be broken and routinely were.

The 1950s is the decade for which it has been easiest to miss the extent of upheaval in America's heartland. In standard accounts, migration peaked in the 1930s as Okies fled the Dust Bowl and then movement temporarily surged again in World War II, after which families settled into sanguine rural and small-town prosperity during the fifties. But understanding how the region changed requires taking a closer look. The farms, towns, technological developments, and home improvements achieved across the Middle West during the first quarter of the twentieth century were seriously disrupted by the Great Depression and the war. Things did not return to normal simply with rising grain prices and better cattle markets. People struggled to rebuild sagging infrastructure and to adapt to changing economic circumstances. Part of why the region prospered later was that marginal farmers who had hung on during the 1930s and 1940s lost out completely during the 1950s. Government subsidies helped some of these families, but large numbers gave up. They took blue-collar jobs in towns and cities, moved to other states, retired, or died.

If habits are shaped by conditions, the people who display these habits play an active role in determining what they mean. Students of social life who seek to objectify the people they observe are constantly reminded of this fact. Heartland residents may have paused rarely to contemplate what writers or filmmakers thought about them, but they were keenly interested in crafting their own interpretations of what it meant to live in middle America. There were myths galore: The heartland was rural America, inhabited by rustics who knew little about city life and rarely traveled or read great literature. Its residents spoke with peculiar regional accents and had little appreciation of fine art. That was one image, and it was sometimes comforting for heartlanders simply to embrace the idea that they were simple, unpretentious, plainspoken people. But that view squared poorly with aspirations to be equal with the rest of America and with the fact that farms and small towns were indeed modernizing and connecting increasingly with the wider world through television and motion pictures. Other available myths needed to be recast. The heartland was—but not quite—Buffalo Bill's Wild West, Laura Ingalls Wilder's pioneer home on the prairie, and Dorothy's Kansas in the *Wizard of Oz*. For the heartland to remake itself, it had first to redefine itself, and this act of self-redefinition occurred mostly in the 1950s and 1960s. The heartland came to be a region defined less by geography alone and more by attributes associated with and transcending a particular place. To be a heartlander, it was no longer necessary to farm or live in a small town but rather to appreciate those who did and even more so to enjoy the landscape's natural beauty, to pride oneself on commonsense ingenuity, to cherish family and friends, and with Dorothy to utter simply, "There's no place like home."

The stuff of movies and television helped Middle Westerners reinvent themselves, and yet their own futures and the region's required practical knowledge. Here were people who had grown up on farms and in small towns far from the great centers of learning. How could a region long dominated by one-room country schools and so recently afflicted by the Depression possibly compete? The truth was that Middle Western states had taken education so seriously from the beginning that by the early twentieth century, the region was often referred to as the nation's education belt. In 1950 the top four states nationally in percentage of adults having completed high school were Nebraska, Iowa, Kansas, and Minnesota. An extensive system of well-financed and well-supervised public elementary and secondary schools gave the region an enormous advantage as it sought to advance economically and culturally. Over the half century that followed, the proportion of adults with high school degrees steadily increased, exceeding the national average, and rising numbers went on to college. As the population became better educated, the region nevertheless faced a new challenge. Could it make appropriate employment opportunities available? Or was it destined to experience a massive brain drain as its best-trained young people took jobs in other regions? One thing was certain: higher education had become a major dislocating force. Young people in their twenties left in massive numbers to attend college and to seek jobs upon graduation. The region's policymakers increasingly wondered how to lure them back and how to attract newcomers.

That worry was compounded by the fact that towns were dying. Or so it seemed. The Middle West had been settled by farmers who needed towns and by entrepreneurs who eagerly catered to their needs. As farms became larger and transportation improved, the dynamics changed. By 1920 many towns were losing population. The baby boom of the 1950s reversed the trend in some communities, but it continued in others. By 1980 the nine Middle Western states ranked first through ninth in having the highest proportion of towns with fewer than fifteen hundred people. And during the quarter century after 1980, nearly two-thirds of the region's towns declined, and few of the others kept pace with population growth in the rest of the nation. Shifting agricultural patterns, uncertainties in oil and gas production, and military base closings all contributed to the decline. Yet the region's established towns proved resilient. The ones that declined most were already quite small. Other communities held steady, experiencing what demographers of the 1970s touted as ideal zero population growth, or declined gradually enough to avoid major increases in unemployment and poverty. Quality-of-life rankings confirmed what residents argued: that their communities were good places to live, make friends, and raise families.

The few rural towns that grew dramatically did so because they became heavily implicated in agribusiness—especially the region's increasing role in packaged-meat processing for fast-food distribution and consumption. The key example of this transition was Garden City, Kansas, which became one of the fastest-growing communities in the 1980s and the home of the world's largest meat-processing facility. With a flood of new immigrants from Mexico, Central America, and Southeast Asia, Garden City became the new face that scholars projected onto the region. Surely the region was remaking itself, they argued, by importing cheap labor to work in conditions reminiscent of *The Jungle* and with ethnic tensions as the expected result. But the restructuring of agribusiness proved to be a more complicated story. It required looking to the first half of the twentieth century to understand the social infrastructure that made agribusiness possible. It also necessitated looking at the complex multinational conglomerates in which meat processing became involved.

With so many farms and small communities losing population, the remaining question was whether enough people would stay to keep the region in business, and if so, what business that would be and where they would live. Edge cities were not expected to emerge in the Middle West to the extent they did in the Sunbelt and on both coasts, but they did appear and increasingly became symbolic of the Middle West's new role in the national economy. By 2005 there were ninety-five independently incorporated edge cities with at least ten thousand residents within twenty miles of the region's eight largest cities. More people lived in these suburbs than in those large cities combined. Logic held that people were attracted by capacious homes with ample yards near shopping malls and interstate highways. But the reality was again more complex. Much of the growth could be traced to World War II, when defense industries expanded onto open land adjacent to the region's cities, and to the manufacturing firms that grew out of these defense industries. At first, commuting to center cities increased, but it later decreased as more employers located in the suburbs. Those employers were the principal architects of the region's new emphasis on avionics, fiber-optic communications, finance, medical technology, and bioscience.

The remaking of a region is a large story that can be told only by combining evidence of the big picture with details about individuals and their communities. The big picture comes from hundreds of datafiles constructed by the U.S. Census Bureau and other government agencies about topics as diverse as the populations of towns and counties, the education levels of residents, the locations and output of meat-processing plants, and the crop yields of wheat farmers and beet growers. This material covers the past half century, and for some topics, it was necessary to examine a much longer period. The fine-grained details resulted from delving into the business records and community histories of selected illustrative towns, from reading back issues of their newspapers, from searching through oral histories and minutes of town meetings, and from conducting scores of interviews with ordinary residents and community leaders.

If there is a single lesson to be learned about how communities remake themselves, it is this: the capacity to change depends on the institutional arrangements that precede it. America's heartland was never as down and out as its detractors in the big cities and elite universities believed. But its transition from the Dust Bowl era to the twenty-first century was not simply a matter of shucking bad habits and rewarding innovators either. Much of its success was attributable to the fact that the U.S. government decided early on to fill it with settlers and to the institutions these settlers created for themselves, including the market towns, the farmsteads, the one-room schools, the townships, the rural cooperatives, and the manufacturing centers that gave the region its identity. These institutions had to adapt as economic and demographic conditions changed, but they had been established as adaptable social forms in the first place, and they served well to provide the incentives, legal frameworks, and support networks needed to make new arrangements possible. What later would sometimes appear to be entirely new was seldom quite as novel as it seemed.

The story of the heartland's transition is, for me, a matter not only of academic interest but also of personal exploration. It is about the road not taken, the region I left behind many decades ago and have always wondered about, always loved, often visited, and never before taken the opportunity to look at through the eyes of an outsider or tried to write about with the heart of a person still there.

ONE

Here in the Middle

Here in Smith County, at the exact geographic middle of the United States, there is a sense of timeless tranquility that can be deceptively seductive. Above the small stone monument that local citizens erected on April 25, 1941, to mark the site, an American flag waves serenely in the Kansas breeze. At one side, a few trees planted on that occasion shade a picnic table and a small white prayer chapel. Several tall pines and a row of overgrown junipers make a home for native jays. The grass has recently been cut, and the litter barrel is nearly empty. A few yards away is a low bluish-gray building that once served as an eight-room motel. Its doors and windows are now covered with plywood. A dirt road extends up over the hill and into the distance. Except for the rustle of wind, the day is palpably quiet.

The location provides a commanding view of the surrounding countryside. To the north and west, a field of rich loam lies ready to be planted with sorghum. Down the hill to the east, an access road dips through a pasture in which a herd of Black Angus while away the warm spring days. To the south as far as the eye can see, across the gently rolling terrain, fallow land and sparse shelterbelts intersperse with fields of undulating wheat. In a few weeks, the fields will turn golden brown in anticipation of the harvest. Several miles in the distance is the small hamlet of Lebanon, its grain elevator and water tower rising tall against the cloudless sky. To the southwest, a grain elevator is barely visible on the horizon, and beyond that lies the town of Smith Center, the county seat. This is the heart of America's heartland.

Visitors travel to this spot to gauge the enduring values that define America. They come from Philadelphia and Chicago, from New York and Los Angeles, from bustling cities overrun with change and uncertainty, and increasingly from other countries. The sojourners detour up from Interstate 70 to break the long haul between Kansas City and Denver. They include hunters who come each fall in search of deer and pheasants. Some are writers sent by newspapers and television stations to record their observations for distant audiences. They are looking to plumb the nation's soul. Perhaps there is wisdom here, extracted from the soil by these folks who still live so close to it, that can inspire people elsewhere whose lifestyles are profoundly different.

A writer in the early 1990s found the local residents compellingly honest, hardworking, sheltered, and a bit disappointed that progress had passed them by. A tourist from Minnesota came about the same time and stood at the grave of her great-grandmother, a rugged pioneer who struggled to establish a life on the open frontier. "We belong to each other," she wept. A few years later, a reporter from Australia stopped on a cross-country tour with his eleven-year-old daughter to see if there was a connection between the landscape and the nation's psyche. Truly this was God's country, he concluded, observing the tiny prayer chapel and the church steeples and cemeteries. But it was an idealized past, he thought, a place with an uncertain future. At the turn of the millennium, a writer for the *Washington Post* spent the day in Lebanon, absorbed by its silence and overwhelmed by its emptiness. Main Street stays so vacant, he wrote, that "a dog could lie down in it for a long nap in no fear of being awakened, much less run over." Standing amidst the crumbling storefronts, he was gripped by the melancholy of what had been lost. Yet he was equally impressed by the stubborn endurance of the people who remained. "It's something you feel if you stop the car," he mused, "get out, stand hip-deep and soaking in the pond of stillness that spreads without a ripple, mile on mile on mile."[1]

It is hard not to conclude that America's geographic center has seen better days. In 1870, three years before Lebanon became a town, only sixty-six settlers lived in all of Smith County. "We earnestly invite emigrants from the Eastern States," one of the residents wrote in 1877, "energetic men and women who are not afraid to do or dare, ornaments to society and occupying useful positions in life."[2] By 1880, the population swelled to 13,883, of whom 1,673 were living in Oak Township where Lebanon was located. Seven years later, when the Rock Island Railroad came through, the citizens moved their town two and a half miles northeast to be on the rail line and started in earnest to create something worthy of their dreams. "The place bids fair to become a town of considerable importance," a visitor wrote a few months later. "It is located in the center of a fertile section, has an immense scope of country to draw trade from, and is already populated by a pushing, go-ahead class of business men."[3] Indeed the town did prosper. By 1910, it had 731 residents—more than twice as many as several nearby towns with rail service. Photos from the era show large, well-kept two-story houses with barns, gardens, and orchards in the rear. Along Main Street and Kansas Avenue, more than forty businesses had been established, including two pool halls and a motion-picture theater, and by the depot stood three grain elevators, a mill, coal sheds, and a stock yard. In 1920, the population reached 822, but it has fallen ever since. By 1980, it had tumbled to 440. Twenty-five years later, it was down to 278.[4]

A slump of such magnitude takes a heavy toll on any community. The boarded-up motel adjacent to the center monument is symbolic of Lebanon's decline. Built in 1956 by an entrepreneur with high hopes of attracting tourists, it closed in 1970. Local schools shut down in the 1980s when consolidation forced the few remaining children to transfer to Smith Center. Along Main Street, the post office, a bank, a small grocery store, and the grain elevator remain, but they are sandwiched between vacant buildings with fading signs reminiscent of earlier times. Adams Clothing, Hobbs Variety, Chadbourne's Shoe Shop, Lammey's Café, and the Ford dealership are all gone. Of the two hundred houses in the community, 30 percent are vacant. Many are in sorry states of disrepair. The talk at the grain elevator is of rising fuel costs and uncertain hog prices. "It's a battle to keep afloat," the farmers agree. Volunteers at the Legion Hall wonder if sausage and pancake fundraisers will keep the building open much longer. The churches are struggling. "We're down to fifteen members," a sixth-generation resident says of hers. "And we're all related."[5] At the grocery store, retirees quietly lament a teenager killed recently in an automobile accident and confess to strangers that times used to be better. After a morning spent listening to aging residents' tales of decline, a writer observed ruefully, "Life is slowly bleeding from America's heartland, leaving an increasingly empty landscape full of graceful widows."[6]

Even its status as geographic center has been emblematic of the town's steady displacement. Located by engineers for the U.S. Coast and Geodetic Survey in 1898, the site is often described metaphorically as the location at which a map of the forty-eight contiguous states would balance if attached to a plane of uniform thickness. In fact, this is exactly how it was chosen. Pasting a map onto a piece of cardboard, the engineers moved it around until it balanced. Fortunately for Lebanon, the method proved surprisingly accurate, and the location (latitude 39'50" and longitude 98'35") has not changed with more sophisticated measuring devices. However, the monument itself does not stand at this location, which is more than a third of a mile to the northwest. Over the years, further ambiguities have arisen about the meaning of "center." The geodetic center, which takes account of the earth's curvature and is better for scientific surveys, is in a pasture in Osborne County to the south of Lebanon. With the addition of Alaska, the geographic center of the continental United States shifted to a location in North Dakota. And the geographic center of U.S. population has variously been located in Illinois and Missouri. Lebanon's claim has long been relegated to that of *historic* geographic center of the United States.[7]

That America's heartland is a thing of the past is a long-standing refrain in treatments of the region. The reigning motif is nostalgia for a pastoral village-based America—a longing that grew among people who had never lived there, or had lived there only as children, and who viewed it from the standpoint of cities and suburbs that were constantly in flux. The image in this rearview mirror is of simpler times, of hayrides and strolls down country lanes, fading into the distance as life speeds ahead. Regret hangs heavy over the scene. The heartland retains only vestiges of that slow-paced time when people were less materialistic than they are now, less worried about crime, better equipped to instill values in their children, and more supportive of and supported by their neighbors. Life then was a Lake Wobegon existence, recognizable as myth and yet held fondly in memory.[8]

The other common perspective on middle America sees the region as a social problem. "The government props up the heartland," journalist Timothy Egan declared after visiting in 2003. "The only growth industries now are pigs and prisons."[9] Entire communities were dead or dying. This, too, is a view that has been around for a long time. Observers came increasingly to regard the region as a vast catastrophe during the Great Depression. As dust storms rolled across the plains, the dimensions of the problem became evident in falling incomes, rising foreclosures, and deteriorating health and housing. Farmers themselves were partly to blame, analysts concluded. Too few were using efficient scientific farming methods; too many were plowing fields that should have remained untilled. They had no idea how to keep track of expenses let alone find ways of reducing them. Many naively engaged in land speculation and too readily turned to the government to bail them out. They worked hard when work was to be done, but otherwise spent their time at the pool hall and exhibited no talent for leadership.[10] Recent studies are generally more charitable but depict a heartland with a feeble pulse. Hardworking farmers are being driven off their land by agribusiness conglomerates, analysts say. Those who remain are destitute, aging, and badly in need of social services that cannot be found in rural communities. Young people leave as soon as they can or have to stay behind because of poor training at lackluster schools. And if that is not enough, the land itself is being destroyed by fertilizer and pesticides.[11]

The idea of an American heartland now beset with problems intertwines easily with nostalgic visions of a better past. Both perceptions play well to the insiders who live in declining rural communities and to audiences who have long since pursued more glamorous lifestyles elsewhere. A man who farms the land adjacent to the geographic-center monument near Lebanon nicely illustrates the point. In an interview for the *New York Times*, he complained that corporate farmers are taking over and that he does not understand the complexities of international trade agreements. He works from sunrise until past midnight but fears he is falling behind. His wife thinks maybe they should throw in the towel. He worries that his son is going to leave for college and never return. He muses that they have had a good life on the farm but wonders if it is all coming to an end. The interviewer lets the farmer's words speak for themselves. Surely an era is passing from American life. A moment of remembrance is in order.[12]

However, neither nostalgia nor an emphasis on social problems adequately captures the complexity of the social forces transforming America's heartland. Declining population in rural communities, vacant storefronts, children growing up and moving away, and farmers fearing that their way of life is ending are significant parts of this complexity. And if this were all that was happening, it would make sense to predict, as a writer in California did, that American agriculture would simply be replaced by imported food from other countries. It would be reasonable to argue, as an editorial in the *New York Times* did, that the heartland should be turned into a vast national park of prairie grass and buffalo.[13] But these notions miss the integral relations between aspects of middle America that are declining and others that are emerging or remain strong. They ignore the fact that stillness in places like Lebanon, Kansas, masks enormous change and massive adaptation. Agriculture has for many decades been only a part of the region's economy, and the growth or decline of communities has been as much shaped by merchants, investors, speculators, and government officials as by farmers and ranchers. Agriculture, too, has proven remarkably responsive to new technologies, changing patterns of ownership and organization, and shifting farm security policies.

The familiarity with change and the necessity to adapt can be heard when observers listen for sounds other than the stillness of the rustling wind. In 1852, two decades before white settlers arrived, a French trapper camping near the future site of Lebanon observed a three-day battle involving more than 16,000 Pawnee, Cheyenne, Comanche, and Arapaho tribesmen. They were battling each other for rights to diminishing hunting lands.[14] In 1859, *New York Tribune* editor Horace Greeley passed through the area by stage coach and recorded seeing large herds of buffalo. "There certainly were not less than 10,000 of them," he wrote, "I believe there were many more."[15] Less than two decades later, the buffalo were gone. In 1878, Riley A. Holmes homesteaded the site that became known as Old Lebanon after the town moved in 1887. Far from federal marshals, the homestead became a hiding place for two of Holmes's former neighbors from Missouri, Jesse James and Cole Younger.[16] The area acquired a different reputation in 1896 when D. H. Hyde, a devout Free Methodist, built a grain elevator along the railroad tracks and embellished it with Bible verses in large print. "Where will you spend Eternity? Decide Now. Jesus invites you," rail passengers read, surely impressed as later visitors would be that they were somehow in God's country.[17]

Communities adapt by taking advantage of the resources at their disposal. At times, those are people organizing in search of political redress. In the 1890s, Lebanon residents overwhelmingly voted Populist and participated in large rallies demanding regulation of eastern business monopolies and reductions of exorbitant freight rates. At other times, adaptation takes different forms. In the 1930s, residents hung sheets across windows to keep out the howling dust storms, planted gardens that withered in the drought, quit eating meat because there was none, and sent hungry children to live with relatives. A few years later they anticipated better times. When the Hub Club of Lebanon erected the center monument in 1941, tourism was being promoted along nearby U.S. Highway 36 as the "great central scenic highway from the Atlantic to the Pacific Coast." In 1952, troubled once again by drought and serious soil erosion, the same Hub Club organized a workday involving fifty bulldozers and earthmovers to demonstrate the advantages of terracing and better land management. Consolidating school districts in the late 1950s and again in the 1980s so that children could receive better training in Smith Center was another response to changing conditions.[18]

In recent decades, seemingly moribund communities like Lebanon have continued to adapt. Consider the following. The farmer in the *New York Times* story about children leaving and corporations taking over was himself the holder of a 100 percent interest in a corporate farm. He ranked twentieth among the more than 1,500 farmers in Smith County receiving crop-subsidy payments. In good years, his total income was approximately four times that of the median household in Lebanon; in bad years, he barely made the payments on his machinery. Times may have been hard and his way of life may have been uncertain, but he was adapting to the current economic environment. Two of his neighbors were also responding. One was honored in the 1980s by the Kansas Bankers Association for an innovative terracing system and later by the Kansas State University Research and Extension service for the use of new corn, soybean, and white wheat technologies and for computerized monitoring of soil fertility. The other, a corporate farmer who owned properties in four counties, played a pivotal role in bringing no-till technology to the area, which reduced equipment and operating costs and increased per-acre profits. All three experimented with crops they would not have considered a few years ago and derive an increasing share of their income from contract farming. They and many of their neighbors farm three to five times as much land as farmers near Lebanon did a generation ago. They own combines that cost a quarter of a million dollars. With high-tech tractors, they apply fertilizer using a GPS tracking system to guide the equipment and adjust application levels to soil conditions.[19]

The point is not that farmers were doing better than unsuspecting journalists may have imagined but that the heartland was quietly remaking itself. The widows who gather for coffee at the market in Lebanon are an important part of the story, but so are the packaged foods that make up an increasing share of the store's inventory and are transforming the region's agriculture. The farmer's son who leaves for college and the father who worries that his son may not return reflect the human drama taking place here in rural America. It is understandable that people mourn the departure of their children, but it is equally important to understand that they know this is the reality they face and have usually played a positive role in encouraging it. Populations decline not only because people are forced to leave but also because they choose to do so, and because those who stay behind are often better able to be productive and efficient as a result.

A business executive in Oklahoma who grew up on a farm near Lebanon says there was never much question that he would go to college after high school and probably settle elsewhere. His younger brother, a college graduate, also lives out of state. Meanwhile, their father and an uncle are earning a good living farming land that has been in the family for a hundred years. Living frugally and working hard, they have gradually expanded the operation to include five thousand acres. In a few years, when his father is ready to retire, the younger son will probably return to the farm. If he does not, a cousin will rent the land.[20]

It is important, too, to ask about the underlying social and economic dynamics taking place in Lebanon that the journalist who stops for a brief visit is likely to miss. Why have the most successful farmers in the township turned to corporate contract farming, and why do they have misgivings about it? What did they learn a few years ago from the shifting fortunes of the U.S. hog market? Why are they diversifying their crops? And in Lebanon itself, further questions must be posed. With population shrinking so dramatically, why does the grain elevator continue to receive record crops each year? How does its membership in the regional Midway Co-op Association affect its operations? With the schools gone, why do even the widows pay close attention to the events over at Smith Center High? How well did the high school prepare the farmers' sons and daughters to go to college? Why has it made headlines in the national media?

A woman who moved here sixteen years ago—and still feels like an outsider—speaks candidly about the changes taking place. "We are in the middle of nowhere," she says, describing the difficulties of attracting newcomers and new businesses. She loves the community but acknowledges the adjustments it is having to make. On the one hand, she says, it is a wonderful place to raise children. People live frugally, work hard, and have genuine "old-school" moral values. On the other hand, there are strong pressures to conform. Neighbors talk about one another behind their backs. "So-and-so got a new car. How can they afford that? They can't!" She says the older people seem to have learned how to get along with one another, but the competitiveness among younger people has surprised her. There is growing tension between those who have better incomes and those who have fewer opportunities.[21]

How do people make sense of the ambivalence they feel about their neighbors and their communities? When population shrinks, what are the appropriate mechanisms for downsizing? Do long-term residents resist change? Do they welcome newcomers and new ideas? What adjustments are required to feel good about where one lives? Are dreams deferred? Are self-images redefined? Have these changes been harder on the women than on the men? on young families? or among the elderly?

Addressing these questions necessitates a broader perspective on the changes taking place in America's heartland. It requires shifting focus, first from Lebanon to the county seat, which provides a clearer picture of heartland farming, and then to other communities that are rapidly gaining prominence as sites of economic and demographic vitality. Like Lebanon, Smith Center is a small community with a declining population. But it is seven times larger than Lebanon, which gives it a very different place in the county's economy. The questions it evokes reflect these differences. Are the fewer people who live here managing to keep the farm economy going? Is the county's history inscribed in their habits? What impact has the diminishing population had on county government and local businesses? As retirees have moved in from surrounding farms and farming communities to be closer to the hospital and nursing home, how has the town's service system responded? What has kept the one manufacturing plant in town prospering? How are the huge tractors and combines for sale at the John Deere dealer on the west edge of town affecting the local farmers? And how did a local entrepreneur manage to start a business a few years ago that was soon valued at more than $100 million?

If some of the changes that are overtaking the heartland are implied in these questions, others come into focus when the lens pulls back to include the wider region. Garden City, a four-hour drive to the southwest, is an important location of these broader dynamics. Fifteen times the size of Smith Center and with a growing population, it is a community surrounded by feedlots and meatpacking plants. Nearly half of its population are Hispanic. Like Guymon in Oklahoma, Lexington in Nebraska, and Marshalltown in Iowa, Garden City is one of the emerging agribusiness centers that has transformed middle America in recent decades. Questions arise from the dramatic change this once-quiet farming community has experienced. How did a community known only as the location of a horrendous crime acquire a new reputation as a center of economic innovation? What were the predisposing factors that led to it becoming an agribusiness hub?

How did community leaders facilitate the expansion? Why did the community become the location for one of the most hotly contested energy initiatives in the state? What tensions have arisen between the Anglo and Hispanic populations? What uncertainties have the new economic conditions created for workers at the packing plants and for farmers in the region?

Traveling northeast from Garden City along Kansas Highway 156 to Interstate 70 and then east to the Kansas City area, a person interested in the region's transformation is confronted with additional puzzles. Along the highway, wheat fields, pastures, and little else dominate the terrain. What happened to all those people who left places like Smith Center? or who fled from Garden City when the ethnic and economic challenges became too great? The answer can be found in a community like Olathe, a town about twenty miles from downtown Kansas City that in 1950 was only half as large as Garden City but fifty years later was almost four times its size. Once prominent only as a stop on the Santa Fe Trail, Olathe has become a massive agglomeration of off-ramps, housing developments, shopping malls, distribution warehouses, and high-tech industries. Like neighboring Leawood, Lenexa, and Overland Park, it has become a major example of suburban sprawl. Its expansion—and the rising prominence of rapidly growing communities as diverse as Woodbury, Minnesota; Omaha, Nebraska; Fayetteville, Arkansas; and Lee's Summit, Missouri—points to the need to understand how these places are transforming America's heartland. Why has population grown so rapidly in these areas? What inducements have businesses been offered to locate here? How are they connected with the hinterland and with the global economy?

Olathe's growth reflects a wider heartland restructuring that has yet to be examined or fully understood. Visitors to declining rural communities like Lebanon come away thinking the Middle West is a place that people usually leave, and the few who stay have been there forever. But that is far from true of the region. U.S. Census Bureau statistics for 2006 showed that four Kansans in ten had moved there from another state. The proportion was about the same in Oklahoma and Arkansas, while in Missouri, Nebraska, and South Dakota one-third were nonnative. These figures were similar to rates in Massachusetts, Michigan, Illinois, and New York. In Johnson County, Kansas, where Olathe is located, 46 percent had been born in another state.[22]

This is a book about the interplay among several developments that dramatically transformed America's heartland during the latter half of the twentieth century and are likely to shape it long into the future. The first is a major redistribution of the region's population. Throughout the Midwest and across the Great Plains, hundreds of communities in rural counties have lost population over the past half century, and in many cases for much longer. These farming communities, like Lebanon and Smith Center, were never large, and they have become smaller. But this emptying cannot be understood without paying attention simultaneously to the growth that has been experienced in places like Garden City and Olathe, some of which has come directly from people flocking in from rural areas, and much of which represents the heartland's changing relationship to the rest of the nation and the world. Second, a profound growth of productivity has occurred in agriculture, permitting fewer people to produce more and altering the relationships among families, communities, and the land. Farm technology and new marketing strategies have played an important role in this transformation. Third, middle America has become the location of numerous innovative business enterprises and a generator of wealth from these ventures that would have been undreamed of a few decades ago. Bioscience, information technology, communication systems, warehousing, wholesale distribution, and food processing have all become important as new sources of capital investment and employment. And fourth, an unsettling of the cultural and political values of the heartland has taken place, resulting less in any straightforward recentering of power and more in new modalities of accommodation, resistance, diversity, tolerance, and self-definition. These moderating cultural changes are often missed in popular depictions of the so-called red states that make up so much of middle America.

The single question that these multiple transformations raise is, how has all this been possible? For communities widely regarded as dying and desperately clinging to outmoded traditions, it is quite remarkable that such change could have happened at all. None of it has been easy for those experiencing it firsthand, especially when it has indeed involved pulling up roots, leaving familiar lifestyles behind, telling children good-bye, relocating, learning new occupations, inventing new revenue streams, exploring new markets, and adapting to new neighborhoods. Yet the remaking of middle America has been overwhelmingly successful in bringing economic restructuring to the region, in redistributing the population to take fuller advantage of changing labor markets, and in strengthening its ties to other parts of the country.

The extent of this success is evident in comparisons between population levels and statistics on state-by-state gross domestic product from the U.S. Department of Commerce's Bureau of Economic Analysis (BEA). Nine states lie between the Mississippi River and the Rocky Mountains and comprise more than three-quarters of the 820,000 square miles of the Louisiana Purchase that Thomas Jefferson obtained from France in 1803. Closest to the Mississippi are Arkansas, Iowa, Minnesota, and Missouri, and to the west, Kansas, Nebraska, North Dakota, Oklahoma, and South Dakota. In 1950, these states were still reeling from the Great Depression and from World War II, and they faced an uncertain future. Only three million of the eighteen million residents of these states lived in cities of 100,000 or more. Half lived on farms or in towns no larger than 2,500. Fewer than half of these rural households had running water or indoor toilets. A quarter of the five million people living on farms did not have electricity. Half the farmsteads did not have telephones. By the end of the twentieth century, the proportion living in rural areas in these states had dropped from 49 percent to 34 percent. Approximately 750,000 farms—more than half—had disappeared. The farm population shrank by nearly 80 percent from more than five million to 1.1 million. Only 3 percent of the total population remained on farms. In nearly two-thirds of the 650 counties that were predominantly rural in 1950, the population in 2000 was smaller than it had been a half century earlier.

At the start of the twenty-first century, these nine Middle Western states were still in many ways the product of their rural past. Although they included 21 percent of the land area of the contiguous United States and nearly a third of its farmland, they accounted for less than 9 percent of its population. On average, there were forty-one people per square mile, compared with eighty for the nation at large. Not one of the country's twenty-five largest cities was located in these states. A mere 19 percent of the nine-state population lived in cities with 100,000 population or more.[23] Much of the region was still defined by population loss. Of the more than five thousand incorporated communities in the region, nearly two-thirds lost population between 1980 and 2000. These were years during which the U.S. population as a whole grew by 24 percent. Some of the loss occurred because of the farm crisis of the 1980s, but in the first years of the twenty-first century, decline was still the order of the day. More than 3,400 communities lost population between 2000 and 2006. In Missouri, Oklahoma, and Arkansas, which fared best, nearly half the towns decreased, while in Kansas, Nebraska, and South Dakota, three-fourths of the towns diminished, and in North Dakota, 90 percent did.[24]

BEA economic data, though, contradict the view that America's heartland is simply in decline. That view is based largely on population figures and reflects arguments in the national media about the waning significance of farming and the undesirability of living anywhere remote from one of the largest metropolitan areas. The population data confirm that fewer people reside in the region relative to the rest of the United States than in the past and that this decrease, which was already evident during the first half of the twentieth century, continued to be significant during the second half. As a proportion of total U.S. population, 17 percent less lived in the region in 2006 than in 1963.[25] But the economic figures do not suggest a similar decline.[26] Trends in GDP per capita for the region divide into three periods: from 1963 to 1980 there was a steady increase for the region relative to the nation; from 1981 to 1990 there was a marked decrease; and from 1991 to 2006 there was overall improvement, except for a drop in 1999. The 1980s decline coincides with the farm crisis of those years, which was a significant setback for the region's economy. Otherwise, the region largely held its own or improved relative to the rest of the nation. The ratio of GDP per capita for the region to GDP per capita for the nation was *higher* at the start of the twenty-first century than in the early 1960s.[27] In the 1990s, growth in GDP per capita in six of the states—Arkansas, Iowa, Minnesota, Missouri, North Dakota, and South Dakota—exceeded the national average.[28] These trends continued into the twenty-first century. Between 1997 and 2006, the BEA estimated that GDP for the nine states grew 25 percent in inflation-adjusted dollars, despite a population increase of only 8 percent. Minnesota's GDP climbed 32 percent; South Dakota's by 41 percent. Thus, despite the many worrisome indications a half century earlier, the region managed to outperform expectations and keep up with or exceed the rest of the nation.

The BEA also discovered long-term convergence between the Middle West and the nation during the latter half of the twentieth century in per capita earnings. The nine-state region was significantly lower than the national average in the 1930s and rose during the 1940s, only to experience relative decline in the 1950s. However, by the end of the century, the region was only slightly lower than the national average.[29] Another report showed that per capita *income*— composed of earnings, dividends and interest, and transfer payments—grew at the same overall rate for the heartland states as for the nation between 1950 and 1999. Arkansas, Minnesota, Oklahoma, and South Dakota exceeded the national average on both earnings and dividends and interest.[30] Having started lower, personal incomes still averaged about 10 percent lower than the national average in 1999. However, the average costs of living were also lower. Housing costs, for example, ranged 18 to 27 percent below the national average, while food and transportation costs were at least 10 percent below average.[31]

The economic data suggest that slower-than-average population growth across the region—and outright population loss in a majority of small towns and rural areas—did not significantly impair the Middle West's overall economic vitality.[32] But the economic picture is only part of the story. Massive population redistribution is dramatically consequential in its own right and was accomplished partly through a reduction in rural fertility rates and largely through outmigration from small towns and farms. Managing population decline to reduce its negative effects is often as challenging as planning for population growth. In the first years after World War II, resources had to be spent to build infrastructure postponed by the war, and by the Depression before that. Later, infrastructure had to be relocated to accommodate the shifting distribution of the population. Organizations were needed to train workers for a changing labor force, and the region underwent further change as it became integrated more fully into the national consumer culture. Churches, schools, leisure activities, and political orientations all changed.

The sources of the relative success of this transformation, I argue, lie in social institutions that were firmly in place by at least the 1950s and often long before. Although the most dramatic developments that have come to define the heartland in the twenty-first century happened during the last quarter of the twentieth century, their origins can be found before World War II and, in many instances, at the end of the nineteenth century, when many of the basic social patterns that came to characterize the region were established. These patterns were not always what local residents thought they were creating or wanted to create, but the people accommodated to the conditions with which they were faced and discovered ways of dealing with the attendant uncertainties. From the start, the region was of intense national importance and developed financial and commercial ties with firms, banks, and investors elsewhere. Its residents developed a sense of themselves as part of a national culture and tempered local interests with these wider outlooks. They inherited an effective system of local government that had been worked out in earlier decades along the eastern seaboard. Much of the region benefited from having been aligned with the winning side during the Civil War. As immigrants from other states and from Europe flooded into the region, these administrative structures played an important role in facilitating assimilation. The people were institution builders who created a coordinated system of local education and founded colleges, normal schools, technical institutes, and asylums. They asked, albeit reluctantly, for assistance from state and federal government when they thought they needed it. They put down roots, and found wealth under the land as well as in the topsoil, but they also recognized the necessity of moving on—and generation after generation did so.

It was these social arrangements and the tacit habits of life that mattered most when Middle Westerners adapted repeatedly to changes in their environment. There was nothing particularly special or romantic or heroic about it, although heroes and heroines could always be found. People were often exploited, knew that they were, and complained bitterly about it. They resented the railroads and the oil companies and the government strictures, and yet their lives were shaped by these forces. They established towns by the thousands, watched as many of these towns died almost overnight, picked up and moved some of them to better locations, and over the years found reason to claim them as their homes. The institutions they brought with them or developed once they came enabled them to educate their children, buy and sell property, protect themselves from each other, worship freely, express their values, and gradually to make use of new technologies, launch new businesses, and secure their livelihoods.

An emphasis on the roots of social transformation in established social institutions is not an argument about continuities outweighing discontinuities. Middle America is profoundly different in the twenty-first century than it was a half century earlier, and this is true even in the subtle ways in which small farming communities in out-of-the-way places have changed. But understanding how existing institutions structure and, indeed, make possible new patterns of life casts these changes in an entirely different light from the more common perspective that has often been advanced. In that view, the heartland has simply lagged behind everywhere else, and if change has happened, it has come from the outside and been forced onto an old-fashioned population who resisted it tooth and nail. Nothing could be further from the truth.

Where exactly is the heartland located? The term itself is vague enough to have acquired a vast range of meanings, from ones that are largely subjective (as implied in the adage "Home is where the heart is") to others defined by precise geographic demarcations. Some of the latter are astonishingly inclusive. An essay a few years ago about the nation's changing demographic characteristics included twenty-eight states and the District of Columbia in the heartland, employing the term to designate everything not part of the dynamically growing Sunbelt and the melting-pot states that served as gateways for new immigrants.[33] For that purpose, the idea was a good one. And yet people living in Baltimore and Philadelphia would likely have been surprised to be identified as part of the heartland. Other designations are quite narrow. The residents of Smith County, Kansas, frequently lay claim to being the heart of America, or its heartland. But clearly the term encompasses a larger region than this. Other geographic definitions, such as Midwest, Great Plains, and Upper Central North, have proliferated and been divided into subregions so often that they have to be used with great care.

One of the more helpful efforts to define something close to what might be termed the heartland or middle America was a study by cultural geographer James R. Shortridge examining perceptions among college students from various parts of the country to see what they included in the region he termed the Middle West. The boundaries varied when viewed from, say, California, New York, or Alabama, but there was widespread consensus that Kansas, Nebraska, and Iowa were at the center of America's heartland and that parts of Missouri, Oklahoma, and Arkansas might be included as well. In some perceptions, it extended into the Dakotas, Minnesota, eastern Colorado, and northwest Texas.[34] My usage is similar. Communities like Smith Center, Garden City, and Olathe are clearly part of the heartland, as is the rest of Kansas, and for consistency in describing statistical evidence and providing comparisons with other locations, I include information about Nebraska, Iowa, Missouri, Minnesota, North and South Dakota, Oklahoma, and Arkansas.[35]

A writer who grew up in South Dakota, went to Princeton, and settled in New England describes the Middle West as the "imaginary home of all Americans"—a place of little towns with farms nearby surrounded by "pure unadulterated heartland." For people who leave or who simply imagine having lived there, she says, "it eventually turns out that all we ever really wanted to do was go home."[36]

Imagination and longing mingle with the realities of change and the passing of time. The heartland is neither the cozy past of childhood memories nor the harsh place from which so many are glad to have escaped. It is a temporally decentered geographic middle of a nation that has required all of its places to pull together and, in so doing, to remake their traditions, refashion their lives, and come to a greater appreciation of what each part contributes.

For people in New York and Los Angeles, for travelers from Chicago and Houston, this is flyover country—a region seldom visited but still vital in the heart of America. It is a place of quiet, vibrant adaptation more similar to the rest of the nation than passersby might suspect. I asked a Smith Countian what she would tell people in the wider world if she could say one thing. "Don't ignore the middle," she replied. "We are the backbone of America."

TWO

Recovering from the Great Depression

The Great Depression was something Americans hoped they would never experience again. In the rural Midwest, foreclosures and sheriff's auctions were common. Farmers postponed purchasing tractors and combines long after they became available because there was no way to afford them. Electric lights and indoor plumbing were present in towns but did not extend to the surrounding farms. The worst drought years devastated the land. Dust storms blew with such intensity that crops failed and machinery broke down. Even the rattlesnakes perished.

World War II sparked the economy, revived agriculture, and coincided with better weather. It left casual observers forever believing that hard times ended about as quickly as they began. But the war took millions of men and women away from their families, necessitated mandatory rationing, and drove up prices. When it was over, rural communities faced continuing challenges. Schools and roads were in disrepair. Soil conservation projects remained sparse. Young families whose lives had been put on hold struggled to make a new start. Good crops and high prices for wheat and corn boosted farm incomes. But mechanization was costly, and opportunities to buy land were scarce. Only the better off could afford to expand. In the 1950s, adverse weather returned, and uncertain markets resulted in wide annual fluctuations in family income. Government programs served less effectively to stabilize prices than policy makers hoped.

Farm communities nevertheless had a long history of adapting. Although the first settlers had come expecting to put down roots, they had moved before and would do so again when conditions required. Many set an example for later generations and did move on. Those who stayed created enduring social institutions. On the open frontier, homespun wisdom and neighborliness were not enough. Homesteaders found land by enlisting the help of agents and government surveyors. Counties, townships, and sections imposed spatial order on the land. Entrepreneurs laid out towns with aggressive strategies for attracting newcomers and businesses. Settlers took competition for granted. Churches, lodges, women's auxiliaries, veterans associations, the Farm Bureau, and the

Grange organized social gatherings. Newspapers and rural mail delivery linked communities to the wider world. Scientists studied rainfall, experimented with hybrid crops, and sent out agents to advertise the results. Farmers learned which crops to plant and how to get into and out of livestock markets. Retailers varied inventories accordingly. When the Dust Bowl was finally a memory, the patterns of life that had sustained the heartland in the past exhibited continuity even as they underwent significant revision.

Smith Center, Kansas, serves well to illustrate the challenges rural communities faced as they overcame the setbacks of the Great Depression and prepared for the era ahead. Located just south of the Nebraska border about 260 miles west of Kansas City and twelve miles west of the U.S. geographic center near Lebanon, Smith Center is smaller by several hundred people than it was in the 1950s, and it has experienced dramatic changes in what people do for a living. But it is still at heart a farming community. On all sides, country roads form perfect mile-length squares. Fields of wheat, corn, and milo and pastureland fill the squares. Most of the fields range from forty to 160 acres. Occasional groves of trees mark the location of a farmstead. A tourist from West Virginia or California might consider the landscape utterly flat, but to local eyes the terrain is gently rolling. Along Beaver Creek to the southwest and Spring Creek to the south, the elevation is about fifty feet lower than it is closer to the Nebraska line. Many of the fields are terraced to deter erosion. "The soil is one of the best in the world," an early visitor declared. "A person driving across the county from east to west," wrote another, "would never travel over three miles without crossing a stream of pure spring water as nearly every stream in the county, except the Solomon river, have their source within the county and are fed by springs which boil up copiously in almost every portion of the county."[1]

The town itself spreads out for a mile or two on either side of U.S. Highway 281, which comes in from the south, runs along Main Street until it joins U.S. Highway 36 at the north edge of town, and jogs east. Most of the businesses are located along these two arteries. Blue and white banners flutter from each of the lampposts along Main. "A City for all Seasons," they proclaim. A large mural in the shape of Kansas adorns the brick side wall of one of the businesses. The inscription reads, "Smith Center, Kansas. Heart of the Nation, Still beating strong!" On the south edge of town is a small hospital, constructed in 1951 with a new wing in the 1990s, and a municipal airport farther out. The county courthouse, a grand three-story structure built in 1920 with a small jail out back, sits two blocks east of Main. A few of the homes are stately, well-kept Victorians on corner lots. Many of the houses are modest one- or two-story frame dwellings dating from the 1920s. As in most farming communities in Kansas, Smith

Center's tall cement grain elevator, with a faded "Co-op" sign near the top, is the most prominent structure on the horizon.

"Sounds like Sleepyville," an acquaintance remarked upon hearing that I had been spending time in Smith Center. Her reaction is not hard to appreciate. Although it is untrue that a dog could take a nap in the middle of Main Street (any more than it could in Lebanon), a person might be ready for one after searching in vain for fine cuisine or urban amusement.[2] Duffy's Tavern, the local watering hole, usually has a pickup truck or two parked in front but is shuttered and uninviting. A Pizza Hut on Highway 36 offers the usual fare. Many of the stores are empty, closed, or without patrons. Second Cup Café & Pastries, with its fifties-era decor, is the place to find coffee and conversation. It sits lonely between a vacant store on the right and the old, red-brick bank building on the corner that is now maintained through a state-run preservation fund. Its regular customers include the As the Bladder Fills Club, a group of retired men who show up every morning, rain or shine. A few women gather occasionally across the street at the Quilted Four Patch to work on handicrafts. Just crossing the street can inspire the thought that one might better have driven. The distance from one side to the other could accommodate a four-lane thoroughfare with room for parking on both sides.[3] When the town was laid out, there was no need to skimp on space. And there still isn't.

The tempo of life is slower here than in many parts of the country, and the pace of change is, too. People do not hesitate to think before they speak. There is no need to form an opinion quickly. Vehicles crawl through town slowly, as if to savor each moment before heading into the vacant countryside toward Osborne, Phillipsburg, or Red Cloud, and there is no hurry at the Second Cup. Yet it would be profoundly inaccurate to conclude that Smith Center is a slumbering town on the verge of collapse. Agriculture in the county has prospered. Average incomes have never been high but have steadily risen. Poverty levels and unemployment are low. A local manufacturing plant has expanded. The high school excels in football, graduates 100 percent of its seniors, and sends more than four-fifths of them on to college.

Bobbi Miles, a retired chemist who moved here with her husband a decade ago to renovate one of the old Victorians, says the slow population decline that began in the 1950s has bottomed out. The town will never be much larger than it is now, she hopes, and it may become smaller. "This is kind of an oasis," she says. "It's a good place to raise wholesome young people. Everything you need is right here." At the bed-and-breakfast she runs, business has been brisk. Mornings she heads to the local workout center, which is forty-five seconds away, and stops afterward at the Second Cup. Evenings she and her husband play cards with their friends or take in a first-run movie at the theater. Tickets are $4.50 and on Tuesdays, $2.50.[4]

The transformation that has taken place here has been incremental enough to be nearly imperceptible unless one pauses to think about it in decade-length chunks. It is most immediately visible when a store closes or a new one opens and when a person dies or a family moves away. Gambles Hardware and the J. C. Penney store are gone, but the John Deere dealership has expanded and the old Safeway has been replaced by a new Heartland Foods. Change has been a constant in the history of Smith Center. The farmers whose big rigs till the soil today are the grandsons of farmers who struggled during the thirties to make anything grow. They, in turn, were the descendants of pioneers. Learning to adapt was their way of life.

The rolling prairie that Smith Countians now call home was once part of the extensive inland sea that covered the continent's center, and it later played an important role in the lives of nomadic hunters. Evidence of the sea has come from numerous fossils, including one identified as the tooth of a shark that lived in the area about sixty-five million years ago. In 1939, a young anthropologist named Loren Eiseley, who would become one of the most distinguished archaeologists of his generation, conducted research near Smith Center. He found evidence that nomadic bison hunters had populated the land thousands of years earlier. In the nineteenth century, the main north-south Pawnee hunting trail passed directly through the area. The Europeans who settled in the 1870s remarked about the abundance of buffalo and the transient presence of native peoples who hunted them. A woman who came to the area as a girl in 1871 recalled large herds of buffalo coming down from the hills to the river for water. She remembered going hunting with her uncle for antelope, wild turkey, prairie chicken, and quail. Another early settler remembered a few Indian families living in the area in 1871 and, on one occasion, about eight hundred Pawnee who came from Montana on a three-week hunting trip. About a year later, Dr. Brewster M. Higley, a settler who occupied a cabin approximately eight miles west of Smith Center, penned the words that became the lyrics of "Home on the Range."[5]

> Oh, give me a home,
> Where the buffalo roam,
> And the deer and the antelope play,
> Where never is heard a discouraging word,
> And the sky is not clouded all day.

Although Kansas became a state in 1861 and some parts had been settled in the 1850s, plans for the region in which Smith Center is located took place mostly in the late 1860s. In September 1865, a U.S. government peace commission appointed by President Andrew Johnson met with five thousand Indians near the present site of Wichita and concluded a treaty that permitted the white settlement of western Kansas. Conflicts continued during the next two summers, including a major battle between four companies of the Eighteenth Kansas Volunteer Cavalry and more than three hundred Kiowas and Cheyennes at Prairie Dog Creek on August 21, 1867. A second treaty was negotiated that fall, and by 1869, armed hostilities in western Kansas largely ceased. The Kansas legislature divided the area into counties by an act approved on February 26, 1867, and surveyors completed the work of creating township and section maps soon after.[6]

The formal organization of Smith County, named after Union Army Major Nathan Smith, was approved in 1872 by the Kansas legislature, and the county seat moved from Cedarville in the southwestern part of the county to Smith Center in November of that year. The town had been incorporated the previous September by the Smith Center Town Company, a group of five investors from Republic and Jewell counties to the east. Like Osborne County to the south and Webster and Franklin counties across the state line in Nebraska, Smith County immediately attracted homesteaders seeking farmland and drew merchants eager to cater to their needs. During its first year, the town became home to a blacksmith shop, post office, hotel, grocery store, doctor's office, newspaper, school, and church.[7]

The massive grasshopper invasion that swept across the state in July 1874 temporarily halted further development. "There are thirty-one counties in Northwestern Kansas that were stripped of everything by grasshoppers," two residents of Smith County wrote to a Chicago newspaper that fall. "We know of a number of families and little children that are suffering and starving in this neighborhood." One family traded a $15 plow for a $3 sack of flour. The state legislature authorized bonds for emergency relief, and when these proved immediately to be inadequate, settlers sent representatives to Kansas City, Chicago, and other cities where private committees organized shipments of food and supplies for the destitute. "Some people lost heart and returned East," one resident recalled, "but the majority of them remained, and finally got a toe-hold and became prosperous farmers."[8]

The following year, hopeful inhabitants poured into the county in large numbers. A census taken in 1875 showed a population of 3,876, nearly all newly arrived. Except in the northern third and far southwestern and southeastern corners of the county, nearly every plot had been claimed. A third of the new residents came from Iowa, and another third came from Illinois, Missouri, Nebraska, and eastern Kansas In 1876, an observer in Junction City, through which most of the pioneers to Smith County passed, wrote that "our roads are and for some time have been literally whitened with the wagon-covers of incoming settlers."[9] That winter, the editor of Smith Center's newspaper lauded the county as a place of "good homes and cheap lands, the best of climates, the richest of soils, schools, churches, factories and all the equipments and adornments of an advanced civilization."[10]

Over the next two years, the population of Smith County swelled to 8,249. A homesteader stopping at Kirwin in 1878, where the government land office was located, wrote that "estate agents and law offices seemed to be located on practically every vacant lot."[11] By the end of the decade, there were thirty-seven businesses in Smith Center, including two banks, three grocery stores, two drug stores, and three hotels. In addition, two doctors and seven lawyers had opened offices. Population in the town had risen to 450 and in the county to more than 13,000. Communities in the southern part of the county, including Harlan, Gaylord, and Cedarville, grew especially rapidly with the advent of rail service in 1879. Countywide, there were 2,717 farms, totaling more than 475,000 acres, of which about a third were in crops and the remainder were in pasture. More than 90 percent of the farms were owner operated, and more than 90 percent of those included 100 acres or more. In 1880, the county produced nearly 270,000 bushels of wheat. It was also the domicile of more than 3,700 milk cows, 5,000 other cattle, nearly 7,000 horses, and more than 24,000 pigs.[12] The county showed every sign of being a place where families could put down roots and stay for generations. Yet in reality, it was a community of migrants. Three-quarters of its leaders had moved at least once before. Four in ten had moved more than twice.[13]

Smith Center's boosters worried about the absence of rail service, which did not come until 1887, and initiated numerous proposals to bring lines up from Gaylord, down from Nebraska, or through from the east. Despite glowing reports of prosperity supplied to eastern newspapers, they endured harsh winters on the nearly treeless plains and scorching summer heat. Willa Cather, who lived for six years just north of Smith County in Red Cloud, wrote, "The sun was like hot brass, and the wind that blew up from the south was hotter still."[14] But in many respects Smith County was fortunate. With average rainfall around twenty-two inches, it was at the western edge of what agricultural economists would later term the Kansas corn belt. Wheat grew in abundance and pastureland was sufficient for livestock. The lack of railroads spared it from the problems that Russell and other counties to the south faced where large blocks of Kansas Pacific Railroad land were held tax free until further settlement drove up prices. Unlike Phillips County to the west, in which large cattle ranches slowed settlement, and Marion County in central Kansas, in which investor William Scully purchased more than 55,000 acres, Smith County offered a location for the average farm family to establish a home.[15]

The families who settled Smith County in the 1880s were part of the vast westward migration that populated the middle United States during the last third of the nineteenth century. Between 1870 and 1900, the U.S. population doubled from thirty-eight million to seventy-seven million, but the nine-state heartland region increased by almost 280 percent from a little over four million to more than twelve million. At the start of the period, the Middle West made up 11 percent of the nation's population, but by the end, it accounted for nearly 16 percent. Growth was especially rapid in the western half of the region. Kansas, Nebraska, Oklahoma, and the Dakotas grew by a total of 730 percent, compared with 220 percent in Iowa, Minnesota, Missouri, and Arkansas. Settlers flooded west from Illinois and Ohio because land was cheap or free. They moved from Iowa and Missouri into Nebraska and Kansas as cavalry regiments pushed back the Indians and railroads crossed the prairie. Often the men came first, but women and children soon followed. In Smith County, men outnumbered women by only a ratio of four to three in the 1870s. In 1880, two-thirds of the adults were in their twenties or thirties. Children and teenagers made up more than half the total population. School attendance through eighth grade was mandatory. In 1882, there were 123 school districts, 120 school buildings, and 101 salaried teachers. Forward thinkers anticipated the need for advanced schooling. At Harlan, local backers announced the opening of Gould College under the sponsorship of the United Brethren Church and with expectations of support from its namesake, railroad magnate Jay Gould.[16]

Agricultural production became successful enough and expectations of future prosperity rose to the point that land in Smith County increased in value to five or six dollars per acre in 1880 and to thirteen dollars per acre in 1890. North central Kansas was also starting to be seen as an attractive location for mortgage loans from investors in the east who earned as much as 10 percent annually. Besides goods for household consumption, a commercial market developed in butter, eggs, wool, wheat, corn, and pigs. Until the Central Branch Railway arrived in Gaylord in 1879, goods were transported 120 miles by team and wagon to and from Waterville for rail shipment between there and Kansas City. The first elevators were grist mills that ground grain for families and livestock and took a share of the grain as payment. Store owners often had farms of their own and generally planted gardens and raised chickens, and it was not unusual for teachers and doctors to accept produce in payment for their services. The largest need was for lumber, most of which had to be shipped in by rail and wagon. A visitor to the area in 1888 remarked that there were "very few houses outside of the towns of any other material than sod."[17]

In later years, people mostly remembered the small details of daily life. A woman who grew up near Gaylord recalled the importance of fending off loneliness. "They made friendly visits with neighbors for miles around, and when any entertainment was planned, everyone was willing to do his part to make it a success." A pioneer who lived about eighty miles west of Smith Center in 1885 described caring for two cows, a calf, and some chickens. "Chickens and eggs had to be saved to buy sugar, salt, beans, soda, molasses, coal oil, feed for chickens, hogs, and cows," she wrote, "but we always had enough to eat." She remembered making "considerable butter" from milk kept cool in a sod milk house and using the income to purchase groceries and fabric. A woman whose family raised corn wrote that four or five sacks of corn would usually be hauled to the miller who took his share in exchange for grinding. Wheat flour was expensive, she said, "so we lived mostly on cornbread." A man whose family homesteaded on the open prairie described pig killing as a time when "we all helped at the scalding and scraping off of the bristles." In winter, he said, the dead pig hung in a cold corner of the house. "We used just to take a hatchet and cut off as much as we wanted to fry." Others wrote of planting watermelon and tomato seeds, of searching for wild gooseberries, and of baking pies. They described plowing, milking, and killing snakes. They were struck by the quiet serenity of the plains, but also by the prevailing wind. "Kept us awake," one settler wrote in her diary after a particularly blustery night. "Shook the house most down."[18]

The start made in those first few years was the beginning of a viable agriculture-based community, but it took another decade to turn the homesteads into fully productive farms. Between 1880 and 1890, the number of farms in Smith County was nearly constant, and the total acreage in farms rose by less than 3 percent, but the number of *improved* acres (fenced or under cultivation) increased by almost 150 percent. In 1880, the average farm had only 57 improved acres; by 1890, it had 141. The typical farmer planted 19 acres in corn at the start of the period; 56 acres at the end. The number of livestock also increased dramatically. The average farm kept nine pigs and one cow in 1880; it kept thirty-four pigs and seven cows in 1890. Among other things, butter production quadrupled as a result. The number of chickens and other poultry increased fivefold, which boosted egg production from fewer than two dozen a week to nearly six dozen. The one thing that did not increase was the equipment, which remained valued at about $90 per farm. But considerably more field work could be done as the number of horses doubled. Overall, the average value of annual farm output rose from $245 in 1880 to $467 in 1890.[19]

Farm prosperity and the arrival of the Chicago Rock Island and Pacific Railroad in November 1887, which ran from Chicago to Denver, resulted in a building boom in Smith Center. By summer of 1888, nearly 500 residences were being built, one brick bank building had been finished, and two others were under construction. Along Main Street, three entire blocks of brick buildings were replacing earlier wooden structures. By 1892, there were four hotels, six general stores, and three drug stores. Five restaurants catered to customers from the railroad, which made Smith Center a regular eating stop. There was also a billiard hall, a photograph gallery, and three newspapers.[20]

By the 1910s, the social and economic patterns that had been established in the 1880s had generated enough business to transform Smith Center into an active commercial hub. These were the years that later analysts would describe as the heyday of Midwestern agriculture. Population in Smith Center climbed from 450 in 1880 to 1,292 in 1910 and rose to 1,567 by 1920. Sixty businesses were open along Main Street, and more than a dozen were located on side streets. Besides restaurants, drugstores, and banks, there were specialty shops for jewelry, candy, and bicycle repair, a place to view moving pictures, and a public library. The store that had been established in the 1890s on Kansas Avenue behind the bank to purchase eggs and poultry had added a cream station next door. The building that would later be the location of Second Cup Café & Pastries was a Masonic lodge, and above the stores next to it was the Opera House. Along the tracks of the Rock Island Railway stood the large Smith Center Mill, Elevator and Light Company and the smaller Smith Center Co-operative Grain Company. Within a few yards of the depot was an icehouse, a hotel, a large lumber company, and the new Standard Oil service and delivery station. The Baptists, Christian Church members, Congregationalists, Methodists, and Presbyterians all had fine houses of worship near the center of town. In the county, there were more than 500 Lutherans, more than 600 Presbyterians, nearly 700 United Brethren, and more than 2,000 Methodists. The congregations were linked federation-style to their denominations with regular meetings that brought pastors and laypeople together locally and regionally.[21]

The farms surrounding Smith Center in the 1910s were mostly quarter sections, but the average acreage per farm had edged up from 182 in 1890 to 214 in 1910 and rose further to 229 in 1920. About a tenth of the farms in the county had more than five hundred acres. L. C. Uhl, an early settler who practiced law and operated a hardware store, owned an entire section north of town, and several of his neighbors had farms of 480 acres or more. But there were no landowning monopolies. Farmers signaled their progressiveness by naming their farms. South of town, one could visit Ideal Home Farm, Cedar Lawn Farm, Grand View Farm, and Pleasant View Farm, while to the north were Sunnyside Farm, Brookside Farm, Golden Crop Farm, and Modern Home Farm. Although the names most often connoted features of the terrain or aesthetic qualities, some—such as Spring Brook Dairy Farm and Poland China Stock Farm—suggested their function. Nearly every farm included a farmstead, and as historians have noted for other areas, these were sometimes located so that neighbors were just across the road from one another, but in many instances, the closest neighbors were at least a quarter mile away. A sense of community came less from daily contact than from participation in meetings of the Farm Bureau and the Grange and through kin networks.[22]

From 1890 to 1920, Smith County farmers adapted to fluctuating weather conditions and broadening market opportunities by shifting the mixture of crops and other commodities they produced. The average farm produced more than a thousand gallons of milk annually throughout the period, and farmers increasingly sold cream and butterfat to creameries instead of producing their own butter. Farm butter production fell by more than two-thirds. With improved breeding and husbandry techniques, egg production increased by 60 percent. Hog production declined, in part because of uncertain prices. The largest shift was in wheat. From an average of eighteen acres per farm in 1900, wheat increased to fifty-two acres per farm in 1920. In 1890, Kansas wheat sold for an average of seventy-seven cents a bushel; in 1919, for $2.14 a bushel. Overall, the total value of farm output in Smith County quadrupled between 1890 and 1920, as did the value of farmland. With mechanization and higher taxes, the costs of farming also increased.[23]

Residents in those first decades of the twentieth century would have viewed themselves as the beneficiaries and promoters of technological change. Smith Center enjoyed telephone service and electricity, and the livery stables were rapidly being replaced by garages and automobile repair shops. The trains that roared through town came more often and had more powerful engines. Countywide, a third of residences had electricity by 1926, and 80 percent had an automobile or truck. On the farms, it would be the 1930s before tractors appeared in any significant numbers, but the big implement dealers—John Deere, McCormick, Deering, Hollinger—became increasingly effective in marketing horse-drawn disks, lister cultivators, row crop equipment, and grain drills. As wheat became more prominent, binders and threshing machines were increasingly seen as necessities. However, a quieter change was also taking place in the county. The first settlers had been attracted by the prospect of owning their land, and in 1880, that ambition was true for all but 7 percent of the county's farmers. A decade later, the proportion of tenant farmers and sharecroppers had risen to 25 percent. In 1890, it was about the same (28 percent) but then rose to 36 percent in 1910 and 41 percent in 1920. By 1930, tenants were farming nearly half (46 percent) of the county's farms. Many were doing well, but the aspiration of landownership had become harder to realize.[24]

After World War II, when the children and grandchildren of those earlier residents had taken their place, the prosperity of the 1910s and 1920s seemed like a distant dream. The 1930s had intervened, halting much of the technological and economic development of the earlier time. The Depression brought severe hardship to Smith County, as it did across the nation. In 1929, Kansas winter wheat sold for an average of ninety-nine cents a bushel. By 1931, the price had fallen to thirty-three cents a bushel. Over the next decade, it averaged thirty cents below the 1929 level. In Smith County, wheat sold for sixty-three cents a bushel in 1930, but only twenty-nine cents in 1932. Corn dropped from sixty-four cents to fifteen cents a bushel. Hog prices fell from $8 per hundredweight to $2.40. Annual precipitation decreased from thirty-one inches in 1928 to ten inches in 1934 and was below average most of the decade. A farmer north of Smith Center wrote in his diary: "I haven't much ambition anymore. When one sees all he has slipping away, his ambition seems to gradually go along with the rest." That was in February 1936. On July 15 he wrote: "It is really too hot, dry, discouraging and devilish to do anything. Over 2500 have died in this 'great middle west' of the effects of this Hellish weather and country."[25]

The dust storms began in the spring of 1935 and came intermittently for the next four years. Residents with telephones looked out for one another by calling neighbors when storms appeared on the horizon. Schools and businesses closed as the sky darkened. "Smith Countians will always remember the chickens going to roost at ten in the morning because it was dark as night," one resident recalled, "of fathers rushing to school to get the students and sometimes not making it home in the car because the dirt got too thick to see to drive, of washing the chickens' nostrils because they were clogged with dirt, helping put adhesive tape around all the windows to try to shut out the dirt."[26]

The drought and sinking prices cut deeply into the local economy. Farmers in Smith County harvested nearly 128,000 acres of wheat in 1919 and 81,000 in 1929, but less than 44,000 in 1934 and only 24,000 in 1935. Wheat that formerly averaged twelve to fifteen bushels an acre yielded three bushels per acre that year. Corn averaged four bushels an acre. The number of pigs fell by two-thirds. Overall, the human population in Smith County decreased by 22 percent during the 1930s. Merchants sold 42 percent less merchandise in 1939 than they had in 1929. No farms were simply abandoned, as they were in Southwest Kansas and Oklahoma, but farmers lost their land to mortgage companies and banks. Farm sales and sheriff's auctions of farm families' equipment and household goods were "held so frequently during 1937, 1938, and 1939 that two or three were scheduled daily," one resident remembered. A study of land transfers showed a fivefold surge in acquisitions by life insurance companies, the Federal Land Bank, the Federal Farm Mortgage Company, and other firms. "It was a time when everyone was at least a little hungry and ragged," a man who lived just across the county line to the east remembered.[27]

The destitution experienced in Smith County in the 1930s was worse than anything since the grasshopper invasion of 1874. Chickens, eggs, and homegrown vegetables became the mainstay of household budgets. People suffered health problems from the raging dust storms. Work was harder to find, weddings and babies were postponed, and educations were deferred. Most people scraped by on their own resources, but more than 250 registered for emergency work programs. By 1939, things were better than they had been in 1934, but farmers continued to struggle. They planted more wheat that year than anytime since 1919, but the crop averaged only seven bushels an acre. Sorghum averaged six bushels an acre, and corn averaged only four. Milk production was 20 percent lower than in 1929. Egg production had fallen by 50 percent; hogs, by 87 percent. The value of total farm production in the county was two-thirds lower than in 1929. Farmers and their wives made do by repairing worn-out machinery and by farming with horses and mules. They went without household appliances, slept in cold bedrooms, and made their own clothes.[28]

In Smith Center and smaller towns like Lebanon, Gaylord, and Kensington, store closings were rarer than might have been expected (the number of stores actually increased during the 1930s). But merchants carried smaller inventories and hired fewer employees. Stores supplying essentials—lumberyards, hardware stores, and drug stores—survived, but general merchandise stores and restaurants declined. Between 1929 and 1935, four of the county's nine banks closed and deposits fell by 50 percent. The largest drop in population was among children, as young families had fewer children or left the area. Seeking employment off the farm, young women left in significantly larger numbers than young men. Other changes were simply put on hold. There were fewer cars and trucks in 1939 than in 1929, only a slight increase in homes with electricity, and tractors remained far less common than horse-drawn equipment. Only 11 percent of the farmhouses had electricity, and 8 percent had running water.[29]

The forties would later be known as a decade of prosperity, but mostly because of what people had been through in the thirties. Setbacks as serious as those of the Depression were not recovered from quickly or easily, even at wartime prices. Between 1939 and 1944, as many farmers went out of business as had during the previous decade. Wheat that sold for sixty-seven cents a bushel in 1939 climbed to $1.49 a bushel in 1944, and reached $2 in 1950. But labor costs tripled, and yields remained uncertain. Farmers planted as much wheat in 1944 as in 1929 but harvested 12 percent less. The crop in 1949 was worse, yielding only 6 bushels an acre. Farmers sold less than half as much corn in 1949 as they had in 1929. Fewer hogs and fewer eggs were produced, and the number of cattle was only slightly larger than it had been two decades earlier.

The rural modernization that had begun in the 1920s was especially slow in developing. Among the 1,501 farm families living in Smith County in 1950, 25 percent did not have telephone service and 61 percent still did not have electricity. Of those who did have electricity, nearly a third were not yet connected to power lines, operating instead from wind chargers and batteries. Electric washing machines had become the most coveted household appliance, but only 30 percent of the farm wives had one. Ninety-four percent lacked a hot water heater, and 86 percent relied on windmills to pump water. Although most of the farms had milk cows, 95 percent of the milking was done without milking machines. Most of the farmers had an automobile, but the average age of these cars was nine years. Two thirds of the rural families lived on unimproved dirt roads. Fewer than half the farms had a truck. There were only twenty-one hay balers in the entire county.[30]

By Depression-era standards, Smith County gave the appearance of doing well in the late 1940s. Local banks held over $3 million in assets, much in government bonds. Population was up, as soldiers returned and started families. The government-financed Agriculture Conservation Program offered assistance in such "scientific farming" practices as terracing and crop rotation. With gasoline and tire rationing lifted, families drove to Oklahoma and Colorado to visit friends and entertained relatives from towns in eastern Kansas. A new Lutheran church was organized, and business leaders purchased land to create a recreational park. Plans for the new municipal hospital were moving forward. The airport hosted a "fly-in" breakfast for area pilots. Members of the 4-H club were honored by the chamber of commerce and children who had gone off to college received recognition from the Rotary club. Prominent farmers were elected to offices in the Farm Bureau and the Kansas State Board of Agriculture.

The stark reality at midcentury was relative prosperity for the few who had come through the Depression unscathed and serious continuing hardship for many others. About 20 percent of the farmers were doing well. They farmed in excess of 500 acres, raised ample acres of wheat and corn, and had sufficient pastureland for cattle. It was possible on that scale to own a combine, a corn picker, and a truck and to employ a hired man. Most of the remainder were less fortunate. Forty percent had fewer than 260 acres and typically rented most of their land. Family incomes averaged only $2,000 per year; a quarter of the farm families lived on less than $1,500. Renters and farmers of small plots fared least well. From 1940 to 1950, the number of farms with fewer than 50 acres fell by 50 percent. In 1940, 48 percent of the farms were operated by tenants; by 1950, only 31 percent were. Those who did not work in agriculture worked mainly in retail stores and in utilities, keeping the telephones, electricity lines, and roads intact, and a few were employed in manufacturing. Unlike neighboring Phillips County, where oil had been discovered and an oil refinery built in 1939, and unlike Russell and Barton counties to the south where oil was becoming a major industry, Smith County remained overwhelmingly dependent on agriculture.[31]

Roy Brown, a third-generation Smith County farmer, remembered vividly what life was like in the late 1940s. His dad owned a small used tractor that sat outside because there was no shed and had to be dug out in winter when snow drifted around it. The family lived in an uninsulated frame house with no indoor plumbing. They chopped their own wood, which was barely sufficient during the cold winters. "We had this bucket of water in our kitchen," Roy recalled, "and there was no way to keep the fire going at night. In the morning there would be about a half inch of ice on the bucket."[32]

It took the 1950s for Smith County to recover and establish an economic basis for long-term growth. Tractors and trucks that had been unavailable during the war were now in plentiful supply, but high demand drove up prices. To make matters worse, drought came again in 1953, 1954, and 1955, reducing farm income and causing farmers to wonder if they were to relive the Dirty Thirties. An index of farm output based on food-grain production fluctuated wildly from a high in 1947 to a low in 1949, then to another high in 1952, followed by lows from 1953 to 1957.[33] Weather and land were the constraining factors. In good years, crops could yield three times as much as in bad years, but there was no way to predict or control the fluctuations. All the land that could be improved had been, and the balance of pasture land and crop land was nearly fixed by the terrain.

The one available option was to expand on capital investment. Farmers who could afford it or who had sufficient capital to borrow money did this by enlarging their land and equipment. From 1949 to 1959, the number of farms in Smith County dropped by 25 percent to around 1,100. The average farm grew to 480 acres, and the number of large farms with 1,000 acres or more increased from forty-eight to eighty-five. Larger farms were not only a way to grow more crops; they were also a good investment. The price per acre rose from $39 in 1949 to $76 in 1959, an increase of more than 20 percent after inflation. The other way of expanding capital was to invest in machinery. A new tractor in 1950 cost about $1,800, which was about 50 percent more than the value of *all* machinery per farm five years earlier. In 1950, there were as many tractors as farms; by 1959, nearly twice as many tractors as farms. The social effect of these changes was a significant decline in the farm labor force. As much land was farmed in 1959 as in 1949 with a labor force of 600 fewer, or about a third smaller. Relying more on machines and less on hired help, the average farmer grew about 20 percent more acres of wheat and raised twice as many cattle. Tenant farming declined from 31 percent in 1949 to 22 percent in 1959.

The other improvements that had been postponed by the Depression were better roads and electricity. In 1938, none of the state or federal highways in Smith County or in any of the adjacent counties was paved. In 1941, only U.S. Highway 36 was paved and that remained the case through the end of the war.

Statewide, Kansas spent less on highways in 1945 than it had in 1930. When the war ended, an aging highway system and demand for better roads necessitated significant new investment. Expenditures on highways throughout the state tripled between 1945 and the end of the decade. In 1950, paved mileage in Smith County was approximately double the 1945 figure. By 1957, paved mileage had doubled again, and nearly all the major county roads were surfaced with gravel. These farm-to-market roads were vital to the increasingly mobile farm population. Electricity expanded along the same roads and over the same period. Between 1950 and 1954, the proportion of farms with electricity grew from 39 percent to 87 percent, and by 1959, rural electrification was virtually complete.[34]

By 1960, the agricultural patterns that would continue to define Smith County during the remainder of the twentieth century were largely in place. Farms would become fewer and larger; tractors and combines would become more plentiful and powerful. The agricultural labor force would shrink, and the total population would decline. Had the Depression and World War II not occurred, the developments that consolidated during the 1950s probably would have taken place a generation earlier. Yet it was also the case that the transition in the 1950s was grounded in patterns that had been established much earlier. The aspiration to own land was as strong in the 1950s as in the 1870s. Wheat and corn, hogs and cattle remained the basis of the county's economy. Retail sales rose and fell with agricultural output. Farmers took pride in being independent but frequently faced hardships. They had looked to government to make land available in the 1870s, to protect them from eastern monopolies in the 1890s, and to provide assistance in the 1930s. That relationship with government was still present in soil conservation and agricultural stabilization programs in the 1950s and would continue in other forms in the coming decades.

At the end of World War II, much of the heartland resembled Smith Center. Although the shift from farms to cities and from agriculture to manufacturing was well under way, farming continued to define the region. In 1950, eighteen million people made the nine heartland states their home, just 2 percent more than in 1940. Five million lived on farms. Another four million lived in rural areas and in towns of fewer than 2,500 people. Most of the remainder lived in small to medium-sized towns. Only 15 percent lived in cities of 100,000 or more. In 656 of the 772 counties, at least half of the population was rural. In half of the counties, 80 percent was rural. Farming was the principal occupation of 1.7 million people and made up about a quarter of the labor force. Farmers operated a total of 339 million acres, which accounted for 84 percent of the land, and produced crops and livestock valued at more than $6.5 billion. Farms were more than five times as numerous as retail stores and more than sixty times as numerous as manufacturing establishments. The largest number of farms was in Missouri, with approximately 230,000, followed by Iowa, with 203,000; Arkansas, with 183,000; and Minnesota with 179,000. Oklahoma had 142,000 farms, Kansas had 131,000, and Nebraska had 107,000. The smallest numbers were in South Dakota, with 66,000, and North Dakota, with 65,000.[35]

Recovery from the Great Depression varied across middle America, but many of the dynamics evident in Smith County occurred elsewhere. People hoped the suffering was over, prayed that better weather would last, and tried to forget the hard times. But recovery was more difficult and often took longer than optimists anticipated. Mortgage payments came due with unrelenting regularity. Land was scarce and machinery prices were high. An infrastructure of roads, schools, telephone service, and electrical power remained to be built.[36] Hundreds of thousands of rural families lived in houses badly needing repair.[37] Indoor toilets were rare. Fires, accidents, and illness were not. Crop yields and livestock prices fluctuated dramatically from year to year. Rural communities struggled to reestablish an equilibrium between land and people. Tenants and farmers without the capacity to make large capital investments found it increasingly difficult to compete.

The national media circulated exuberant stories—almost as fanciful as boosters' glowing reports in the 1870s—and missed most of the details. "Money is pouring in on Western farmers," declared a *New York Times* headline in 1947. The "happy condition" in Kansas was like a California gold rush, the article noted. Bank vaults were piled high with cash. Farm youngsters were heading off to college in shiny automobiles, and new machines were "rolling into farmyards as rapidly as they can be produced."[38] *Time* painted a rosy picture of bright skies over the Midwest with farmers enjoying "bonanza" crops, "dollars galore," and unaccustomed pleasures. Some were "buying airplanes and putting landing strips in their fields."[39] Stories of farm prosperity continued in 1948 and 1949. If anything, prices were too high, analysts argued. Farmers were producing too much and government support programs were artificially boosting farm incomes. Everywhere barns and sheds were jammed with new tractors, combines, plows, harrows, and grain drills, journalists discovered. "Farmers," one wrote, "had the relaxed air of men who have plenty of meat in their smokehouses, though they weren't the kind to crow about it."[40]

That winter, on December 15, 1949, Clarence Seibel and Mary Koslowsky began their life together as farmers near Benedict in southeastern Kansas. With 320 acres of rented land, they felt fortunate. Three-quarters of the farms in their county were smaller. The average was 216 acres. As tenants, they paid the landlord a third of the wheat, soybeans, and milo they produced. Median family income countywide was $2,000. Only 6 percent of the families earned $5,000 or more. Nobody owned an airplane or had a landing strip. It would be another two years before the Seibels had electricity. Clarence worked part-time at a brick plant and in the winter cut firewood and hedge posts to bring in extra income. A well supplied water, which Mary carried to the house and barn in buckets. Until the 1960s, the unpainted farmhouse was heated with a wood-burning stove. "One could find the side of his body nearest the stove blistering hot," their son Eugene remembered, "while his backside was frosty cold from the drafty old farmhouse." Clarence nailed plastic over the windows each winter to keep out the wind. Mary heated wash and bath water on a kerosene stove that once exploded and set the wash house on fire. There was no bathroom and no telephone.[41]

The Seibels were not alone in lacking conveniences that most townspeople took for granted. In Iowa, where rural electrification projects had begun early, one farm in ten still lacked electricity in 1950. That was true of one-sixth of the farms in Minnesota and more than one-fifth of those in Nebraska and Kansas. In Missouri and South Dakota, 31 percent of the farms lacked electricity, while in North Dakota, Arkansas, and Oklahoma 33 percent did.

In 1942, the prestigious *American Journal of Sociology* published an overview of rural life in the United States drawing information from the 1940 decennial census. "With electricity," the author wrote, "came the electric lights, iron, radio, washing machine, refrigerator, vacuum cleaner, range, sewing machine, churn, pump, and all the smaller electrical equipment such as toasters, percolators, roasters, waffle irons, fans, dishwashers, heating pads, and curling irons." Besides these household conveniences, the sociologist observed, the husband "received many new services and implements such as electric fences, water pumps, milking machines, elevators, grinders, and the like which had previously been absent or operated by far more clumsy tools than the electric motors."[42]

It was fine to think that all this had already come about in 1942, but the truth was that a sizable minority of farm homes still lacked access to any of these conveniences in 1950, and a large majority enjoyed only a few. The extent of rural electrification varied significantly from county to county. In north central Kansas, only half of the 4,300 farms in Smith, Osborne, and Republic counties had electricity in 1950. Less than one-third had electricity in parts of western Kansas, southeastern Missouri, northern Nebraska, and central South Dakota. In principle, all counties had become eligible for rural electricity programs in 1936 when Congress passed the Rural Electrification Act. In practice, counties with larger land areas, where the cost of installing lines was higher, lagged behind smaller counties. Counties that experienced population decline or slow growth in the 1940s also fell behind.[43] Telephone service was even slower in reaching farmers like the Seibels. In 1950, service was lacking for 32 percent of the farms in Kansas, 35 percent in Nebraska, 40 percent in Minnesota, 44 percent in South Dakota, 54 percent in Missouri, 58 percent in North Dakota, 68 percent in Oklahoma, and 90 percent in Arkansas.[44]

In 1951, most of the Seibels' land flooded when heavy rain caused the Verdigris River to overflow. The water came all the way to their doorstep. In other low-lying areas many families lost their homes. The flood of 1951 left large sections of Topeka and Wichita underwater and alerted officials to the need for a system of dams, reservoirs, and levees. But it would take more than a decade to develop that system.

Too much water was not the problem in western Kansas, where drought was a recurring presence. Memories of the Dirty Thirties were still vivid there. Farmers remembered the measures they had taken to survive and worried about having to repeat them. On a farm near Coldwater in Comanche County in 1939, the Pepperd family sealed the dining room windows as best they could with strips of cloth, covered the table with layers of sheets, and huddled underneath as a massive dust storm rolled in from the west. "Grandmother wet a washcloth and told me to hold it over my nose and mouth. When it got brown spots on it, she would rinse it out in the pan and give it back to me," Margaret Pepperd recalled. "There has never been a lonelier sound for me than to hear the moans and screams of the prairie wind. All afternoon the wind howled and railed and hammered at the big old farmhouse." When the storm finally passed, the floor was covered with several inches of dust; outside, the fence posts were half buried. Margaret's father scooped dirt out of the house with a shovel.[45] Mary Lou Stewart's recollection was similar. Her mother also covered the dining room table and stuffed rags around the windows and doors. "The dust was like talcum powder and almost magnetic," she said. "You couldn't get it off the furniture or wipe it up." People suffered from dust pneumonia. Three children in her community died.[46]

Haskell County, south of Garden City, had experienced some of the worst devastation. In the 1920s, Haskell farmers had prospered, purchased automobiles, and driven regularly to town to watch a movie or spend an evening with relatives. But in 1940, the land lay gray and barren. Houses were unpainted, the farm yards were piled with dust, tumbleweeds rolled across the fields, and the granaries were empty. Earl H. Bell, a researcher from Nebraska, spent four months studying the county. "Nature in western Kansas had not changed," he wrote. "[S]he had only more masterfully, more cunningly, and more viciously than ever before succeeded in raising man's hopes to the clouds and then dashing them into the ground." An old man told him, "We had two feet of snow last year. Maybe the wheat will come up yet." The man's optimism worried Bell. When the rain became more plentiful, he predicted, land values would rise and speculators would return, but other dry spells would come and the people would again be sorely tested.[47]

By 1949, the economic situation in western Kansas was markedly improved. Median family income in Comanche County was $2,550 and in Haskell County, $4,200. Twenty percent of families earned more than $5,000 in Comanche, and 41 percent did in Haskell. Comanche's population had declined by only 12 percent during the 1940s, but Haskell had lost 30 percent. Most of the Comanche farms had electricity and telephones, but in Haskell more than 40 percent lacked electricity and only half had telephone service. Near Wilmore, about ten miles northeast of Coldwater, Buck and Wendell Ferrin had earned enough money growing wheat to buy a new LA model Case tractor and a Gleaner Baldwin combine. The first Ferrins had homesteaded the farm, and the next generation had struggled to save it during the 1930s when money was too scarce to pay the taxes. Wendell was away when he learned that a tornado had swept through the area. The storm somehow spared the tractor and combine but slammed seven large cottonwood trees into the house, damaged the barn, and destroyed the granary, chicken house, and shed. It took Wendell two years to clean up and repair the damage.[48]

Intermittent drought continued to plague the region. Rainfall was above average in 1949 but below average from 1951 through 1954 and again in 1956. In Haskell County, Paul and Evelyn Brown began farming a few months after their wedding in August 1949. They rented 160 acres and farmed another 320 acres owned by Evelyn's father. They lived in a small aluminum trailer house while Paul remodeled the old two-story farmhouse. Paul planted wheat that fall and again the next fall but with disappointing results. "With the drought, hail, wind and jackrabbits, we weren't harvesting anything," he recalled. Until 1960, he kept food on the table by hiring himself out as a carpenter and plumber, selling cream and eggs, hauling sand, and working for a custom harvesting crew each summer.[49]

The worst dust storm since 1939 swept through the region on February 19, 1954. In the Texas panhandle, visibility was cut to zero. An eighty-foot radio tower crashed across Main Street in Lubbock. Southeast Arkansas was hit by a tornado, and warnings were issued in Oklahoma and Texas. Schools were closed in parts of Colorado, Nebraska, and Kansas where winds blew in excess of sixty miles an hour. In Coldwater, Garden City, and Dodge City, shopkeepers shoveled dirt off sidewalks like snow.[50] As the drought continued that winter, wheat died and pastureland turned to dust. Fences blew down and livestock suffered from inhaling dirt. Residents in Missouri hauled water by truck as local wells dried up. Crops failed in Iowa and the Dakotas. An engineer in Oklahoma City estimated that one of the storms deposited 185,000 tons of dirt on the city, enough to fill a large auditorium.[51]

The drought continued in 1955 and 1956 with occasional dust storms that stalled motorists and turned day into night. A farmer in Missouri described the five-year drought that dried out his pasture and shriveled his corn as an insidious "wearing-away process that leaves the farmer's pocketbook, and very often his temper, thinner and thinner."[52] On January 14 and 15, 1957, President Eisenhower toured the drought-stricken areas, making stops in San Angelo, Texas; Woodward, Oklahoma; Clovis, New Mexico; Pueblo, Colorado; and Garden City and Wichita, Kansas. He talked with farm men and women, saw parched fields and underfed cattle, and heard experts discuss the economic consequences. Aides reported that he was thoroughly depressed. At a meeting in Wichita attended by representatives from fifteen states, the president promised to ask Congress for $25 million in emergency drought relief, $25 million for soil conservation programs, and $26 million for refinancing farm indebtedness.[53]

Federal programs were already an important—but often controversial—part of the postwar recovery. Farm loans from various federal agencies totaled about $511 million in 1940, grew to $1.8 billion by 1950, and topped $3 billion in 1956.[54] Government, Eisenhower told the assembly at Wichita, should be a "cheerful, willing partner," adding that "responsibility and direction of action" should be at the "local scene." Sensitivities to being dependent on government ran strong in a region proud of its self-sufficiency. From a business standpoint, it was seldom clear whether the government programs made sense. Farmers were leary of federal bureaucracy from what they had experienced thus far. In the 1930s, frustration with the government loan system had simmered into open protests.

Elmer G. Powers, a farmer in central Iowa, wrote for months in his diary about wasted trips to the loan office and poor communication "I do not wish to always be 'throwing cold water' but it is pretty certain that before things are over some branches of the New Deal will 'stink to high heaven,'" he wrote in 1933, "and possibly a number of them will." Two years later he wrote, "This evening I am rather bitter toward the local, State and National agencies that are supposed to assist the farmer. I know something about how thousands and thousands of farmers have been treated and how they feel."[55]

In Kansas, farmers participated reluctantly in federal soil bank and relief programs or did not sign up at all.[56] In 1936, Edna and Bill Heim wrote from Smith County to their landlord in Topeka that they were "not going to take the soil program" because it "would be less than $160 altogether" and they would have to "plow up some wheat." On August 31, 1938, Edna wrote about the new government conservation program scheduled to take effect in 1940. "We have been to S. Center also talked with several of the Committee men & all we are allowed to plant on your farm is 26 [acres]." The letter explained that sixty acres would have to remain idle in order to qualify for a seed loan. "There are very few who are taking it," she said.[57] A decade later, soil conservation efforts had become more popular; yet in 1950, the county agriculture agent reported that only 200 of the county's 1,500 farmers were participating.[58]

The debate after the war focused on government price-support programs. Price supports aimed to prevent a recurrence of the dramatic declines in crop prices that farmers had experienced in the early 1930s. A guaranteed minimum price was established through a formula for determining "parity." The formula was based on prices paid by farmers from 1909 to 1914, a period judged to have been favorable to agriculture. A farmer who could purchase a year's supply of coffee in 1910 by selling fifty bushels of wheat, for example, was to be able to purchase the same amount in 1949 by selling the same amount of wheat. If wheat prices rose higher than parity, farmers were well off, but if wheat prices sank to about 90 percent of parity, the government stepped in and purchased wheat to keep the prices from falling lower.[59]

The program was popular with farm organizations because it provided a safety net without interfering in farmers' decisions about what to raise or purchase. The debates focused on small but important details. Which crops should be covered? Major field crops in the Midwest, such as wheat, corn, and milo, were included—as was cotton in Arkansas, Oklahoma, and the South—but many of the crops raised on smaller farms (such as vegetables) were not. Livestock was not included, which meant that farmers who purchased grain to feed cows and pigs sometimes paid prices they regarded as excessive. Urban consumers complained that they were paying to subsidize farmers both through taxes and at the grocery store. The government also faced perplexing questions about what to do with the grain it purchased.

Assistance programs notwithstanding, a massive relocation of the rural population occurred during the 1940s and 1950s as part of the post-Depression and postwar restructuring. Nationwide, the farm population dropped from thirty million in 1940 to twenty-five million in 1950 and stood at just over twenty-one million in 1959. The raw figures implied that each year, one farm family out of every fifteen quietly moved to town and took up some other means of earning a living. But broad statistics concealed the extent of the change involved. Data assembled by the U.S. Census Bureau in 1960 showed that the farm population was ten million smaller in 1959 than in 1936. However, during this period, natural increase—births minus deaths—had enlarged the farm population by 9.3 million. In addition, a cumulative total of 20.8 million people had moved *to* farms. In all, a cumulative total of 41.1 million had moved *from* farms—considerably more than the number who remained.[60]

The census figures also revealed dramatic annual fluctuations in farm migration. Between 1936 and 1940, net migration from farms was driven by the Depression but was relatively small by later standards. About 5 percent of the farm population left each year, and this number was offset by in-migration of about 3 percent each year. World War II reduced the farm population far more significantly. In 1942, out-migration exceeded in-migration by 1.4 million; the figure rose to nearly three million in 1943 and was still higher than 1.5 million in 1944. The war's end set in motion a new dynamic. In 1946, the number of people who moved to farms jumped by nearly 300 percent, while the number moving off farms sank to prewar levels. In 1947, in-migration and out-migration effectively canceled each other. Then, as if time gave people a chance to see that farming was no longer possible, out-migration in 1948 rose to a higher level than at any time except 1943. Another large exodus occurred in 1950 and again in 1953 in conjunction with the Korean War. Relatively few net departures occurred in 1955 and 1956, but another significant exodus occurred in 1957 as a result of that year's drought.[61]

Residents liked to describe their rural communities as bastions of settledness where families came and stayed in one place for generations. An observer in Smith County wrote in 1960, for example, that nearly everyone could claim to have descended from some of the original homesteaders.[62] Smith Center's newspaper printed stories about these ancestors, and community organizations hosted pioneer days and old settlers' picnics in their honor. But in reality, a shifting population was often characteristic of rural communities. A study of Presho, a prospering community in central South Dakota, for instance, found seeming stability between 1910 and 1920, when the population declined slightly from 635 to 597; yet closer inspection showed that only 15 percent of the 1910 residents were present in 1920.[63] At the start of the twenty-first century, the Bureau of Labor Statistics devised a metric it called the thirty-six-month turnover rate, which added the number of separations and openings and divided that number by the total jobs in a particular industry or occupational category. By that metric, the thirty-six-month turnover rate for farm population averaged 36 percent during the 1940s and 27 percent during the 1950s.

Movement from farm to farm and temporary relocation from farm to town or town to farm were harder to measure but were significant among segments of the rural population. A rare compilation by local historians in Mitchell County, Iowa, just south of the Minnesota border, demonstrated some of these shifts. The county had suffered during the Depression, when corn sold for 10 cents a bushel and loans on more than 350 of the county's 1,600 farms were in arrears or foreclosed, but was faring much better in the 1940s.[64] The area around Meroa in the southwestern part of the county was homesteaded by immigrants from Norway in the 1850s and remained heavily Norwegian a century later. Its residents prided themselves on close ties with neighbors and extended families. The information assembled in 1977 was meant to commemorate those ties but revealed another aspect of what longtime residents also knew to be true. Farmsteads were in flux. Farmers died or retired and were replaced by sons or sons-in-laws. Widows stayed and hired renters to farm their land. Sons tried farming in partnership, and one bought out the other. A tenant family lived in rented buildings on another farm and worked as hired labor until an opportunity for better work opened elsewhere.

Each farm near Meroa carried a distinctive genealogy. The Norbys had a 200-acre farm purchased from the U.S. government by one of the community's first settlers in 1861. They lovingly referred to it as the Old Homestead. The settler's son had farmed the land from 1885 until he retired in 1938. After several short-term renters left, the Norbys arrived in the early 1940s. There were two houses on the property. They lived in one and rented the other to a family who helped with the farm. The hired help included at least three different families who came and went between 1943 and 1948. The Norbys' son worked the farm after the war until his death in 1959, upon which his widow rented out the land. The Larson farm told a different story. Avilla Larson inherited the 85-acre farm in 1949 from her father, who had rented it to a tenant farmer in 1947. The tenants lived on the place one year but moved to another farm the next year and continued to work the land. Avilla rented out the farm to another family who lived on it for six years and farmed it for two more. New tenants arrived in 1955 and purchased the farm in 1957. An equally complicated pattern of occupancy was evident down the road at the Olson farm. Julius and Inga Olson purchased the 104-acre farm from an uncle in 1942 after having lived on it for two years. Julius did some of the farming, but was known mostly as a refinisher of antique furniture. He relied on a series of tenants and hired helpers to work the land. Tenants included the Christiansens, Husets, Olsons, Andersons, Lees, Ericksons, Lindleys, Maakestads, Bakers, and Amundsons. Hired workers included the Brocks, Wherrys, Lindleys, and Amundsons.[65]

During this period, Steve Sanger was growing up in Cedar County, the birth-place of Herbert Hoover, in eastern Iowa. His father worked for farmers as a hired hand. Steady work was difficult to find. Between 1933 and 1940 the family moved fifteen times, "living in places with no electricity or running water." Heating, Sanger recalled, was usually a "hand-fired coal furnace with one big grate in the middle of the living room floor." By 1945, the Sangers had moved seven more times, and after that lived in nine different places.[66]

Families fortunate enough to stay put lived with the uncertainty that they *might* have to move after working hard to put down roots. Tenants were especially vulnerable. Jeanne and Arie Van Kley felt lucky in 1945 when they found a farm to rent near Ocheyedan in northwest Iowa after farming with his relatives for four years. The landlord, Charlie Strayer, was known locally as a self-made millionaire who treated his tenants fairly. Yet there were frequent difficulties. Charlie would accuse Arie of not giving him his half of the corn and Arie would argue that Charlie should pay for building a better crib. Electricity was available, but the farm buildings had not been wired. Charlie bought the supplies, but asked Arie to donate all the labor and then berated his work. Jeanne feared they could lose their lease at any time, especially if a relative of Charlie's or a more prosperous neighbor wanted the farm. After fifteen years, that happened. Before the Van Kleys could remove all of their possessions the new tenants came and burned what remained.[67]

Movement and uncertainties like these were accompanied by another sort of adaptation: supplementing on-farm income with off-farm work. Across the Middle West, an average of 12 percent of the farmers worked at least 100 days off the farm in 1949. The proportions ranged from 4 percent in the Dakotas, 6 percent in Nebraska, and 7 percent in Iowa to 11 percent in Minnesota, 12 percent in Kansas, and 19 percent in Missouri, to 22 percent in Oklahoma and 25 percent in Arkansas.[68] Just south of Smith Center in Osborne County, Lowell Guyer was a teenager in the late 1940s. Being a younger son, he stood no chance of inheriting the family farm, even though farming was what he knew best and wanted to do. He took welding classes in high school and after graduation worked as a welder at $4 an hour in the winter and as a hired hand for his uncle in the summer. They worked as custom wheat cutters following the harvest from Texas to the Dakotas. After five years Lowell had enough money to purchase a used tractor and was able to rent some land. He eventually relocated to Sherman County in western Kansas and by the time he retired was farming 10,000 acres.[69]

Sherman County suffered relentless drought and periodic dust storms during the 1930s. Rainfall was significantly below average in all but one year from 1930 to 1941. A detailed study conducted by airplane in 1937 identified 752 occupied farmsteads. A follow-up study in 1950 found that 222, or about 29 percent, had been razed or were seriously deteriorated and were no longer occupied. "Scars of abandoned places, such as concrete foundations and small dilapidated sheds, can be seen by the score," the authors wrote.[70] Some of the better houses had been moved to Goodland, the county seat; others were already in poor condition in the 1930s and by 1950 were still on unimproved roads. Telephone service came through wires nailed to fence posts, if it was available at all. An examination of land deeds showed that 66 percent of the farms had changed owners at least once in the previous thirteen years; nearly a third had transferred more than once. An increasing share of the land was in the hands of so-called sidewalk farmers who drove out from Goodland. Suitcase farmers from other counties were also showing up. For years, Lowell Guyer slept on a cot in the tractor shed when he came out to Sherman County.

Sidewalk and suitcase farming were modes of adapting to changing agricultural conditions. Both were more common in dry land, wheat-growing counties than in areas with livestock and dairy operations. Sidewalk farmers could enjoy the relative comforts of town residence and hold alternative off-farm jobs. Suitcase farming hedged against local crop failures by scattering production across a wider region. But there were costs. Sidewalk farming concentrated people in central locations at the expense of smaller towns. The Sherman County study found no clubs, churches, or stores anywhere in the county other than in Goodland. Suitcase farming, it was feared, reduced earnings and investment in local businesses and left farms untended during dust storms. A 1952 study of Sully County in western South Dakota, found that about a third of the wheatland in the county was in the hands of suitcase farmers, the majority of whom lived in Texas, Oklahoma, and Kansas. Nearly 80 percent of the suitcase-farm land was owned by absentee landlords. The county's population had dropped by half since 1930.[71]

Across the Midwest, about a third of the families who left the farm during the late 1940s were in their late fifties or older and moved because they were ready to retire, in poor health, widowed, or stepping aside for their children. Another third were young adults leaving to attend college or seek better opportunities elsewhere. Some moved to be closer to schools, to get away from run-down farmsteads lacking electricity and indoor plumbing, or because they lost their lease. Economic considerations invariably played an important role. Whether young or old, poorer people left the farms, while those who were better off stayed. In 1950, when census takers asked people if they had moved off a farm in the past year, 618,000 in the nine heartland states said they had— approximately 12 percent of the farm population. On average, family incomes of those who left were 11 percent lower than among those stayed on the farm (ranging from 7 percent lower in Oklahoma and South Dakota to 14 percent in Arkansas and Missouri). Families with incomes less than $1,000 were two and a half times more likely to have left the farm than families with incomes of $3,000 or more.[72]

Carl Swensen graduated from high school in a central Kansas farming community in 1951. His father farmed 160 acres that had been in the family for three generations and raised four children during the Depression by operating a portable gristmill and wiring houses for electricity. Carl's class took an overnight graduation trip, and the next day Carl packed his work boots and hat in the old family sedan and went looking for a job. He had learned to drive a tractor, repair machinery, cut wheat, and milk cows. But generational succession was always problematic on small family farms. The meager acreage was his parents' livelihood and Carl had no money to buy land of his own. He took a job at a construction site. "When could you start?" the foreman asked. "I have my work clothes in the backseat," he replied, and began working that morning. When the project was finished, he worked as a filling-station attendant for a year, at an oilfield supply store for another year, and then at a nearby oil refinery for more than three decades. He eventually inherited his father's farm but never again lived there.[73]

On average, incomes in the heartland states were about 25 percent higher for town dwellers than for farm families and ranged as high as 50 percent more in Arkansas and Missouri. Moving to town was no guarantee of better wages for those who moved, but it did create opportunities to buy or rent more land for those who stayed behind. A study in Minnesota showed that approximately 4 to 5 percent of the state's farms exchanged hands annually. Twenty-five to 30 percent of the sales involved bequests and other transfers to heirs. Nonfarm investors accounted for another sixth. Farmers made up the rest, purchasing complete farm units or adding to their own acreage. Interviews with real estate brokers and loan agents showed strong demand for "good land" throughout the state but also revealed that many who wanted land could not afford it. As one agent remarked, "There are a lot of buyers, but 95 percent of them don't have sufficient down payments." Rising prices exceeded the reach of lower-income farmers, leaving most of the expansion to buyers with larger holdings.[74] Across the nine-state region, the total number of farms declined by 88,000 between 1945 and 1950, and average farm size grew from 309 acres to 331 acres.

Movement from farms to towns and from the Middle West to other regions would have been even greater were it not for another significant adaptation occasioned by the Depression: smaller families. In 1900, a typical farm woman in the Middle West aged forty-five or older had given birth to six children. That number varied only slightly from state to state, averaging 5.4 in Iowa and 5.6 in South Dakota and being the highest in Arkansas at 6.3. In 1910, the numbers were, if anything, slightly higher, ranging from 5.5 in Iowa and 5.6 in Missouri to 6.2 in Arkansas, Minnesota, and the Dakotas, and 6.3 in Oklahoma. When the Census Bureau next tallied the number of children ever born to each woman (in 1940), the numbers were significantly lower, averaging only 3.7 per farm woman aged forty-five or older in the nine-state region. Iowa, Kansas, and Nebraska were the lowest, with 3.2, 3.4, and 3.5, respectively; and Arkansas, South Dakota, and North Dakota the highest, with 4.1, 4.1, and 4.5, respectively. The numbers remained nearly constant between 1940 and 1950, with only South Dakota registering a significant decline.[75]

The Depression was one of several factors resulting in the decrease in number of children by more than two per average family. In the 1930s, women had fewer children because they could not afford to have more and in some cases because they remained single or married later. By 1940, 11 percent of Midwest farm women aged forty-five or older remained childless, whereas that was true of less than 4 percent in 1910. The proportion of farm women with only one child rose from 4 percent in 1910 to 12 percent in 1940. The proportion with four or more children fell from 76 percent to 47 percent.[76] Besides economic considerations, families opted for fewer children as farming became less labor intensive or as pressure increased to provide each child with larger acreage. This shift was evident in the fact that farm families in the Midwest had one more child on average in 1910 than nonfarm families, but by 1940 that difference had narrowed slightly and over the next half century declined further. The fact that fertility rates declined among nonfarm as well as among farm families underscored additional sources of change, such as better medical care and families having fewer children because more were expected to live.[77]

The consequences of rural families having fewer children in the 1940s than a generation earlier included both economic and social adjustments. Fewer children meant that stable or declining family incomes could be stretched further. That was increasingly significant as farmers relied less on homegrown food and sought more often to place their children on larger farms or send them to college. The social adjustments included lower rates of out-migration than would otherwise have been necessary for a smaller population to manage larger farms. The growing number of farm families with no children or only one child meant an increasing likelihood that those farms would be sold or turned over to tenants. As other factors continued to encourage a declining farm population, smaller families also meant that communities were likely to become smaller, that rural schools would close, and that the average age of the population would increase.

Had the years from 1950 to 1960 been as good for farmers in the Midwest as pundits imagined, the economic attractions of farming would have been strong and the decline in farms and farm labor probably would have ended. However, the decline that had been present in the late 1940s and evident in other parts of the United States continued. Between 1950 and 1959, the average county in the nine-state region experienced a 34 percent decline in agricultural workers and a 19 percent decline in number of farms. The agricultural labor force in 20 percent of the counties was only half as large in 1959 as it was in 1950. In 20 percent of the counties, the number of farms dropped by at least a third.[78]

The shrinking farm population prompted speculation among policy makers about the possible sources of this trend. The arguments typically emphasized the impact of machines, magnet pull, and marginality. The machines argument suggested that tractors, combines, corn and cotton pickers, and electric milking machines were replacing horse-drawn equipment and hand labor and making it possible for fewer agricultural workers to care for larger farms.[79] The magnet-pull theory emphasized the attraction of more abundant and better-paying jobs in the towns. The marginality explanation held that inefficient farmers on small plots were being replaced by larger and more prosperous operators. The arguments were not mutually exclusive but offered competing interpretations of what was going on—and indeed surfaced repeatedly in subsequent decades as observers sought to interpret the continuing decline of rural America.

A comparison of counties experiencing larger declines in agricultural workers and farms during the 1950s with counties experiencing smaller declines provides a simple test of the various arguments. According to the mechanization argument, counties in which a higher percentage of farms had tractors in 1950 should have experienced a greater percentage loss in agricultural workers and number of farms during the 1950s than counties with a smaller percentage of farms with tractors in 1950 (taking into account other differences, such as total population, number of farms, and share of the total labor force employed in agriculture). However, that was not the case in any of the nine states. Indeed, just the opposite was true in six states for agricultural workers and in five states for number of farms. It was counties with a *smaller* percentage of farms with tractors that experienced the most decline.[80] It was, of course, true in general terms that machines made it possible for fewer farmers to care for larger farms, but greater mechanization did not explain why some counties lost more farms and farmers than others. Less mechanization provided a better explanation. The large capital outlays necessary to purchase mechanized equipment and to modernize and expand buildings and facilities were simply beyond the reach of lower-income farmers. As an educator in Wisconsin observed, mechanization involving a tractor, tractor-drawn equipment, and a few other essentials required an expenditure in 1950 of more than $6,000, an investment that needed to be used on at least 300 acres to be economical.[81]

The magnet-pull argument served similarly as a broad generalization. The stereotypic farm boy saw Paris during the war and decided to seek his fortune in New York or Chicago. However, migration statistics showed that it was more likely for people to stay in the same county, if they moved at all, or to remain in the same state.[82] The relevant pull was from jobs in nearby towns. The magnet thesis could be examined by comparing counties in which the average wage for manufacturing jobs was higher and counties in which these wages were lower. Counties with larger or smaller urban populations could also be compared. Larger urban populations offered more opportunities and served more visibly as alternatives for farmers who wished to escape the rural life. Neither factor, though, was associated with a greater decline in farms or agricultural workers. The relationships were either insignificant or ran in the other direction. For example, *lower* average manufacturing wages were associated with higher rates of decline in the farm labor force in Kansas, Missouri, and Oklahoma, as was *lower* percentages of urban population in Arkansas, Missouri, and Minnesota.

In contrast, the marginality explanation was strongly supported. In six of the nine states—Arkansas, Iowa, Kansas, Minnesota, Missouri, and Oklahoma—the less prosperous counties experienced the greatest agricultural decline. This was also the case for some measures of prosperity in Nebraska and South Dakota. In the six states that showed consistent relationships, counties with *lower* median family incomes in 1950 had higher rates of decline in agricultural workers and number of farms than counties with higher median family incomes. Other predictors of high decline in agricultural workers and number of farms included lower average farm values in 1949, lower total value of farm products in 1949, lower value of crops sold in 1949, and lower value of livestock sold in 1949.[83]

That marginal farmers were being squeezed out by larger landowners who could afford bigger equipment and achieve more efficient economies of scale was clearly evidenced in comparisons of trends among farms of varying sizes. In Oklahoma, where farms in the eastern part of the state that raised cotton remained small, the number of farms with fewer than seventy acres fell by more than 18,000 during the 1950s. In Minnesota, where small farms were also plentiful, farms of that size declined by more than 9,000. In Kansas, where farms were larger, the number with fewer than 260 acres dropped by more than 25,000, and in Iowa, by more than 35,000. Nearly a third of farms in the region with fewer than 260 acres in 1950 were absorbed into larger farms by the end of the decade. In comparison, the number of farms with 260 to 500 acres declined by only 7 percent, while the number with 500 to 1,000 acres grew by 31 percent, and those with more than 1,000 acres grew by 52 percent.[84]

The county in which the largest percentage decline in farm operators and farms occurred was Saline County in central Arkansas. During the 1950s, the number of farmers fell by 82 percent and the number of farms dropped by 59 percent. The county had been hard hit during the 1930s. Hundreds were without work, and farms sold for a fourth of their pre-Depression value. Although nearly all the farms were owner operated, the land was hilly, wooded, and better suited for livestock and poultry than for crops. In the early 1940s, a majority of the farmers were supplementing their incomes by working at second jobs, a situation that continued in the 1950s. Many worked in the Alcoa and Reynolds bauxite mines or commuted to Benton or Little Rock. Off-farm wages were low but necessary to supplement below-subsistence farm earnings. Less than

10 percent of the farmers owned tractors in 1945, and only 20 percent did by 1950. Electricity lines reached most of the farms between 1945 and 1950, but few families owned electric washing machines, milking machines, or chicken brooders. More than half the farms were on dirt roads, and two-thirds lacked telephone service. It was not surprising that the farm population dwindled in the 1950s.[85]

The county-level evidence reinforces the conclusion from census data that a large-scale realignment was taking place. The reduction in agricultural workers and in overall number of farms involved the displacement of thousands of lower-income farm families. They left because they owned or leased less productive land, because they were unable to afford the machinery needed to make them appealing tenants, and because low-wage jobs in town were better than meager earnings on the farm. Observers sometimes referred to them as inefficient farmers who refused to capitalize their farms or engage in scientific agricultural methods. They were certainly less fortunate than many of their neighbors. The difficulties often dated back to the Depression.

Wayne Ninemire was 22 in 1948, when he returned to the farm in southwestern Missouri after serving five years in the U.S. Navy. In 1930, his parents were operating a successful dairy farm in South Dakota. They milked fourteen cows, raised wheat, kept horses and pigs, and made enough money to buy an automobile and keep food on the table for a family of five. In 1932, the drought began. "The dust would drift against fences, groves of trees and buildings up to four feet deep," Wayne recalled. His father borrowed money to plant wheat, but nothing grew. The next spring, the family packed up and moved to a rented farm in Missouri. Unlike their home in South Dakota, the old farmhouse in Missouri had no electricity. The Ninemires used kerosene lamps and carried water from a well. In 1935, Wayne's father was badly injured in a farm accident, spent four months in the hospital, and was severally crippled the rest of his life. Wayne's mother got a job through the WPA as a seamstress in a garment factory. A year later, the family returned to farming, now on another rented farm, and then moved again in 1939. The farm was hilly and the soil was filled with rocks, but it was the best farm they could find. With his father disabled, Wayne did most of the work. Each day before and after school, he fed and milked eight cows and took care of two hundred chickens, four horses, and several hogs; on weekends and in the summer, he tended the crops. During the war, his parents and a younger brother continued farming, and from 1946 to 1948, Wayne attended college in California while working nights at a laundry.

Wayne's return to the farm in 1948 coincided with his father's death. Wayne and his brother hoped to continue farming and to live in the rented farmhouse with their mother. Their only vehicle was a 1929 Model A Ford sedan. When they took calves to market, they loaded them in the backseat. Lacking a tractor, they tried using the car to pull a plow but quickly discovered that was impossible. Wayne and his brother farmed for three years, during which Wayne held an off-farm job at the Veterans Administration hospital, took flying lessons, got married, became a police officer, and worked nights at a dry cleaners. In 1951, he was recalled to active military duty for the Korean War. In 1952, he relocated with his wife and mother to Washington state. They never returned to the farm in Missouri.[86]

As farmers like Wayne Ninemire turned to other pursuits, those who stayed behind faced serious fluctuations in net income throughout the 1950s. In Iowa, total net farm income was $725 million in 1949, jumped to more than $1 billion in 1950, and stayed at that level for the next year. But in 1952, it fell by more than 20 percent to just over $800,000. In 1954, it returned to the $1 billion level, only to fall by more than 40 percent to $592 million in 1955. The next year was only slightly better. In 1957, the figure was back to more than $900 million, but it fell slightly in 1958 and then plummeted to $580 million in 1959. During one of the downturns, CBS newscaster Edward R. Murrow sent a camera crew to Corning, Iowa, to document an auctioneer selling Dale Peterson's machinery, livestock, and household goods. Peterson was one of three thousand small farmers in Iowa to quit that year.[87]

The annual fluctuations in other states were just as serious. In Kansas, total net farm income in 1956 was a third what it was in 1952. In South Dakota, the 1951 figure was twice that of 1949, but nearly all the gain was wiped out the next year, and the 1955 figure was lower than it had been in 1949. The variation in Nebraska from peak to nadir, respectively, in 1950 and 1955 was more than 260 percent. Total net income in Oklahoma in 1956 was two-thirds less than it had been in 1949. Across the nine-state region, realized net income per farm was about the same in 1959 as it had been in 1949.[88]

On July 14, 1958, the cover of *Life* magazine showed a farmer elbow high in a field of ripening wheat. The farmer was young, wore a straw hat cocked proudly on the crown of his head, and smoked a cigar. He looked pleased. "Best wheat in lifetime for an Oklahoma farmer," the caption read. The contrast with an earlier *Life* photo was striking. The May 27, 1946, cover was a black-and-white photo of an aging, leathery-faced farmer leaning wearily on his hoe. The man's hard life was evident in the calluses on his hands and apprehension about the future showed clearly on his face. Side by side, the two covers suggested that farming in the Midwest had progressed dramatically in the intervening twelve years.

But recovery from the Depression and World War II was not that simple. There was a saying in rural communities that people ran harder just to stay in place. The truth of that observation was evident in national statistics. Net farm income totaled $15.1 billion in 1946, and after rising to $17.7 billion in 1948, sank to $10.7 billion by 1959. To keep from falling further behind, farmers amplified gross revenue by producing crops valued at 34 percent more in 1959 than they had in 1946 and livestock valued at 37 percent more. An index of farm productivity that began in 1948 showed an increase of 77 percent between that date and 1959. Farmers managed on lower total net income by dividing it among a smaller farm population.[89]

The social adjustments that accompanied and facilitated these changes were considerable. Prosperous farmers and outside investors bought the land that poorer farmers and retirees put up for sale. Tenants and low-income farm families moved away. But economic inequality remained a prevalent feature of rural life. In 1960, the bottom 30 percent of farm families existed on less than $2,000 a year and often lived in substandard housing.[90] In the nine-state region, 54 percent of these families lived in houses without plumbing facilities in 1960, 52 percent did not have indoor toilets, and 39 percent did not have telephones.[91] Farmers who were better off purchased larger tractors, better corn pickers, and faster combines and accomplished more with fewer hired hands and tenants. They increased productivity by caring for larger farms and raising more livestock. Rising land prices made it possible to anticipate a nest egg at retirement, and in the meantime, they provided the tax base necessary to maintain and upgrade schools.[92]

Rural residents got used to driving longer distances to county seats and other commercial hubs, or they lived in town, commuted to farms, and did less of their business in smaller communities like Lebanon, Kansas, and Meroa, Iowa. Some found part-time work to supplement farm incomes, and a few started businesses of their own. Even in the most rural counties, about a hundred employees on average worked in small manufacturing plants.[93] As farms required fewer agricultural workers, employment shifted toward service occupations, automotive repair, machinery sales, construction, health care, government, and the professions. Long-term residents adjusted to the likelihood that their children would move away but also found reassurance in the fact that living costs remained low in their rural communities, that they were finally connected with electrical and telephone service and had better roads, and that chain stores and television were bringing them the same products and ideas that people enjoyed elsewhere. They had also learned that government was a permanent partner in their lives.

In 1960, heartland residents turned out in record numbers to cast ballots in the presidential election. Had it been up to them, Richard Nixon would have won by more than half a million votes. The 1950s, though an improvement over the 1930s, had been difficult for small farmers, tenants, sharecroppers, and merchants in low-income communities throughout the Middle West. But government price-support programs provided some stability against fluctuating markets, and federally guaranteed loans assisted with farm modernization and capital improvement. Highways and schools were markedly better, and rural electrification was nearly complete. In good years, families hedged against downturns by investing in land and equipment or putting money in savings accounts. In 1960, bank deposits were higher in inflation-adjusted dollars in 80 percent of the counties than in 1950, and land values per acre had risen by more than 50 percent.[94]

A visitor to Smith Center in the twenty-first century would likely conclude that little had changed since 1960. Wheat was still the dominant field crop, followed by sorghum, which largely replaced corn in the 1950s, and about a third of the county was pastureland. Cattle and pigs were probably less abundant, though it was hard to tell, and livestock was still present on most of the farms. However, there was one dramatic change: about half the farmsteads were gone. Heading east from Smith Center, a traveler would pass only eight farms on the way to Lebanon, where once there had been more than twenty. Countywide, there were 1,141 farms in 1959, but only 546 in 2002. Since 1960, people had become fewer, too. Smith Center's population had dropped by 20 percent; the county's, by 40 percent.[95]

In 1969, there were 1,095 farm proprietors in Smith County, but that number declined by an average of twenty-nine per year during the 1970s and eleven per year during the 1980s and 1990s. As the number of farm proprietors fell, the average acreage per farm increased from 579 in 1969 to 949 in 2002. Only 15 percent of the county's farms exceeded a thousand acres in 1969 but 36 percent did in 2002. In short, the pattern of farms becoming fewer and larger continued.

The uncertainties that characterized the 1950s also continued. Wheat yields increased, but prices fluctuated from just over $2.00 a bushel in 1962 to $1.25 in 1969 before jumping to $4.09 in 1974, only to fall back to $2.42 in 1986. Farmers hedged by adjusting wheat acreage up or down by as much as 20 percent, reducing pastureland by nearly a third, and investing in livestock. Raising cattle became popular in the late 1960s and early 1970s; the number of hogs varied from highs in the middle 1960s, late 1970s, and early 1990s to lows in the middle 1970s and late 1990s. Overall proceeds from livestock exceeded proceeds from crops by a margin of two to one in 1969 and again in 1978 but fell below the value of crops by the late 1990s.[96] Countywide, farm incomes grew between 1969 and 1973, declined steadily until 1978, registered net losses in 1980 and 1981, and then fluctuated over the next quarter century with increases occurring in fourteen of those years and declines in the rest.[97]

Farmers nearing retirement or with other sources of income had good reason to sell by the end of the 1970s. Adjusting for inflation, land purchased in 1950 was worth four times as much in 1978. Those who did not sell may have wished they had. In real terms, land was worth half as much in 1987 as it was in 1978 and was only slightly higher at the end of the century. Adjusted for inflation, the value of farm production doubled between 1964 and 1974 but declined steadily after that. In 2002, its value in real terms was 37 percent its value in 1974.

Smith County, though, was in no danger of dying. Although it remained a farming community, it exemplified the restructuring that was taking place in rural locations across the region. Fewer farms meant that larger shares of the population were living in town, working there full- or part-time, sending children to school there, and perhaps commuting to the scattered fields they owned in several different townships. Nearly half the county's population lived in Smith Center, and two-thirds of those who lived in any of the county's towns did so. Several new businesses were open along U.S. Highway 36 and revenue from local sales taxes was on the rise. Importantly, fewer farms and fewer people were producing more at the end of the century than their predecessors had in the 1950s. The county grew three times as much wheat in 1997 as it had in 1959, three times as much sorghum, and despite fewer acres, twice as much corn.[98]

Several factors were responsible. The competitive market in which farmers participated encouraged continuing interest in technological innovation. Besides fertilizer, which was being applied more effectively to more acreage, hybrid wheat was being planted that grew shorter stalks and larger heads and was more resistant to drought and disease. Similar improvements were made with corn and sorghum. As a result, wheat, corn, and sorghum averaged more than twice as many bushels per acre in 1997 as in 1959.[99] Economies of scale played a role as well. The number of large farms with more than a thousand acres doubled. Farms that formerly had one or two tractors now had three. The big John Deeres for sale in Smith Center sported up to 530 horsepower, compared with models in the 1950s that had no more than 40. More farmers were also experimenting with no-till methods that involved sowing new crops in fields minimally cultivated from the previous season. No-till farming conserved more of the soil's moisture, saved on fuel and labor costs, and was conducive to greater crop diversity. As one farmer explained, "My major concern when going into no-till was, 'Is it economically justifiable?' And the answer is a qualified 'yes.'" The qualification was that weather still posed a risk and crop insurance was a necessity.[100]

These and other efficiencies in agriculture resulted in a dramatic restructuring of the local labor force. With fewer farms and larger tractors, employment in agriculture fell by 75 percent. Fewer people and fewer houses led to declines in construction and retailing. Slightly more people commuted to jobs in neighboring counties. But the labor force grew substantially in other sectors. The number employed in government jobs was almost three times as large in 2000 as in 1960. Trucking and utilities employed twice as many people as in the earlier period, and manufacturing grew almost as much. Teaching and other jobs in education increased by 80 percent. Overall, five-sixths of the labor force worked in nonagricultural jobs, up from only half in 1960.[101]

Like so many heartland towns, Smith Center prides itself on home-grown talent, self-sufficiency, and personal relationships. Patrons at the Second Cup greet one another by their first names. Residents know their neighbors and notice if a stranger passes through town. But Smith Center is integrally connected with the outside world. From almost the start, it depended on the railroad to ship the grain and livestock it produced, and that artery continues to be vitally important to the local economy. Its farmers borrowed money from eastern investors, and those connections continue. Daily wheat prices at the Co-op reflect changes in transportation costs to Kansas City, and the market there is influenced by the supply in Canada or Argentina and demand in Japan or Europe. Farmers discuss the latest farm bill's progress through the House and Senate. They can check it by cell phone from their tractors. The Farm Service Agency used to send a man out to measure fields qualifying for government payments. Now the measurements are made by satellite.

THREE

Reinventing the Rustic Life

Historian David B. Danbom observes in *Born in the Country* that generations of Americans who lived on farms and in rural communities grew up hearing that they were residentially deficient. They learned from journalists, writers, and even educators that country folk lacked sophistication, opportunities, and intelligence. Geography kept otherwise well-meaning people from exercising ambition and imagination, deprived them of enlightened morality, and stunted their creativity. Their dull surroundings generated an inferior existence. Farm women developed unfeminine muscles, used outdoor privies, and wore unfashionable clothes; their yokel husbands told crude jokes and chewed tobacco. Townspeople in rural areas were not much better. They knew nothing of fine art and exotic cuisine. Theirs was a dull white-bread and mashed-potatoes world. An entire region could be afflicted. In middle America, hicks, hillbillies, and hayseeds drove down the cultural barometer. They spoke in a nasal dialect and perpetuated peculiar locutions, like "crick" and "warsh." The picture was almost a mirror opposite of the Jeffersonian ideal that saw agrarian life as the taproot of civilization. The heartland was a national embarrassment. Rustics were simpleminded, ignorant, usually boring, and sometimes downright comical. They were certainly not the kind of people who could transform a region or bring it prosperity.[1]

Shorn of these negative connotations, a rustic was merely someone who lived on a farm or in a small village located in the country. The term was as common in England as in the United States. People of means found it charming to mingle for brief stints with rustic fellows devoid of high breeding and given to colloquial speech. A day in the country amidst cow meadows and simple folk, experiencing the "farm-field's rustic grace," as John Greenleaf Whittier once described it, could be refreshing. Londoners might tour into the Cotswolds in search of rustics, and New Yorkers could visit them in rural New Jersey or Vermont. As cities grew, retreat centers advertised escapes at rustic cabins with country cooking; antique dealers displayed rustic wares; artists searched for rustic fences, barns, and bridges. It became vaguely appealing to associate with something passed over, discarded, or left behind. A region of farms and small country towns was easily perceived in these ways. Yet it did not sit well with rural Midwesterners to think that they were merely the remnants of a bygone era.[2]

Between the 1940s and 1960s, heartland residents gained exposure to newer and more positive interpretations of the rustic life. Books, newspaper columns, farm magazines, and films depicted rural Midwesterners as progressive farmers and townspeople who provided a wholesome, secure, and yet simple environment for their families. Rural electrification, off-farm work, and consolidated schools dramatically reduced the gap separating farm families from residents in small towns. Television exposed rural and urban communities to the same sitcoms, newscasts, and films. Middle Westerners came increasingly to be regarded as ordinary members of the American middle class, distinguished by a tradition in which home life and self-sufficiency were especially valued. The heartland was a place of can-do optimism, straight talk, and neighborliness. It provided safe communities in which to raise children, a familiar space that held few of the dangers or temptations of the city. The land itself came increasingly to be seen not only as a source of income but also as scenery, as an appealingly serene landscape in which residents could take delight. To be rustic was to understand and appreciate these simple pleasures.

But redefining the self-image of a region takes place in fits and starts, draws on cultural repertoires that sometimes have little to do with regional identity at all, and entails the selective relocation of competing images. Ambivalence is inevitable. Heartland writers in the 1950s viewed their neighbors as progressive Americans who lived in modern houses, enjoyed the same consumer conveniences as everyone else, went sightseeing and took vacations, worried about national economic and foreign policy issues, favored scientific and technological advancement, and wanted their children to receive a good education. They appreciated the opportunity for short visits to big cities and to know that friends and relatives in distant places were watching the same television programs and listening to the same music as they were. Yet they had also known for a long time that their communities were becoming smaller and that the action, excitement, and coveted opportunities for profitable jobs and self-development seemed increasingly to be elsewhere. Against this sense of displacement, there were distinctive regional traditions on which to draw and from which to craft an identity well-supplied with virtue. These legacies connected middle America with its real past but offered mythologized versions that served better to inspire fantasy than to define reality. The Wild West of adventuresome gunslingers and Indians was one such legacy. The pioneer spirit represented by courageous homesteaders was another. There was also the legacy of the Depression, of displaced Okies and beleaguered Dust Bowlers, who were often a source of embarrassment but, in the right telling, could be viewed as emblems of sacrifice and determination. These possible identities were readily available in the region's history and in books, on television, and in motion pictures. It was necessary, though, to rework them. As time passed, cowboys, pioneers, and Depression survivors faded as realistic role models and were replaced by portable personal identities emphasizing resourcefulness and conviviality.

By the late 1960s, regional identity in the Middle West had lost much of its earlier distinctiveness. The old stereotypes about rural Americans lacking intelligence had largely been put to rest. Fewer Middle Westerners were in fact rural, and far more were better educated than in previous generations. Local speech was closer to the standard inflections heard on radio and television than in places like the Bronx, New England, Texas, or the Deep South. Nationally recognized brands available since the 1920s from General Mills, Procter & Gamble, Sears, and Penney were now supplemented by food from McDonalds and cartoon characters from Disney. Becoming part of the national culture was associated with the region's economic growth and with upward mobility for individuals and families. Yet Middle Westerners also found ways to maintain a local and regional identity. They did this by shaping the meaning of the various traditions at their disposal. The Wild West shifted further west geographically and further into the realm of fantasy. Pioneers became settlers, who valued their families and modeled simple virtues of honesty, ingenuity, and hard work. The Depression came to be a story about the value of home and neighborliness. The heartland was a place in which simple values, children, and an appreciation of the land could flourish. None of these traits was distinct to the Middle West, which meant that the heartland could be almost anywhere Americans wanted it to be.

Until his death in 1917, few people had done more to shape a popular image of the American frontier than William F. Cody, the legendary Buffalo Bill. Cody was born in 1846 in Scott County, Iowa, and moved with his family in 1854 to Kansas Territory where his father was shot for making an antislavery speech. Cody rode for the Pony Express, fought in Missouri during the Civil War, found work at Salina and Ellsworth in Kansas, killed buffalo for the Kansas Pacific Railroad, served at Fort Hays as a scout in campaigns against Plains Indians, and owned a ranch in Nebraska. If anyone could associate the Middle West with frontier excitement, it was Cody. By the late 1870s, newspapers and dime novels had made him a folk hero. In 1883, he organized the "Wild West" show, a four-hour spectacle that included sharpshooters, wild animals, and Indian raids. The traveling show toured the United States and Europe for thirty years and was seen by millions. In the 1920s, five motion pictures included portrayals of Buffalo Bill. That number grew to sixteen by the early 1940s, and ten more appeared in the 1950s.

Cowboys and Indians held a continuing fascination in the Middle West, as they did throughout America. In the 1950s, children played with bows and arrows and six-shooters, read books about Trigger and Flicka, named their dogs Bullet and Rin Tin Tin, imagined themselves as Roy Rogers or Dale Evans, begged their parents to take them to rodeos, and watched *Gunsmoke, The Lone Ranger, Hopalong Cassidy, Gene Autry,* and *Death Valley Days* on television. In the Middle West, where places like Dodge City and Deadwood were located and where Indian battles had actually been fought, the legends of gunslingers and outlaws might have played a special role in countering the view that the region was boringly rustic. But the Wild West, as it was increasingly portrayed, was not the Middle West. Between the 1890s and 1930s, the distance grew. The Middle West became a region settled by farmers and townspeople who had no direct connections with cowboys and Indians and who regarded themselves as civilized people with as much refinement as anyone else. After World War II, they had more reason than ever to think this was true. Television and motion pictures relocated Westerns to the Southwest, West Coast, Mexico, and Canada. Children in the Middle West who played cowboys and Indians may have been unaware of local frontier history, and they certainly knew that in real life, the heroes never visited their farms and towns. The excitement was elsewhere. If a new definition of their communities' special qualities was to be drafted, it would have to be from other stock.

Shifting perceptions of the Wild West, already evident in the 1880s, could be traced in the stories of two Nebraskans: William F. Cody and Polly Spence. According to his biographer, Cody became a Nebraskan on February 4, 1878, with the purchase of 160 acres near North Platte in Lincoln County. Although Cody himself spent much of his time traveling, his wife and family lived in Lincoln County for the next thirty-five years, and Cody made numerous trips to oversee the ranch that grew to more than 4,000 acres. Polly Spence was born in 1914 in Bladen, Nebraska, forty miles north of Lebanon, Kansas, and as a young woman moved to northwestern Nebraska, where she married a man whose family had lived there since the 1880s. She died in 1998, leaving a detailed autobiography.[3]

Polly Spence's family by marriage, the Levi Richardsons and James Brittons, were living in eastern Nebraska in 1883, north of Omaha, where the Richardsons farmed and the Brittons operated a ferry across the Missouri River. As talk of railroad expansion and homestead opportunities in northwest Nebraska spread, the families discussed moving to the White River Valley and then, the following summer, headed to the new community of Bethel, seventeen miles east of the future town of Crawford in the northwest corner of the state.[4] The Crawford area was as close to being the Wild West as anyplace in Nebraska. Until 1876, it belonged to the Oglala and Brule Sioux. Nearby Fort Robinson, established in 1874, was the site of Sioux chief Crazy Horse's fatal stabbing on September 5, 1877. An 1882 report found approximately 800 white people in all of northwest Nebraska. Several large ranches specialized in raising horses, and there were an estimated 300,000 cattle in the area.[5] Crawford was known for its saloons, prostitutes, lawlessness, and fights between soldiers and cowboys. Polly Spence's relatives told stories of killers disposing of bodies in wells.

On May 19, 1883, as the Richardsons and Brittons contemplated their move west, William F. Cody staged a show that the two families would likely have heard about and possibly attended at the new Omaha fairgrounds. Cody had been appearing in smaller performances for several years, but the Omaha show, which he named "The Wild West Rocky Mountain and Prairie Exhibition," was his first large-scale production. The event began with a parade of Indian warriors, squaws, and papooses; cowboys; elk, burros, goats, and mules; and two marching bands. The spectacle proceeded with an Indian race, an exhibition of Pony Express riders' rapid-relay methods, an Indian attack on a stagecoach, a sharpshooting demonstration by Buffalo Bill, a steer-wrestling contest, and a buffalo chase. Cody insisted that everything be authentic. He recruited Sioux Indians from western Nebraska, Wyoming, and South Dakota. The stagecoach was from a route to Deadwood in the 1870s. The attack was so real that the stage driver was nearly unable to bring the mules under control. Cody concluded the program with a speech in which he described the program as "a thoroughbred Nebraska show." It was not hard to imagine that the 8,000 cheering Nebraskans saw it that way.[6]

Through the end of the decade, the "Wild West" show's proximity to real life continued. Sharpshooters and cowboys were recruited among the acquaintances Cody made in Kansas and Nebraska during his own exploits on the frontier. Sitting Bull joined the exhibition in 1885, earning $50 a week and a $125 bonus, and brought with him several Sioux warriors who received lesser salaries. In 1890, when soldiers were sent from Fort Robinson to the Pine Ridge Indian Reservation in South Dakota to investigate rumors of a Ghost Dance resurgence, Sitting Bull was suspected as an instigator. On December 15, 1890, Sitting Bull, his son, and twelve others were killed when an arrest order turned into a gunfight. Two weeks later, the Seventh Cavalry massacred 120 men and 230 women and children at Wounded Knee. Following the attack, members of the Ninth Cavalry—the famous "buffalo soldiers"—at Fort Robinson were sent to assist in securing the area. Audiences in New York, Chicago, St. Louis, and New Orleans read about these events in the newspapers. Cody's extravaganza brought the excitement of the Wild West to life.[7]

But in the 1890s, the Wild West and the Middle West gradually parted company. In 1893, as spectators thronged the Wild West exhibition across the street from the World's Columbian Exposition in Chicago, the historian Frederick Jackson Turner gave his famous speech declaring that the frontier epoch was over. No longer, Turner argued, would America be defined as a struggle between savagery and civilization on the open prairie. The legacy of that era would rather be evident in a "softening down" characterized by "coarseness and strength combined with acuteness and inquisitiveness." Anticipating arguments that would be heard again and again, Turner predicted that heirs of the frontier would be practical and inventive, "lacking in the artistic," but individualistic and buoyant. As if sensing the same shift, Cody's version of the Wild West became wilder, less concerned with authenticity, and more focused on pure entertainment. The show included Roman chariots; starred stage shooter Phoebe Mozee—better known as Annie Oakley—from Drake County, Ohio; employed horsemen from England, Germany, and Russia; and featured Arabs and Cossacks in musical drill. Cody seemed to have taken as his model P. T. Barnum, whose rail coach he purchased in 1891.[8]

Back in northwest Nebraska, residents hoped to capitalize on their claim to being part of the Wild West. In 1893, realizing they were almost exactly one thousand miles from Chicago, the locals organized a race to see who could cover the distance to Chicago by horse the fastest and enlisted Cody to publicize the event. The race began on July 27 at Chadron, a few miles from the Richardson and Britton farms. The race, though, proved an embarrassment for all concerned when several of the entrants, including the winner, were discovered to have traveled part of the journey by train. The "Wild West" show continued until 1913 with declining gate receipts and several mishaps, including a train wreck that scattered buffalo and elephants near Lowell, Massachusetts. Residents in North Platte counted Cody as one of their own, but as time passed, it was doubtful that the same was true in much of the Midwest. The Buffalo Bill legend was associated less with Nebraska or Kansas and more with the Little Big Horn in Montana, a town named Cody in western Wyoming, and his gravesite in Colorado.

When Polly Spence moved to northwest Nebraska in the 1920s, there were 11,000 people living in Dawes County; horses were common (more than 7,000), but farms had become the foundation of the local economy, producing nearly 700,000 bushels of wheat, 400,000 dozen eggs, and more than two million gallons of milk. In the 1930s, she and her husband settled into raising cattle and wheat on the farm his grandfather homesteaded and continued in that routine through the forties and fifties. But in the early 1960s, the area's intermittent association with the Wild West returned when Polly opened the ranch to guests and began advertising in the *Saturday Review*. Her sense of what mattered about the area's identity was revealing. She felt it would be wrong to bring in horses and wagons or pretend to offer an exciting Wild West experience; she disdained Buffalo Bill, whose marksmanship she likened to shooting fish in a rain barrel. The authentic identity of the region, she believed, lay in its natural beauty. "In the spring," she wrote, "flowers bloom in every crevice. . . . [T]he meadowlark breaks the silence with her sweet, piercing, gurgling song; overhead a golden eagle wheels, and a vulture sails, tipping this way and that." As guests arrived from New Jersey, Connecticut, and California, she took them on walks, showed them how a farm works, and persuaded them that the area was rich in neighborliness. She wanted people "who'd like us because of our remoteness and quiet, our history and natural beauty and our laid-back cow country atmosphere."[9]

Spence considered Nebraska special because it was rustic, and that meant simple, old-fashioned congeniality and loving appreciation of the landscape. It made sense to think of northwest Nebraska this way because the area had long ceased being the Wild West. That was a given. But the cowboy heritage had also been relocated and redefined. Buffalo Bill had become too much of a mythic figure to take seriously or to regard as a local hero. A similar trajectory followed other frontier celebrities. Wild Bill Hickok grew up in Illinois, farmed, served as a constable in Kansas, and lived in Nebraska and South Dakota. Wyatt Earp spent his childhood in Illinois and Iowa, received wounds during the Civil War in Missouri, served as a constable in Missouri, hunted buffalo in Kansas, and was a law officer in Ellsworth, Wichita, and Dodge City. George Armstrong Custer was stationed at Ellsworth and Fort Hays. Sitting Bull lived in South Dakota. Jesse James lived in Missouri. All were featured in popular films during the 1930s and 1940s. Yet the West of Western films was increasingly situated in Arizona, New Mexico, Texas, Colorado, Wyoming, Montana, and California, not the Middle West.

By the early 1940s, critics also observed that Western films were shifting from depictions of the Old West to a New West in which cowboys were tamer and more civilized. The Old West was a raw space of open prairie, buffalo herds, Indians, cattle drives, and lawlessness that largely preceded settlement or statehood. The New West included towns, ranchers, fenced land, and small farmers. Often the townspeople and farmers were struggling to persevere against land grabbers, conniving railroad and mining interests, and outlaws. During the Depression, residents of the Middle West could identify with these struggles. However, the films showed cactus and sagebrush more often than wheat fields and pastures. Cowboys chased through barren hills that looked far more like California, where they were in fact filmed, than Kansas or Nebraska.

In the 1950s, when children in the Middle West played and watched television programs about cowboys and Indians, the action was no longer realistically part of their own history but a kind of fantasy that existed elsewhere in a fictional world, if at all. *Death Valley Days*, one of the longest running series, televised from 1952 to 1975, was filmed in Arizona, Utah, and California. *Tales of the Texas Rangers* and *Sergeant Preston of the Yukon* were identifiably non-Midwestern. *Fury*, which aired from 1955 to 1960, was set on the Broken Wheel Ranch in California. *Sky King*, a children's Saturday morning favorite from 1951 to 1962, was filmed in Lone Pine and Apple Valley, California. *The Lone Ranger* television series that ran from 1949 to 1957 took place in Bronson Canyon, California, as did the *Adventures of Rin Tin Tin, Bat Masterson, Have Gun Will Travel*, and *Rawhide*. The most successful adult Western, *Gunsmoke*, ran from 1955 to 1975 and was set in Dodge City, Kansas, but was filmed at ranches in southern California. *Bonanza*, from 1959 to 1972, was filmed at the same locations in Simi Valley, near the future home of Ronald Reagan.

If television's thrilling Western adventures did not inspire children in the Middle West with regional pride, the episodes did convey stories of families who worked hard, expected little, faced danger, pulled together, and found courage within themselves. The buoyancy and individualism that Frederick Jackson Turner described was perhaps communicated in Roy Rogers's "happy trails" and in the Lone Ranger's persistent refusals to stay in town. There were traditional rustics, like *Wagon Train*'s Charlie Wooster, whose naive simplicity provided comic relief, but critics worried that children were learning violence from the frequent fistfights and gun battles or finding reason to hate Indians. The most obvious lesson, though, was that children who watched these programs did not realistically expect to grow up to be buckaroos or cattle drivers, any more than they expected to be pirates or princesses. The most direct connection a person could hope for with the Wild West was a visit to Frontier Days in Wyoming, a rodeo in Colorado or Texas, or a movie set in Arizona or California.

M. J. Andersen, whose 1950s childhood took place in a small town in South Dakota, was probably typical of many children when she recalled with fondness the excitement of pretending her bicycle was a horse, donning cowboy clothes or war paint, watching *Fury*, and doting on Roy Rogers. "For an American child of the 1950s," she wrote, "the seminal romance was the West—the West of the cowboys and unfenced terrain, of rangeland where you could ride for days and encounter no one." It was a world for her that existed only in fantasy on film and television, not a reality that sparked pride in her hometown or state. "Roy Rogers was far more useful to me in dream form than he would have been in person," she realized later. "Imagining him was a necessary type of work, the work a child does to stave off nothingness."[10]

Compared with the Wild West, the Middle West of homesteaders and pioneers was a legacy with which heartland residents could more easily identify. Families like the Norbys in Iowa and the Ferrins in Kansas lived on the actual farms homesteaded by their ancestors. Residents west of St. Louis could readily imagine pioneers streaming across Missouri and Kansas or into Nebraska and Oklahoma or up to Minnesota and the Dakotas. Markers tracked the location of the Missouri, Oregon, Mormon, and Santa Fe trails; statues of pioneer women and men punctuated the way. "Old settlers picnics," discontinued during World War II, resumed in the 1950s. Minnesota commemorated its centennial by reenacting an oxcart drive and reissuing the territorial seal showing a pioneer breaking sod. Kansas's centennial celebration turned as "corny as August," the *New York Times* declared, when it tried to rehabilitate the legends of Wild Bill Hickok and Wyatt Earp, but local communities celebrated with women costumed in frontier dresses and sunbonnets and men in beards and straw hats.[11] Nebraska celebrated by issuing pioneer recognition certificates to anyone who could claim one hundred years of continuous residence and forming thirty new historical societies. In the 1950s, more than 300 new books appeared with "pioneer" in the title, and in the 1960s that number climbed to more than 500. Children's books set the Middle West as favorite locations as rarely as television series did, but included such frontier classics as the *Courage of Sarah Noble, Old Yeller,* and *Frontier Living.*

The most popular literary depiction of pioneer life was Laura Ingalls Wilder's *Little House on the Prairie* and its several prequels and sequels, four of which received Newbery Honor awards.[12] *Little House* was published in 1935 and went through twenty-four printings before an equally popular illustrated edition was released in 1953, which was printed fourteen times between then and 1971. The *Little House* television series began in 1973 and won Emmy Awards in 1978, 1979, and 1982 and Best Young Actress Awards in 1983 and 1984. In 2000, a survey conducted by the National Geographic Society showed that Wilder was among the fifteen most popular American authors of all time. A study by sociologists Wendy Griswold and Nathan Wright found that *Little House on the Prairie* was particularly popular among Midwestern readers.[13]

Unlike fictionalized portrayals of the Wild West in which the location was often difficult to identify, Wilder's stories were unmistakably set in the Middle West. As Pa, Ma, Mary, Laura, and Baby Carrie headed west in the book's opening from their home in Wisconsin in 1869, they came to the Missouri River, crossed into Kansas, and settled southwest of Independence, Kansas, near the Verdigris River. Other books in the series were set in Walnut Grove, Minnesota, where the family lived briefly in 1874, and in De Smet, South Dakota, where they homesteaded in 1879. Wilder wrote the books with her daughter's editorial assistance at a farm in the Ozarks near Mansfield, Missouri, where she lived from 1894 until her death in 1957. Readers often remarked that they knew her characters as intimately as their friends. "I found a family much like my own," wrote one, recalling his 1950s childhood on an eastern Kansas dairy farm. "Out the west-facing windows of my own little school on the prairie, I could see the windswept buffalo grass and feel the vastness of the land on which the Ingalls family pioneered."[14]

Little House gave readers an authentic and yet selective view of rustic life on the prairie. The narrative features the Ingallses' intermittent dangers—high water that nearly sweeps them away while crossing the river, wolves following Pa and surrounding the house, severe illness, Indians, and a prairie fire—all of which they survive more from luck than heroism. Told from Laura's perspective, each threat is scary but ends happily. Much of the story, though, is simply a description of the flora and fauna of the Plains. Like Polly Spence, Wilder interprets the land as scenery with a distinctive natural beauty. While Pa selects the home site because of the presence of wild game and timber in the creek, Laura is overtaken with the immense blueness overhead, the pearly clouds, and billowy grass. In a representative passage, she observes: "Hundreds of meadow larks were rising from the prairie, singing higher and higher in the air. Their songs came down from the great, clear sky like a rain of music. And all over the land, where the grasses waved and murmured under the wind, thousands of little dickie-birds clung with their tiny claws to the blossoming weeds and sang their thousands of little songs." Following a description of low, rounded hills covered with trees and open grassy spaces with deer grazing in the sunshine, she continues: "All along the road the wild larkspur was blossoming pink and blue and white, birds balanced on yellow plumes of goldenrod, and butterflies were fluttering. Starry daisies lighted the shadows under trees, squirrels chattered on branches overhead, white-tailed rabbits hopped along the road, and snakes wriggled quickly across it when they heard the wagon coming." Throughout her books readers are treated to vivid portraits of rich, garden-like abundance.[15]

The chances that Wilder recalled any of these specific details from the short time she lived in Kansas are slim. Her character in *Little House* is six years old at the time; in real life, she was three.[16] But Wilder did extensive research while writing the book, and an appreciation of natural beauty was a recurrent theme in her work, appearing repeatedly in essays she wrote for the *Missouri Ruralist* from 1911 to 1923, well before the Little House series. Although she was thoroughly familiar with the daily toil farming required, it was the emotional and spiritual appeal of the land to which she returned again and again. In a 1911 essay, for example, she described "smooth, green, rolling meadows and pastures, the good fields of corn and wheat and oats . . . the orchard and strawberry field like huge bouquets in the spring." In another, she marveled at the "delicate tints of the early spring foliage, the brilliant autumn leaves, the softly colored grasses and lovely flowers." In yet another, she mused that children are particularly attuned to nature: "I am sure old Mother Nature talked to me in all the languages she knew when, as a child, I loitered along the cow paths, forgetful of milking time and stern parents waiting, while I gathered wild flowers, waded in the creek, watched the squirrels hastening to their homes in the tree tops and listened to the sleepy twitterings of birds." Wild sunflowers, plum thickets, and daisies in meadows made her homesick, she wrote, and yet were "soul satisfying."[17]

In these essays, Wilder also consistently praised simple, inexpensive, practical ideas that revealed the commonsense ingenuity of Middle Western pioneers and farmers—basic mechanical tools, plain cooking, functional furniture, old-fashioned games for children, better-fitting work clothes, and labor-saving devices. Observing that most farms did not have electricity or gasoline engines, for example, she described in minute detail how a farmer she knew rigged pipes from an outdoor pump to a tank in the barnyard and then to the cellar and kitchen, and with a series of corks and faucets provided running water with this "simple, inexpensive contrivance." Other essays discussed homemade kitchen utility carts, garden-grown beauty tips, a neighbor's method of reducing time spent cooking, ideas for growing apples and increasing egg production, and tricks for saving money when purchasing from a mail-order catalog. Although she wrote favorably about scientific experiments and technological advances, the ingenuity of ordinary people impressed her more. Simple folks came up with clever ideas because they valued frugality and paid close attention to their work. These were traits, not just of Americans in general, but of neighbors in Missouri and especially of people who lived on farms. Repeatedly she admonished country folk to resist imitating city dwellers, especially bankers and merchants, and to cultivate the distinctive rural virtues of thrift, hard work, and sharp-witted inventiveness.[18]

In keeping with these emphases, the theme that dominates *Little House* is Pa's ingenuity. Ma plays a supportive role, tender in her affection for the girls and humanized in the sprained ankle she suffers early in the story. She affirms Pa's decisions and is courageous in her quiet way, while dutifully carrying out the household tasks of cooking and cleaning, about which Laura says surprisingly little. In contrast, Pa is Laura's hero. She follows and helps him, observes when he acknowledges being afraid, and is reassured by his strength. But it is his resourcefulness that impresses her the most. No challenge is too great for him. He has natural skills, honed while farming in Wisconsin, which he quickly adapts to each new situation on the prairie. A long passage describes him fitting the wagon for the journey. Another shows him felling trees, hauling them to the home site, and building much of the cabin singlehandedly before meeting the neighbor, Mr. Edwards. An entire chapter details Pa's cleverness in constructing a stout door for the cabin using no nails and crafting leather hinges and a latch string that can be pulled in at night. Pa's native ingenuity comes through again and again as he adds a chimney to the cabin, constructs a hearth, digs a well, and devises a windlass.

Appearing in the 1930s during the Depression, *Little House* offered readers a picture of better times and of continuing possibilities. A land of dust storms and tumbleweeds had in Wilder's description once been verdant and would be again when the rain returned. Good people experienced bad luck, and it was legitimate to worry, but ingenuity and perseverance would prevail. Readers familiar with the region's history could recognize the story's authenticity. Indians did enter settlers' cabins uninvited and prairie fires were a constant danger. But *Little House* was also distinctive in what it did not emphasize. Roderick Cameron, another early settler, described Kansas as a "desolate [land of] chalk hills that the rains had cut up into gullies and deep ravines . . . without a sign of life anywhere."[19] Wilder herself wrote elsewhere of the barrenness, drought, and failed crops she experienced in South Dakota. Other homesteaders wrote of torrential rain and hail, relentless heat, wind, dying cattle, and loneliness. Laura's account mentioned none of these. Neighbors came and went, were sometimes helpful, but never lived too close, and the Ingallses preferred being where people were scarce. When the family moves on before soldiers come to evict them for homesteading on Indian land, they are cheerful that the covered wagon is again their home. The book hints that they may have inadvertently settled in Indian territory or received misguided information from Washington but spares readers of the long controversies involving squatters, preemption, and uncertain treaties on the Osage reserve in southeastern Kansas. The Ingallses' buoyancy in the face of setbacks is something that Depression-era readers could appreciate more than depictions focusing only on frontier conquests and manifest destiny.[20]

Little House and other stories of pioneer settlement in the Middle West are often interpreted as narratives of rugged individualism. But it is important to understand how social relations were portrayed. The Ingallses are a family whose members work and play together, not lone cowboys, and they get along with help from their neighbors. They exemplify love of home, family loyalty, and devotion to neighbors. Lacking other amenities, they enjoy one another's company and spend long hours working and playing together. Individualism is most clearly evident in Pa's ingenuity. Pioneers get ahead by being smart in a commonsensical way and by making the best use of whatever resources and opportunities are available. In a revealing episode, the Ingallses meet a family down on their luck because their horses have been stolen. Pa promises to send soldiers from Independence to help them, but to Ma he says the unfortunate settlers were stupid for not having a watchdog and not tying their horses securely. "Tenderfeet," he snorts. "Shouldn't be allowed west of the Mississippi."[21]

For Middle Western readers in the 1950s and 1960s, the Little House books were a way to preserve and update aspects of the pioneer experience. Farmers with tractors and electric milking machines and rural families with automobiles and televisions were increasingly removed, culturally and technologically, from the open frontier. They nevertheless could admire the early settlers' courage, viewing it among the Ingallses if not in their own family histories, and they could take pride in imagining that they, too, exhibited native ingenuity. They prided themselves on being neighborly, like the Ingallses, and took pleasure in the rolling meadows and rich sunsets. They appreciated household conveniences and yet valued frugality and old-fashioned simplicity. A rustic did not have to farm or be unsophisticated to appreciate these virtues. Living in a region of farms and small towns was enough. "The real cultured, social, and intellectual life," Wilder wrote, was not in cities but "in the country."[22]

A third tradition on which Middle Westerners could draw in crafting an identity was the Great Depression. It was present in eastern cities where large numbers of unemployed workers gathered in soup lines and in the South where rural poverty was acute. However, the Dust Bowl that defined western Kansas and parts of Oklahoma and Nebraska and the drought that ravaged most of the region was popularly associated with the Middle West in family stories, films, books, and history lessons. To have lived through it, had relatives who did, or resided later in one of the states most affected earned heartland residents a badge of distinction. "It burned a resolve and sacrifice into them," observed a man whose parents struggled against the dust storms in northeastern Nebraska in the 1930s.[23] To be a proud Midwesterner could mean having learned to work hard and pinch pennies from parents or grandparents who survived the Dust Bowl. Wrote another, "Family members of mine who were children in the dustbowl area during the Depression are cautious to this day about money, food debt, property—the underlying thought being you never know when it will disappear. They've prospered because they had an unbelievable work ethic and fragile security."[24] Later generations could view the thirties as a starting point against which to measure their own success. But the hardship could also be a source of embarrassment and anxiety, or a story of decreasing relevance. As Middle Westerners became more affluent, they needed to reshape their stories of the Depression.

The most famous telling of heartland life during the Great Depression was John Steinbeck's *Grapes of Wrath*. Published in 1939 and released as a motion picture a year later, the story memorialized the tragedy so many in the

Middle West had recently experienced. Readers and viewers could recognize the barren fields as their own or their neighbors' and imagine what it must have been like to lose everything. They could argue, as reviewers did in Oklahoma, that Steinbeck erred on important facts—that he should have located the Dust Bowl in the western part of the state instead of the east, that he misunderstood landownership and foreclosures, and that his portrayal of ignorant Okies was offensive—and, in registering these objections, affirm their regional pride. They may have noted, as historians would show later, that the Joads were an atypically large family, that most Middle Westerners who fled to California were not farmers at all, that they would have journeyed along paved Route 66 instead of dirt roads, and that few worked in migrant labor camps when they arrived in California. They may have even heard that the story had socialist overtones and was banned in some libraries. Yet it was hard to deny that Steinbeck had created anything less than an epic account reminiscent of the biblical Exodus narrative and, in the person of Jim Casey, had presented a Christ figure whose compassion and sacrifice added themes that Middle Westerners could easily understand. The story was ultimately about courage in the face of oppression, family relationships, hope, and the will to survive. The film won two Academy Awards and was nominated for five more. Steinbeck received the Nobel Prize for Literature in 1962. The book perennially ranked high in lists of best American novels and, by the late 1940s, was being assigned widely in high school and college literature classes.[25]

But if Steinbeck sought to reveal the hardship of the Depression, another story, written earlier, filmed in 1939, and concerned only loosely with hard times had far greater appeal. The *Wizard of Oz*, starring Judy Garland as Dorothy, told the story of an orphaned girl living on a Kansas farm with her aunt and uncle. A tornado carries Dorothy and her dog, Toto, to the fantasy world of Oz, where she meets a scarecrow, a tin man, and a cowardly lion, and searches for a way to return home. The movie followed the narrative of L. Frank Baum's *The Wonderful Wizard of Oz*, published in 1900, and based on Baum's experiences in drought-ridden South Dakota from 1888 to 1891 as the founder of an unsuccessful general merchandise store and editor of a local newspaper. The book was an instant bestseller, and Baum followed it with thirteen children's novels featuring the same characters. A musical adaptation toured widely after 1902 and two films were attempted before the successful MGM version in 1939. Although the film was nominated for an Academy Award and earned an immediate profit, its popularity grew dramatically when it was re-released in theaters in 1955 and shown on television in 1956 to an estimated audience of forty-five million.[26]

The most memorable lines in the Wizard of Oz were "We're not in Kansas anymore" and "There's no place like home." Literary and film critics who dissected the story drew connections with prairie populism, saw the scarecrow as a symbol of the American farmer, and debated whether the plot was a critique of the national government or a brief for apolitical self-help. They agreed that themes of courage, authenticity, and selflessness evident in the film were universal and at the same time that the story spoke especially of the American heartland. Dorothy's remark about not being in Kansas was repeated so often that the American Film Institute judged it one of the most memorable in all of film history. Dorothy's preference for a humble clapboard house on a dusty Midwestern farm and her innate goodness—that of a "pert and fresh-faced miss with the wonder-lit eyes of a believer in fairy tales," as one reviewer wrote—suggested something peculiarly appealing about the simple life. South Dakotans claimed Baum as a native son, and Kansas anointed itself the "Land of Ahs."[27]

The heartland as a symbol of home had much more to offer than memories of the Depression itself. People who remembered that era or heard family stories about it came to identify it as a time of home, hearth, and family solidarity. It was a moment when families came together as out-of-work relatives returned from cities and parents and grandparents worked hard to preserve the family farm. "I think through all of this time I had a sense of security," one woman recalled. Others remembered "the closeness with family and friends that made those years livable and even enjoyable," as historian Pamela Riney-Kehrberg noted among southwestern Kansas Dust Bowl survivors.[28] But people experienced the Depression in different ways, and those who were most seriously affected often had conflicted emotions that they would just as soon forget. For many, it was a painful low point psychologically as well as economically. "The last six years have been tough," a North Dakota farm woman wrote in 1936, describing her "inability to get a good paying job, illnesses, a thousand petty discouragements, crop failures, drouth, dust storms, poor cattle market."[29] A government agent, she wrote, was running around trying to buy up land at ridiculously low prices. A farm woman in Kansas, whose son sought work in Oregon when the dust storms devastated their land, mourned his death in a logging accident.[30] Besides the heartbreak and personal loss, Midwesterners found themselves at the mercy of wealthy landlords, as Steinbeck emphasized, and sometimes of neighbors with whom relationships remained strained for years. C. Hugh Snyder was a boy near Haviland, Kansas, when a neighbor took over the mortgage on his father's farm, collected the government allotment meant for the farmer, and left them with little more than a place to live.[31] Elmer Powers wrote of neighbors stealing turkeys, of others driving shiny new cars, and of his own embarrassment at having to part with farm machinery to make ends meet.[32] Polly Spence recalled with some chagrin that her father-in-law paid a sack of flour for a neighbor's 160 acre farm.[33] Noting that "farmers practically had to give away" their livestock, a writer in Minnesota acknowledged that anti-Semitism grew rife in his predominantly German community. "The fact that the buyers were Jewish somehow gave the perception that they were the cause of the poor prices." The sentiments died hard, he recalled, even though they were expressed less openly after World War II.[34]

The Depression was too firmly marked in regional memory to be ignored, and yet, as with all experiences, what people remembered about it was selective. It was only natural that they recalled the good times as much as the bad. Not only were they proud to have struggled and survived, much like the pioneers before them; they also associated it with the warm enveloping homes from which they had come. As the *Oz* mythology moved further from its original telling, it expressed the lingering ambivalence of having both suffered and been sustained. Dorothy's wide-eyed "not in Kansas anymore" spoke as much of non-Midwesterners' gratitude for having escaped (or of having never lived there) as it did of regional loyalty, whereas "no place like home" signaled a longing for roots wherever they might be found. Midwesterners could think of their own homes—their childhoods, the Depression era fading into the past, the families they were now raising—and imagine that their towns, their farms, their more comfortable dwellings were the special places where all this was true. They knew that it was true at least for them. Dorothy's ultimate discovery, M. J. Andersen wrote, recalling the movie as an annual late 1950s ritual, is that "there is no finer place in the world than her own backyard—than the farm in Kansas, U.S.A., where she belongs and, most important, is loved."[35]

Although surviving the Depression can be a tale of rugged self-sufficiency, its legacy for Midwesterners was often more nuanced, tempered by acknowledgment of family support and ambivalence toward more fortunate neighbors, but also set against the better times that followed it. Like the pioneers, Depression survivors and their descendants stood tall by having exercised resolve, making the hard decisions to stay put or move on, and then using their wits to confront the challenges they faced. For many who chose in the 1950s to abandon the farms of their parents and grandparents, the 1930s provided a rationale. They were either incapable economically of staying or unprepared psychologically to endure the same hardship. For others, whatever advancement they made was cherished more because they had started from nothing.

Delmer and Evelyn Hodge got married and moved to a rented farm near Blackwell, Oklahoma, upon his return from serving in the infantry during World War II. Both came from families who had little schooling and were dirt poor. Delmer remembered a banker in his hometown committing suicide during the Depression because of bad loans to farmers. He also saw the elderly standing in soup lines and vowed that would never happen to him. The newlyweds paid

$10 a month for an old rat-infested farmhouse that had no plumbing or electricity. Many years later, Delmer remembered the exact month when electricity came and they hung their first lightbulb. "I love electricity," he said. The couple farmed eighty acres of rented land, raised chickens, and milked cows. Although they never prospered quite as much as they hoped, Delmer and Evelyn earned a modest living, reared three children, and sent all of them through college.

The key was ingenuity. It could have been Yankee ingenuity or just plain American ingenuity, but in the Hodges' case it was part of their understanding of the heartland. A rustic—though they would not have used the word—was someone who had simple-enough tastes and worked hard enough to make it, as the saying went, "from scratch." When Delmer and Evelyn got married, they had $85 and no automobile, but Delmer qualified for a veteran's loan, which was enough to purchase a small tractor, five cows, and some chickens. "We just kept clawing," he recalled. Clawing was in no way ruthless, aggressive, or self-promoting. It was 10 percent luck, 30 percent native talent, and 60 percent being willing to seize opportunities that became available. Raising chickens and milking cows was something he could do with relatively little investment and a lot of patience. When money was tight, he worked at an airplane plant, did carpentry jobs, and baled hay for the neighbors. Later on, Evelyn worked outside the home, too. They lived frugally. Ingenuity inhered in being wise about the daily decisions of ordinary life. Taking pride in doing simple tasks well was another mark of the rustic life. In small towns, self-sufficiency meant taking care of one's family and one's property, earning the respect of one's neighbors, and doing one's part to keep the community in good order. Delmer always made sure the weeds were kept in check on his property and the grass mowed. The community took pride in productive farms that looked good. "If you don't have pride," Evelyn explained, "you don't have very much."[36]

Gunslingers, homesteaders, and Dust Bowl survivors were all more heroic than the ignorant rustics that writers so often associated with the rural Midwest. Rustics were young men left behind for want of the marvelous ambition, intelligence, and enterprise evident in East Coast cities, a Harvard professor declared in 1897. Rustics were stupid, idle, and shiftless.[37] Readers of the *Daily Inter Ocean* in Chicago in the 1890s amused themselves with "A Racy Ravel of Rustic Rants and Rural Revelries and Roundelays"—a column about life in the rural Midwest.[38] The *St. Paul Daily News* treated readers with comic quips contributed by a columnist known as "The Rustic."[39] In 1893 an article in *Science* described the average farmer as "ignorant of the most vital laws that underlie farm husbandry" and concluded that "his city brother has outwitted him in every department." Referencing the ineluctable survival of the fittest, the writer argued that farmers were incapable of surviving in any other vocation, suffered from a "low intellectual standard," and were properly "held in derision."[40]

Despite the technological advances and increasing productivity of Middle Western agriculture in the first decades of the twentieth century, writers saw modernity as a fact of city life and resistance to it as a feature of the countryside. The great engine of progress was manufacturing. Enterprising young people were finding new opportunities in the cities, while farmers remained socially and culturally isolated. This was the true source of the "farm problem," a 1905 essay in the Chicago-based *American Journal of Sociology* argued. Rural habits were ingrained. Farmers' tendency was to "tread the well-worn paths," that is, to be suspicious of outsiders and skeptical about innovation. Farm life encouraged too much self-sufficiency and not enough understanding of politics and social organization. Even the idea that farm life promoted high moral standards, the writer suggested, was "mere silliness." Rural clergy were inferior, and farmers were known for their vulgarity and coarseness of thought.[41] In contrast, urban life was socially and intellectually stimulating. "A typical man of the town," another sociologist wrote, "knows about a vast number of things" and is "more alert" than a countryman "who contemplates the slow cycle of the seasons."[42]

Writers in the rural Midwest sometimes went to great lengths to combat these images of the ignorant countryman. Laura Ingalls Wilder's emphasis on farmers' ingenuity could be understood as an example. Another was Margaret Hill McCarter, a Kansas author whose popular novels featured the adventures of early settlers. McCarter reacted strongly to urban stereotypes of the prairie in her 1911 novel *Peace of the Solomon Valley*. The story, set on a farm not far from Smith Center, Kansas, is a tale of urban encounter with rural life. An Eastern businessman sends his son to the Kansas farm to recover from rheumatism, whereupon the son, initially disdainful of rustic ways, discovers that the farmer was his father's academically superior classmate at Yale and falls in love with the farmer's daughter, a sophisticated college graduate herself.[43] Nebraska writer Wright Morris pictured the difference between urban and rural life as a stark contrast: "There is no grass in New York, no yards, no trees, no lawn swings—and for thousands of kids not very much sky," rural-born Clyde Muncy explains in *The Home Place*. His rustic uncle replies, "Seems to me a man with any sense, or any kids, would live some place else."[44]

But the time-worn stereotypes of benighted farmers did not die easily. The Country Life Commission, created by President Theodore Roosevelt in 1907 to study rural problems, focused on technological efficiency, mechanization, and rural school consolidation, and, when met with considered indifference to these top-down recommendations, concluded that farmers were indeed resistant to new ideas.[45] By the 1920s, some analysts of rural problems blamed farmers for too readily conceding that they were indeed inferior. Quoting an anonymous publication, a writer sympathetic to farmers observed that urbanites frequently looked down on the countryman because of "his rough dress, his tousled hair and beard, sometimes bearing chaff and straws, his lack of polish in social approach and conversation, his ignorance of city ways and manners." As long as farmers accepted these views, it would be difficult, the observer believed, for progress to occur.[46] Other scholars employed psychological tests to examine the inferior "mental capacity" of farmers and noted tendencies in popular culture to associate rustics with simple-minded foolishness.[47] In the 1950s, sociologists and psychologists still thought it valuable to learn if farm children were less intelligent than city children.[48]

Nevertheless, the social conditions that gave credence to traditional stereotypes of the rustic life were changing. Observers of the American farm population noted a gradual evolution "from folk-mindedness to scientific-mindedness" in the 1940s among better-off farmers. Machinery, fertilizers, animal breeding, and hybrid crops required greater knowledge than in the past. As farm families recovered from the economic setbacks of the 1930s, automobile use, visits to cities, and shopping increased. Subscriptions to farm journals and daily newspapers grew steadily. Farm youth more often attended town schools and continued through high school. They saw the same picture shows and listened to the same music as town youth and often attended the same churches.[49]

The distinction in rural communities between those who farmed and those who did not remained important. "The world was two worlds, divided into country kids, who lived on farms, and town kids," M. J. Andersen recalled of her childhood in South Dakota.[50] As M. J. played with her friend down the street or helped her father put out the town newspaper, ten-year-old Carol Bodensteiner, a farm girl in northern Iowa, was watching cows give birth and learning to lift heavy five-gallon pails of milk.[51] Yet the gap was never complete. Farm families' incomes averaged less than townspeople's, but farmers' land and machinery gave them a higher net worth. Poor people lived in town as well as in the country, and the more affluent could be found both on and off the farm.[52] The gap had less to do with economics than with lifestyles—and these differences were diminishing. Andersen lived in town, but she loved horses, could see the open prairie from the end of her street, and often visited farm relatives. Bodensteiner played frequently with town cousins and listened to the same music as Andersen. Nearly everyone's livelihood was rooted in the land. "You either farm," Andersen observed, or "provide what farmers need: groceries, hardware, clothing, implements."[53]

The new force in cultural self-understandings that further eroded the town-country divide in the 1950s was television. Farm families and residents of small

towns across the Middle West watched the same programs and both participated increasingly in common viewing experiences with audiences in other regions and in large cities. Like radio and electricity, television came later to rural
communities than to metropolitan areas and thus contributed temporarily to
the perception that rustic life lagged behind the times. Commercial broadcasting began in 1930 in New York, Boston, Chicago, and Los Angeles but remained
limited until after World War II, when the number of television stations shot up
nationwide from seven in 1947 to 108 in 1952, tripled to 349 in 1954, and then
rose to 517 by 1960. In parts of the Midwest, broadcasting appeared early: a
station in Milwaukee received a license in 1931, stations in Kansas City and
Minneapolis began broadcasting in 1933, an educational station was founded
at the University of Iowa the same year, and experiments in broadcasting were
conducted at Kansas State University in 1935. But viewing on a large scale lay
well in the future.[54]

Network television, guided by master plans devised at NBC and CBS in the
late 1940s to concentrate on the Northeast and markets with 100,000 families
or more, spread unevenly to the rural Middle West during the 1950s. In 1952,
no stations were located in Arkansas, Kansas, Oklahoma, South Dakota, and
North Dakota; only one was present in Iowa and Nebraska; and only two were
in Minnesota and Missouri. Reception was weak, especially in rural areas, and
television sets were expensive. In 1954, the proportion of farm households with
a television ranged from only 12 percent in South Dakota, to 16 percent in North
Dakota and 18 percent in Arkansas, to 24 percent in Kansas, 27 percent in Nebraska, 31 percent in Missouri, 32 percent in Minnesota, 33 percent in Oklahoma, and 54 percent in Iowa. Owning a television set was strongly associated
with other aspects of rural modernization, such as the proportion of farmsteads
with running water, and with living close to a metropolitan area. Upward of
70 percent of farm homes near Kansas City, Minneapolis, and Omaha, for example, owned televisions, compared with 10 percent in Smith County, Kansas,
and fewer than 2 percent in parts of western Kansas, northwestern Nebraska,
and the Dakotas. By 1960, television was nearly universal. The nine-state region
boasted eighty-seven television stations, and more than 80 percent of all occupied dwellings included a television set. Nationwide, broadcast revenue was
more than $1 billion that year, and families spent more purchasing black-and-
white televisions than they did on any other home appliance.[55]

Television communicated a common repertoire of newscasts, sitcoms, and
dramas to farmers and townspeople and across the nation, but it also tailored
content to regional tastes and sometimes reinforced unflattering stereotypes of
rural life. Drawing lessons from radio, network executives instructed local affili-
ates to pattern programming differently in the rural Midwest than in metropolitan

markets. Local performers and themes, hillbilly and Western music, and community news were to be aired in preference to programs deemed too cultured or cosmopolitan. Station managers walked a fine line between viewers who enjoyed the down-home programs and those who felt condescended to and wanted to be part of a larger picture.[56] While it was good to see people like themselves on television, the mirror was not always what viewers wanted. As one observed, "Wives look like an ad for fertilizer sacks, and about the only thing the farmer can say is 'Yep' and 'Nope.'"[57]

Complaints about television portrayals of rural life resembled negative reactions toward Hollywood films that catered too much or too little to agrarian tastes. As the notable 1935 *Variety* headline, "Sticks Nix Hick Pix," put it, filmgoers in the Iowa and Nebraska "Silo Belt" considered farm stories less appealing than dramas and mysteries in glamorous settings.[58] Yet they flocked to theaters for *Oklahoma* and *The Grapes of Wrath*, even if they did not agree with all they saw, and laughed at the city sophisticates who tried to operate a chicken farm in *The Adventures of Ma and Pa Kettle*.

Through the 1960s, rural Midwesterners were treated to two motifs on network television that, on the one hand, absorbed them into a national and largely placeless culture and, on the other hand, gave them a comedic caricature of the rustic life that they could easily disown despite a resonance with their past. The national culture was communicated in Edward R. Murrow's and Walter Cronkite's newscasts, which appealed to Americans as a whole and not to particular regions, and in coverage of presidential speeches and political conventions. Popular sitcoms and variety shows—*I Love Lucy, Red Skelton, The Jackie Gleason Show, Leave It to Beaver, Ozzie and Harriet, Father Knows Best*—took place in cities and suburbs, and yet the action occurred almost entirely on stage sets of living rooms and kitchens that could have been anywhere. Light-hearted portrayals of rustics included *The Beverly Hillbillies, The Real McCoys, Mayberry R.F.D., The Andy Griffith Show, Green Acres*, and *Hee Haw*. The comedy came from juxtaposing city and country ways and occurred at the expense of urbanites as often as of rural folk. Plots spoke to the fact that Americans remained close enough generationally and geographically to farms to see the humor and yet were sufficiently removed to escape being offended. In what became known as the Rural Purge, all of the country-based programs still on the air in 1971 were canceled, signaling executives' belief that the nation was past this transitional stage.[59]

Although television offered an exciting new mode of entertainment, it was by no means the only or even the most important source of information in rural areas. Popular magazines, such as *Life* and *Reader's Digest*, reached families in small towns as well as in cities. Farm magazines, catering distinctly to an agricultural niche, were particularly important in reaching rural readers. Dating to the early part of the twentieth century, and sometimes to the nineteenth, dozens of these magazines continued in the 1950s and were especially prominent in the Middle West. Many, like *Cappers Weekly, Farm Weekly, Front Porch, Oklahoma Country, Arkansas Farm Research, Farmers Independent, Gobbles,* and *Show Me Missouri,* focused on issues of limited geographic interest, but others appealed to larger audiences and competed in content and glossy color format with such periodicals as *Better Homes and Gardens* and *Saturday Evening Post.*[60] Farm families in the Midwest may have been entertained by *I Love Lucy* and influenced by the repetition of commercials for Folgers coffee and Ipana toothpaste. But a farm magazine brought hundreds of pages of reading material into their homes each month, lay on coffee tables and in bathroom racks to be read again and again, offered diagrams for use in the farm workshop and recipes for the kitchen, provided full-page color advertisements, and featured farmers and farm families with whom readers could easily identify.

By far the most important of these rural-market magazines was *Farm Journal,* founded in 1877 by Wilmer Atkinson, a Quaker farmer and publisher who was also the originator of *Saturday Evening Post.* With more than 3.4 million subscribers in the early 1960s, *Farm Journal* claimed to be the nation's "most influential farm magazine." One survey in the Midwest suggested it was present in more than 70 percent of farm homes and that 78 percent of subscribers claimed to read "all or most" of every issue.[61] For a dollar a year, subscribers received twelve monthly issues of approximately 125 to 150 pages each. In 1955, *Farm Journal* absorbed *Country Gentleman* and for several years carried both titles on the cover. Its only significant competitor was *Successful Farming,* which cost 50 percent more and offered similar content. *Farm Journal* was published in center city Philadelphia, and for part of its history was owned by Sun Oil magnate J. Howard Pew, but nothing about the magazine betrayed its urban location. By the 1950s, the magazine had regional editors in Iowa, Kansas, Colorado, Georgia, Texas, California, and Washington and produced different editions (Eastern, Southern, Central, and Western) with special "farmcasts" and advertising targeted to each region.[62]

Farm Journal was much more than a magazine of news, agricultural bulletins, and opinion. It was a highly competitive business enterprise that left no stone unturned in soliciting reader involvement and selling advertising space. Its staff conducted marketing surveys in which every third household in selected communities was systematically telephoned and farm women were asked to rate each section of the magazine, compare the content with other magazines, and say whether they owned each of a long list of household items, ranging from deep freezers and electric ovens to fry pans and toasters and to men's shavers and power lawn mowers. Based on these responses, households were assigned to one of six socioeconomic categories. Field staff visited farms, took photographs, and interviewed farmers about crops, livestock, and machinery. The magazine sponsored contests and offered monetary prizes to farmers and farm wives who sent in letters, essays, and news items. Half of each issue was devoted to "The Farmer's Wife" and included recipes, fashion suggestions, home decorating tips, a section about parenting, inspirational stories, and advice columns for teen girls and boys. With cartoons, classifieds, weather forecasts, and movie reviews, there was something for every member of the farm family.

The magazine earned three times as much revenue from advertising as it did from subscriptions. In 1961, when total advertising revenue was $10.7 million, more than 500 companies were clients. The journal's business department worked with twenty-five major advertising agencies, whose contracts provided about two-thirds of the total advertising revenue. Deere and Company, the makers of John Deere tractors and farm implements, and International Harvester each spent more than $400,000 that year on advertisements in the magazine; ads for Fordson tractors totaled nearly that much, and ads for Massey Harris equipment, more than $200,000. Many other companies specializing in agricultural products—such as Case and Allis-Chalmers tractors, Gehl and Holland corn pickers, Kewanee discs, and Monsanto and American Cyanamid chemicals—advertised regularly in the journal. While these products reinforced readers' unique identity as farmers, other advertisements increasingly communicated that rural people were no different from other Americans. New York Life Insurance and Purina Dog Chow each purchased ads worth more than $100,000; Winston-Salem spent $230,000; Ford advertised automobiles to the tune of $200,000; General Foods ads ran more than $300,000; and General Motors topped the list at more than $800,000.[63]

As the magazine promoted consumer products to its readers, its staff campaigned aggressively to persuade corporate executives that farmers were indeed a market worth reaching. One strategy involved direct lobbying among the nation's major corporations. *Farm Journal* sponsored speakers to make presentations to corporate boards and at conferences, conducted marketing surveys on special topics such as hog breeding and farmers' interest in stocks and bonds, published a free newsletter called *Rural Marketing* with information about farm economics and consumer purchases, kept detailed files on each of its clients, recorded correspondence about their products, and hosted numerous publicity events. In 1959, as one example, a "Farmer's Wife" editor produced a twenty-page pamphlet titled "How to Be Queen," offering tips for young women about fashion, posture, and etiquette; conducted live demonstrations at supermarkets; followed these with in-store interviews; and held a contest in which "queens" were selected to promote products.[64] The journal's other promotional strategy with prospective advertisers was to depict farmers and farmers' wives as progressive Americans who traveled, drove new cars, lived in modern houses, used the latest appliances, and sent their children to college.

The new image being promulgated in the pages of *Farm Journal* was aptly summarized in the January 1959 edition of *Rural Marketing*. "If we stop speaking in terms of the average farmer—since he's a mythical person anyway—and start thinking of the successful, prosperous farmer who is our best customer," the writer observed, "we find a more responsive businessman, better qualified to judge the usefulness of our product in terms of its economic returns to him, less inclined to haggle over price, [and] more willing to spend."[65] The writer was an executive at Monsanto, the pesticide manufacturer that would come under attack three years later by conservationist Rachel Carson, but the statement could have been made by *Farm Journal* editors, who also understood that rural life was changing. The families featured each month were among those whose acreage and equipment were increasing. News stories and advertisements depicted neatly dressed farmers wearing coveralls, jeans, starched open-collar shirts, and caps or hats. They could have been suburban dads out mowing the lawn or bringing in firewood. Women and children appeared often, but never on tractors or doing barnyard chores. Barns were pictured with electric lights and milking machines; homes, with refrigerators and televisions. "We either go forward into a new life or will be left by the wayside as times change," a reader in Kansas observed. "Who really wants to stay in the days of the kerosene lamp and home-made lye soap?"[66] Except for an occasional reference to declining farm subsidies or drought, there was no mention of hardship or of the quarter or so of the farm population at the bottom of the income scale. The response received in one of its surveys—"I'm just a poor housewife. No money. Mine all goes for eats and clothes, taxes, and insurance"—was not what the journal printed. The image projected was of farmers who were making money and thinking of ways to make more. If it did not always reflect reality, it was an attractive portrayal of what farmers hoped they were or could be.

Although consumer products of every conceivable kind—from Wyeth chemicals for animal infections to Lysol, Colgate toothpaste, Remington rifles, and Spalding basketballs—were an important part of the new images depicted in farm magazines, there was continuing emphasis on the traditional values that had long given residents of the rural Midwest a sense of identity. Negative stereotypes (stupid, dull, sweaty, dirty), to which sensitivities remained, were balanced by positive self-perceptions focusing on family loyalty, frugality, simplicity, and self-determination. Some of the rustic characteristics of rural life, such as plain living and commonsense values, were preserved but were now updated and associated positively with technological advances and scientific farming. As a letter to *Farm Journal*'s editors in 1956 noted, "The farmer has been called so many names from hick and clod hopper to country jay, but he really isn't so dumb these days." Today's farmer, the writer argued, was a gentleman with expertise in business management, soil conservation, and animal care.[67]

Contrasts between urban and rural life were inevitable, since the magazine's niche was among farmers. Fears of being looked down on and aspirations to be viewed as equals were evident in letters from farm readers. "We had city guests over the last holiday weekend," a woman wrote, "and one of the teenagers among them said, 'You don't look like a farm woman.'" The writer acknowledged that she drives the tractor and sometimes cleans the barn but explained, "I keep order in the house, have an up-to-date hairdo, and spare the time to don a street dress and makeup before going to town for groceries."[68] Another woman remarked that men who work in offices shave and shower daily, but she had to nag her husband because of his "infrequent hair cuts and untidy nails" and "greasy overalls and frayed caps."[69]

Yet it was equally common for articles and letters to tout farm life as preferable to city living, to mention products and activities that would also have been present in urban homes, or to ignore cities entirely except as places to visit for shopping or on vacation. A writer in Kansas was one of many who praised the advantages of rural life, especially for families with children. "I'll bet my best bottom land that 90 percent of the mothers in the city would like to bring their children up in the countryside," she wrote.[70] A reader who sent a letter from her farm in Iowa nicely illustrated the desire to keep up with other middle-class Joneses, wherever they might live. Describing a recent home expansion project, she added, "We've bought a movie camera and movie projector, we've taken a trip to old Mexico, and built a swimming pool."[71]

The rustic image of country life with which readers were invited to identify emphasized grassroots ingenuity as much as *Little House* and other stories of pioneer or Depression-era life had. Only now, ingenuity was illustrated in practical, up-to-date farm and household tips. One farmer had figured out a way to build calf shelters from hay bales; another offered instructions for constructing an easy-to-operate loading chute; yet another showed how to make better use of pulleys and levers. Each monthly issue included a section titled "Homemade and Handy" offering short articles and photographs about devices to make in the farm shop, uses of scrap metal and worn-out parts, tips for keeping tools organized, ways to make lifting easier, and so on. Many of the devices reflected the era's increasing reliance on motors, engines, and electricity. Helpful hints dealt with power saws, silage lifters, electric grinders, paint sprayers, and numerous other machines. Longer articles described how to remodel a basement or kitchen or featured a farmer's success with breeding leaner beef cattle or more productive milk cows. An ingenious person in these accounts was someone with imagination, given to new ideas, and yet a nonexpert who used simple skills, tinkered, poked around, puttered, and came up with a device that was cheap, time saving, practical, and easy to understand. "Among farm people there is more wisdom, more plain common sense, more perspective," the journal's editor declared, "than you could get from any number of 'experts.'"[72]

For farm women, articles discussed ingenious home canning techniques, simple remedies for children's ailments, budget-stretching recipes, and methods for easing muscle pain and relaxing. Professional advice had its place, readers learned, but was no substitute for practical common sense. A "Slick Tricks" column demonstrated readers' ingenuity in thinking of uses for leftovers, devising kitchen utensils, keeping houseplants alive, improvising recipes, and running an efficient household. Women's ingenuity was often expressed in stories about ways to support—or in some instances, outsmart—their husbands. A woman in Iowa, for example, wrote that she had been raising specialty iris in her garden, found a market for them, and earned enough profit to pay for their 107-acre farm. A woman in Missouri, who secreted money from selling cream and eggs, was able to pay for emergency medical bills. A reader in Michigan said her husband never liked car trips, so she took the children and drove to the beach herself.[73]

Editors selected letters, which appeared in a special section of the magazine, based on the letters' chances of receiving favorable votes from readers, and awarded the letter receiving the most votes a $25 savings bond. Articles attributed ingenious ideas or inventions to a specific farmer or farm wife whose name and location were given. Although the magazine's tone toward agricultural scientists and extension agents was always respectful, it credited readers themselves with having the best ideas. Other readers could send their own suggestions or responses, identify with the farmers whose suggestions were published, or tell themselves that their own inventions were just as important. Homemade and handy ideas also complemented the advertisements for manufactured products. An article about home renovation would be accompanied by advertisements for a new furnace or gas range; tips about a homemade farm device often presupposed owning one of the electric welders advertised.

The do-it-yourself emphasis in farm magazines was evident beyond the rural Midwest in such publications as *Popular Mechanics*, in Boy and Girl Scout manuals, and in the growing interest in hobbies, crafts, and home repair. However, it mattered to *Farm Journal* readers, its staff had determined, that a farm shop tip came from a farmer named Floyd Smith in Nebraska, that the loading chute pictured was common on livestock farms in Kansas, and that a letter to the editor was from a farm woman named Mabel Jones in Iowa. Ingenuity was local and specific, easily identifiable and identified with. Stories of farm resourcefulness drove home the point that farmers were their own bosses, knew better how to fix things than an expert did, and usually had nobody to explain how to do things; they worked alone, often without urban services and supplies, and they tried hard to be frugal. Homemade and handy ideas fit well with farmers' emphasis on self-reliance. "You can" or "one man can," articles declared, underscoring the point by picturing a man alone in the farmyard or a woman alone in the kitchen. It was possible for readers to imagine that ingenuity was a distinctive feature of agrarian life as they knew it.

Midwestern neighborliness was a second theme emphasized repeatedly in the pages of *Farm Journal*. Handy ideas facilitated self-sufficiency by making it possible to do more things alone and needing less help from one's neighbors, but they did not preclude the value of neighborly conviviality. Illustrations featured community picnics, farmers talking over the back fence, and women attending club meetings. Advertisements suggested that men might go hunting together, that women might share ideas about new appliances, and that an insurance agent was like a good neighbor. Advice columns encouraged teenagers to participate in 4-H and told them how to get along with their friends. Readers commented on the warmth, assistance, and frequent volunteering in their communities. "If you asked almost any farmer here how many times he's gone out of his way to help a total stranger (for free)," a reader in South Dakota remarked, "he couldn't tell you. He doesn't keep count."[74]

However, there were cues that neighborliness was changing, sometimes becoming more problematic and requiring more effort. The heartland was no longer where neighbors could be found merely working together, but a place where people valued neighborliness enough to work at making it happen. "During the depression," one essay recalled, all the neighbors used the same threshing machine and "women would get together" to cook for the harvest crew. "Swapping work usually isn't necessary or even feasible in today's farming," the writer noted. "But, *neighborliness* is feasible, and more necessary than we sometimes realize."[75] The forces making interaction among neighbors more difficult were implicit in do-it-yourself tips showing how one farmer could accomplish a task without relying on assistance, and in the many advertisements showing individuals alone on their tractors, in their trucks, or in their kitchens. More explicit difficulties in being neighborly were evident in letters from farm women saying they were now working at jobs in town or spending longer hours helping their husbands farm larger acreage. Complaints about the built-in surveillance of traditional neighborliness sometimes surfaced as well. For instance, a woman whose son and his fiancée were having a baby out of wedlock wrote that "rural communities are often very cruel," noting how people gossiped and expected rigid conformity to moral codes.[76] Most evident was the fact that the new rustic of the 1950s led an organized life and sought social interaction through organizations. Neighborliness may have still happened spontaneously, but it increasingly involved participation in formal community activities, and members wanted these organizations not only to provide companionship but also to be edifying. A reader from Kansas, for example, wrote about weekly meetings she and others held in her neighborhood. The meetings were religious—a topic *Farm Journal* seldom broached—but were appropriately "nondenominational," better than old-fashioned "coffees," and involved sharing inspirational articles or poems.[77] A new mother wrote that she was having to manage her time better now that she had a baby, but said her club activities not only helped solve home and community problems but also helped "stimulate and relax me."[78]

Home demonstration units (HDUs)—monthly meetings organized by county agricultural extension offices for farm women—were a frequent *Farm Journal* topic, as women remarked favorably about opportunities to get out of the house, mingle with their neighbors, and learn to decorate their homes or put on holiday dinners. Articles encouraged women to participate in HDUs, said they would be known as pikers if they didn't, and provided ideas to use at meetings and to take home. But HDUs also revealed the changes accompanying efforts to combine old-style neighborliness with progressive images of what rural life should be. "I hoped that we might occasionally look beyond the sewing machine and the kitchen range," one HDU member lamented. "I hoped that we might find time to review a good book, or that we might try to learn more about our own community problems and problems in other countries. Too many of us go through life so busy we hardly have time to read the daily paper. . . . Our programs could, in short, cater to the whole woman—wife, mother, business manager, artist and citizen."[79] Another HDU member supplied a more favorable view. "We study and play records of operas, review books," she wrote, "very refreshing after a diet of buttonholes and string beans."[80]

The other prominent theme was an appreciation of natural beauty. Farms and small country towns were depicted, not as sites only of arduous toil, but as quiet retreats where a person could go fishing or enjoy the cool evening breeze after a hot summer day. "Just thinking about our quiet peaceful creek, beautiful in its solitude, makes me feel good," a woman in Missouri wrote. "I feel sorry for a boy who grows up without a creek to explore," echoed a writer from Oklahoma. Musing about the passing seasons, another recalled "cloud shadows moving across the green wheat on a windy March day, and moonlit summer nights when the pasture lay under silver mist."[81] The images were similar to Laura Ingalls Wilder's descriptions of spring flowers, birds, and autumn landscapes.

As was true of articles about barns and kitchens or letters about neighborliness, where gender differences were always evident, references to the land revealed stark differences between men and women. For men, the land and the crops and animals it sustained were topics of instrumental importance. Men used fertilizer and pesticides on the land, tilled it more aggressively than ever with larger tractors and plows, cross-bred animals for high productivity, milked them with new equipment, and treated them with new vaccines and antibiotics. They undoubtedly appreciated the land in other ways and perhaps said so to their wives—"how he misses watching moist, dark furrows fold over neatly behind the tractor," one woman wrote when her husband gave up farming—but this was not how they discussed it in public. Women who may have been less directly involved in daily care of the land perhaps viewed it less instrumentally all along. Certainly they wrote about it in farm magazines as an aesthetic experience. "Living and working on our farm is one long, continuous sensory adventure," declared one. "You can watch the wheat chaff dance with the breeze" at harvest time. "Rays of heat rise magically from the fields; watching them, you can drowse into the dreamland of your choice." Wrote another, "I like the distinctive odors of animals; the pungent smell of fresh silage, dust in the barn and new-mown hay; perfume of dew-covered lilacs and the light spring rain that emphasizes their essence."[82]

The sensory pleasures of farm life featured in other writing as well. A study of newspaper columns written by rural Iowa women in the 1950s, for example, found frequent depictions of natural beauty. "He who has an eye to see, a heart to appreciate beauty can not long live in Iowa without learning to love the corn," one writer observed. Another described the wintery scene from her northwest Iowa window: "The crisp white snow covers the ground and drapes itself about shrubs and trees. The glistening blanket shines through tracks and mounds. Bare trees in lacy pattern silhouette themselves against a sky that is a shade of blue not seen anywhere else." Others wrote of berry bushes, black birds and robins, green foliage, fresh garden lettuce, and the scent of spring lilacs. The descriptions explained the writers' love of Iowa, embellished with fond references to good eats, good people, and folksy living.[83]

There was a timeless quality to statements about wafting breezes and new-mown hay. If farm life was becoming more dependent on technology, the landscape remained as a connection with the past. Words like *serenity, tranquility, peacefulness,* and *calm* appeared often. The picture was of nature's benign beauty, just as it was for Laura Ingalls Wilder. Rolling green landscapes and mist-filled valleys provided the setting for graceful swaying wheat, tall corn, freshly cut grass, and pink geraniums in the garden. It was the same peaceful scene that Rachel Carson evoked in describing "the heart of America where all life seemed to live in harmony with its surroundings . . . of prosperous farms, with fields of grain and hillsides of orchards, where, in spring, white clouds of bloom drifted above the green fields."[84]

Continuities with earlier writers notwithstanding, descriptions of rustic beauty in the 1950s often differed in one important respect. Wilder's prose depicted a landscape rich, alive, teeming with brilliant colors in midday under the bright sun, punctuated with the restless activity of snakes and rabbits, and filled with the melodious music of thousands of birds. Willa Cather's descriptions were similarly vivid. In *O Pioneers!* she portrayed the wheat and corn as a checkerboard of light and dark dotted with "gayly painted farmhouses" and "big red barns." The fields were green and yellow, the phone wires hummed, and the windmills trembled and tugged.[85] It was a busy landscape of right angles and shimmering color. In contrast, the later writers' scenery was quieter and muted. The settings were more often dawn or dusk—the in-between times before and after work, when the sky was barely lit and the hues softer. The gaze was not of an engaged person running through the fields or busily at work but of a relaxed spectator looking dreamily across the valley and absorbing its stillness.

Leonard Hall, a Missouri farmer who wrote a regular column for readers in St. Louis during the late 1940s and 1950s, focused much of his attention on the serenity of rural life. His favorite scenes were the farm pond and other "peaceful places" to which he retreated in early morning or in the evening around sunset for an hour of enchantment. The sounds were muffled and soothing, the sky between dusk and darkness was a mellow haze interrupted only by the lazy silhouette of a lonely hawk or barn swallow. Avoiding gadgetry, seeking simplicity, and pausing to reflect on life in these quiet moments yielded wisdom. He mused, "Where can man turn for some sense of tranquility and certainty? Where can he look to find a source of spiritual direction? For some inspiration upon which to build a core of inner security? My answer is to Nature—to the unchanging verities that can be found there, to the basic rhythms of life in plant and living creature."[86]

The pleasure of farm life was not in the roar of a powerful combine or in the whoosh of a vacuum milking system but in a quiet evening enjoying a landscape that might have been imagined during the early nineteenth century by Hudson River School artists. The same hint of nostalgia was present. Farm writers of the 1950s could appreciate the land's serenity even if they were among the growing number who worked off the farm and raised children who would not return. In a few years, they could look back with longing on the pastures where "freeways slice through" and remember the "once-blue sky, now gray with smog."[87]

Each of the themes characterizing rural Midwestern identity in the 1950s and 1960s served both as a bridge to the wider culture of the nation and as a distinguishing source of local identity and pride. For those who may have taken the time to read about cavalry and Indian battles, to visit Boot Hill and Deadwood or stop at cattle town replicas in Wichita or Abilene, the Wild West held some local resonance at the same time that Roy Rogers and the Lone Ranger became heroic personalities on the silver screen for audiences everywhere. Pioneers and Dust Bowl survivors conveyed dual-sided messages in the same ways that motherhood and apple pie did. One side had personal meaning while the other was universal. A pioneer was likely to have been a distant relative, the first settler of one's town, a mythic larger-than-life figure after whom the town was named or in whose honor a parade was celebrated. A pioneer also symbolized aspirations less tied to any particular place: freedom, the spirit of adventure, ingenuity. Depression stories brought the pioneer legacy closer in time, commemorating the same struggles to rise from a barren land.

Emile Durkheim, the great French sociologist whose writing at the turn of the twentieth century was profoundly shaped by observing the transition from rural to urban life, argued that ideas become more abstract in cities because people no longer share the same backgrounds and thus of necessity communicate at a higher level, as it were, speaking not of loyalty to *their* village but of loyalty as a *value*, and referring less often to their love of a particular tree or animal and more to their shared appreciation of nature.[88] Something similar is evident in the reshaping of identities in the American Middle West during the middle decades of the twentieth century. On farms and in small towns, each bend in the road, each view of the valley, each aging barn, and each meandering creek was etched indelibly in memory. Yet as people read farm magazines or heard stories about pioneers, they could identify with descriptions of other families and other places.

The ingenuity of homemade and handy farm ideas was perhaps the least explicitly identified characteristic of the heartland. There was nothing very special about a barn door latch or a kitchen utility cart other than the fact that it was useful. The devices may not have been that practical, either, at least not enough to have been widely adopted. It was rather what they stood for that mattered. They were thoroughly democratic. They demonstrated that any person, any individual with common sense, even with few resources, could come up with a good idea. Training and equipment were, in principle, unnecessary. Inventive devices could be created by a solitary individual and indeed could help that individual accomplish things without the help of others. There was once again the link between an artifact that was local, unique, tailored to the needs of a particular person and, at the same time, of wider interest. Handy home-crafted ideas were part of the do-it-yourself movement that observers saw sweeping the nation in the 1950s as thousands of people bought power tools and plywood, installed their own water heaters, put up wallpaper, built birdhouses, and planted gardens. The farmer's shop and the suburban resident's basement or garage shop bore similarities. In both, a person could tinker, retreating into the imagination and away from the mandates of large-scale organizations. However, the rustic life into which suburban crafts and gardening provided only brief excursions was something that rural residents could proudly regard as an integral feature of their lives. A farm or small town in a rural area was preferable to a large city because no zoning ordinances prevented one from feeding chickens in the back yard or fixing an antique engine in the driveway. If it were true, as some argued, that office workers needed to do something with their hands to reconnect with the physical world, farmers were the ones who still had this connection.[89]

In the twenty-first century, residents of the rural heartland continue to express many of the sentiments about rustic life that were evident in the 1950s and 1960s. They like their neighbors—these adopted descendants of pioneers— because they are down-to-earth, unaffected, content with simple pleasures, and helpful but also self-reliant. "The people who came to northwest Kansas were not weenies," a northwest Kansan says. "They're tough. They're pioneers. And you can see the people who live here now. They're happy persevering like dogs with a bone."[90]

Residents pride themselves on being resourceful. Stories of personal accomplishments have less to do with success, perfection, recognition, or awards than with having done something all by oneself. "I built these two buildings, plus I restored a 1948 Dodge pickup that is sitting in the garage," a man in his fifties says. "Bought a cement mixer and poured all that cement myself. I put every nail and screw in. Didn't pay anybody." One of his neighbors is in her early thirties, raising four children, and struggling financially. She and her husband are not self-sufficient, but they aspire to be. The desire has roots in her childhood. "The farm I grew up on was completely self-sufficient," she says. "We butchered our meat, we grew our own wheat, we grew our own vegetables."

Living in a rural community, residents say, is enjoyable because they know everybody. Having neighbors who "know you by name" gives a sense of location in the world. Being known in the community makes it less necessary to be known for one's accomplishments or to take pride in having a high-power job. If they have grown up in a different community, their current residence still reminds them of the past. They had friends growing up and they enjoy having neighbors now. The continuity provides a feeling of security. Residents nearly always mention the lack of fear about crime. They say children can play safely outside, and if someone has trouble a neighbor will be watching. Security also comes from knowing one's way around. They know the postal carrier, the café owner, and the filling station attendant by name. There is no danger of feeling lost.

An aspect of the rustic tradition that has been preserved is its sense of irony. Rustics are often wiser than their interlocutors realize. Simplicity masks an underlying awareness that things are not always as simple as they seem. The image that emerged over the years is of a heartland that is a romanticized place, to be sure, and yet one that does not deceive its residents. They embrace the reality that in one instant seems ideal and in the next breath distance themselves from it. A man who regards his farmstead as a haven and loves nothing more than spending a week there without having to go anywhere says, on the one hand, that he enjoys his "place," considers it "home," and thinks it is something "everybody should have." But, on the other hand, he laughs about the family ties that link him to the land and suggests they should not be taken too seriously. "It's a lot of one-upsmanship," he says, "this was granddad's, my family has been here longer than yours," and so on.

Although the land is sometimes a source of ambivalence, it is valued in a way that people from other regions often find difficult to understand. In farming communities, residents talk about the land as a possession, something that people own or lease, buy, sell, and make money from. Land can be rich or poor, productive or unproductive. "A farm," David Hamilton writes in his memoir of rural Missouri, "is land to grasp."[91] But people are also grasped by the land. Farmers say they are tied to their land and have an obligation to it. They are attached to the land because it is the source of their livelihood. They feel good about it when the return on investment is high. When it betrays them with crop failures, weeds, muddy fields, or rocky terrain, they hate it. As a former farm wife put it, she was relieved when they quit farming because it had taken everything she and her husband could earn both on and off the farm to support it. Yet the land is valued even in bad times because of the blood and sweat that farmers put into it. They take pride in the struggle to hang on to it, especially if it has been in the family for a long time. The land is part of their genetic makeup, the sacred source of their being. Carl Swensen, the oil refinery worker who grew up on a farm that had been in the family for three generations and eventually inherited it, drives into the hills where the farm is located on evenings when the weather is nice. Sometimes he takes a visitor to see the area. "Take off your hat," he says. "You're entering God's country now. These hills are special. I was raised out here."

A terminological distinction reduces the ambiguity inherent in farmers' complicated relationship to the land. *Land* can take on an almost mystical quality as part of a family's identity. "I don't know how to explain it," a woman says, "but you feel tied to the land because you've lived with it and you've endured the hardships, you lived through the droughts, you lived through the blizzards, you lived through the ice storms, and you've done everything you can to save that piece of land your granddad gave you. People will sell everything but the home place."[92] But what is actually farmed is *ground*. Referring to it as ground helps blur the fact that much of the farmer's land may be rented rather than owned. A piece of ground is seldom the land on which one lives. Ground is closer to *dirt* and is easier to place beneath one's feet. It can be treated as an object. Whereas the land can hold a person hostage, requiring sacrifices to keep it from being sold or repossessed, a piece of ground can simply be measured, fertilized, sown, irrigated, and harvested.

Perhaps it is the monetary connotation of landownership that encourages residents to focus more on the *landscape* in conjunction with rustic life. A woman in her forties who helps her husband tend a thousand acres of cropland and 150 cows says her favorite times are in the evenings when things get quiet. She and her husband drive out to the pasture. Like Leonard Hall, she enjoys the soothing stillness. "We just sit up there and shut the pickup off and listen. We watch the cattle and listen and just do nothing." The man who poured his own cement and restored a 1948 pickup enjoys the more rustic aspects of his environment by avoiding the busier towns and highways. "I stay off the main roads as much as I can and drive country roads. I like the slower pace." Delmer Hodge enjoys sitting outside on summer evenings, looking at the trees, and feeling peaceful. "We're farmers," he says. "We don't need all that hustle and bustle."

The land, people, and pace of life intermingle to define what rural residents say they especially like about the region. It is a quality they expect outsiders, especially those from cities, to find uninviting. To enjoy a rustic life is to have most of the conveniences a person might want without many of the accompanying hassles. Beauty is better when it is subtle enough to be missed by someone in too big a hurry. "During the winter," a resident of western Kansas explains, "I always say, okay, how many shades of brown can we count, because it is kind of brown. There's nothing like watching a storm come in from sixty miles away. The open space has the beauty of the storms, the clouds, and the stars." Evenings, he too drives into the country, turns off the motor, listens for the wildlife, looks at the stars, and revels in the quiet. Friends come out from Kansas City, he says, and complain about the slow pace of life. "I tell them, we're not in a hurry. That's what you learn when you live out here. We're not in a hurry."[93]

Remarks about beauty in shades of brown and unhurried lives are vivid reminders that contentment, as the saying goes, can be found anywhere. Or not found. Although Middle Westerners have updated the old arguments about the virtues of a rustic life, the region continues to evoke disparaging and dismissive remarks, especially from disgruntled current and former residents. Unflattering statements are revealing, not only of the dissatisfaction present in any community, but of the continuities they represent. Stereotypes die hard. The negative images of rural Midwesterners that writers expressed a century or half century ago are part of the region's lasting identity. The difference is that it has become less acceptable to express these sentiments in the pages of prominent newspapers and scholarly journals.

In the quasi-public, largely anonymous world of Internet forums, candid opinions emerge that would rarely have appeared in print before. Prohibited from making personal attacks or using profanity, bloggers nevertheless vent openly and in strong terms about their grievances and dislikes. "It was like going back in time at least 40 years [and] after awhile we grew to despise the place," writes Cactus Sam of Iowa. "It is backwards, dirty, moldy and decrepit." "Oh, and did I say ignorance?" Wrote another, "Iowa stands for Idiots Outside Walking Around." "What a mistake," another said of the Midwestern town he lived in for fifteen years. "Town was a culture shock. No intelligents [*sic*], no culture all truckers." Yet another cautioned of "old-boy attitudes" and being run out of town "if you do not succumb to the way they want to live or behave in their town."[94]

But Middle Westerners are more likely to post glowing accounts of their communities than they are to add or agree with negative remarks. What they like is largely what people talk about in personal interviews. They find it appealing to escape from the bustle, traffic, and crime they associate with cities, and they write fondly of friends and neighbors they know well in their communities. They like neighbors who are laid-back, hospitable, and unpretentious, and yet who are hardworking and resilient. Although they acknowledge harsh winters and threats from tornadoes, they often find pleasure in quiet landscapes and open fields. Simple beauty is enhanced by well-tended parks and lakes and by farmers and homeowners taking pride in their property. They realize the rustic life is not for everyone. "We don't mind if you come visit and don't like it," said one. "We're not going anywhere."

FOUR

Education in Middle America

It was 1972, and Iowa had just implemented legislation to improve funding for rural school districts. Susan McAlister, a junior in high school that year, was contemplating her future. The country school she had attended through eighth grade was like a second home. The twenty farm families who lived nearby gathered monthly for fried chicken and homemade pie. The men played cards by the old pot-bellied stove while the women made quilts. The economy in northwest Iowa was suffering. Corn and cattle prices were low, and fuel and fertilizer costs were high. Susan remembers her parents didn't say much about the hard times. "They never made me feel like we were poor, but we did eat tons of bologna when I was a kid." Education in their small rural community could easily have been a casualty of the economy. But contributions from the state supplemented declining local tax revenue. Susan did well in school, graduating near the top of her class. She especially loved her classes in history and politics. The students read Plato, Aristotle, and Kant. Another class examined Supreme Court decisions. It awakened her interest in law.

Neither of Susan's parents had gone to college, but they cherished education. Her mother states emphatically, "Education is a really, really big thing for me. Although I didn't get to go to college, I wanted to go on." Her father recalls serving for years on the school board. Susan says it was simply taken for granted that she and her brother would go to college. He went to the state university, majored in agriculture, and eventually returned to the farm. She decided in high school that the rural life was not for her. "I'd read too many books and was looking for my knight in shining armor," she says. "I'd already dated all the boys that I was interested in during high school. I was looking for something more interesting. I was ready to move on, see what was out there, what opportunities there were." Passing up advice to attend a small college more like her high school, she opted for a large university, a "snob" school, where she could pursue her interests in history and politics. Her parents, gambling that crop and cattle prices would increase, let her go. She wound up majoring in journalism ("a marketable degree"), worked for several years in broadcasting, got married, and went to law school. Today she is a successful attorney in Houston.

But the transition from a small rural community to urban Texas left her deeply conflicted. Although she would make the same choices again, there is much she would like to have preserved. Her high school, she is convinced, was far better than the one her children would attend if she and her husband had not sent them to a private school. "I really miss family," she says. "I love having a meal and then everybody sitting around for hours and doing things together." She recalls Christmases with grandparents and cousins and weekend visits with aunts and uncles. "I loved the freedom of growing up on the farm. It is my kids' misfortune that I can't live there. You don't know it until you move away." After the 9/11 attacks, she thought for a while about moving back. The rural community seemed safe. People there were self-sufficient, but they also cared for one another. "Cities are terribly social in a superficial way," she muses, "but not in a meaningful way."[1]

Education fitting the needs and aspirations of its citizens was an important aspect of life in heartland states from the start. Country schools, private academies, public high schools, and colleges were founded in such numbers during the first few decades of the twentieth century that the region came to be known as the "education belt." After World War II, state and county boards of education mounted a massive campaign to improve and consolidate public schools. Officials promoted education, technological improvements, and research as means of advancing their communities and the region. Colleges and universities throughout the Middle West expanded. Parents like the McAlisters encouraged their sons and daughters to attain higher levels of education than they themselves had achieved.

Yet the question of how much to invest in education posed a quandary for families and community leaders alike. On the one hand, inexpensive, high-quality, universal secondary education and widely available higher education were easily promoted as facilitators of opportunity, economic advancement, and responsible citizenship. It was not surprising that Susan McAlister grew up believing she could be anything she wanted to be and that education was the key. On the other hand, realists argued that education was costly and that it made little sense for young people to attain more education than they could possibly use, at least if they stayed in rural communities. Parents balanced wanting their children to have new opportunities through better education against the likelihood of their departing to live in other places. Citizens took pride in institutions of higher learning that increasingly symbolized the prowess of their states but wondered if these colleges and universities were mostly training young people at taxpayer expense to leave and work in other parts of the nation. By the end of the twentieth century, schooling was profoundly different than it had been at midcentury both in levels of attainment and in how it was organized. Its development had required the heartland to face not only its desire for economic and cultural enrichment but also its attitudes toward place, work, family, and race.

In 1950, only 33 percent of the United States population aged twenty-five and over were high school graduates. Across the nine heartland states, where many of these residents were Dust Bowl survivors and where country schools were deemed so inferior that most had already been shut down or would be in the near future, the proportion with high school degrees exceeded the national average in four states and came close to it in four others. In 1960, despite the massive restructuring of farm life that took place in the 1950s, five of the nine states still exceeded the national average. Over the next four decades, as the percentage of adults who were high school graduates grew from 41 percent to 84 percent nationwide, the proportion in the nine Middle Western states rose from 41 percent to 88 percent. By the early twenty-first century, the proportion of high school graduates was above the national average in six of the nine states and matched it in two others.[2]

Although the region as a whole progressed dramatically in educational attainment, sizable differences from state to state remained. Iowa emerged in the nineteenth century as a leader in primary and secondary education and was soon joined by Kansas and Nebraska, and eventually by Minnesota. These states took pride in innovative educational reforms and invested heavily in supporting schools. During the second half of the twentieth century, they consistently ranked in the top third of states nationally having the highest proportions of high school graduates. In contrast, Missouri, which instituted an education system about the same time as Iowa, ranked in the bottom third of states, and Arkansas routinely placed near the bottom. Why several of the Middle Western states outperformed much of the rest of the nation—including such states as New York, Pennsylvania, and Maryland—was a question meriting consideration, and why Missouri and Arkansas did less well posed an interesting comparison.

The story was different for higher education. Between 1950 and 2006, the percentage of adults nationally with four or more years of college rose from 6 percent to 28 percent. College attainment grew in the Middle West at about the same rate, but few of the Middle Western states consistently exceeded the national average. The two that did were Minnesota and Kansas. In 2006, Minnesota ranked seventh in the nation for percentage of adults having graduated from college, and Kansas ranked twelfth. Minnesota had moved up from twenty-fifth in 1960 and Kansas from eighteenth. The other Middle Western states did less well. Despite its high percentage of high school graduates, Iowa ranked thirty-fourth in percentage of adults who were college graduates in 2006. Missouri ranked thirty-seventh and Arkansas ranked forty-ninth. How Minnesota and

Kansas managed to train and retain high percentages of college graduates was especially worth considering, as were the reasons for Iowa's lower success, along with Missouri's and Arkansas's. Whether the heartland could educate and attract residents in the professions and with other advanced degrees also remained an important question.

Research consistently demonstrates that educational attainment is a strong determinant of entry into higher-paying occupations for individuals and that it affects the economic well-being of communities and regions. For the Middle West, keeping up with or outdistancing the rest of the nation in educational attainment presented a dual challenge. The first involved mobilizing a largely rural population, whose livelihoods traditionally required only minimal schooling, to value public education and to provide it in small communities with few resources. The second involved retaining enough of the residents who attained higher education and placing them in attractive jobs, so that the region would benefit, rather than only preparing them to depart. Both challenges reflected the region's distinctive history, its patterns of settlement, and its effectiveness in transitioning through successive programs for providing public education.[3]

Public schools spread westward during the nineteenth century as quickly as settlers established new towns and townships. The congressional township system established by the Land Ordinance of 1785 set aside a square mile of land—designated as Section 16—in each thirty-six-square-mile township for the support of public schools. That system covered most of Ohio by 1803; extended a year later to the territories that would become Indiana, Illinois, and Michigan; applied to Missouri in 1820 and Arkansas in 1836; and was modified for later territories and states to include the revenue from Section 36 as well. Coupled with subscription academies that often preceded the effective implementation of legislative plans, this provision of public funds facilitated the development of an extensive and, for the most part, inexpensive program of education.[4]

Ensuring that public funds for education were well spent nevertheless presented a daunting challenge. Qualified teachers were hard to find, and it was sometimes difficult for citizens with little education themselves to judge the relevant qualifications. The story was told of one prospective teacher who, when asked if the world was round or flat, said he wasn't sure and would be happy to offer either view, upon which the hiring committee deliberated and decided he should teach that the world was flat.[5] In other instances, teachers were known to arrive inebriated or to spend the day engrossed in a book of their own while children played.[6] Some townships misused public funds or failed to construct adequate buildings. "A miserable, good for nothing school house," noted an Iowa county superintendant about a building where the wind whistled in and the front door was gone. A "burning shame" to its township, he wrote of another.[7] In other states, white residents resisted public education because it meant establishing schools for blacks or was regarded as charity for the poor. Wealthier citizens often preferred private academies subject to no external supervision. These were especially popular in Arkansas and Missouri, where nearly three hundred private academies were established by 1850 and made up a large share of the enrollment around St. Louis and Little Rock and in several counties with sizable black populations.[8]

Schools varied in size and quality and adapted to local conditions, but state administrators and county officials increasingly shared information with one another and passed laws that encouraged uniformity. By the middle of the nineteenth century, numerous educational experiments, including gender-separated schools, had been tried and largely rejected, while other practices, including public funding, county-level supervision, and common curricula, had become relatively standard. State and local school boards debated and adopted rules governing the number of weeks schools should be in session, how much teachers should earn, when morning classes should begin and afternoon classes should end, the length of recess, what constituted truancy, and how to punish rude behavior. These measures went partway in curbing the "boyish spirits," as one resident termed them, which resulted in at least one teacher's resignation after being tied to a fence post where she was left all day.[9]

The Middle Western states benefited from being settled a generation or two after the widespread development of public education in the northern states from which the majority of their inhabitants came. The adult literacy rate in 1850 was 94 percent in New York, 93 percent in Pennsylvania, 92 percent in Ohio, and 81 percent in Indiana. More than five-sixths of children aged five to fourteen in New York, Pennsylvania, and Ohio were enrolled in school and three-quarters were in Indiana.[10] Residents from these states who headed west carried both the advantages of being literate themselves and the practical knowledge of having founded or supported public schools for their children. "These newcomers," a writer in Iowa observed, "having arrived from states which had succeeded in establishing a school system, were familiar with the benefits of free schools and were therefore eager to secure the same privileges in their new home."[11]

Iowa's early emphasis on education was particularly indebted to these precedents. Provision for common schools in each county, "open and free for every class of white citizens between the ages of four and twenty-one," was made in Iowa Territory in 1839, and following a Michigan law, the establishment of schools was determined in 1840 to be a township function. As few townships yet existed, schools developed largely through village sponsorship and private subscriptions until Iowa became a state in 1846. Three years later, the legislature established a school fund with proceeds from 500,000 acres of public land. That year, census takers counted 742 public schools and thirty private academies with a total enrollment of nearly 45,000 students. Wapello County, with a population of 8,000, had forty-six public schools, for example; Linn County, with a population of 5,000, had thirty-eight public schools and five academies. In 1856, the state established a commission, chaired by the distinguished educator Horace Mann, president of Antioch College in Ohio, to conduct a far-reaching study of the prospects for public education in Iowa. The commission studied programs in other states and developed a plan emphasizing both the need for public funding through taxes and coordinated organization at the state, county, and township levels to promote uniform standards.[12] By 1859, the number of schools in Iowa mushroomed to 4,200, an increase of more than 500 percent in nine years. There were approximately 5,000 teachers and 143,000 students, representing 60 percent of the school-age population. A few years later, a resident in one of the new western counties observed farmers eagerly starting schools to qualify for public funds. "Revenue for the support of these schools is ample," another resident wrote, noting that it included "11,520 acres of choice lands which will be sold" and revenue from the state school fund "now amounting to over four millions of dollars."[13]

Other states adopted educational policies similar to Iowa's. In 1849, the Minnesota Territorial Legislature authorized the establishment of school districts and a permanent school fund. In 1855, the Kansas Territorial Legislature stipulated that common schools be established in each county "open and free for every class of white citizens between the ages of five and twenty-one years," and three years later adopted revised wording prohibiting exclusion because of color and any inclusion of sectarian instruction. The same statute specified the subjects to be taught, called for as much uniformity in the use of textbooks as possible, put school districts under the authority of local trustees and divided them by township, and affirmed that the proceeds of land in Sections 16 and 36 of each township would be used for school support. Subsequent legislation prohibited discrimination on the basis of gender, authorized local tax levies for school support, and established normal schools to train teachers. As counties were established, county superintendents of public instruction were elected and boards of examiners were created to certify teachers. Similar provisions were included in Nebraska's territorial legislation and in the Enabling Act of 1864 that led to statehood in 1867. A report by the territorial commissioner of education in 1860 showed thirty-four schoolhouses in Nebraska Territory, 131 schools, 139 teachers, and 2,930 students. Kansas became a state in 1861, enrolling nearly 5,000 children in 217 schools. Five years later Kansas employed more than a thousand teachers in 986 school districts, teaching more than 31,000 children for terms of approximately 4.3 months.[14]

These territories and states aggressively promoted public education in the years immediately prior to and during the Civil War as part of abolitionists' and free-staters' emphasis on democracy and in opposition to what they perceived as an aristocracy ruling over an untutored population in the South. "Knowledge is power," Kansas educator Grosvenor Clarke Morse declared. "Should learning be confined to a few that few would soon [have] an unbounded influence or authority over the ignorant rabble." Northern writers poked fun at Southern slaveholders who lacked schooling. Essayists took pride in statistics showing that white children in the North were three or four times as likely to attend school as white children in the South. As the war continued, women increasingly filled teaching positions vacated by men. School officials called it a patriotic duty to provide public education for soldiers' children.[15]

By 1870, approximately 60 percent of children aged five to thirteen across the Middle West were enrolled in school. Iowa, with 73 percent, had the highest proportion, followed by Minnesota with 67 percent, Missouri with 55 percent, Kansas with 53 percent, and Nebraska with 48 percent; Arkansas trailed with only 32 percent.[16] The years following the Civil War witnessed exceptional growth not only in students but also in the construction of school buildings. For example, in Iowa nearly a thousand buildings were erected from 1866 to 1868, and about the same number went up from 1872 to 1874. In Kansas, schoolhouses shot up from about 700 in 1867 to more than 3,500 in 1874. In Nebraska, there were fewer than 300 in 1870 and more than 2,000 in 1875. The number of teachers also increased dramatically. Iowa had more than 13,000 in 1872. Kansas had about 3,800 that year, triple the number five years earlier. Nebraska had 1,500, triple the number two years earlier. It was not surprising, in many respects, that expanding populations drove up the need for schools and teachers. Yet it was also testimony to the value citizens in the Middle West attached to education, and to the benefit of organizational models from which to borrow and mechanisms to provide funding, that the need was addressed with such determination.

Nowhere was the development of Middle Western education more clearly illustrated than in Vinton, Iowa, a small town on the Cedar River midway between Cedar Rapids and Waterloo in the eastern part of the state. Following a treaty ratified in 1838 with the Sacs and Foxes, the first white settlers arrived in the area in 1841, attracted by its rich timber- and farmland. The town became the Benton County seat in 1846, survived several years of lawlessness and vigilantism, and after going by two other names, officially became Vinton in 1853. In 1854, it had 200 inhabitants. A census two years later showed a population of 766. Nearly half the residents were from Ohio and Indiana, and many of the remainder were from New York, Pennsylvania, and New England. There were six doctors, six lawyers, five clergy, five teachers, two pharmacists, and a dentist. By 1861, with a population of 1,010, Vinton's establishments included a newspaper, a handful of doctors' offices, a public library, several law offices and banks, five churches, and a three-story flour mill. After the Civil War, the town grew rapidly, reaching 2,460 in 1870. The Burlington Cedar Rapids & Minnesota Railway came through in 1869 and established a freight house at Vinton in 1876. Another rail line extended west in 1872. In the 1870s, pioneers heading west in covered wagons made Vinton a stopping point. The Fairview Country School was situated at the intersection of two roads. "If you were in a covered wagon going to Kansas," a Vinton resident recalled, "you went south at that road, or if you were going out to Nebraska or North Dakota you went north."[17] A corn-canning factory, founded in 1879 and enlarged in 1892, helped the population grow to 3,449 in 1900. A button factory was established in 1904 but was abandoned two years later. The population topped 4,000 in 1940 and leveled off at around 5,000 after 1970. By the end of the twentieth century, Vinton's small-town charm, complete with refurbished antique-style streetlamps and rustic murals, and its convenient location—just twelve miles from Interstate 380—made it a favorite stop for presidential candidates, supporters, and journalists during the highly publicized Iowa caucus campaigns. "If you like Iowa," residents said, "you'll love Vinton."[18]

Formal schooling in Benton County began in 1846, when settlers living near Hoosier Point northeast of Vinton constructed a log schoolhouse and opened it on a subscription basis that fall for a dozen or so children. The U.S. census of 1850 showed Benton County, population of 672, having three schools, three teachers, and sixty pupils, representing about four-tenths of the school-age population. The county raised $106 for education that year, $59 from taxes and $47 from other public funds. Officials eased the burden of supporting public schools by taxing unimproved land held by nonresident speculators at the same rate as improved land owned by local home builders. Ninety-four percent of the adult population was literate. The first school opened in Vinton in 1852, meeting at the courthouse and then at a store on Main Street prior to moving into its own building the following year. In 1858, legislation declared each of the county's twenty townships a school district with responsibility for initiating schools and organizing teacher-training institutes. Fifty-two teachers attended the first institute in 1859, and eighty participated the following year. "Our present school system," an official wrote that year, "is giving universal satisfaction." By 1870, one school had been established for every four square miles in the county, each with its own board of directors. H. M. Hoon, the county superintendent, traveled 2,300 miles by horse and buggy in discharging his duties that year.[19]

A pioneer who settled in the 1850s explained the county's early commitment to public education. "Massachusetts had had in successful operation a common school system that had been copied by Ohio and other states and that could be easily adapted to the conditions of Iowa and under the most favorable circumstances." Settlers' children were able to receive an education at practically no cost. Schools were constructed and teachers hired almost as quickly as new towns and townships were formed. "There was no excuse for the children growing up in ignorance," he said.[20] Even the most uninformed visitor would have assumed that to be true. Entering Vinton from any direction, visitors passed a country school within a mile and a half of the edge of town, and throughout the county one came to a school at precise two-mile intervals.

Opportunities for advanced education in Benton County developed early, as well. The Iowa College for the Blind—where Mary Ingalls, Laura Ingalls's sister, came to enroll in 1881 after losing her sight from an illness two years earlier—opened in Vinton in 1852.[21] In 1862, the Irving Institute, a preparatory academy founded by a Baptist minister from Massachusetts, opened in the southwest corner of the county and raised $5,000 from local citizens to construct a building. Six years later, leaders of the Evangelical Society founded a preparatory academy at Blairstown, south of Vinton, and dedicated a building costing $4,000 several years later. Meanwhile, plans initiated in 1858 resulted in the founding at Vinton of the Tilford Collegiate Academy in 1871 with an initial enrollment of one hundred students. Vinton's public high school building opened in 1877.[22]

By 1880, Benton County's population had grown from only 11,000 at the end of the Civil War to nearly 25,000. Agriculture was prospering. There were more than 3,000 farms, totaling more than 438,000 acres, and more than three-quarters were owner operated. Farmland and improvements averaged $3,500 per farm, or approximately $25 per acre, and the typical farmer owned $700 in livestock. In 1879, output per farm averaged $871. Countywide, that included the revenue from 30,000 cattle, 122,000 pigs, more than a million pounds of butter, and nearly six million bushels of corn. Benton County was one of the most productive in the state, ranking fifth in overall farm productivity.[23] By the end of the decade, the population had stabilized, output per farm had risen by another $100, and farmland was selling for $35 an acre. That year, the county supported 369 teachers, who taught nearly 6,000 students, representing more than 80 percent of the school-age population.

As the twentieth century began, more than 98 percent of Benton County's adult population was literate. Its educational system included twelve village school districts, the largest of which was Vinton with twenty-one teachers; ten township districts, and eighty-seven rural schools. Eighty-nine percent of children aged six to fourteen were enrolled in school, and among those aged fifteen to seventeen, 62 percent were enrolled. There were, nevertheless, large differences between village schools and country schools. Villages had grown to the point that the typical teacher was in charge of thirty-six students, whereas in township and rural schools, that number was sixteen. Attendance rates further accentuated the differences. In village schools, average daily attendance included 80 percent of enrolled students; while in township schools, the figure was 67 percent; and in rural schools, only 57 percent.[24]

The state curriculum included standard training in reading, writing, grammar, geography, and arithmetic and made allowances for local needs and interests. Benton County's program specified that "the effect of stimulants, poisons and narcotics" should be taught, that vocal music should be offered, and that "the Bible shall not be excluded." Each school yard was to include twelve trees to shelter the building, and the doors of all schools were to open outward to facilitate escape in case of fire. In elementary schools, children sat two to a desk and came forward to a recitation bench grade by grade. One student recalled that the day usually began with the Lord's Prayer, singing, and recess, and ended by helping the teacher dust and bank the fire. At the high school, pupils studied algebra, geometry, history, English, and social studies. Girls took domestic science, learning to sew, knit, and cook; and boys studied breeds of cattle and horses, the names of different crops, and methods of agriculture. During the six months when schools were in session, girls were often absent on wash days and when younger siblings were ill, and boys missed sessions when needed to pick corn and tend animals. But poor attendance in rural schools was a function of weather as much as of chores. Heavy rain and snow kept children at home. A woman who attended one of the country schools remembered her brother pulling her the half mile from their farm each morning on a sled. Another said getting there was easier in winter, when she could walk on the frozen creeks, than in the fall or spring with muddy fields to cross and fences to be climbed. The difficulties increased in high school, especially for farm youth with greater distances to travel. Some took jobs and boarded in town or roomed with relatives. Nira Geiger, a farm girl in Benton County, for example, paid $5 a week for room and board while attending high school in Vinton, earning the money babysitting and cleaning. Two of her classmates at the rooming house held jobs at a restaurant, and a third worked at the dry-goods store. Iowa girls that year were almost 50 percent more likely to attend high school than boys.[25]

Conditions similar to those shaping public education in Benton County played an important role across the Middle West. Among other factors, high literacy in the first generation of settlers encouraged residents to provide better schooling for the next. These effects were evident even within Iowa. Among the thirty-six

Iowa counties in 1850 with adult literacy rates of at least 80 percent, 50 percent of children aged five to fourteen on average were enrolled in school, compared with only 32 percent in the thirteen counties with lower adult literacy rates. Taking account of differences in population, the former counties employed twice as many teachers as the latter and raised nearly four times as much tax revenue for public schools.[26]

Twenty years later, Iowans took pride in evidence from the 1870 census that the state's literacy rate of 93 percent among adults aged twenty-five and over was among the highest in the nation. Surely this was proof, some argued, that the state's school system was working effectively. What this interpretation missed was the fact that Iowans aged twenty-five and older—born before 1845—were very likely to have been educated elsewhere. Indeed, only 2 percent of the state's population aged twenty-five and older in 1870 had been born in Iowa. The same was true in Kansas, Minnesota, and Nebraska, where less than 1 percent was born in the current state, and even in Arkansas and Missouri, where the rates were 11 percent and 19 percent, respectively. Thus, the better way to think about literacy was as a *source* of interest in public education—a source that, in turn, needed to be understood in terms of the patterns through which the Middle West was populated.[27]

Literacy in much of the Middle West was high in 1870 for several reasons. First, a significant number of immigrants to the region came from northern states, where public schooling was well established and literacy was already the norm. Nearly half of Iowans aged twenty-five and older in 1870 had been born in Ohio, New York, Pennsylvania, and Indiana. These states also sent large numbers to Kansas and Nebraska. In all, 60 percent of Iowans, 54 percent of Kansans, and 48 percent of Nebraskans had been born in northern states. In Minnesota, with a larger number of foreign-born residents, 37 percent nevertheless came from northern states. Missouri differed in this respect, with only 22 percent from northern states, as did Arkansas, with only 6 percent.[28] Second, those who migrated had higher literacy rates than those who stayed behind. The difference was in some instances due to migrants being younger than nonmigrants. However, even among younger adults (aged twenty-five through forty-five), a higher proportion of migrants was literate than of nonmigrants. This was true in Iowa, Kansas, Minnesota, and Nebraska, where literacy was quite high and where many had come from northern states that also had high literacy rates.[29]

Migration from southern states, where literacy rates were lower, partly resembled the northern pattern and partly differed from it. White migrants to Kansas, Missouri, and Arkansas from Virginia, Georgia, Kentucky, and Tennessee were more likely to be literate—or at least as likely to be literate as people who had been born in those southern states and remained living there. This was also the case for black migrants, among whom literacy was relatively rare. For instance, 14 percent of black residents in Arkansas born in Tennessee were literate, compared with 10 percent of those born in and remaining in Tennessee. Differences in literacy between whites, who had not been denied schooling, and African Americans, who had been, underscored a third reason for high literacy in much of the Middle West: the preponderance of white settlement. Ninety-nine percent of residents aged twenty-five and older living in Iowa in 1870 were white, as were 99 percent of Nebraskans, 99 percent of Minnesotans, 95 percent of Kansans, and 93 percent of Missourians. Arkansas's population, which was 25 percent African American, differed significantly in this respect.[30]

Foreign migration into the Middle West lowered literacy rates less than stereotypes of ignorant Swedes, Norwegians, Irish, and Germans often suggested. Literacy rates among adults in Iowa were 6 percentage points lower among residents whose parents or who themselves were foreign born than among native-born residents. In Kansas, the difference was also 6 points, and in Minnesota, 13. However, it was only 2 points in Nebraska, and white residents in Missouri whose parents or who themselves were foreign born were 6 percentage points *more likely* to be literate than white native-born residents. In Arkansas, white residents of foreign birth or ancestry were 17 percentage points more likely to be literate than white native-born residents. Literacy also varied significantly by country of origin. Seventy-eight percent of immigrants in the Middle West from Norway and Ireland were literate, for example, whereas 84 percent of Swedes and 95 percent of Germans were literate.[31]

The cumulative effect of these various factors reinforced high literacy rates in the Middle West but also accounted for differences among its population. On average, the odds of being literate were about twenty times greater among whites than among blacks, about four times greater among Middle Western residents born in northern states than among residents born elsewhere, and slightly higher among younger adults than among older adults. The odds of being literate were about twice as high for men than for women and about that much higher among people living in urban areas than among those living on farms. State by state, Iowa and Nebraska had the highest literacy rates, followed by Minnesota and Kansas, with lower rates in Missouri and Arkansas. About half of these statistical differences were attributable to the effects associated with race and with birth in northern states.[32]

School enrollment in the Middle West in 1870 was influenced by the same social and demographic characteristics that affected literacy among adults. But the efficacy of state programs promoting universal education was evident in the fact that some of these characteristics did not matter as much. Boys and girls were about equally likely to be enrolled in school. Enrollment among African

American children ranged from 30 percent of the white rate in Arkansas and 42 percent in Missouri, to 65 percent in Kansas, 72 percent in Iowa, and 79 percent in Minnesota. Having been born in a northern state had much less of an effect on school enrollment than it did on adult literacy. Being foreign born lowered the chances of being in school, but having foreign parents was only a minor factor. What continued to matter when these other factors were taken account of was the state of residence. Children were most likely to be enrolled if they lived in Iowa or Minnesota, followed by Missouri, Kansas, and Nebraska, and least likely to be enrolled if they lived in Arkansas.[33]

Within each state, school enrollment varied considerably from county to county, and it was at this level that the effects of literacy, race, foreign birth, and other factors were most evident. The strongest predictor of a high percentage of children enrolled in school, taking account of other differences, was the percentage of the county's adults who could read. School enrollment was significantly lower in counties with a larger foreign-born or African American population. The other factors that mattered were economic. For example, counties in which the average total value of farms was higher had higher rates of school enrollment. These counties also had higher local taxes, which in turn facilitated the support of local schools.[34]

Together, the effects of favorable migration, high literacy, and a strong economic base were considerable. By the end of the 1870s, the clear leader among Middle Western states in commitment to public education was Iowa. It was the only state in the region with a seven-month school calendar. Total public expenditures on schooling averaged nearly $12 per pupil, matching Connecticut's and exceeding New York's and New Jersey's. The other Middle Western states offered schooling for terms ranging from five months in Kansas and Nebraska to four months in Minnesota, Missouri, and the Dakotas to only three and a half months in Arkansas. Approximately two-thirds of the school-age population across the region were enrolled in school, and average daily attendance ranged from 65 percent in Nebraska to 46 percent in Missouri. Nebraska's expenditures per pupil were similar to Iowa's, while Kansas, Minnesota, and Missouri spent about a third less. Arkansas's investment per pupil was a mere $1.33 for the year.

On a farm near Manchester, Iowa, a town of 2,200 fifty miles northeast of Vinton, a mother of two illustrated the value that many in the region attached to education. She wrote in her diary on October 8, 1881, "It seems to me we are placed here on this earth for something higher than merely to use our hands, toil and toil—merely to eat, and die in debt to our brains. [The children] love to go to school. With God's help I will try to educate them that they may through life have the advantage of a good education, with their noble hearts, their virtue and industrious habits." At age seventeen, she had taught school briefly herself but had been unable to complete a high school education. It was a matter of pride that her children did well in school. She wrote often of what they were reading, how many ciphers they could do, and how she wished their teacher were better trained. "We can not too highly prize an accomplished well educated mind," she wrote on another occasion, "and we are thankful indeed for the knowledge we possess, and would that we might gain more." Her daughter became a teacher a few years later and taught for the next fifty-two years.[35]

Despite numerous changes in school policies and population characteristics, the imprint of earlier patterns remained evident across the Middle West a generation later. In 1910, total school enrollment in the nine heartland states was 3.5 million, up from 1.2 million in 1870, and average daily attendance had grown from fewer than one million students to 2.5 million. The typical school year had risen from four and a half months to seven months, and all of the states had passed compulsory attendance laws.[36] County differences in school enrollment in 1910 could still be explained partly by factors that had been present in 1870. The effect of 1870 differences in literacy had diminished but were still statistically significant, taking account of other factors. The percentage of a county's population that was black in 1870 had as strong an effect on school enrollment in 1910 as it had in 1870. The percentage that was foreign born in 1870 still had a small but significant dampening effect on enrollments in 1910. Net of these effects, state to state differences were also evident. Iowa remained at the top in school enrollment as a percentage of school-age population, and Minnesota continued to be above average. Kansas and Nebraska both moved up, surpassing Missouri. Arkansas remained well below the others. Of the new states, North Dakota resembled Iowa in proportion of school-age children enrolled, while South Dakota and Oklahoma resembled Arkansas.[37]

Seventy-seven percent of schoolchildren aged five through eighteen in the nine-state region lived in rural areas in 1910. Country schools offering first-through eighth-grade education in one- or two-room schoolhouses were prevalent. In Iowa, nearly 3,000 of the state's 5,000 schools were in rural independent districts, and another thousand were township schools. In Minnesota, 9,000 of the state's 14,000 teachers were employed in one-room schools, as were two-thirds of Nebraska's. Forty-five percent of Kansas students attended one-room schools. A study of Oklahoma estimated that three-quarters of its children did.[38]

Rural schools were an integral part of farming communities, serving not only as places of instruction but also as meetinghouses for potluck suppers, holiday pageants, worship services, political debates, and family reunions. John Edgar, who attended a country school in Page County, Iowa, recalled spelling bees, community programs with recitations and playlets, and his favorite—the annual box socials when "women and girls prepared gaily decorated boxes packed with sandwiches, pie, cake, fruit, and other goodies." An auction of the boxes was usually followed by a contest to pick the "most popular young lady and the homeliest man," he remembered.[39]

As agriculture prospered, school administrators found it easier to purchase books, globes, maps, better desks, and writing equipment. "There were a few library books, including a set of *The Book of Knowledge*," John Edgar recalled, plus a map case, a globe suspended by a rope from a pulley on the ceiling, and a coal heater.[40] Better conditions also made it possible for administrators to lengthen the school year, and sometimes to attract better teachers by offering higher wages. Salaries at one-room schools in Kansas, for example, climbed from $38 a month in 1900 to $70 in 1911—with women, who constituted the majority, receiving 20 percent less than men. Pupils studied an enlarged curriculum that included state and national history, spelling, geography, physiology, geometry, and civics and were tested on these subjects in a standardized eighth grade exam.[41]

Many former students would later write fondly of their experiences and their teachers, recalling not only the long walks on cold mornings but also the happy memories of playground activities, favorite teachers, and friends. "My sister and I would always help her after school with the work like dusting and sweeping or washing the water bucket," a woman who attended a rural school near Vinton, Iowa, from 1902 to 1909 said about the teacher—"a neighbor girl"—she had for seven of those years. "Then she'd walk home with us. She lived three-quarter mile past our place and she'd walk back and forth too. We always thought that was a great treat walking home with the teacher." A former pupil at a rural school in Calhoun County, Iowa, who went on to become an educator himself remembered his first teacher: "She was a very young person to have the responsibility for a country school [but] she personified wisdom, maturity, maternal protectiveness, and kindness." "Through the years," another Iowan summarized, "a great feeling of esteem for the rural school has grown in the hearts and minds of people."[42]

The quality of rural education was nevertheless one of mounting concern. A study in Iowa demonstrated that children in rural schools attended significantly fewer days per year than children in town schools. Another study concluded that rural students lagged behind town students on tests, fell behind their grade level more often, and were more likely to drop out. A detailed investigation of twenty-two schools in rural Iowa found heating, lighting, and ventilation prevailingly unsatisfactory and concluded that the only teachers who stayed more than a year or two were unqualified for more attractive positions elsewhere. Other reports observed that school grounds frequently fell short of state standards, that rural teachers often had little training, and that country schools cost more to operate than town schools.[43]

Proposals for improving rural education presaged arguments that would appear repeatedly in coming decades. One argument emphasized the need to bring schools more clearly in line with the changing demands of Middle Western agriculture. Proponents of this view drew inspiration from the Country Life Commission, which concluded that better schools could play a central role in revitalizing rural communities. Besides elevating children's appreciation of literature and history, schools could do a more effective job, some argued, of training youngsters for scientific farming. "The rural school must aim to make better farmers and better helpmeets for these farmers," one writer observed, "must make the occupation more remunerative, and the whole life more worth living and free from city domination." Accomplishing this aim would require educators to recognize the distinctive skills needed in farming communities. School administrators should avoid taking cues from cities and should discourage local youth from migrating to cities by concentrating more on "field and meadow," manual training, domestic science, and farm accounting. "We shall never solve the farm problem," another writer declared, "as long as the most energetic and ambitious leaders of country life are being forced into cities to provide educational advantages for their children."[44] Other proposals focused less on curricula and more on efficiency. If the overall quality of rural education was to improve, they argued, school districts would need to be reorganized. Fewer farmers and smaller farm families, they predicted, would necessitate closing many one-room country schools. Transportation by team and wagon to town schools could be arranged. Studies of school consolidation were promising. With lower per-pupil costs, better teachers could be hired, more subjects covered, and longer school terms budgeted. State officials offered financial incentives for consolidation in the form of subsidies to larger districts.[45]

The decline in rural school enrollment that reformers foresaw in 1910 took place as expected. Compared with 3 percent growth in the 1910s, total enrollment among farm youth aged five through eighteen declined in the nine-state region by 5 percent in the 1920s, fell by 17 percent in the 1930s, and dropped another 23 percent in the 1940s. Nearly all of the loss was due to smaller school-age cohorts, although the proportion enrolled also dropped slightly—from 79 percent in 1920 to 76 percent in 1940. Fewer students in rural areas spelled the end of many one-teacher country schools. Nationwide, approximately 96,000 remained in 1944, compared with 200,000 in 1915. In some areas, the Depression and World War II postponed school consolidation until the late 1940s. The number of one-teacher schools in Kansas, for example, held steady at approximately 7,250 from 1928 to 1945 but declined by more than half to 3,140 in 1951.[46] Fewer children throughout the region also reduced the demand for town schools. Total enrollment of nonfarm youth aged five through eighteen rose 17 percent in the 1910s and 15 percent in the 1920s but declined by 1 percent in the 1930s and rose by only 3 percent in the 1940s. The Depression also reduced teachers' salaries, which were lower in 1940 than in 1930 in eight of the nine states.[47]

After World War II, school administrators in the Middle West focused on reorganizing rural districts and providing new and improved schools at both primary and secondary levels for an expanding school-age population. Consolidation of districts facilitated the closing of smaller schools and the construction or expansion of others. Between 1950 and 1960, elementary school enrollment in the nine states grew by 24 percent, while the number of elementary schools declined by 35 percent. High school enrollment increased by 15 percent, with the number of high schools falling by 13 percent.[48] The number of school districts decreased from approximately 38,000 to 16,000, the largest declines occurring in Iowa, Kansas, Minnesota, and Missouri. The trajectory in Iowa was illustrative. Having invested heavily in establishing and maintaining strong country schools, residents resisted school consolidation in the 1920s. In the 1930s, when Iowa extended compulsory school attendance through age sixteen, as did all of the Middle Western states except Missouri, students were often exempted from attending high school if they had successfully completed eighth grade or were lawfully employed. Although school consolidation continued through the 1940s, it was not until 1957, with passage of legislation requiring every school district to offer a full four-year high school course, that the majority of rural schools closed. Counties that may have had seventy or eighty school districts in 1942 had only three by 1960, each with a high school in the largest town and several elementary schools in smaller towns.[49]

The shifting center of gravity from farms to towns and the need to reorganize districts was evident in the region's changing demographics. In 1930, 48 percent of youth aged five through eighteen in the nine-state region lived on farms; by 1960, only 23 percent did. During the 1950s, as overall school enrollment increased, the number of students from farms declined by 9 percent while the number of nonfarm students mushroomed 62 percent. The challenges these changes posed were compounded by differences between farm and nonfarm youth in secondary school attainment. The proportion of youth aged fourteen to seventeen in high school rose from 31 percent in 1920 to 60 percent in 1930, after which it remained relatively stable, rising only to 70 percent in 1940 and 71 percent in 1950.[50] However, farm and nonfarm youth diverged during the 1920s and 1930s to the point that by 1940, the former were significantly less likely to be in school at age seventeen than the latter. During the 1940s, the rates converged, but farm youth were less likely than their counterparts to have been raised in contexts where adults had graduated from high school. This difference was evident in the fact that among adults aged twenty-five and over in 1940, only 10 percent of those on farms had finished high school, compared with 22 percent of those not on farms. In 1950, the ratio remained about the same, with 16 and 32 percent of farm and nonfarm adults, respectively, having finished high school. Although the farm population was declining, the fact that nearly a quarter of the region's children were still being raised on farms, coupled with these lasting differences from the Depression, presented issues with which the region's school administrators, parents, and young people had to contend as they considered how much and what kinds of education were most desirable.[51]

The upgrading of education to prepare a growing segment of the Middle West population for college required vast increases in public and private investment. Expansion had always generated ambivalence. Earlier in the century, school officials sometimes accused farmers of earning profits by keeping their children at work, and there were plenty of instances when citizens resisted school redistricting and tax increases. But these concerns were more about efficiency, community identities, and providing quality instruction than about the merits of education itself. The gradual rise of secondary education was revealing in this regard. High schools served local communities by training teenagers in history and civics, teaching domestic science and agriculture, and offering courses in algebra, chemistry, and Latin as preparation for future teachers and store managers or for the occasional student aspiring to become a doctor or lawyer. Parents accommodated the added cost, and public officials found creative ways to enlarge school budgets and adjust attendance requirements to farm schedules.[52] The school was seldom farther than the nearest town, and there was little danger that a student would meet a future marriage partner there who would lure him or her away from the community.

By 1910, rural prosperity made it easier for some farmers and townspeople to send children to high school and for these institutions to offer training in shop, vocational arts, bookkeeping, athletics, and music. In Iowa and other states with strong primary schools, legislation required counties to provide public secondary education and to pay for it through a combination of local taxes and state funds. Families took pride in being able to participate to this extent in what they regarded as the civilizing process. County agricultural extension agents and local farm bureaus worked with parents and school officials to demonstrate that secondary education was necessary for successful farming. Research in Iowa suggested that secondary education elevated occupational opportunities and earnings.[53]

In the 1920s, automobiles and better roads facilitated students' commutes and made it easier for farmers to forgo the loss of free labor. An ethnographic study of Shell Rock, Iowa, a town of eight hundred residents sixty miles north of Vinton, found families having fewer children and expecting to send them to high school. "Four children," the author wrote, "are considered an indecently large number, and usually only ne'er-do-wells have such large families. Birth control is taken as a matter of fact and is not even considered a debatable matter."[54] A study in western Kansas, where school taxes rose 50 percent between 1920 and 1935, found farmers planting more wheat and raising more cattle to cover the added cost. "Education," the writer observed, "is the modern force to which the people look for a solution of their problems. They say that any given problem—social, economic, or political—must be solved through education."[55] When crop yields were uncertain and opportunities to purchase land were declining, sending children to high school was the preferred way to invest in their futures. As the Depression reduced the number of farm youth able to attend high school, regret strengthened their conviction that the next generation would have it better. Through the WPA and then after World War II, community construction projects frequently included school expansion. In 1947 alone, Kansas and Arkansas each devoted more than $3 million to capital outlay for new schools, and Minnesota, Iowa, and Missouri each spent more than $4 million.

In 1950, four of the Middle Western states—Nebraska, Iowa, Kansas, and Minnesota, respectively—ranked first through fourth nationwide in percentage of twenty- to twenty-five-year-olds having completed four years of high school.[56] The figures showed that most teenagers in these states—between 70 and 80 percent—went to high school. There was also little variation from county to county in rates of attendance in these states. In Iowa, for example, only three counties fell significantly below the state average, whereas, in comparison, seven did in Arkansas and nineteen did in Missouri.[57] The high-ranking states were relatively homogeneous in social composition, but they also had state education systems that encouraged uniformity. County-to-county variations in these states were less affected by race, median incomes, and other factors than they were in Arkansas and Missouri. In consequence, some counties in Arkansas and Missouri rivaled those in the top-ranking states in rates of high school enrollment, while other counties dramatically lowered the state averages.[58]

Overall successes notwithstanding, education in the Middle West remained deeply divided and unequal along racial lines. The problem had deep roots in the region's history. Although much of the region had been settled by abolitionists and others opposed to slavery, white settlement was so predominant that many communities failed to confront questions about race, while in others slavery was present. In 1850, Missouri's population included more than 87,000 slaves, and Arkansas's included more than 47,000. Slaves accounted for more than a quarter of the population in six counties in Missouri and twelve counties in Arkansas. Twenty years later, African Americans made up 40 percent of the population in those eighteen counties. But African Americans accounted for only 2 percent of those counties' school enrollment, and they were 76 percent of the total number who could not write.[59] Elsewhere in Missouri and Arkansas, educators argued that it was impossible to start schools for African Americans because they were too few and too widely scattered. It occurred to no one that blacks and whites might attend the same schools.

The effects of these early patterns continued in subsequent years and were not limited to Arkansas and Missouri. In 1880, only 37 percent of African American children aged five through eighteen in Kansas were in school, compared with 63 percent of white children the same age. In Missouri, 29 and 55 percent, respectively, were in school; and in Arkansas, 17 and 38 percent, respectively. Thirty years later, the gap in Kansas had closed to 8 percentage points, in Missouri to 9, and in Arkansas to 12. Not until 1940 was the difference erased in all three states. Among adults, the earlier disparity nevertheless continued. In 1940, only 9 percent of African American adults aged twenty-five and older in the nine-state region had finished high school, compared with 19 percent of white adults. In 1950, the respective percentages were 14 and 30; and in 1960, 20 and 38.[60] Local variations also mattered. In Missouri, two counties— Mississippi and Pemiscot—had a large minority of African Americans, and both had lower percentages of young people aged fourteen through seventeen in school than in the rest of the state. In Arkansas, the lowest percentages of high school–age youth in school were in five counties with high proportions of African Americans.[61]

During the 1950s, the Middle West gained notoriety for two of the most widely publicized civil rights episodes of the era: the *Brown v. Board of Education* Supreme Court case in 1954 and the struggle in Little Rock over school integration in 1957. *Brown v. Board* arose from a class-action lawsuit in Topeka, Kansas, charging that the city's four elementary schools for black children were inferior to the eighteen schools white students attended and that the distances involved required excessively long walks and bus rides for young children. In 1951, the U.S. District Court of Kansas ruled against the plaintiffs on grounds that the schools' inferiority had not been demonstrated. The case was combined with four others involving more than two hundred plaintiffs in South Carolina, Virginia, Delaware, and the District of Columbia, and appealed to the Supreme Court. On May 17, 1954, the Court ruled that segregation in public schools solely on the basis of race violated the Fourteenth Amendment and in a subsequent case decreed that efforts to end segregation should proceed with all deliberate speed. The conflict in Little Rock three years later occurred as Arkansas governor Orval Faubus used National Guard troops to impede integration of Central High School.

The irony that the nation's landmark school desegregation case would foreground the Middle West rather than the South was not lost on contemporary observers. Of the 2.5 million African American students in segregated schools in 1953–54 nationally, only 12 percent were in the Middle West, and three-quarters of those were in Arkansas. Fifteen schools in Kansas were segregated, representing 7,500 of the state's 362,000 pupils. Iowa and Minnesota prohibited segregated schools, Nebraska and the Dakotas had no legislation pertaining to the issue, Kansas permitted it as a local option in cities, and Arkansas, Missouri, and Oklahoma required it. Kansas had long taken pride in its history of abolitionist support, leaving some citizens puzzled, as one wrote, "how we suddenly find ourselves represented before the Supreme Court opposed to those human rights for which our early settlers bled." Embarrassed by the furor, Topeka's school board ended segregation in September 1953, eight months before the Supreme Court's decision. "We feel that segregation is not an American practice," one board member explained. Yet it was also the case that Kansas's policies were at best ambivalent about race. Nearly a dozen previous cases had unsuccessfully challenged the state's optional segregation law, including three in Topeka itself, and numerous instances of local conflicts, discrimination, and white flight had been documented.[62]

The episode in Little Rock emerged in September 1957 when segregationists blocked nine African American students from attending previously all-white Central High School. Following a court injunction ordering Governor Faubus to withdraw the National Guard, municipal police and soldiers from the 101st Airborne Division of the U.S. Army successfully escorted the students. With tension continuing throughout the year, the school board canceled the 1958–59 session instead of proceeding with integration. The schools integrated the following year. The struggle not only catapulted Little Rock into the national spotlight and elevated tensions between state and federal authorities, but it also polarized the community and reshaped the public's image of Arkansas. News analysts estimated it to have been the most heavily reported story of the year, both domestically and abroad.[63]

Although media coverage increasingly cast Arkansas as a southern state solidly aligned with the Deep South and thoroughly backward in educational policies and racial attitudes, closer analyses of the Little Rock controversy revealed the continuing importance of long-standing economic and cultural differences within the state. Resistance to school integration was comparatively low in the northwestern half of the state, where farming, relative equality in incomes and education, and racial homogeneity prevailed, as it did in much of the Middle

West. Support for Governor Faubus and for school segregation was significantly higher in the southeastern half of the state. These counties included most of the areas in which slaveholding had been common in the 1850s, where black tenant farmers had outnumbered white tenant farmers by more than two to one during the first decades of the twentieth century, and where cotton acreage and production was highest. They had the greatest economic disparities between whites and blacks, the largest percentages of adults with low levels of education, and the least favorable traditions of support for universal public education.[64]

Besides racial differences, the Middle West faced the continuing challenges of inequality between wealthier and poorer school districts. The purpose of school-equalization legislation was to ensure that children had access to elementary and secondary education of reasonable quality no matter where they lived, whether it was in a remote farming community, small town, city, or suburb. Equalization policies were the late-twentieth-century equivalent of nineteenth-century public land allocations to townships for school funding. By the 1960s, equalization efforts were increasingly shaped by the fact that rural populations were shrinking, school districts were geographically larger, and expectations about school programs were higher. Schools continued to be funded by a combination of local and state revenues. But the question was how much those respective contributions should be. Was it equitable for tax rates to be lower in some areas than in others? Was it equitable for the state to contribute more when local revenue was sparse, even if this meant in effect transferring funds from wealthier districts to less wealthy districts?

The legislation in Iowa that benefited rural students like Susan McAlister in the early 1970s was typical of efforts throughout the Middle West to provide equal access to high-quality education. The legislation sought to balance two objectives: equity in per-pupil expenditures and equity in taxation. Neither objective could be accomplished exactly or simply. In the McAlisters' community, local funding for schools came from property taxes, which supplied a growing revenue stream as land values increased, but which strained farmers' budgets when land prices remained high and income from farming declined, as it did in the early 1970s. To ease the burden on rural communities, the base for tax levies in some areas shifted from property values to productivity, but doing so increased the likelihood of annual fluctuations. The preferred solution was to allocate state funding more generously to communities in which local revenue was declining. Affluent taxpayers seldom found it appealing, though, to anticipate revenue being redistributed to poorer districts. Not surprisingly, school finance legislation was frequently revised and sometimes challenged in the courts. The Iowa General Assembly, for example, passed laws modifying the method of allocating state funds for the aid of schools in 1967, 1970, 1972, and 1989, and again in 1998. Revenue for schools in Iowa in 1998 totaled almost $2.9 billion, of which 61 percent came from the state and 39 percent was raised locally, nearly all through property taxes.[65]

All of the heartland states instituted school-equalization legislation in the 1970s and made periodic revisions through the remainder of the century. Although the simplest measure of how well objectives were achieved was per-pupil expenditures, complex formulas reflecting differences in competitive salaries, construction costs, transportation, and needs for special education resulted in considerable variation from district to district. Data compiled for the 1998–99 school year showed an average expenditure of $6,345 per pupil for the nine-state region, with Minnesota, Iowa, Kansas, and Nebraska spending the most, and Arkansas and Oklahoma spending the least. There was also significant variation within states. In Minnesota, for example, district expenditures per pupil ranged from $5,000 to more than $16,000, and in South Dakota, from $4,000 to more than $15,000.[66]

In Vinton, Iowa, quality education remained as much a priority at the turn of the twenty-first century as it had been in the 1850s. There were 114 full-time teachers and more than 1,900 students in the consolidated Vinton-Shellsburg district. Expenditures per pupil were approximately 50 percent above the state average. Besides its friendly small-town atmosphere, residents especially took pride in the community's schools. Two of the older buildings were recently renovated, and the high school was brand-new. Eighty-six percent of the community's residents were high school graduates in 2005, up from 68 percent in 1980. The elementary and middle schools were focusing more of their effort on reading skills and students' professional development. At the high school, annual graduation rates ranged from 93 percent to 98 percent. Vinton was still home to the state's primary learning center for the blind, now called the Iowa Braille and Sight Saving School. In 2008, the community was selected to serve as the North Central region's training center for AmeriCorps.[67]

Growth in college enrollments was the other significant development in heartland education during the second half of the twentieth century. Between 1952 and 2005, enrollment in institutions of higher education in the nine-state region grew at an annual rate of 28,000 students—enough to fill a large new campus every year. Yet it was by no means certain in the years immediately following World War II that the heartland could—or would—support this kind of commitment to higher education. Although it was evident that doctors and lawyers and a few others required advanced schooling, it was doubtful that many in the region could reasonably aspire to these occupations. For every thousand people living in Kansas, Nebraska, or Oklahoma in 1952, only fifteen were going to college, and in Arkansas, only nine were. For every thousand adults in these states old enough to have finished college, fewer than sixty had done so. Despite the G.I. Bill, which later observers sometimes argued sparked a huge influx of postwar enrollees, less than 10 percent of college students in 1952 were veterans. Indeed, the total enrollment in 1952 was not much more than it had been in 1940.[68]

Unlike high school, the cost of which was borne almost entirely and universally by taxpayers, the expense of college fell heavily and unevenly on individuals and families. Although tuition at public universities would seem bargain-cheap by later standards, it was only part of the cost involved. Housing, transportation, food, and other living expenses doubled or tripled the overall cost. For the 40 to 45 percent of families in many Middle Western towns and rural areas whose gross family earnings were less than $3,000, spending a third of that on college represented a nearly imponderable investment. For aspiring students, going to college meant postponing income from full-time employment and, in many cases, drawing from parents' contributions and savings accounts. Farm boys wondered if anything they might learn in college would be useful for farming. Girls pondered the trade-off between spending time in college and starting families earlier. Compared with high school, college was more likely to encourage young people to move away from their families and to leave farms and small towns for cities. For public officials, selling higher education to parents and taxpayers was a different proposition than promoting local schools.

Yet the sales effort proved overwhelmingly successful. By 1962, college enrollments in the Middle West mushroomed to 473,000, double the number a decade earlier. Thirty thousand students were attending college in Arkansas and Nebraska; more than 60,000 were enrolled in Iowa, Kansas, and Oklahoma; and nearly 100,000 were in Minnesota and Missouri. Total population in the region rose by only about 10 percent in the 1950s, but there were more young people of college age, and a significantly larger proportion were in school. For every thousand residents, twenty-four were now in college, and the number continued to climb steadily during the 1960s. By 1971, total enrollment nearly doubled again, to 865,000. For every thousand residents, forty-one were in college. Sparsely populated as they were, North and South Dakota each had more than 30,000 students. Arkansas had more than 50,000, and Nebraska had 67,000. Iowa, Kansas, and Oklahoma each enrolled more than 100,000, Minnesota had 159,000, and Missouri had 188,000.[69]

Several aspects of the region's history facilitated the growth of higher education. Entrepreneurial religious leaders competed to spread the morally uplifting effects of advanced learning to an expanding frontier. "Surely if the early colonies of the Atlantic coast needed Christian colleges at the very outset of their slowly developing Commonwealths," a Congregationalist educator told a Minnesota audience in 1880, "much more do these Western States into which the swelling tides of immigration are pouring, and wherein are already multitudes of youth for whom the best education of the times should be provided."[70] By that year, more than fifty colleges and universities had been established in the Middle West. Iowa had nineteen, Missouri had fourteen, Kansas had eight, Minnesota had six, and Nebraska and Arkansas each had four. Many were private, founded by Congregationalists, Methodists, Presbyterians, Baptists, and Catholics, each group sensing the need for a college in every state. These small western colleges, historian James Bryce wrote in 1888, "set learning in a visible form, plain, indeed, and humble, but dignified even in her humility, before the eyes of a rustic people in whom the love of knowledge, naturally strong, might never break from the bud into the flower but for the care of some zealous gardener." Bryce found their diverse, decentralized rural locations appealing. "They light up in many a country town," he wrote, "what is at first only a farthing rushlight, but may finally throw its rays over the whole state in which it stands."[71] In addition, there were the public universities in each state, beginning with the University of Missouri in 1839, nine of which received a congressional land grant through the Morrill Act of 1862 to establish schools of agriculture and mechanical arts. The grants ranged from 136,000 acres in Nebraska to 600,000 acres in Oklahoma.[72]

The number of colleges and universities in the Middle West grew from about 100 in 1910 to more than 200 in 1930 and topped 300 in 1940. In the 1950s, the total remained just slightly above 300, as a few of the smaller church-related colleges closed and several public institutions opened. Iowa, Kansas, and Missouri each had about fifty colleges and universities, Minnesota had more than forty, Oklahoma had about thirty, Nebraska and Arkansas about twenty, and each of the Dakotas about a dozen. While the number of campuses remained constant, funds devoted to new facilities signaled the expansion taking place. In 1950, expenditures on plant expansion in the nine states totaled $58 million, or an average of $186,000 per campus. By 1960, the total was $99 million for an average of $324,000, and by 1970 the figure rose to $372 million and averaged more than $1 million per campus.[73]

But young people did not stream to the ivied halls quite as eagerly or as free of misgivings as later writers would sometimes imagine. Many young people were on paths that simply ruled out thinking about college. Others tried it and found it not to their liking or experienced great difficulty knowing what to make of it and where it might lead. Whether the region's farm youth could—or should—be enticed into going to college was a matter of particular debate. Some argued that farming itself required advanced training. "Technical ability is in big demand now and for the foreseeable future," a writer for *Farm Journal* declared in 1956. "A youngster with a bent for mathematics and science will do well to develop himself in those directions. He'll be a better farmer if he does, for farming will grow more technical."[74] Fewer opportunities to remain on farms presented additional reasons to seek higher education. Jobs in industry, engineering, agribusiness, and the professions would require it. An informal survey of farm boys suggested that most saw value in attending college. "I plan to go to college," said one. "Dad regrets he did not and has encouraged me to go." Said another, "A college education is just like a high school diploma 20 years ago. You need it to get ahead."[75] Yet observers recognized that college was not for everyone. Vo-tech training, shop and auto repair courses, or on-the-farm mechanical skills might be more reasonable alternatives. "It's true that 40 percent of you boys growing up on farms these days won't ever be a farmer," one writer advised, adding: "Think of the opportunities in the 18,000 food processing firms, 1,360 farm machinery and tractor companies, and the 75,000 firms serving as assemblers, brokers and jobbers of farm products!" A boy in Kansas told his dad, "I guess I'll take a short course in aviation mechanics. Maybe I can get an airlines job or work at the aircraft factory in Wichita. This drouth every year has cured me of ever wanting to farm."[76] A boy in Iowa commented, "My relatives have all discouraged me from thinking of college; my uncle says it would be a waste of time and money." The opportunity to "start earning money right way," he said, was more appealing.[77]

A young person growing up on a farm anywhere in the United States during the late 1940s and 1950s was at a considerable disadvantage in attaining a college education. In 1962, the U.S. Census Bureau conducted a survey in which men were asked not only about their own educations but also about their father's education. Among young men aged twenty-five through thirty-nine whose fathers farmed, only 17 percent had fathers who had attended high school at all. In comparison, among those whose fathers did not farm, 40 percent had fathers who had attended high school. For the young men themselves, it mattered both if their fathers were farmers and if their fathers had been to high school. If a young man's father farmed and had not been to high school, that young man had only a 9 percent chance of attending college and a 4 percent chance of graduating. If the father farmed and had gone to high school, the young man's chances of going to college rose to 26 percent and of graduating, to 13 percent. If the father did not farm and had gone to high school, the young man's chances of going to college increased to 47 percent and of graduating, to 26 percent. In short, a young man from town with a moderately better educated father was more than five times as likely to go to college than a young man from a farm with a less educated father, and he was six times more likely to have graduated.[78]

Those who argued that farm youth should go to college because many would have to seek off-farm employment had a point. In the 1962 survey, fewer than half (only 42 percent) of men aged twenty-five through thirty-nine from farm backgrounds were currently employed as farmers or farm laborers. Twelve percent were in white-collar occupations, such as the professions, managerial jobs, or sales. Forty-two percent were in blue-collar occupations, such as skilled or unskilled jobs in factories and manufacturing. This meant that nearly three-fourths of those who left the farm were working in blue-collar jobs. Education was the ticket to white-collar employment. Among those from farm backgrounds who had earned some college training, 18 percent were doing white-collar work, and among those with college degrees, 63 percent were.[79]

But lacking family experience with higher education, youth from farms and rural communities who did aspire to further schooling often faced frustrating decisions. A farmer who tried college for a semester on the G.I. Bill recalled, "I tried to do the pharmacy thing and it didn't work out." He had no idea what was required. Chemistry had not been taught at his high school. It was "literally impossible" for him to continue. A man who grew up on a farm near a town of 500 people and whose father had only an eighth-grade education picked a college for no reason other than knowing a boy from his high school who went there. Teaching was the one white-collar job he knew about, so he majored in education and became a teacher. But he always wondered how things might have turned out if he had known a little more. He recalled a geology course that he discovered too late to guide his choice of majors. "I guess I envy those people who say 'I just love my job and wouldn't give it up for anything,'" he remarked.[80] Other young men found it simply more attractive to stay on familiar turf than to venture into the unknown. Parents able to send their offspring to college were also in the best position to enlarge farming operations enough to absorb an interested son.

Young women in rural areas often received even less encouragement from their families to seek education beyond high school. Martha Fallows, a farm girl who finished high school in the mid-1950s was typical. "I always wanted to be just a mom and a housewife," she said. After a short beauty school course she began working at a beauty shop in a town of about 2,000 people, driving fifty miles when the roads were too muddy to cut across the hills in her 1939 sedan. Almost immediately she began dating a young man working at a temporary construction site. "Back in the fifties, nice girls did not go with the transients," she explained, but fortunately for her, he lived in a neighboring town and the romance continued. The couple got married soon after. He settled into a regular round of construction work, and she devoted herself to their children. Two decades later, with family expenses rising and her husband's work less steady, she resumed working, first at an appliance store, then at a five-and-dime, a flower shop, a doctor's office, and a greenhouse. Would she do anything different? "I wouldn't get married right away, and I would get a really good education," she replied, "a very good education probably in a medical field."[81] By the end of the 1970s, only 8 percent of women in the nine Middle Western states who had grown up on farms or in small towns were college graduates, compared with 16 percent of men with similar backgrounds.[82]

Research underscored the educational difficulties many rural youth encountered. Surrounded by family and friends who had not gone to college, they were less likely to aspire to higher education or understand the necessity of strong academic performance in high school. Low family incomes and living farther from campuses made it harder for many to consider college a serious option. If they did contemplate college, they realized they would very likely be leaving their families and communities behind, or they made an early vocational choice that limited what they felt valuable to learn. They lacked what scholars later would term "cultural capital," such as books, music, and paintings in the home, opportunities to attend concerts, and networks including men and women in the professions.[83]

By the end of the 1960s, rural Middle Westerners nevertheless more often expressed interest in gaining higher education than they had a decade earlier—and found it more troubling when these aspirations were postponed or went awry. Karen Hartman grew up in a town of about two thousand people, thinking her love of sewing and involvement in the annual 4-H fashion show would take her someday to a big city where she would work in fashion design and the clothing industry. Instead, she got married and returned to her home county. There were no regrets, she said. "I decided that this was the kind of life I wanted for my kids, and I wanted to raise them in an agrarian environment. It was a choice." However, she wished she had finished her college degree sooner than she did. After a few community college courses, she dropped out to have children and did not return for nearly a decade when the need for a second income became urgent. She eventually completed a degree in education, taught science, and managed the school library. She said going to school and working full-time turned out to be good for all concerned. Her children became more self-sufficient and better organized. For herself, receiving the degree was one of her proudest moments.[84]

Going to college proved increasingly attractive, not only because of the earnings potential it represented, but also because of what it symbolized. For students themselves, it was the necessary rite of passage through which one entered the middle class. Going to college meant coming of age on one's own, learning to be independent of one's family, and especially discovering one's identity by exploring new experiences and opportunities. For young people from small towns and rural areas in the Middle West, like Susan McAlister, college was the ticket away from places and faces that were all too familiar, the passport to life and work elsewhere. College opened doors to the glamorous world that small-town young people saw on television and in motion pictures. Even before they left, high school students preparing for college signaled their intent to depart. College was the reward for doing well in school. It cast them in a different light than their classmates who might be hometown heroes on the football field or dance floor but who were going nowhere. For small-town parents, a son or daughter at college was a talking point, a news item, a mark of distinction, just as a new car or a lavish home might be, but in communities where ostentation was judged harshly, educating one's children was a more legitimate form of conspicuous consumption.

For all its attractions, higher education nevertheless related uneasily to the fact that heartland America was hardly the place for college-educated young people to seek the most alluring jobs in high finance and aerospace or to bask in the grandeur of Broadway or Hollywood. Indeed, a few inhabitants of the rural Middle West had always felt keenly that the region was not an ideal location in which to realize the finer virtues that higher education provided. Pioneer women with training at eastern colleges, who were dragged by adventuresome husbands to the barren frontier, wrote in their letters about the absence of refined conversation and the complete unavailability of good music and books. Small-town newspaper editors, doctors, and teachers tried the Middle West and either left discouraged or stayed with quiet misgivings. While avoiding the disdain with which city dwellers sometimes viewed the rustic life, they wondered if it was possible to enjoy the benefits of civilization quite as much in the hinterland as people did in urban centers. In this "age of oratory and music and art," a college-educated Kansan who returned to a small town to teach school in the 1890s observed, "our village offered nothing except a market and a loafing place for boys." Finding no newspapers, few books, and little social life other than church, he considered whether death might be better than life.[85]

As growing numbers of young Middle Westerners went to college, the likelihood that they would leave their communities of origin, if not the region itself, increased. Primary and secondary education had always been marketed as benefits to the local community. Residents who could read and write, who had studied civics and arithmetic, and who knew something about animal husbandry or home economics were better local citizens. They stayed in the community and made it stronger. A fine high school building symbolized that strength. Earlier arguments about higher education had been similar. The small western colleges that inspired James Bryce were beacons shining from country towns. They trained clergy, Christian laypeople, teachers, doctors, lawyers, and dentists who would return to the small towns where they would serve as moral leaders. This was the role of the educated minority. Good government, Alexis de Tocqueville had written in the 1830s, depended on it.[86] The Morrill Act, followed up decade by decade with appropriations for agricultural extension programs and institutes for technical training, aimed to benefit local communities as well, not by removing farmers and laborers from them, but by making these inhabitants more productive. But the growth of higher education during the last half of the twentieth century was different. Insofar as it contributed to the region, its benefit was popularly associated with individual achievement and with national well-being more than with local communities. The demographics of the baby boom, together with long-term decline of the agricultural sector, dictated that college-educated young people from rural areas would seek employment elsewhere. Going away to college became the means through which social relocation was accomplished. Although two-year community colleges and branch campuses partly reversed the trend in the 1980s, higher education in the 1960s and 1970s came increasingly to be concentrated on large campuses populated by students in residence. It was to these places that young adults fled if they wanted to escape, or went to reluctantly if they did not. Campus administrators prided themselves on recruiting students from afar. Mixers and dormitory assignments encouraged students to move past their parochial horizons. Attending college and leaving home became synonymous.[87]

The relationship between better schooling and moving away was, to a degree, reminiscent of earlier patterns. The Middle West prospered in the nineteenth century from the fact that literate people with more schooling were especially likely to move into the region. As secondary education emerged, being able to attend high school sometimes required young people to move from farms to towns, and graduation opened opportunities to seek employment in other communities. Yet the extension of compulsory education through age sixteen and the wide availability of high schools necessarily reduced the chances that secondary education would be associated with greater geographic mobility. By 1940, exactly the same proportion of Middle West residents aged twenty-five through thirty-nine who had graduated from high school lived in their birth states as did their counterparts who had not finished high school.[88] In this respect, college was different. A relatively small fraction of young people went to college, and those who did usually left their communities to do so. Having left, they were also more likely to continue living elsewhere when they finished.

The extent to which college was associated with moving was evident in the 1970 U.S. census. Among people born in any of the nine Middle Western states, the likelihood of residing out of their birth state increased slightly (by less than

0.2 percent a year) for ages three to eighteen. At age eighteen, 8 percent were no longer living in their birth state. For ages twenty-one through twenty-nine, the rate of out-migration among those who graduated from college rose to 0.6 percent a year, while the rate of departure among those who did not graduate from college was 0.1 percent a year. Thus, at age twenty-nine, 17 percent of those with college degrees no longer resided in their birth state, compared with 11 percent of their counterparts without college degrees. Then for ages thirty through sixty-five, the likelihood of living in their birth state remained almost constant for both groups, meaning that those with college degrees were still about 5 points less likely to be living in their birth state than those without college degrees. This pattern continued to be evident, and indeed, the differences became more pronounced in the 1980, 1990, and 2000 censuses. In 2000, for instance, the rate of departure from one's birth state was 0.7 percent for ages three through eighteen; it shot up to 2.4 percent a year for ages twenty-one through twenty-nine among college graduates, compared with less than 0.2 percent among those of the same age not graduating from college; and then increased at a modest rate of 0.4 percent for both groups for ages thirty through sixty-five. At age twenty-nine, nearly half of the college graduates had left their birth state, compared with a third of the non–college graduates.[89]

A report by the U.S. Census Bureau in 2003 underscored the extent to which state-to-state migration was taking place among college-educated young people. Nationally, one-third of all movers between 1995 and 2000 were young adults aged twenty-five to thirty-nine. Within this age group, those who were college educated were especially likely to have moved. About three-quarters had done so. Seventy-two percent of those who had college degrees and were married had moved, as had 75 percent of those who were single and had college degrees. About one-quarter had moved to a different state, and the Middle West was losing population as a result. Out-migration exceeded in-migration in all but one of the Middle Western states. Minnesota was the exception, with a net gain of 1,700 people aged twenty-five to thirty-nine, single, and college educated.[90]

One reason young adults in their twenties moved was to attend college in another state. But data reported by the National Center for Education Statistics in 2006 showed that residents of Middle Western states were not leaving at especially high rates to attend out-of-state colleges. Approximately 269,000 residents of the nine states were attending postsecondary institutions that fall, and approximately 225,000 of these were attending colleges in their home state. This proportion—84 percent—was the same as for the nation as a whole. In addition, out-migration had to be compared with the number of young adults from other states who came to the Middle Western states to attend college. This number was approximately 60,000 in 2006, meaning a net gain of about 16,000 students. In short, the Middle Western states were disproportionately attracting college students but losing college graduates.[91]

By the start of the twenty-first century, the loss of college graduates from the Middle West had become a matter of profound concern to the region's educators and policy makers. A report for the Federal Deposit Insurance Corporation (FDIC), for example, argued that a brain drain from low-population rural states in the Middle West was occurring, with adverse effects possibly similar to those of out-migration of educated people from developing countries. Among other things, states' budgets would suffer from the loss of residents most capable of earning high salaries. The supply of high quality education might itself be a casualty as states faced "comparatively high per capita costs for university-level education but are able to capture only a small fraction of the benefits for their local economies." Local communities lacking better-educated residents with professional training and leadership skills might also find themselves in a downward spiral. "Like the small size of the labor force in many depopulating counties," the report said, "the quality of the labor force may raise concerns that shorten the list of companies willing to locate in those communities."[92]

A comparison of birth states and states of current residence provided the best approximation of how many college graduates the Middle West was losing. Approximately 1.5 million college-educated Americans aged twenty-five to thirty-nine in 2000 had been born in one of the nine heartland states. Of that number, 800,000 (52 percent) were no longer living in their birth state. By that estimation, the brain drain was huge. Had these states been able to keep everyone who eventually went to college, they would have had twice as many college-educated young adults as they did. When those who moved in from other states were considered, the story remained troubling but was less grim. Of the 1.4 million college-educated persons aged twenty-five to thirty-nine *currently* living in one of the nine states, 659,000 had moved there from another state. Subtracting these 659,000 in-migrants from the 800,000 out-migrants meant a net loss of only 141,000. That was a net brain drain of about 9 percent in relation to the 1.5 million who had been born in these states.

However, there were significant differences among the nine states. Minnesota had a net gain of college-educated immigrants; Arkansas, Kansas, Missouri, and Oklahoma broke even; and Iowa, Nebraska, and the Dakotas experienced a net loss. It is in these numbers that the answer to the riddle was to be found of how Iowa had historically ranked near the top of all states in educational achievement—from high literacy rates among its first settlers to strong programs of primary and secondary education to excellent public and private colleges and being a magnet for out-of-state college enrollees—and yet fell among the bottom third of states in percentage of residents with college degrees. The reason was Iowa's loss of a large number of its residents by birth who eventually earned college degrees and a failure to attract college educated residents from other states.

The comparison between Iowa and Kansas was revealing. Both states lost more than half (58 percent) of their college-educated birth residents aged twenty-five to thirty-nine. But Iowa had a larger number of birth residents with these characteristics, which meant a loss of 137,000, compared with Kansas' loss of 93,000. Iowa also attracted fewer college graduates from other states. Of college-educated residents aged twenty-five to thirty-nine living in Iowa in 2000, only 37 percent were from another state, compared with 58 percent in Kansas. Iowa gained 59,000, while Kansas gained 88,000. Thus, the net loss of college-educated young adults for Iowa was nearly 79,000, while for Kansas it was only 4,200.[93]

Efforts to retain the region's better-educated residents or to lure them back emphasized everything from business opportunities to tax breaks to advertisements about lifestyle amenities. In 2005, Iowa state senator Jeff Lamberti proposed offering a tax break of $600 to every resident under thirty years old. In 2007, Iowa passed the Generation Iowa bill, which established a commission to advise on attracting residents to the state through student loans and aggressive marketing in bioscience and other high-technology fields. Nebraska initiated a microloan program to encourage small business start-ups. Kansas forgave student loans for graduates of its medical programs for each year spent in a rural community and launched a "Come Home to Kansas" initiative targeting entrepreneurs in technical fields. Oklahoma introduced bills to provide tax incentives to graduates in aerospace and engineering. Private initiatives appeared as well, such as the Dakota Venture Group, which offered expertise in investing, and Dakota Roots, which linked former South Dakota residents with local business opportunities.[94]

While it remained to be seen how the Middle West would fare in retaining better-educated residents, there was little question that education at all levels would play an important and continuing role in the region's local communities. In town after town, the high school was the largest, newest, and best-maintained public building. In other communities, an elementary school occupied a similar place. Like the one-room country school for an earlier generation, these were the centers of social life in their communities. People came there to visit their children's and grandchildren's teachers, to attend concerts and school plays, and to vote. They gathered there for blood drives, vaccinations, and family reunions, and they flocked in large numbers to root for the home team.

That was especially true for the Redmen, the vaunted football team of Smith Center, Kansas. A visitor looking for the town's center of action quickly realizes that it is not on Main Street but several blocks east at the high school. District 237 covers six hundred square miles of taxable property, from which it receives more than $5 million a year. The district has more than seventy employees, including forty-two teachers, half of whom are at the high school, where they instruct approximately 225 students. A majority of the eleventh graders meet or exceed national standards in math and reading. The graduation rate is 100 percent, and 89 percent go on to college.[95] The building is the largest and most modern structure in town and often doubles as a location for community gatherings. To its left, just past the baseball field, is Hubbard Stadium. On Friday evenings each fall, this is where the Smith Center Redmen play football, often to crowds that exceed the town's population. The games are televised throughout the state, and the scores are reported on CNN and in major newspapers. One season, the Redmen set a national record by scoring seventy-two points during the first quarter of a game. That same season, they outscored their opponents 844-20 and won their fourth straight state championship. "What we do around here real well is raise kids," the coach told a reporter from the *New York Times*. "In fact, we do such a good job at it—and I'm talking about the parents and community—that they go away to school and succeed, and then pursue opportunities in the bigger cities."[96]

The coach was a keen observer of life in Smith Center as well as a decisive influence in the community. To instill discipline in his players he made them promise not to drink or smoke, had them give testimonials at the elementary school about their pledge, and cut those from the team who broke it. Life was not about winning, he taught them, but about working hard. He could point to former players who had gone on to the National Football League and to occupations as doctors, lawyers, and scientists to prove it. He and his wife—a community leader—knew they were preparing young people who would mostly earn their livings elsewhere. [97] But they were also carrying on a legacy. Farming and agriculture had been the community's center of gravity for more than a century, and despite periodic difficulties, it would remain so. The people who stayed knew how to adapt.

FIVE

The Decline of Small Communities

The snow is finally melting in this west Nebraska town of two hundred people. But it has been a difficult winter. More than forty-two inches fell, twice the annual average, causing fuel bills to rise and discouraging residents from venturing outside. On mornings with the windchill below zero, farmers bundled their children in heavy coats and drove them by tractor to meet the school bus. Some days, the drifts were so high even the tractors were unable to navigate the country roads.

Madge Schmidt has been driving the school bus since 1975. She inherited the job from her dad, who became the bus mechanic and part-time driver when the Case farm equipment dealer he worked for closed its doors in 1966. "Bus driving has its trials," she says, referring to the noisy children on her route. "But there are a lot of good days, too" she says. " I enjoy seeing the sunrise, windmills silhouetted in the sunrise, deer, antelope, turkey buzzards, and sometimes an eagle." The job is also a necessity. For ten years, she and her husband lived on a rented farm. Then the owner died and his son took over the land. Her husband worked for the grain company, climbing high in the tall cement towers to keep the machinery running smoothly. He earned $14 an hour. After twenty years, when the company consolidated and relocated most of its business to a larger town, he was laid off. He now works for the county road department.

Life here in this nearly treeless prairie town is similar to that of many small communities across the Middle West. The population was twice as large in 1960 as it is today. Madge remembers classes of thirty to forty pupils when she was in school. Now the average is six. Located on one of the nation's major coast-to-coast highways, the town benefited for many years from motorists stopping for gasoline and lodging. But that business died in the 1960s when the interstate missed the community by fifty miles. By 1980, so many of the old stores on Main Street were abandoned that the townspeople got together and tore most of them down. Twenty five years later, all that remained were a small café, a bank, several auto repair shops, and a boarded-up hotel that hunters camped in during pheasant season. Madge laments the lack of a grocery store or a decent restaurant. "Sometimes you really would like to go out and eat supper without having to drive twenty miles," she says. "Just having a good coffee shop would be nice."

Small communities like this one sputter along as business dwindles. Some become ghost towns. Yet most of them do not. Despite the limited opportunities, people find reasons to stay. Madge lived in Denver when she was first married, and she much prefers living here. The house she and her husband own was built in 1970. They can afford it even though their salaries are low. She was glad to be near her father as his health deteriorated. Her parents had raised a large family and never been able to save money for retirement. Family ties have meant a lot. So have neighbors. "My neighbor and I yard-talk over the fence while we're both pulling weeds," she says. "She was my son's teacher and is older than me. Her daughter is about my age."

People who grew up here, moved away, and returned decades later, Madge says, would feel an extreme sense of loss. "You always want to feel that you can go home again. Coming back and seeing how small the town is getting would be a jolt." An insider, though, experiences it differently. Sentiments are more nuanced. Store closings used to remind residents that the town was shrinking. Funerals more often do that now. Happier chords are struck not only by yard talk but also by the new fire station the town is building and the fact that Walmart is only thirty miles away. Change is a gradual thing, Madge explains. "You adjust to it and in the meantime you still have a strong sense of security."[1]

In 1980, 76 percent of all the incorporated towns and cities in the Middle West had fewer than 1,500 people. The region's nine states ranked first through ninth nationally (not counting Alaska) in having the highest proportion of small towns this size. North Dakota, South Dakota, and Nebraska, where 88 percent, 86 percent, and 85 percent of the towns, respectively, had fewer than 1,500 residents, ranked first through third. Iowa came in fourth with 79 percent, followed by Kansas with 76 percent, and Arkansas with 72 percent. In Minnesota and Missouri, 71 percent of the towns had fewer than 1,500 people, and Oklahoma ranked ninth with 70 percent. A third of the region's towns—like the one Madge Schmidt lived in—had fewer than 250 people. Only 2 percent of the towns had 20,000 people or more. The region was clearly defined by its small communities.[2]

A visitor traveling through the region in 1980 would have come to a town every ten miles if they had been located equidistant from one another—every eight miles in Iowa, where towns were most abundant, and every fourteen miles in the Dakotas, where towns were less common. On average, there were seven towns in every county. Twenty-five years later, the visitor may have noticed that nearly all the towns still existed. But two of every three would have been smaller. Overall, 64 percent of towns in the region had smaller populations in

2005 than they did in 1980. The proportion was highest in North Dakota, where 89 percent of all towns became smaller between 1980 and 2005. In the other eight states, a majority became smaller. In Kansas and Iowa, 70 percent were smaller, and in South Dakota and Nebraska, 68 percent were. Sixty five percent of Oklahoma's towns were smaller, as were 54 percent of Missouri's, 52 percent of Minnesota's, and 51 percent of Arkansas's.[3]

Population was most likely to have declined in the communities that were the hallmark of the Middle West: its smaller towns. Among communities with at least 500 people in 1980 but fewer than 1,500, 62 percent were smaller twenty-five years later. That figure rose to 70 percent among towns between 250 and 500 people in 1980 and to 75 percent in towns with fewer than 250 people. Becoming smaller nevertheless was characteristic of many of the larger towns as well. Fifty-one percent of the towns with 1,500 to 5,000 people had fewer residents in 2005 than in 1980; 40 percent of the ones with 5,000 to 20,000 people did. Even among towns with more than 20,000 people in 1980, 37 percent declined.[4]

The fact that many Middle Western towns were getting smaller did not escape residents' attention. When asked about change in their communities over the past twenty or thirty years, townspeople frequently mentioned something about the town's size—either its decline or lack of growth. Bobbi Miles, the bed-and-breakfast owner in Smith Center, Kansas, was one such resident. Being a newcomer to the community, she had examined its history and thought a lot about its future. "The county has been declining in population since 1900," she said. "Beginning about then, the size of the farms began to increase, and as the farm size increased, it required fewer and fewer people." That decline, in turn, affected the town, whose population peaked in the middle of the twentieth century. "Since the fifties or sixties, it has declined until, I think, the last year or so."[5]

In the living room of an elderly couple in a town of nine hundred—about half the size it had been in 1960—neighbors discussed how their community had been changing. Several were lifetime residents, one was a newcomer, and one had returned after living in a city. "The stores closing on Main Street" was the biggest change, one said. "The John Deere and the department store were huge, and now things are closed." There used to be six grocery stores, and now there was only one. "The population's dropping in town, and that's because people's kids don't want to come back," the speaker continued. "There's no jobs for them here," said another. "It's getting to be an older community," added another. "Well, Carol came back," interjected another. "But her parents were here. That's the only reason they come back. They don't come back to work at a store. That doesn't happen. There's not that many stores left." It was not just the stores they missed, but the social life the stores facilitated. "Anymore people don't come to town in the evening just to visit," one explained. "In the past, people would come to town just to meet and greet. They don't do that anymore."[6]

But residents of small Middle Western towns were seldom glum about their communities. They regretted children moving away and waxed nostalgic about better times on Main Street, and yet their communities were still the places they lived in and cherished. Like Madge Schmidt, they held nuanced views that acknowledged both the shortcomings and the benefits of their towns. Population loss was troublesome but did not spell doom. The good times of the past when the town was larger were matched by the favorable developments residents saw taking place in their communities. A new store came to town. The school had been renovated. Neighbors were friendly. Crime was low.[7]

At a gathering in another town, the conversation was decidedly upbeat. This town was a hundred miles from the nearest large city, and residents traveled the distance whenever they made major purchases or picked up relatives at the airport. They all worked locally and felt a strong attachment to their community. Several expressed concerns. "When they took the highway and bypassed us, that really hurt the town," a longtime resident noted. "I used to run a store here," a woman said," but we don't have the businesses we used to." "We've got a Walmart eight miles from here," a man explained, "and that's really killing the town." "People come to town and see our business district with buildings that are boarded up and think, well, this town isn't doing very well," a woman responded. They began listing the stores that had "gone out." The clothing store. The furniture store. An "electric store." Four drugstores. Yet they were uniformly optimistic about what was happening in their town. "Our schools are really updated," a young mother said proudly. "We have that truck bed company," said another. She did not know how long it had been in operation but knew it employed about 140 people, which she thought was "big for a little town." They appreciated shopping at Walmart and felt fortunate being as near as they were to the airport. With almost 1,900 residents and having declined by only 20 percent since 1980, their community seemed relatively stable.[8]

It is not surprising that residents ponder with interest the changing size of their communities. From the start, Middle Western states required towns to surpass population thresholds before qualifying for incorporation and then categorized them as villages or third-, second-, or first-class towns according to their size. Boosters hoping to attract new inhabitants often cited growing populations as evidence that their communities were indeed desirable. By the 1920s, franchise chains such as Penney's, Woolworth, and Ben Franklin stores were taking note of town sizes in determining where to locate stores. During the 1930s, bank failures proved especially devastating in smaller towns. As school consolidation plans took effect, declining population often meant losing a school and having to bus children to another town. With each decennial census, town newspapers printed stories lauding or lamenting the latest results. If population faltered to the point of losing one of the town's longtime businesses—the John Deere dealer or a furniture store—that was sure to prompt headlines. In more recent years, population trends and demographic characteristics appeared prominently on Web sites describing various towns' opportunities and amenities.

Community leaders paid particular attention to how their towns were being affected by and responding to stable or declining populations. Lacy Gregory, a mother in her twenties, was doubling as Smith Center's director of economic development and head of its chamber of commerce. Lately she had been working to bring an ALCO store—like a "small-town Walmart"—to town and was negotiating with the state transportation department to secure a minivan to transport the community's elderly residents. She was impressed with the community's willingness to pitch in when something needed to be done. "They don't want to see the town go under, and they will work hard to see that this town survives," she said. "They have such pride about living in Smith Center that they'll do whatever it takes."[9] Over at the bank, one of the loan officers who served on the Economic Development Committee and helped arrange the ALCO deal noted how difficult it was to attract new businesses. They "look at population," he said, and figure it "doesn't provide enough people to shop in a store." He knew ALCO had made a careful assessment of the community before deciding to locate there.[10]

Being small or getting smaller should not be equated, some insisted, with lacking strength or ingenuity. Smith Center's prowess in football, for instance, was not its only resource. Although the town had never been particularly prosperous, its residents over the years had been community-minded. The trust department at the bank handled $260 million in assets, including charitable accounts totaling nearly $25 million. There were numerous scholarship accounts to help students go to college or gain vocational training, charities to benefit the hospital, and various family foundations. The town benefited, too, from its many volunteer organizations—4-H, Lions, Rotary, Kiwanis, and two dozen others.[11]

Other leaders emphasized recent improvements in their communities. Pam Barta, the football coach's wife in Smith Center and a member of the chamber of commerce, said the new ALCO was just one of several important developments, including a bigger grocery store, new housing for senior citizens, and better care at the hospital.[12] In nearby Osborne, a town of fourteen hundred about twenty-five miles south of Smith Center, leaders were also upbeat. Not only did the townspeople look out for one another, they said, but there was a healthy spirit of generosity about community improvement projects, such as new sidewalks and lighting. "We had a campaign at Christmas to put big snowflakes on each of the light posts along the highway," Laura McClure, a volunteer who helped organize the campaign, recalled, "and people came in with their checkbooks, and they'd write out a check for $250 for a snowflake." She said the townspeople just wanted to do good things for their community.[13]

The questions evoked by small size and stable or declining populations were complex, though, and the answers were seldom straightforward. Although it was generally the case that changes in small communities reflected the region's overall demographic and economic restructuring, it was harder to say why some towns held steady or grew in population while others declined. It was unclear whether the downsizing many towns experienced during the last quarter of the twentieth century represented something new or whether it was merely a continuation of trends begun much earlier. Nor was it evident how exactly this downsizing was affecting life in small communities. Was it leaving them without vital services? Was it dampening the rich associational networks that had kept these towns strong in the past? Was it leaving residents poorer or more economically divided? Or were small communities faring better than fiscal projections alone may have suggested?

These questions, in turn, suggested others. Why did so many towns exist in the first place, and what role did they play in the social and economic fabric of the region? As conditions changed, was it inevitable that towns would become fewer and smaller? Was it perhaps beneficial to the region's long-term future that many of these communities would decline? And for the inhabitants who continued to call small towns their home, why did they stay? How resilient were these places? Was an attractive quality of life being sustained? What new opportunities and resources were available?

In retrospect, it seemed evident that towns would have proliferated as soon as white settlers moved into the Middle West. Many of the new residents came from towns and had skills as shopkeepers, clerks, and artisans that required living in towns. Everyone needed the services towns provided. However, far more towns started than survived. Daniel C. Fitzgerald, a historian who spent years collecting information about early towns in Kansas, determined that as many as six thousand existed at one time or another in that state, and a majority became extinct.[14] Smith County was the home in 1882 not only of Smith Center and Lebanon but of Harlan, Gaylord, Cedarville, Kensington, and fourteen other towns. Vinton, in Iowa, was surrounded at the end of the nineteenth century by twenty other towns. In Nebraska, two thousand towns were founded at one time or another, four times the number that survived.[15]

Strong forces encouraged the establishment of towns. Entrepreneurs like the ones who founded Smith Center stood to make a handsome profit if the town succeeded. It was often possible to purchase land for as little as a dollar an acre, plat it into twenty or thirty lots, and sell each lot for $100. Many of the towns were established by the railroad companies needing places every ten miles or so to take on water and coal and hoping to attract people to purchase railroad land. Farmers sometimes opened a store, secured a post office, and called it a town. Few of these ventures ever amounted to much. They failed because hopes for rail service vanished or because another town had a better grist mill or because the expectation that farmers would move into the area were too high. But a small percentage became incorporated towns under county and state law. Many of these towns grew.

The growth among Middle Western towns at the end of the nineteenth century was evident from census tallies. Several states—Arkansas, Iowa, Kansas, and Nebraska—reported relatively complete population figures for incorporated towns in 1880. There were 843 that year. In 1890, these states reported figures for 1,159 towns, an increase of 37 percent. The average population of incorporated towns in Arkansas increased 54 percent during the 1880s; in Iowa, 21 percent, in Kansas, 59 percent; and in Nebraska, 92 percent. During that period, 83 percent of the incorporated towns in these states gained population. In 1890, 91 percent had at least 250 people, up from 74 percent in 1880.[16] During the 1890s, growth continued. Among more than 1,200 towns, 76 percent were larger at the end of the decade than at the beginning. Fifty-six percent had at least 500 residents in 1890, while 65 percent did in 1900. The number of incorporated towns was also increasing. That number grew 32 percent in Arkansas, 45 percent in Iowa, 5 percent in Kansas, and 47 percent in Nebraska.[17]

The rapid growth at the end of the nineteenth century lasted until 1910 for most towns and until 1920 for others. However, many of the smaller towns peaked in these years. The first long-term decline in town populations occurred between 1910 and 1950. In Kansas, Missouri, and Nebraska, between 50 and 55 percent of the towns were smaller in 1950 than they had been in 1910. In Oklahoma, 40 percent were smaller, and in North Dakota, 36 percent were. Thirty-three percent of Iowa's towns became smaller, 31 percent did in South Dakota, and 26 percent did in Arkansas, while only 11 percent declined in Minnesota.[18] These changes would set the stage for what was to follow between 1950 and 1980 and again after 1980. The boomtown expectations that inspired earlier entrepreneurs faded in town after town, especially in the five states farthest from the Mississippi. Construction of new store buildings ground to a halt in these towns, and housing starts dwindled. Residents came to realize that their towns would always be small and might well become smaller. Businesses often closed or relocated to larger trading centers. And yet the decline that occurred in many towns by no means affected all of them. As some towns became smaller, others grew. On average, Middle Western towns were 65 percent larger in 1950 than they had been in 1910.

It was to be expected that many small towns would decline in population during this period, as families bore fewer children and as the economy shifted from agriculture to manufacturing. In addition, towns declined simply from being in the wrong place at the wrong time. Frederick, Kansas, for example, a town near the center of the state with 151 people in 1910, was well situated along the Missouri Pacific Railroad, had a grain elevator, a bank, two churches, and half a dozen stores. But in 1914, the town was struck by a tornado that flattened several buildings and carried a baby a quarter of a mile away, depositing the unharmed child under an overturned wagon box. Exactly twenty years later, a fire started in a wooden grain elevator and gutted most of the stores on Main Street. By 1950, only the Baptist church, the grain elevator, and fifty-three residents remained in Frederick.[19]

But population declined in many towns for broader reasons. Generally speaking, smaller towns were at significantly greater risk of becoming even smaller, while larger towns were more likely to grow. Communities with 250 to 500 residents in 1910 had the highest chance of losing population. Fifty percent of them would become smaller by 1950 (even more than among the smallest villages). Larger communities were in a stronger position to hold their own. Among towns with 1,500 to 5,000 inhabitants, for example, 81 percent were larger in 1950 than in 1910, and among communities with 5,000 to 20,000 residents, 89 percent were larger.[20]

When towns were being settled, residents often campaigned aggressively—and sometimes violently—to determine where the county seat would be located. The thinking behind these county-seat wars was that being the county seat meant better chances for a town to grow, attract law offices, and acquire rail service. That expectation turned out to be true. By 1910, county seats in the region averaged more than 6,000 residents, while towns that were not county seats averaged only 600.[21] Being larger, county seats were more likely to hold their own or grow between 1910 and 1950 than other towns. However, even taking account of initial differences in size, the county seats were likely to fare better. For example, among towns with populations between 500 and 1,500 in 1910, only 15 percent of the county seats were smaller in 1950, while 40 percent of the other towns this size were smaller. The same was true among towns of 1,500 to 5,000 residents, where decline occurred in only 10 percent of the county seats, compared with 35 percent of the other towns.[22]

It also mattered a great deal where a town was located. Logic held that towns near cities and in more populated parts of a state had a better chance of holding their own than towns in remote or less populated areas. But that was not always the case. Smaller towns closer to cities were sometimes at a disadvantage as cities and larger towns grew. In Kansas, for example, 62 percent of towns in the northeast (closer to Kansas City and Topeka) and 54 percent of towns in the southeast (closer to Wichita and Hutchinson) lost population between 1910 and 1950, whereas in the southwest only 24 percent lost population, and in the northwest, only 16 percent did. The same pattern was true in Nebraska, where 70 percent of towns in the southeast (near Omaha) became smaller, compared with 55 percent for the state overall.[23] In Iowa, 46 percent of the towns closest to Des Moines declined, compared with 30 percent in other parts of the state. In Oklahoma, 43 percent of the towns nearest Tulsa declined, compared with 36 percent of other towns. Across the nine-state region, towns located closest to the region's largest cities were about 3 percent more likely to decline than towns farther away. Among towns with fewer than 500 people, the difference was 7 percentage points, and among towns with 500 to 1,500 people, 5 points.[24]

Another aspect of a town's location that affected its future was how many competitors it had nearby. Community leaders paid close attention to the relative standing of their towns. As transportation improved, it was a genuine drawback for some towns to be located too close to rival towns. In most areas, communities with fewer competitors did, in fact, fare better. Except in Iowa and Minnesota, where towns were numerous in nearly all parts of the state, towns in counties with only one or two competing towns were in the best position to grow. For instance, in Arkansas, only 18 percent of towns located in counties with one or two other towns lost population between 1910 and 1950, whereas 37 percent of towns located in counties with seven or more towns declined. The differences were even greater in Kansas, Nebraska, and the Dakotas where, on average, a fifth of the towns with only one or two competitors in the same county lost population compared with one-half to two-thirds of the communities in counties with seven or more competitors.[25]

The likelihood of losing population was especially high for towns whose population in 1910 was below the average of other towns in the same county. In these instances, it was particularly likely that customers would gravitate to the larger towns, that businesses in the smaller towns would fail, and that people would move away. Across the region, 42 percent of the towns in counties where the average town was larger than they were lost population between 1910 and 1950; and in Kansas, Missouri, and Nebraska, upwards of two-thirds did. In comparison, only a fifth of towns that were above average in size within their respective counties lost population.[26]

In a region in which agriculture was the dominant industry, towns were also deeply affected by changes in farming. As farms became larger, the declining number of farm families in these areas meant fewer people needing the goods and services available in nearby towns. Nearly 1,000 towns were located in counties in which the number of farms declined by 25 percent or more between 1910 and 1950. Among these towns, nearly half (49 percent) lost population. In contrast, among the 1,200 towns located in counties where the number of farms held steady or increased, 82 percent gained population. Towns were most seriously affected in Missouri and Nebraska, where two-thirds of the towns in counties where farms decreased by 25 percent or more lost population.[27]

Whether the number of farms was declining or not, towns were also affected by how well the farms were faring economically. As a rule, towns grew during this period if agriculture prospered but declined if agriculture did less well. Overall, the value of farmland, buildings, and equipment—a strong indicator of performance and expectations—rose on average from about $11,000 in 1910 to about $18,000 in 1950. The rate of increase in farm values nevertheless varied from county to county. Four percent of the region's towns were in counties where farm values remained constant, 34 percent were in counties where farm values rose by less than 50 percent, 32 percent were in counties where farm values increased between 50 and 100 percent, and 27 percent were in counties with farm values rising more than 100 percent. In every state except Oklahoma, towns were significantly more likely to decline if they were in counties where farm values rose slowly. For example, in Kansas, 72 percent of the towns declined in counties where farm values rose by less than 50 percent, whereas only 31 percent declined in counties where farm values rose by more than 100 percent. In Nebraska, two-thirds of the towns declined in areas with low rises in farm values, but only 4 percent declined in areas with the highest increases in farm values. Across the region, 49 percent of towns declined when they were located in counties with farm values that increased less than 50 percent, while only 26 percent declined when farm values increased more than 50 percent.[28]

Decade by decade, *fewer* towns lost population during the 1930s than before or after—indicating that the Great Depression was by no means the principal cause of towns' decline between 1910 and 1950. During the 1920s, 51 percent of Middle Western towns lost population; during the 1940s, the same proportion declined; but during the 1930s, only 41 percent became smaller. Some towns, though, were affected more than others. Whereas the proportion of small towns (fewer than 5,000 residents in 1930) that lost population *decreased* during the 1930s, the proportion of larger towns (more than 5,000 residents in 1930) that lost population *increased*. State by state, Kansas and Nebraska were affected the most, with the percentage of towns losing population during the 1930s rising by 17 percent and 12 percent, respectively.

In combination, the various conditions to which towns were subject had a powerful effect in determining whether they gained or lost population between

1910 and 1950. Taking into account the differences among states, the odds that a town declined in population were more than twice as great if it had fewer than 5,000 people in 1910 than if it had more at that date. Its chances of declining were more than four times as great if it had not had the good fortune of being selected as a county seat, three times as great if the number of farms in its county declined by more than 25 percent or if their value increased by less than 50 percent, and about 30 percent greater if it faced more than two competing towns in its county or was below the average size in its county. When none of these conditions was present, 96 percent of the towns grew, but when four or five were present, about two-thirds of the towns declined.[29]

Harvard, Nebraska, eighteen miles east of Hastings, was typical of the towns that lost population between 1910 and 1950. Founded by the South Platte Town Company in 1871 on the main line of the Burlington & Missouri River Railroad (and named by a railroad official who had gone to Harvard), the town narrowly escaped being destroyed by a large prairie fire in 1872 and was buried by a massive snowstorm in 1873. It nevertheless attracted settlers and grew to a population of 768 by 1880. "How wonderful the progress!" a resident declared in 1882. "With what spirit of satisfaction must the pioneer and early settler, supplied as he now is with comfort and plenty, look back to the time when in the canvas-covered wagon, he made his way across the monotonous prairie." Census takers in 1890 counted nearly eleven hundred residents, and despite a temporary decline during an economic slump in the late 1890s, the population in 1910 remained at approximately eleven hundred. After that, Harvard's population declined steadily, reaching 774 in 1950, a drop of 30 percent.[30]

Harvard's troubles began almost as soon as the town started. Between 1875 and 1879, it lost in three successive bids to become the county seat. Clay Center, selected as the dark-horse candidate because it was in the middle of the county, grew 474 percent between 1880 and 1890, while Harvard grew by only 40 percent. "Alas for the uncertainties of human affairs," the same resident who lauded the town's progress wrote. Lacking sufficient numbers to be classified as a city, Harvard remained a "village," henceforth "robbed of the glories she had assumed." Although Harvard in 1880 had been the largest town in Clay County, by 1910 it was one of five competing towns of nearly similar size. Over the next four decades, its population was affected by the region's changing agricultural base. The number of farms in Clay County declined 38 percent. Income from poultry, dairy, and cattle was significantly higher in 1950 than in 1910, but revenue from wheat and corn was not. Average farm values rose only 19 percent, not adjusting for inflation. In 1942, an army air force base opened just north of town, temporarily doubling the community's population, but the base closed in 1946 and the buildings were dismantled and sold for lumber. Also in 1942, the U.S.

Navy established the Blaine Naval Ammunition Depot in Clay County, but even the presence of this large facility did not significantly affect the long-range trajectory of the county's towns. All were smaller in 1950 than in 1910. Meanwhile, the population of Hastings—the largest town in the region—doubled from less than 10,000 to more than 20,000.[31]

In 1950, community leaders in the Middle West looked forward to better times than they had experienced during the Depression and World War II. The post-war baby boom was in full swing, new automobiles were cheap, and demand for home appliances was at a record high. Although most towns remained small and many had become smaller, nearly half (49 percent) had grown during the 1940s and would continue to grow during the 1950s. On average, towns in the region increased in population during the 1950s by 7 percent. During the 1960s, growth continued, with towns on average increasing in population by 8 percent. By 1980, 56 percent of Middle Western towns were larger than they had been in 1950, and 44 percent were smaller. Arkansas, where only 21 percent were smaller, fared best. Missouri and Oklahoma, with only one town in three losing population, did relatively well too. In Minnesota, 37 percent of the towns declined, and in Iowa, 41 percent did. Fifty-two percent declined in population in Nebraska, and 55 percent in Kansas did. In South Dakota, 63 percent lost population, and 73 percent did in North Dakota.[32]

Among the towns that lost population, some declined, as they had earlier, for idiosyncratic reasons. Republican City, Nebraska, for example, a small town in the south central part of the state about forty-five miles north of Smith Center, Kansas, was a flourishing community of 570 residents in 1950. But the construction of a dam that year for the new Harlan County Lake forced the town to relocate several miles away. Many chose to move farther. In 1960, only 189 residents called the new location home. Redbird, Oklahoma, declined by more than 50 percent during the same period. Settled by African Americans around the turn of the twentieth century, its residents were frequently subjected to discrimination. With Tulsa only thirty-two miles away, many of them found the larger city more attractive.[33] Other towns lost population simply because of wider changes in the region. Blanchard, Iowa, a farm town straddling the Missouri border seventy-five miles north of St. Joseph, tumbled from 214 residents in 1950 to 98 in 1980. Ambrose, North Dakota, three miles south of the Canadian border in the northwest corner of the state, lost more than two-thirds of its population. Okolona, Arkansas, a few miles west of Interstate 30 southwest of Little Rock, declined by more than 50 percent.

Just as some towns became smaller for reasons distinctive to their location, others grew dramatically for equally particular reasons. As the aircraft industry in Wichita expanded, nearby towns like Park City and Valley Center shot up almost overnight as bedroom communities. Reversing its long-term decline, Harvard, Nebraska, began attracting residents who worked in Hastings, and the town experienced a 43 percent surge in population between 1950 and 1980. The same reservoir that spelled decline for Republican City elevated Alma's population from two hundred to nearly a thousand. Alma was among dozens of lakefront towns in the region benefiting from tourists interested in boating and fishing. Between 1950 and 1980, 77 percent of these towns grew, averaging a 64 percent increase in population.[34]

On a larger scale, the characteristics that had been associated with towns' growth or decline from 1910 to 1950 continued to matter, although with some modifications. Towns with fewer than 250 residents in 1950—of which there were still nearly 1,500—were in greatest danger of losing population. By 1980, 58 percent of these towns were smaller than in 1950. Among slightly larger towns of 250 to 500 people in 1950, about half grew and half declined. Two-thirds of towns with populations between 500 and 1,500 grew and a third declined; three-quarters of towns between 1,500 and 5,000 or between 5,000 and 20,000 grew and a quarter declined. Among towns larger than 20,000, only 20 percent lost population. Of these larger towns, nearly all the decline came in the 1970s, as inner-city populations shrank relative to surrounding suburbs. Otherwise, it was by far the smaller communities that stood the greatest risk of declining further. This was especially true for towns of fewer than 250 residents in North Dakota, where five of every six lost population, and in Kansas and South Dakota, where nearly three-quarters did.[35]

County seats continued to retain or attract population better than other towns. On average, only a quarter of the county seats declined. Other factors mattered as well. If a town had declined between 1910 and 1950, it stood a better than even chance of declining further between 1950 and 1980. If it had not declined in the earlier period, its likelihood of gaining population from 1950 to 1980 was two in three. Unlike the gains or losses between 1910 and 1950, town populations from 1950 to 1980 were less affected by change in numbers of farms. That change amounted to 50 percent fewer farms across the region in 1980 than in 1950, but towns were less influenced by the rate of decline than by the number of farms in existence in 1950. In counties with fewer than 500 farms, 58 percent of the towns declined, whereas in counties with 1,500 to 2,500 farms, 43 percent declined, and in counties with more than 2,500, only 29 percent declined. The lowest number of farms per county was in Kansas, Nebraska, and the Dakotas—and towns in those states were at the highest risk of losing population.

In 1910, many parts of the Middle West had only recently been settled, raising the chances that towns in those areas would continue growing at least in the near term. For instance, in northwest Kansas, northwest South Dakota, and northwest Nebraska, five towns in six gained population between 1910 and 1950. But by 1950, the earlier growth had peaked, leaving towns in these areas especially vulnerable to decline.[36] The other notable difference from the earlier period was in the effect of being located near a city. Across the region, 68 percent of towns in the vicinity of a large city gained population between 1950 and 1980, compared with 51 percent of other towns. The difference was especially notable in Minnesota, where only 9 percent of towns near the Twin Cities declined, compared with 51 percent elsewhere in the state. In Kansas and Missouri, towns near Kansas City, Wichita, and St. Louis grew more often than other towns, and the same was true in Nebraska for towns near Omaha.[37]

Growth or decline in population usually implied other changes as well. Median family incomes in growing towns were 17 percent higher in 1980 than in other towns, taking account of differences in town sizes in 1950. The poverty rate was 24 percent lower. In towns with declining populations, compared with other towns, the housing vacancy rate ranged from 29 percent higher in larger towns to 80 percent higher in smaller towns. While there was never a one-to-one relationship, growth usually meant better conditions for retail establishments, while decline was associated with store closings.[38] Residents of declining towns would also have found it harder to obtain services such as medical care. On average, there were 29 percent fewer doctors in 1982 in counties with declining towns than in other counties.[39]

Whether towns had grown or diminished in the past, though, revealed little about residents' perceptions, the loyalty they may have felt toward their communities, or what they may have imagined about the future of their towns. It would have been perfectly reasonable to imagine that one's town would grow. More than one in four towns had increased by at least 30 percent over the past thirty years, and in parts of Arkansas, Missouri, and Oklahoma, the proportion had been considerably higher. Nor was it necessarily the case in other towns that declining population was significant enough to have shaped these communities' identities. One thing was clear: towns in the Middle West continued overwhelmingly to be small. In 1980, three-quarters had fewer than 1,500 residents; nine in ten had fewer than 5,000. In whatever way the region might change over the next twenty-five years, these small communities would be an important part of the story.

The two-thirds of Middle Western towns that lost population during the quarter century after 1980 was a higher proportion than in any similar period since 1910. This was partly because of the erosion that had already taken place. Towns that remained small or had become smaller were especially vulnerable to continuing depopulation. Among towns with fewer than 250 residents in 1980, for example, 75 percent were smaller twenty-five years later. Larger towns fared much better. Among towns with 1,500 to 5,000 inhabitants in 1980, 49 percent grew. And among towns with 5,000 to 20,000 residents, 60 percent grew.[40]

The growth or decline of communities continued to reflect broader changes taking place in the region. Some towns lost population because of volatility in farming. Growth or decline also bore the imprint of changes in the oil and natural gas industry and of developments in infrastructure, such as the construction of interstate highways and the opening or closing of military bases. Community leaders often worried about past or anticipated population declines. Many residents, though, found reason to stay in small communities and to take advantage of new opportunities. Through it all, even towns that lost population often demonstrated remarkable resilience and a strong commitment to the quality of their communities.

Mayville, North Dakota, illustrates the changes that occurred after 1980 in many farming communities. Mayville is located in the fertile Red River valley twenty-five miles west of the Minnesota border and approximately forty miles southwest of Grand Forks. The first white landowners—mainly from Norway, Minnesota, and Wisconsin—settled in 1870 on flat, unbroken sod thick with tall prairie grass. Mayville came into being in 1879 and by the following year included six stores, two blacksmith shops, a lawyer's office, and three carpentry shops. About three dozen of its inhabitants worked for the Northern Pacific Railroad. A large number of farmers settled there between 1882 and 1885, bringing Traill County's population to more than 8,000. Thirty-nine percent of the land claims were homestead patents, 8 percent were military script warrants, and 53 percent were cash purchases.[41] In 1885, 371 people lived in Mayville. Two-thirds of the town's residents were members of nuclear families; a quarter were boarders and servants. Mayville was second in size only to Hillsboro, the county seat eleven miles east and six miles south, which had 500 residents. There were five smaller towns in the county as well. Portland, with 200 residents, was only two miles away. A century later, all of these towns still existed, but in 1885, there was considerable uncertainty about which ones would survive. Three towns—Newburgh, Little Fork, and Stony Point—were already gone, and over the next decade a dozen others would be attempted and eventually fail.

From the start, Mayville's existence depended on agriculture. Its workforce in 1885 included three farm-machinery agents, three blacksmiths, a tinsmith, five harness makers, and five butchers. The town offered the services needed in any late nineteenth-century farming community—a doctor's office, post office, mill, depot, livery stable, bank, several general merchandise stores, and a saloon. With farmhouses and barns still under construction, a handful of carpenters kept busy and more than a dozen of the farmers lived in town. Neighboring communities offered similar services, but there was a division of labor as well. The sheriff's office, the largest lumberyard, and the veterinarian were in Hillsboro. The telegraph office was in Portland. The county's three prostitutes lived in smaller towns.[42]

By 1890, Mayville's population reached 634, still second to Hillsboro, which exceeded 700. A photograph taken in 1895 shows large two-story houses on corner lots, many with recently planted trees, and a one-room school. In the surrounding area, wheat was the dominant crop. In 1909, the county produced more than three million bushels. Farmers in the area also produced large quantities of eggs and milk which they sold in Mayville and neighboring towns for rail shipment to Grand Forks and Fargo. "Just as their city cousins had replaced business buildings and homes with new and attractive ones," a resident observed, "so had the homesteaders replaced their log cabins and tar paper shacks. Farming was now a good life."[43] With large families and a majority of the farmers employing hired laborers, the county's population grew to more than 12,000 by 1910, with nearly three-quarters living on farms. Mayville, Hatton, Hillsboro, and Portland—the four largest towns—grew steadily. In 1920, Mayville was the largest of the four with more than 1,200 residents.

Mayville's growth continued, climbing to nearly 1,800 in 1950. Crops were good, housing was in short supply, and the community collected enough revenue to construct a new hospital. As the town grew, businesses expanded. Traill County Electric put up a new building. Harrington Brothers enlarged its livestock operation. The Mayville Grain Company became part of the International Elevator chain. Archer Daniels Midland, the emerging agribusiness conglomerate, contracted with Mayville farmers to sell their goods in Minneapolis. Investors bought the telephone company, and the Kaiser dealership promoted its newest line of fashionable automobiles. Growth lasted another two decades, bringing the population in 1970 to 2,500. After that, the population gradually diminished to about 1,900 in 2005, a drop of nearly 25 percent. That matched the decline in Traill County, a third of which resulted from deaths outnumbering births, and two-thirds from people moving away.[44]

In 1980, Mayville's leaders were already worrying about the community's decline. The *Traill County Tribune* carried a front-page story about the preliminary results of the decennial census. Mayville's population was down 14 percent, the report said. To be sure, the news was not all bad. Several of the smaller towns nearby had lost more, but one or two had grown. In Mayville, plans were moving ahead to resurface the streets, and a new jewelry store announced its grand opening. But the local auctioneer was keeping busy with farm sales as people left the area. It was unclear if a proposed increase in the school tax would pass, and south of town, farmers were predicting a poor crop for the third year in a row. There would need to be belt tightening, the editor advised.[45]

Mayville's declining population reflected changes in the area's farms. A study of the county's agriculture in the 1950s had shown markedly few changes to that point. "Crop and crop combinations that prevailed in 1899 [and] kinds and number of livestock kept by local farmers reveal no new directions in farming or sharp breaks from the past," the study concluded.[46] In the early 1960s, there were still more than a thousand farms in Traill County, only slightly fewer than in 1910. By the end of the twentieth century, though, that number had fallen by nearly 60 percent. The average farm was more than a thousand acres. Earlier in the century, tractor power had permitted farmers to operate with fewer tenants and hired hands, but during the closing decades of the century, the role of mechanization shifted again. In 1964, there had been nearly 2,700 tractors, each requiring a driver. Three decades later, there were fewer than 1,500 tractors. Each tractor was larger and capable of tilling more land. By 1992, the average farmer had more than $150,000 invested in machinery. A decade later, that figure had risen to $275,000. Larger and more expensive machinery meant that the average farmer could do more work alone, but also required larger debt and entailed greater risks during economic downswings. The farm workforce declined further as labor-intensive care of livestock and poultry diminished. Between 1964 and 2002, the number of cattle fell by three-quarters, the number of hogs by 90 percent, and the number of chickens by 99 percent. Livestock accounted for 26 percent of farm income in 1964 but only 3 percent in 2002. At the start of the twenty-first century, farm earnings still contributed a third of the county's revenue, but farmers now made up only 2 percent of the county's labor force. All of this meant fewer farm families living in the area, fewer coming to Mayville to shop, fewer sending children there to school, and fewer needing the town's services.[47]

Mayville was in a better position to withstand these changes than many of the towns in North Dakota. With more than three dozen schools in the county, Mayville's founders had recognized the need for a teachers' training institute and successfully petitioned the state to establish the Mayville Normal School in 1889. In 1925, the school became a four-year teacher's college. After World War II, it continued to serve the county's teachers, of whom more than sixty were still employed in country schools, and by 1950 enrolled more than two hundred full-time students. In subsequent decades, the campus not only brought jobs and revenue to the community but also contributed to training its labor force. The town's early prominence and relative size allowed it to maintain itself much longer than smaller communities, such as Hatton and Reynolds, that began to decline earlier. Its proximity to Grand Forks, where the large North Dakota Mill and an Armour packing plant were located, proved advantageous as an outlet for farm products and later as a source of employment. Unlike Hillsboro, Mayville no longer had direct rail service to Fargo, but indirect service continued and other means of transportation were readily available.

But none of these advantages fully protected Mayville from having to downsize. Bad weather and dramatically rising production costs forced a number of farmers with large loans to quit farming and seek employment outside the area. Farmers in the county had a particularly bad year in 1980, suffering a net loss of more than $5 million, and again in 1988, when total net income fell by nearly 80 percent. Five times during the 1990s, net farm income was less than it had been the previous year. In 1991, when North Dakota lifted its hundred-year-old blue laws prohibiting Sunday shopping, stores in Mayfield followed suit, but the mayor called Sunday shopping "one of the dumbest changes" the people of North Dakota had made and predicted that residents would shop more often at the mall in Fargo than in Mayville. Although Sunday shopping had little to do with it, taxable sales and purchases in Mayville fell from $15.8 million in 1996 to $12.4 million in 2005, and in Traill County from $36.4 million to $30.6 million. Residents commuting to work in Grand Forks and Fargo found it easier to shop there as well, and farmers were more often bypassing local merchants and buying directly from wholesalers. Countywide, there were still more than 800 businesses in 1996, but by 2005, that number had fallen to 670. Old photos on the wall at Paula's Café show a town busy with commercial life. The photos are a vivid reminder of how much things have changed.

Following a consolidation with Portland's schools in 1963, parents were relieved that enrollment at the Mayfield elementary and high schools held steady during the 1990s, in contrast to nearby Clifford and Galesburg where declining enrollments caused the schools to close. However, taxpayers twice rejected bond issues for renovation projects, and after 2000 enrollments steadily fell. The municipal swimming pool closed in 1996 due to high upkeep costs and remained closed until 2000, when volunteer efforts and private donations covered a significant share of the cost. In 1998, following a worrisome edict from General Motors about declining sales, the Mayville Motors dealership closed after being in business for more than fifty years. By 2005, Mayville also lost two hardware stores, two grocery stores, a drugstore, a furniture store, a clothing store, a tavern, and several full-service restaurants. On Main Street, about half the buildings were vacant.[48] With more than half its students from Traill and adjacent counties, Mayville State University was in jeopardy from the area's declining population. In 1990, the campus eliminated its music and art programs, and in 1994, it joined forces with Valley City State University seventy-five miles away to save money by sharing administrative costs and coordinating classes.

Despite rumors that it might close, Mayville State remained open but, by 2003, was running a sizable annual deficit. Enrollment was down, and fuel bills were straining its budget. Fewer of its faculty lived in town.[49]

Many Middle Western farming towns experienced what Mayville did. Two aspects of their relationship with farming were especially important. If a town was located in an area where farming was a large share of the local economy, that town was more likely to lose population than if it were located elsewhere. This was true whether a town was small, medium, or large. These towns were significantly affected by volatile farm incomes, which fell in as many years between 1980 and 2005 as it rose—sometimes by 25 to 50 percent.[50] Then, as farms increased in acreage and became fewer, the decline in the number of farms affected the towns in their vicinity. Among towns the size of Mayville, 60 percent lost population when located in a county where the number of farms declined by 20 percent or more, compared with only 40 percent where the number of farms did not decline. No matter how small or large the town was, its chances of losing population were higher if it was in a county with a shrinking number of farms.[51]

The factors that contributed vitality to Mayville were also evident more generally. Having a college or university was clearly an advantage. In the nine-state region, about 160 towns had at least one college or university, and another hundred were the site of community colleges. The majority of these institutions were in the region's larger towns and cities, but thirty-five were located in small towns the size of Mayville. On average, 49 percent of towns this size gained population between 1980 and 2005, but that proportion was 55 percent among the thirty-five towns that had an institution of higher learning and rose to 72 percent if that institution was a four-year college or university. These were towns like Sterling, Kansas, home of Sterling College, where population rose from about 2,300 to 2,500; and Mount Vernon, Iowa, location of Cornell College, where population grew from 3,300 to 4,000. Fifteen colleges were located in even smaller towns (of 500 to 1,500), and these towns registered similar patterns: 60 percent grew, compared with only 31 percent of noncollege towns the same size. In larger towns of 5,000 to 20,000 residents, 59 percent without colleges grew, 65 percent with universities grew, and 85 percent with private liberal arts colleges grew.[52]

As was true for Mayville, location was a significant factor in whether towns gained or lost population. In North Dakota, where nearly 90 percent of towns lost population, the extent of decline was less severe in the southeast near Fargo and Grand Forks than elsewhere in the state. On average, towns in the state's southeast quadrant were 14 percent smaller in 2005 than in 1980, compared with 24 percent smaller in the southwest, 30 percent smaller in the northeast, and 32 percent smaller in the northwest. These differences reflected geographic variations in agricultural productivity, with farms in the Red River valley producing crops of significantly higher value than elsewhere in the state, while counties to the west depended to a greater extent on declining earnings from livestock. Towns in southeastern South Dakota and southeastern Nebraska also fared better than towns elsewhere in their respective states for similar reasons.

As the number of farms declined, towns' ability to maintain themselves or grow depended not only on agricultural productivity but increasingly on proximity to metropolitan areas as well. Across the region, small towns located near cities fared better than small towns situated farther away. For instance, among towns with fewer than 1,500 residents, 41 percent grew between 1980 and 2005 if they were in or adjacent to a metropolitan area, while only 17 percent did if they were located elsewhere. Among towns with 1,500 to 5,000 residents, the differences were even larger. Sixty-four percent of those in or near metropolitan areas grew, while only 17 percent did elsewhere.[53]

Mayville's other advantage was being close—ten miles—to Interstate 29. Mayville did not benefit to the same extent as Hillsboro, which was adjacent to the highway, but was one of more than a hundred towns in North Dakota that stood to gain by being located in one of the counties through which I-29 and I-94 passed. The Interstate Highway System, authorized in 1956 and begun later that year in Missouri and Kansas, brought new opportunities for tourism, trucking, and related transportation industries. Although the routes generally paralleled existing U.S. highways, which in turn followed major railroad arteries, and thus ran close to many towns, communities lobbied authorities to avoid being bypassed and to ensure that exit ramps were conveniently located. The value of being located near the interstate was evident in differences between towns, like Mayville, located in counties through which an interstate passed and towns in counties lacking an interstate. Fifty percent of the former grew larger between 1980 and 2005, while only 31 percent of the latter did. The differences were especially pronounced among smaller towns. For communities with 1,500 to 5,000 residents, those near an interstate averaged only about three-fourths as many people in 1950 as towns farther away, and this difference continued in 1960; but by 1980, towns near an interstate had caught up, and by 2005 were 40 percent larger than the others. Even towns with fewer than 1,500 residents benefited from proximity to an interstate.[54]

Although Mayville was smaller in 2005 than it had been in 1980 and some of its stores were gone, the community—like many others—showed signs of continuing vitality. Median household income had risen more than threefold and was now about 5 percent higher than in Fargo. A good starter home could still be purchased for $25,000 or less. The proportion of Mayville residents with college degrees climbed from 23 percent in 1980 to 34 percent in 2000, the same percentage as in Fargo. A study conducted by the North Dakota Department of Commerce in 2004 found Mayville's labor force was well educated, aspiring to better jobs in computing, information processing, and technology. Three-quarters of the labor force worked in Traill County, but a majority of those surveyed said they would commute farther if better work could be found.[55] As farm employment declined, new jobs were being created in finance, information services, and health care.

Like Smith Center, Mayville had attracted an ALCO store and enlarged its senior citizens center. It still had a hospital, a hardware store, three banks, an assisted-living center, and numerous other businesses. Mayville's merchants benefited, as they had from the start, by serving people who lived in the county's smaller communities. Between 1994 and 2005, Hatton lost its hardware store and pharmacy, grocery stores closed in Buxton and Portland, and a filling station closed in Galesburg. More of those residents now shopped in Mayville. There was a new Subway sandwich shop, a tanning salon, a Verizon Wireless store, and a new regional trauma center at the hospital. Despite the county's declining farm population, Mayville continued to provide essential agricultural services, including two airplane crop-spraying companies, two farm-implement suppliers, a commodities dealer, the farmers' co-op, a new hydroponics business, and numerous repair shops. In all, the town's 1,900 residents were supporting more than 150 businesses with more than 1,200 employees. Mayville State University was the largest establishment in town, with more than 150 employees.[56]

Like other towns of its size, Mayville's residents worried about its future. Few jobs were available to attract young people. The students at Mayville State knew their opportunities were mainly in Grand Forks, Fargo, or Minneapolis. Among teenagers, binge drinking was high, and with only one sheriff in the county, it was hard to combat drug use. Declining population reinforced the conviction that people who stayed were somehow to blame for the community's troubles. As one community leader put it, "I guess we have a hard time saying there's anything good about us."[57]

The quality of life in Mayville was nevertheless strengthened by an abundance of civic organizations and opportunities for voluntary service. These included many well-established organizations, such as the VFW, Knights of Columbus, Lions, the Farm Bureau, a Masonic lodge, the Mayville Civic Association, the Sons of Norway, and three Lutheran churches. In any given week, a civic-minded person could attend a Kiwanis lunch on Wednesday, help at the hospital or public library, take in a cultural event at the university or at the Goose River Heritage facility, and sing in one of several church choirs. On special occasions, there were the Sons of Norway pancake breakfasts, the annual 4-H fair, tractor pulling contests, holiday parades, and lutefisk dinners. Although many of the older organizations had fewer participants, their work was being supplemented by a school support foundation, a hospital society, a housing assistance program, an affordable rural health board, and a multipurpose social assistance and community event center. There was a communitywide food pantry for the needy, a group called Caring Club that sponsored volunteer benefits for the hospital, a monthly book-discussion group, and an active hospice network.

Civic-mindedness in Mayville, as in many small towns, worked reasonably well as long as it conformed to strong unspoken norms. The community aspired to be progressive in terms of social services, roads, business, and schools, but chafed at raising taxes. That shifted responsibility for more of the community's needs to voluntary organizations, which were effective because the population was small and residents were well acquainted. "People are very friendly once they know who you are," one community leader explained, "but very reserved if they're not sure who you are."[58] At the churches, for example, deacons' committees helped needy families they knew to be trustworthy and did so with little in the way of formal procedures or structure. Among farmers, there was an implicit rule against asking for help. It was up to the neighbors to learn through the grapevine that someone needed assistance and to provide it voluntarily. It was common to give of one's time to help a sick or bereaved neighbor but unusual to offer cash assistance unless it could be channeled through a community organization. Helping, moreover, did not preclude disagreements. Neighbors might argue vehemently at the café one day and then pitch in the next day to provide assistance.

A farmer described the prevailing sentiment this way: "When we have problems, we don't publicize them. We don't advertise them. The community is small enough that people know when members are in need and will make their donations or provide their labor." It was his view that neighbors more often provided labor than money, not because they were "tight fisted," but because they recognized one another's pride and "don't want to step on that." He said his own pride is such that if something breaks he rarely hires somebody to fix it, and then only as a last resort. "It really doesn't have anything to do with money," he said, "it has to do with the need to prove to myself that I can take care of things."[59]

One of the more innovative civic efforts in Mayville—Partners in Progress—vividly illustrates the community's capacity to abide by these norms and still respond to the challenges it faces. In 1985, North Dakota's Agricultural Extension Service mounted an effort to help farmers keep better track of their expenses. The program lasted two years and assisted some of the farmers in Mayville, but it ultimately was too little and too late. Farm incomes had already deteriorated to the point that farmers were losing their land, and the situation was not improving. In 1991, eleven of Mayville's farmers were about to go under. A men's prayer breakfast had been meeting on Wednesday mornings for many years at one of the Lutheran churches, and the members decided it was time to act. One of the men, who had banking experience and farmed, knew from working with the extension service program that short-term loans were often the key to avoiding foreclosure auctions and that farmers were often too proud to ask for assistance even though others in the community were willing to help. The group went to the bank and cosigned a loan for one of the farmers, worked out a lease agreement with another farmer, and over the next year organized a loan committee to assist other farmers. Partners in Progress became a 501(c)3 tax-exempt nonprofit organization in 1995. Over the next decade, it quietly worked with approximately 450 farmers in North Dakota and Western Minnesota, a third of whom would have lost their farms had it not been for the organization's assistance in raising contributions, providing short-term loans, helping identify strengths and weaknesses in their operations, and serving as mediators with local banks. By 2005, Partners had become a model for dozens of similar organizations in other towns.[60]

If changes in agriculture forced farming communities like Mayville to adapt, the region's towns were also affected by a seismic shift in their relation to another of its resources. This shift was especially evident in parts of central Kansas. In 1936, Minnesota geographer George J. Miller toured the area to examine the effects of the Dust Bowl. His journey began in Salina, Kansas, wound south on U.S. Highway 81 through McPherson and Hutchinson, turned west on U.S. Highway 50 through Stafford and Garden City, and continued on to New Mexico. Much of what he saw in Kansas that summer could have been in the Red River valley around Mayville. Wheat fields were parched, and the photographs he took showed weathered farmhouses and shriveled shelterbelts struggling to survive against the dry wind. Miller could not have known it, but east of Stafford he passed within a mile of something that was quite different from anything in Mayville and would influence the region as much as the Depression ever did. That was an enormous repository of crude oil some 3,800 feet below the surface.[61]

In 1884, Bart and Mary Hartnett began farming in Stafford County. His family had come as homesteaders in 1877, and hers in 1883. Bart and Mary owned a quarter section near Zenith, a village six miles east of Stafford, and on their modest farmstead raised eleven children. Bart died in 1923, and Mary continued working the farm with the help of a daughter and son-in-law. On August 1, 1937, Standard Oil of Indiana, also known as Stanolind, began drilling a wildcat well on her farm. On September 15, the drillers struck oil at a depth of 3,807 feet. It was not the first well in the area, but it was one of the best. The No. 1 Hartnett well came in at 800 barrels a day. Over the next thirty years, it produced more than 381,000 barrels of oil. It was the first of more than three hundred wells in what became known as the Zenith–Peace Creek field. By the century's end, more than forty million barrels had been pumped from the field.[62]

Oil shaped the development of Stafford, a farm town of about 1,600 inhabitants in the late 1930s. Stafford, like Mayville, was settled in the late 1870s and early 1880s by farmers who grew wheat and raised livestock. By 1886, it benefited from being at the intersection of the Santa Fe and Missouri Pacific railroads, which helped it outpace St. John, the county seat twelve miles northwest. Bad weather and several years of poor crops left residents wondering if the community would survive, but by 1910, Stafford was the largest town in the county with approximately 1,900 residents. Agents for Stanolind came through the county in the 1920s buying leases from farmers at $10 an acre. For families like the Hartnetts, that was more than they made from farming in an entire year. For some it was enough to purchase more land or to pay off the mortgage. When George Miller, the geographer, visited Stafford in 1936, the land was suffering from drought and had been stripped bare by locusts. The town's dentist that year felt fortunate to be making $34 a month. The doctor was being paid mostly in eggs and milk. Soon after, the Hartnetts and their neighbors were able to resume paying their bills. Even with the oil companies taking most of the profits, a farm family with a good well could double its annual income. For the townspeople, drilling itself meant added business. The drillers needed food and lodging, their trucks required fuel and repair, and as the wells started to produce, pump servicers and tank installers were needed.[63]

Stafford was one of many towns in Kansas affected by the discovery of oil. The first commercially successful well was drilled in 1882, and by 1903, more than 1,100 wells were in operation across the state. Production peaked in 1906 at more than twenty-one million barrels, only to decline by more than 90 percent two years later. Then between 1914 and 1917, large-scale pools were discovered in Butler County near Augusta and El Dorado, east of Wichita. Production shot up from three million barrels in 1914 to more than fifty million in 1920. The populations of Augusta and El Dorado tripled. Exploration leading to even larger discoveries in central and western Kansas began in Russell County in 1923, extended to Stafford County in 1930, and included more than a dozen other counties within a few years. Drilling continued and intensified after World War II. Statewide, the number of wells attempted rose from 400 in 1946 to 1,900 in 1956 before declining to fewer than 1,000 by 1962.[64]

Towns in the region were shaped by many factors, including changes in agriculture, but oil was an important influence. By 1970, thirteen counties had emerged as the leading oil producers in Kansas, each yielding at least two million barrels annually and averaging more than four million. Stafford ranked seventh; Barton, to its immediate north, ranked third; Ellis and Russell, north of Barton, ranked first and second, respectively; and Rice, northeast of Stafford, ranked fourth.[65] Nineteen towns in these counties had grown to include at least 1,500 residents by 1950. The extent to which they had been affected by oil could be seen in comparisons with fifteen towns of similar size in counties where no oil had been discovered.[66] In 1920 and 1930, the towns in both sets of counties averaged about the same number of residents. But during the 1930s, towns in the oil-producing counties grew by 15 percent, while towns in the non-oil-producing counties grew by a modest 3 percent. These differences continued over the next two decades. During the 1940s, growth was 16 percent in the former, compared with 2 percent in the latter, and in the 1950s, it was 14 percent, compared with 2 percent. By 1960, the towns in oil-producing counties had grown an average of 52 percent since 1930, whereas the comparison towns had grown only 7 percent. Among the towns in oil-producing counties, the ones where oil had been discovered earlier—Augusta, El Dorado, and several others—increased less than the others, while the largest growth occurred among towns in counties that became the top producers. Great Bend in Barton County grew from about 5,500 residents in 1930 to more than 16,000 in 1960. Hays, Russell, and Ellinwood doubled in population during the same period. Lyons in Rice County grew 56 percent. Even in Chase—a small town eight miles west of Lyons—the population tripled.

"Oil is jobs. It's a whole bunch of jobs," a man in Pratt County south of Stafford told a writer for the *New Yorker*.[67] But many of these jobs were ephemeral. Drilling required roustabout crews working round-the-clock on the rigs, truckers to haul equipment, construction workers to make roads to the wells, surveyors, inspectors, and geologists. When the drilling was finished, a much smaller labor force was needed to service the wells. The drilling and well-servicing companies established themselves closer to active fields and in larger towns. Activity in the Zenith–Peace Creek field east of Stafford peaked in 1942, when forty-eight wells were drilled. Twenty-three were drilled in 1949, but only one in 1950, and nine more over the next eight years. The more active drilling continued in the northern part of the county.

In 1948, Paul Brown, the farmer who appeared in Haskell County several years later struggling with drought and failed wheat crops, was attending high school in Stafford. His father had come there from Oklahoma to form the Post and Brown Well Service Company. Working in the oil fields after school and on weekends, Paul earned enough money to attend junior college, get married, and begin farming. He was one of many who benefited from the temporary oil boom. At midcentury, the *Stafford Courier* carried weekly reports of wells being drilled in the county, many with success, and there was clear evidence of its financial impact on the community. The Baptist church constructed a new building in 1952, a new intermediate school opened in 1954, and the United Presbyterian Church in Zenith moved into new quarters in 1959. Expansion continued into the next decade, with a new hospital in 1961, a new Presbyterian church the same year, and a new post office in 1963.[68] But much of the drilling and well servicing was conducted by companies in Barton, Russell, and other counties to the north. Oil's impact on Stafford was less significant than on towns such as Great Bend and Russell in those counties. In 1950, nearly 2,000 employees worked for oil companies in Barton County, more than 1,000 did in Rice County and Russell County, but only 200 did in Stafford County.

Revenue from oil production was ephemeral too. Wells in Stafford County were still producing more than 3.5 million barrels in 1970, but production declined steadily to approximately two million barrels in 1987 and then fell to little over one million by 1998. The decline in production was temporarily offset by the OPEC oil embargo of 1979, causing domestic crude to rise from $14 a barrel to almost $36 dollars a barrel in 1981, but prices fell back to $14 by 1986. Stafford's revenue from oil was lower in 1999 than anytime since the 1960s.[69] Similar trends took place in Kansas's other top producing counties. Those thirteen counties produced nearly fifty-two million barrels in 1970 but only thirty-two million in 1980, dropped to twenty-eight million in 1990, and fell to sixteen million in 2000. Stafford County was producing one-third as much as it had in 1970, Barton and Russell counties were producing 28 percent as much, and Rice County only 17 percent as much.

In addition to declining production, the oil industry experienced several changes as early as the 1960s that held long-term implications for small communities like Stafford. One was the increasing market for natural gas, which in Kansas resulted in Grant, Stevens, Morton, and Finney counties in the southwest corner of the state—where a huge reservoir of natural gas had been discovered—becoming the strongest centers of the oil and natural gas industry by the early 1970s. Another development was the merger and consolidation of small petroleum companies, along with their increasing centralization. In Kansas, revenue from oil and gas remained relatively decentralized, although Wichita's revenue more than doubled during the 1960s and employment in the mineral industry held steady in Sedgwick County, while declining revenue and employment characterized most of the oil-producing counties. In Oklahoma, where centralized coordination of the industry began in 1929 and deepened in 1955 with the formation of the Oklahoma Independent Petroleum Association, the trend was even more evident. In 1958, only 3 percent of the state's oil companies and 9 percent of the oil industry's revenue were located in Oklahoma

City, but by 1972, 17 percent of the establishments and 69 percent of the revenue were concentrated there.[70]

The effect of declining oil production and revenue on Stafford County—in which only 5 to 6 percent of the labor force was employed in the industry—was relatively minor. The effect was considerably greater in the other counties. Ten percent of Russell County's labor force was in the oil industry in 2000, down from 17 percent in 1970; the proportion in Barton County declined from 13 percent to 8 percent; and in Rice County, from 9 percent to 5 percent. Of the towns in these counties, Hays was large enough and its economy sufficiently diversified by 1960 that it continued to grow, and Great Bend was nearly able to maintain its population, but almost all the rest declined. Ellinwood's population fell by a quarter between 1960 and 2005, as did Lyons's. Hoisington's, Russell's, and St. John's declined by a third; and Stafford's dropped by nearly half. At the turn of the new century, another geographer came through Stafford, retracing Miller's journey six decades earlier, and noted nothing of oil's impact on the town. The trees around the few remaining farmsteads had grown taller. The wheat fields were producing better. The town itself appeared to have seen better days.[71]

There was ample evidence of decline in Stafford. The population numbered just over 1,000 residents in 2005, down from 1,400 in 1980 and a high of 2,000 in 1950. Countywide, deaths exceeded births by more than 300 during the 1980s and 1990s and out-migration exceeded in-migration by nearly 400. Total employment fell by nearly 500. For anything but routine shopping, Stafford residents drove thirty-seven miles north to Great Bend or forty-three miles east to Hutchinson. Many of Stafford's longtime establishments—Curtis Café, Farmers National Bank, Basye Well Servicing, the lumberyard, and the funeral home—remained, but between 1994 and 2005, annual payrolls fell by 10 percent and ten of the community's businesses closed, including two restaurants, a grocery store, and a pharmacy. School enrollment declined at a rate of ten to fifteen students a year, and as an indication of the community's financial difficulties, more than 50 percent qualified for free or reduced-fare lunches.[72]

Stafford was like Mayville, though, in having become smaller and yet finding a way to sustain its identity as a community. Lacking a college, Stafford was unable to attract or retain as many college-educated residents as Mayville, and in this respect, it was more typical of many Middle Western communities. Instead of promoting jobs in technology and the professions, it became a community in which lower-income working-class families could earn a modest living, keep expenses within reason, and find satisfaction in local amenities and friends. Unlike Mayville, where one adult in three had a college degree, only one in eight did in Stafford. Among younger adults aged twenty-five through forty-four, even fewer (6 percent) had college degrees. Associate degrees were also rare (held by 5 percent of younger adults), despite the availability of community colleges in Great Bend, Hutchinson, and Pratt. As the oil industry and farming declined, workers found jobs in construction, in trucking, pumping gas, and as employees of the Postal Service or the county. Nearly a quarter (mostly women) were employed at the hospital or at assisted-care facilities in Stafford and St. John. Twenty percent of the labor force commuted to jobs outside the county. Median household income in 2000 was $27,000. But housing was also inexpensive. Four families in five owned their homes, the median value of which was $23,000. Among those who did not, monthly rent averaged $225.[73]

Craig Anderle moved with his parents to Stafford when he was in high school. His dad worked for an oil company, and they moved every year or two as the drilling shifted from field to field. They would have moved again, except his dad died that year and the family had nowhere else to go. Craig joined the army after high school and then worked in several states before returning to Stafford. He works as an electrician for the utility company, and his wife has a job at the hospital. They raised four children, all graduating from college and now working in cities in other states. Jeff Jansen is one of the Anderles'neighbors. Younger than they are, he drives a truck on long-distance hauls and is helping on the farm until his dad retires. Craig and Jeff tell similar stories. Neither did well in school and were glad to be doing something else after high school besides study. Jeff attended community college for a year but felt he was wasting his time. Both say finances are tight, especially as gasoline prices increase the cost of driving to Great Bend or Hutchinson for supplies. Yet they have steady jobs and own their homes. Stafford has changed very little in recent decades, they say, although Craig notes that the Main Street stores have been trying to think of ways to attract more business. Both say what they like best about Stafford is the people. They like seeing people they know on the street and being able to greet their neighbors on a first-name basis. They go to church on Sundays and enjoy fishing at a nearby lake. Neither thinks about moving.[74]

Dixie Osborn's father worked for one of the oil companies, too, and that brought her family to Stafford in 1951. She married, moved away, and returned after her husband's death to care for her aging mother. Dixie expresses values typical of residents in small Middle Western towns. "I don't toot my own whistle," she says. "I'm not materialistic. I feel that I am responsible for my family, for their care and well-being. I just do what I am supposed to do quietly and go on with my life." She wishes she could afford health insurance, hopes she can stay healthy enough to keep working, and is glad she can help her mother and an uncle whose health is also declining. "The good Lord seems to be taking care of me," she says. She has a quote on her desk that sums up her attitude toward life. It reads, "I make myself rich by making my wants few."

In 1999, the award-winning director Kirsten Tretbar produced a documentary film for television about Stafford. Her parents had grown up in Stafford, and as a child, Kirsten visited cousins on her uncle's farm. "I was raised to love the land as if I had been a farm girl myself," she recalled. As an adult living in Los Angeles, she returned periodically to Stafford, rediscovering her roots, finding inspiration and meaning. The film captured the struggles and hopes of the community's residents. Wheat prices for the local farmers were low, barely covering expenses. In a particularly poignant scene, a farm woman watches from her front porch as a hailstorm destroys her crop. At the Co-op, men like Craig Anderle and Jeff Jansen gather when work is slow. One of the group tells of being on drugs when he was younger. It was a way of coping with the feeling that his life was going nowhere. Another man talks of getting his life together after attending a religious revival meeting. The contrast between despair and hope sets the stage for the film's main event, an annual Passion play initiated by the pastor at the church in Zenith. Dozens of the local residents enact parts, and dozens more help with props and costumes. The play symbolizes the community's coming together to resurrect itself.[75]

Stafford's collective life was being held intact not only by its churches but also by a stock of organizations that provided basic services even in the absence of demographic growth or economic prosperity. Despite the fewer residents, an abundance of transfer payments, retirement benefits, and property taxes were sufficient to cover the costs of maintaining the roads and schools, and the state covered a larger share of school and highway expenses. St. John shared the cost of law enforcement. Enough of the residents found the community desirable that medical services continued to be available. The community benefited from its proximity to better hospitals in Hutchinson and Wichita. It also made increasing use of new technology, such as a Telemed health-screening program at the school that linked through fiber optics with technology at one of the state's best medical centers.[76]

The community's greatest assets were its social relationships. Residents contributed faithfully to the Boy Scouts' annual clothing drive, helped with the food bank at the Methodist church, and supported the Lions club's sausage and pancake fundraiser. They watched out for one another, and life was regular enough that routine surveillance was often effective, as it was for one elderly resident whose neighbors got him to the hospital after noticing his absence at the café for his usual morning coffee. With neighbors eager to help, there was a strong ethos of self-sufficiency even among the elderly. Nobody wanted to be viewed as a burden. It was important to work if one was able, to keep up one's property, and to visit those who were sick. Respect was vital. Townspeople spoke dismissively of residents in large cities who were unacquainted with their neighbors.

"We not only know our neighbors," said one, "we know their sons and their daughters and their grandmas and their grandpas."

Still, there were concerns, as inhabitants put it, that the town might just dry up and blow away. When one of the community's two doctors retired, residents wondered if a new one could be found. Businesses on Main Street suffered as more of their customers shopped in Pratt or Hutchinson. When the population dropped below a thousand, as it was expected to, funding from the state would decrease accordingly. Teenagers complained that there was nothing to do in town on weekends and no jobs in the area during the summer. A meth dealer was servicing some of the residents' frustrations. The pastor who started the Passion play fell ill and died. With his passing, the Passion play also became history.

It was unlikely that Stafford was ever going to recover the prosperity it enjoyed in the 1940s when oil was being discovered almost daily. Even if high crude prices fanned new exploration, it was more likely that Stafford would remain small and even become smaller. Residents were skeptical about economic development plans and saw little hope of attracting newcomers. Poverty was higher than in many larger communities, and although unemployment was low, jobs did not pay well and opportunities for young people were scarce. Yet the community was maintaining its roads and bridges better than many larger places were. It was providing adequate fire protection and rescue service, and in 1999, Stafford constructed a modern state-of-the-art school building that served more than two hundred students. Like Mayville, Stafford and St. John benefited from being the large towns in the county where people from smaller towns like Macksville and Sylvia came to shop, see the doctor, or visit someone in the hospital. High gasoline prices, ironically, seemed to be helping the community more than hurting it, as one resident pointed out, because people were shopping in Stafford instead of driving thirty or forty miles to one of the larger towns.[77] Housing costs in Stafford relative to income were half what they were in Hutchinson, Wichita, or Kansas City. More important, the community was working with the sparse resources it had, its members helping one another through the churches and civic organizations and at the school to address the realities it faced. One leader put it particularly well when she summarized, "I think we've embraced the fact of who we are."[78]

Besides oil and agriculture, one other large factor was significant in shaping the trajectory of Middle Western towns. That was the military. During World War II, air fields, aircraft production plants, ammunition depots, and training camps emerged throughout the region. They were located on sites with good drainage, easy access to railroad and highway transportation, and plentiful acreage. They appeared in scattered places like Hutchinson, Kansas, where a naval air station was established in 1942 on nearly four thousand acres, including the town's municipal airport; Grand Island, Nebraska, site of the Cornhusker Army Ammunition Plant, which produced artillery shells and bombs from 1942 to 1945; and McAlester, Oklahoma, where civic leaders successfully petitioned the War Department to establish a naval ammunition depot in 1942 in hopes of boosting the area's depressed economy.[79] Many of these installations (such as the air base near Harvard, Nebraska) closed at the end of the war, leaving few reminders of the past, but some continued to operate much longer. The Cornhusker plant, for example, resumed production during the Vietnam War, and the McAlester facility expanded, especially after 1995 as plants in Kansas, Texas, and California were closed. While other communities erected monuments to the fallen and honored them once a year on Memorial Day, these towns continued to be central to the nation's preparedness for armed conflict.

During the cold war, dozens of Middle Western communities found themselves squarely engaged in the country's long-range air and missile defense systems. Strategic Air Command (SAC) airfields with B-52 bombers were established in South Dakota near Rapid City, in North Dakota near Grand Forks and Minot, and in Kansas near Wichita. Other SAC bases were located in Arkansas near Little Rock, in Nebraska near Omaha, and in Missouri near Knob Knoster, the home of Whiteman Air Force Base where stealth bombers in later years would embark on missions to the Persian Gulf. At the end of the cold war, all of these bases remained active. Besides these installations, there were army bases at Fort Riley, Kansas, and Fort Leonard Wood, Missouri, and an air reserve station near Minneapolis–St. Paul. With the exception of the two bases in Missouri, these facilities were located near cities or larger towns with populations of thirty thousand or more. However, nearly a hundred smaller towns were within a ten- to fifteen-mile radius of these installations. In addition, bases near Altus and Cherokee, Oklahoma, continued to serve support functions, and other bases had been officially inactivated near Clinton, Oklahoma; Blytheville, Arkansas; Salina, Kansas; and Grand Island, Kearney, and Lincoln, Nebraska.

Although communities were affected by their proximity to these and other government installations, it was less often the influence on population growth or decline that became most evident—sometimes considerable in the short run—than on how a community configured its businesses and its workforce. Larger communities were, in most instances, sufficiently diversified that they could withstand the financial impact of losing a defense contract or having a nearby base closed. Smaller towns were sometimes able to take advantage of their proximity to military installations by specializing in aviation and electronics or procuring government grants. Base expansion provided job opportunities sorely needed in some communities. Bases that closed left valuable infrastructure, such as runways, hangers, and housing, that could be developed for civilian purposes, but the use of these facilities was often hindered by uncertainties about military needs and by the presence of toxic materials.[80]

In 1983, federal expenditures for defense-related activities in the nine Middle Western states totaled $15.6 billion. By 2005, that figure had climbed to $25.5 billion. The largest increase was in Oklahoma, where expenditures grew from $1.8 billion to $4.7 billion. One of the more instructive examples of towns being shaped by their relationship to the military occurred in southwest Oklahoma about ninety miles from Oklahoma City at Clinton—the only town in the Middle West that could boast having a commercial facility for space tourism. Clinton was the location of Clinton-Sherman Air Force Base, which originated in 1943 when the government purchased five thousand acres of farmland and established a naval air station to train pilots. The military constructed four runways, three hangars, and two dozen barracks in which it housed more than thirty-five hundred soldiers. A year after the base closed in 1946, the town of Clinton acquired the land, leasing it to the Sherman Iron Works, which named the facility Clinton-Sherman Airport and used it for dismantling and salvaging parts from World War II aircraft. In 1954, the air force resumed operations at the site, turning it into a SAC base, constructing housing for nine hundred families, and completing a new runway nearly three miles long for B-52 bombers, which trained and deployed from the facility until 1969. The air force closed the base that year but continued its maintenance until 1971, when the property was again deeded to the town of Clinton, which leased it to a four-county development organization. In 1974, the facility became the Clinton-Sherman Industrial Air Park, with twenty-five firms bringing an estimated fourteen hundred jobs to the area.[81]

The towns most directly affected were Burns Flat, a community that came into existence in the 1950s adjacent to the SAC facility, and Clinton, which became involved through its ownership of the property. Two smaller towns (Foss and Dill City) were within a seven-mile radius of the airfield, and three others (Bessie, Canute, and Cordell) were within fifteen miles. Clinton had been founded in 1903 at a railroad crossing known as Washita Junction when the United States Congress gave special permission to members of the Cheyenne-Arapaho reservation to sell land to the Washita Townsite Company. Clinton's location on two of the main railroads through the state facilitated the town's growth, which by 1910 included a flour mill, a cotton mill, two cotton gins, a broom factory, three banks, two weekly newspapers, and more than 2,700 residents.[82] Clinton was one-third larger than its closest rival in the county, Cordell (also known as New Cordell), and nearly four times larger than Arapaho, the county seat. Two communities that the railroads missed were already becoming ghost towns. Between 1910 and 1920, Clinton's population declined by about

200 people, but growth returned in the 1920s when the town became the site of the Western Oklahoma Tuberculosis Sanatorium. It also became the location of an arms-storage facility and an important stopping point for truckers, tourists, and emigrants to California along the main route from Chicago to Los Angeles that in 1926 was designated as U.S. Highway 66. Clinton served, too, as the principal market town for Custer County's thriving farm economy, which included nearly 3,000 families who annually produced livestock valued at more than $2.5 million and crops valued at more than $5 million. By 1930, Clinton's population tripled to more than 7,500. With the Depression, its population was about 10 percent smaller in 1940 than in 1930 but returned to the earlier level by 1950. Its most significant growth corresponded with the years in which the Clinton-Sherman SAC facility was in operation. In 1960, Clinton's population was approximately 9,600, a 27 percent increase from 1950. Meanwhile, Burns Flat, which had earlier been the location only of a post office and a school, became an incorporated community with 2,280 residents. Even several of the smaller towns experienced significant population growth. Foss and Dill City increased 37 percent, and Cordell grew 22 percent.[83]

The reduced operations and eventual closing of Clinton-Sherman Air Force Base as a SAC facility had a significant negative impact on Clinton and its neighboring communities. By the time the base closed, it employed fewer than four hundred civilian workers. Clinton's population in 1970 was 12 percent smaller than in 1960, Cordell's declined 10 percent, Foss's fell 48 percent, and Burns Flat's tumbled 57 percent. During the worst years, 1969 to 1972, unemployment benefits in Custer County increased more than two and a half times, reaching a new high again in 1975. Those difficulties were only partly overcome by the end of the decade. As the air base became an industrial park, Burns Flat's population recovered, slightly exceeding its level in 1960, but Clinton's remained lower.[84] "Any time you suck that many people away," a longtime resident recalled, "it makes a difference."[85]

Starting in the 1980s, Custer County embarked on a relationship with the U.S. Department of Defense that proved to be a veritable roller coaster. In 1983, federal defense expenditures in the county totaled only $2.1 million, or about a tenth as much as the forty-eight businesses at the Clinton-Sherman Industrial Park were contributing in annual payroll. By 1985, business at the industrial park had fallen by two-thirds, and the development authority in charge of the park registered a net loss. In 1986, federal defense expenditures in the county jumped nearly twentyfold to $86 million due to a resumption of B-52 training at the airfield and a contract for jet fuel from a local refinery. A year later, the figure plummeted 80 percent. It continued to fluctuate over the next decade, exceeding $80 million again in 1991, only to fall below $14 million in

1993 and then sink to a deficit in 1996. In subsequent years, defense expenditures in the county averaged only $3.2 million and exceeded $3.8 million only once. Meanwhile, agriculture and oil fluctuated, too. Farmers experienced net losses in 1981, 1983, and 1985, and again in 2001 and 2002. Between 1980 and 2005, net farm income relative to the previous year declined twelve times. Oil production fell from 1980 to 1982, rose from 1982 to 1986, and declined steadily from then until 1998. Employment in the county fell each year from 1982 to 1986, declined slightly again in 1990 and 1997, and dropped again in 2001 and 2002. The effects were evident in population figures. Burns Flats was less than half as large in 1990 as in 1980. Clinton experienced a net increase of five hundred between 1980 and 1990, but its population remained lower than it had been in 1960. The smaller towns declined by 20 to 30 percent. Countywide, the population remained constant as births significantly outnumbered deaths, but out-migration exceeded in-migration by more than 3,600.[86]

Although Clinton was smaller in 2000 than it was in 1960, it developed an increasingly diversified economic base that largely stabilized its workforce and enabled its firms' payrolls to expand. Its Cherokee and Arapaho legacy provided the basis for 200 jobs at the Lucky Star Casino, which took in approximately $4 million annually and supported the tribes' diabetes and prevention programs. As hardware stores, drugstores, and restaurants in the county's smaller towns declined, businesses in Clinton benefited. Other than Cordell and Thomas, it was the only place in the county to see a doctor, dentist, or lawyer. Clinton's continuing role as an agricultural center, serving more than 900 farm families in the county, was evident in the presence of United Agricultural Products, Meacham Farms feedlots, Highland Dairy, the Sky Land & Cattle Company, and Bar-S Foods—a meatpacking plant with 450 employees. Seven oil-well servicing and drilling companies were in operation. The town's historic relationship with rail transportation continued with a locomotive-servicing shop for Farmrail System, operator of the former Santa Fe line through a lease agreement with the state. The community's location on Route 66 was commemorated through a museum and visitor's center, drawing tourists traveling through town on Interstate 40, which also served the community's six trucking companies and nine motels. Health care played an increasing role in the local economy, employing more than 500 workers among the regional hospital, a Methodist retirement community, an Indian health services center, and several assisted-living facilities. In all, there were more than 350 commercial establishments with nearly 4,000 employees.[87]

Despite its uncertain relationships with the military, Clinton found ways to build on that legacy as well. In 1971, leaders in Clinton, Burns Flat, and several other communities formed the South Western Oklahoma Development Authority (SWODA) to facilitate business expansion in the region through state and federal grants and programs. SWODA expanded to include forty-six towns in eight counties with a combined population of more than 100,000. Through its experience at the Clinton-Sherman Air Force Base, SWODA was able to develop pilot-training and crash-rescue programs at Altus Air Force Base, about eighty miles southwest of Clinton, where the Defense Department continued to spend more than $100 million annually. Other SWODA projects included securing grants for sewage and water systems at Clinton-Sherman and in Clinton, Cordell, and several other communities; facilitating the financing of Western Oklahoma Area Vocational Technical School at the industrial park; and developing an enhanced 911 emergency telephone service for the region. A few businesses in the area maintained contacts with the military, as well. One such business was Price Prints, a T-shirt printing company in Cordell that brought in more than $20 million in subcontracts for military uniforms.

The most ambitious project was the commercial spaceport. In 1998, a delegation of business leaders and public officials from Oklahoma, including Clinton's mayor, visited Lockheed Martin's headquarters in California where they learned that the company was seeking a launch site for a reusable spacecraft that it hoped to have ready for the National Aeronautics and Space Administration (NASA) by 2004. The massive eighteen-inch thick, 13,550-foot runway at Clinton-Sherman Air Force Base was one of sixteen sites the company was considering. To further the base's chances of being selected, the Oklahoma legislature created the Oklahoma Space Industry Development Authority and commissioned SWODA to develop the site. But after repeated technology failures, Lockheed canceled its VentureStar program in 2001. Following this setback, development plans shifted to the private sector. In 2004, Pioneer Rocketplane of Solvang, California, signed a contract to build a commercial spaceport at the base for civilian tourists. Four years later, Rocketplane officials said they hoped to bring 200 employees to the site, where they expected to develop $30 million in annual revenue.[88]

"It's kind of a tongue-in-cheek joke," a resident in Burns Flat said of the spaceport. "The thing is moving so slowly that it might be a spaceport twenty-five years from now, but at the moment Burns Flat is still a small town with one stoplight." Residents in Clinton were equally pessimistic. "They get millions of dollars of tax credits to start up out there," said one. "They pay a CEO a big salary, and after they get all the tax credits used up, they disband the company and move on. That's happened a couple of times. The spacecraft is really just an old jet hull they've repainted. I don't look for anything to happen out there."[89]

With all the ups and downs it had experienced, Burns Flat adapted by staying small even in good times. There were a couple of convenience stores, the stoplight, and not much else. Oil crews and military personnel came and went, mostly living in Clinton when they were there. Clinton, in contrast, was large and diverse enough that its residents were confident about the town's future. As people left for better jobs in Oklahoma City, others arrived to work at the meat plant, the casino, Halliburton, and the oil companies. If their dealings with the military had left them pessimistic, the people of Burns Flat and Clinton at least had created a regional development plan that gave them a chance to bid for future business with the federal government.

In 2006, an online business journal published a list of one hundred "dream towns"—communities of 10,000 to 50,000 residents that the magazine considered ideal places to live. Although only 21 percent of the 577 towns rated were in the Middle West, forty-four of the top 100 were. The highest-ranking towns included Pierre, South Dakota; Rolla, Missouri; Hays, Kansas; Mankato, Minnesota; and Stillwater, Oklahoma. The rankings were based on quality-of-life indicators that aimed to identify "well-rounded communities where the economy is strong, traffic is light, the cost of living is moderate, adults are well-educated, and access to big-city attractions is reasonably good." Towns ranking the highest received above-average scores on population growth, income growth, small-business growth, employment in management and the professions, ease of commuting, low taxes, high levels of education, and proximity to a major metropolitan area.[90]

Pierre, South Dakota, three hours west of Sioux Falls, scored near the top of the list because its 14,000 residents commuted short distances to work, lived in relatively inexpensive housing, and enjoyed incomes two and a half times as high as in 1980. Thirty-five percent of its adults were college graduates, and 41 percent worked in management or the professions. It was also the state capital. Rolla, Missouri, halfway between St. Louis and Springfield on Interstate 44, was the home of the Missouri University of Science and Technology with 6,000 students. Thirteen percent of the town's adults had advanced graduate degrees. Hays, Kansas, in the western part of the state, midway between Kansas City and Denver on Interstate 70, had grown from 16,000 residents in 1980 to nearly 20,000 in 2005. It was the location of Fort Hays State University. These communities' distinctiveness in employment, education levels, and growth made them dream towns. Others high on the list stood out for similar reasons. A large majority—thirty-three of the top forty-four—were college towns. Twenty-six percent of adults in these communities were college graduates, 9 percent held advanced degrees, and 30 percent worked in professional or managerial jobs. Median family incomes were more than twice as high in 2000 as in 1980, and average population had grown 12 percent. On average, the dream towns had populations of approximately 20,000 residents.

The rankings demonstrated that several dozen Middle Western towns could hold their own in a national competition of desirability. Towns the size of Pierre, Rolla, and Hays with colleges and cultural attractions, good wages, low-cost housing, and light traffic were the kinds of communities the region's leaders boasted about when urging prospective residents to relocate. But what of the smaller towns that made up the majority of the region's communities? What constituted an attractive quality of life in towns of 500, 1,500, or 5,000? What did residents value about their towns?

Residents of these smaller communities were plainly aware that a person had to travel elsewhere to find museums and attend concerts. The lack of these cultural amenities in smaller towns or their abundance in cities was not an issue. Residents went to the city often enough visiting friends and relatives or on vacation. It was not difficult to take in cultural events from time to time. "My girls are interested in dance," a mother in rural Minnesota explained, "so we drive into Minneapolis, see something, and do some shopping while we're there." Or they were content doing other things. "I'm 74 years old," a neighbor of hers said, "so I'm perfectly happy to stay here and go to the barber shop and talk to my buddies."[91]

What mattered was whether the local stores stayed in business. If the barber shop closed, this man would feel it. His buddies would have to reconvene elsewhere—perhaps at the Dairy Queen, like a group in another town did. If the drugstore, the hardware store, or the only grocery store in town closed, the loss would be greater. "My sister was here last week helping do some housecleaning," the first woman said, "and she asked, 'Can we get a paintbrush and some nails?' 'Nope, can't do that.'" The grocery store reopened after being closed for three years, but it was struggling. Having a Dollar General where they could find household necessities was important. Having to drive fifteen miles to fill a prescription was a significant deficit.

In the smallest towns, concerns about store closings were well founded. In 1994, only 20 percent of Middle Western towns with fewer than 500 residents had a drugstore. By 2005, that proportion fell to 13 percent. Over the same period, the proportion of towns this size with hardware stores declined from 21 percent to 12 percent. And the proportion with grocery stores tumbled from 55 percent to 29 percent. This trend was one of the reasons residents felt their communities were declining.[92]

Yet many businesses were continuing in these towns. Small-town pharmacies and hardware stores had been especially hurt over the years by large retail chains (such as Ace, Walmart, and Home Depot), and grocery stores were sometimes replaced by convenience stores at filling stations. But banks were staying in business, often by keeping branch offices open in small towns. In 2005, half of the smallest towns still had banks, down only from 56 percent in 1994. Eating establishments were relatively abundant, too. Although it was true, as residents noted, that opportunities for fine dining were limited, 45 percent of the smallest towns had at least one restaurant. About the same proportion (47 percent) had a filling station.

In towns that were only modestly larger, the chances of having basic stores available were considerably greater. In towns of 500 to 1,500, 63 percent had grocery stores, and that proportion rose to 85 percent in towns of 1,500 to 5,000. Among the latter, 75 percent had a drugstore, 51 percent had a hardware store, and nearly all had banks, restaurants, and filling stations. To be sure, there were concerns—about 10 percent of the group had lost a grocery store or hardware store. But it was still possible for residents in these towns to shop for routine items in their own communities. In the smaller communities, it was common for people to travel seven or ten miles to shop in a larger town anyway because the grocery store there was better, or they had to be there to see the doctor or dentist. In 2005, doctors' offices, dentists' offices, nursing-care facilities, and law offices were present in approximately one-sixth of the towns with fewer than 500 residents, whereas one or more of these services were present in about two-thirds of the towns with 1,500 to 5,000 resdients. In this respect, the smallest towns were part of a larger network of communities that involved shared shopping and services.

A community's quality of life is often associated with its ability to attract new businesses and services. However, the likelihood the smaller towns could do so was low. A widely used commercial service for businesses seeking new consumer markets estimated the "spending potential" for various products through index scores ranging above 100 for attractive markets and below 100 for unattractive locations. Scores in 2002 for Middle Western towns with populations of 1,500 to 5,000 ranged well below 100: from 76 for apparel and furniture, 77 for dining, and 80 for electronics to 82 for home repair and 86 for appliances. Only in Middle Western towns with more than 20,000 residents were any of the scores above 100.[93]

Although new stores were unlikely to open, it was not true that they were nonexistent. The new ALCO stores in Smith Center and Mayville were examples. There was also one in Vinton, Iowa, and in all, there were ninety-five across the Middle West. ALCO was an outgrowth of the Duckwall five-and-dime variety-store chain founded in 1901 by A. L. Duckwall in Abilene, Kansas. Duckwall stores flourished well into the 1950s, but by the late 1960s, they were facing stiff competition from Kmart and other discount stores and were experiencing the consequences of population decline in many of the small towns where stores were located. In 1968, Duckwall management entered the discount market by opening its first ALCO store and, over the next two decades, closed many of its Duckwall stores. By the end of the century, the Duckwall in Stafford was one of only thirty-eight remaining in the Middle Western states. ALCO stores accounted for 92 percent of the company's sales.[94]

The location of Duckwall and ALCO stores provided an interesting comparison. Twenty-two of the Duckwall stores (58 percent) were in towns with fewer than 1,500 residents. On average, these towns were smaller by about 300 residents than they had been in 1980. In contrast, the newer ALCO stores were in larger towns. Seventy-four percent were in towns of 1,500 to 5,000 residents, and 18 percent were in larger towns; only 8 percent were in smaller towns. Whether the ALCO stores would succeed in the long run was anyone's guess, given the history of franchises—including Gambles, Woolco, and Oklahoma Tire & Supply—that had tried and eventually failed. But ALCO was betting that business in the region's small towns would continue.

Walmart was a bigger player in the region and, compared with ALCO, nearly always played in larger towns. In 2005, there were 446 Walmart stores in the Middle West. Missouri had more than a hundred, Arkansas and Oklahoma each had more than seventy, and Iowa and Minnesota each had more than fifty. South and North Dakota, with ten each, had the fewest. There were six stores in Wichita alone, nine in Tulsa, and twelve in Oklahoma City. Only three of the stores were in towns with fewer than 1,500 residents, and less than 20 percent were in towns with populations below 5,000. Fifty-one percent were in towns of 5,000 to 20,000 residents, and 31 percent were in towns larger than 20,000. On average, towns with a Walmart had populations of approximately 8,000 in 2005.

Although Walmart stores were located in larger-than-average towns, they were widely scattered and usually within easy commuting distance. There was at least one Walmart in three-fourths of the counties in Arkansas and Oklahoma and in nearly two-thirds of the counties in Missouri. In the other states, more than half the Walmarts were located near an interstate. People in the smaller towns sometimes worried that Walmart was stealing business and dampening the community spirit they associated with seeing one another on Main Street, but they conceded it was good having abundant merchandise in range. "We travel for everything," a resident of a town of three hundred explained. "We're just part of the Walmart scenario." Another resident said she often ran into her neighbors at Walmart, even though the store was thirty miles away. Yet another said driving to Walmart was just a fun thing to do—and much better than living in a city with noisy neighbors and traffic jams.

As much as the availability of stores and services mattered, the quality of life depended more than anything else on social relationships. Residents like Bobbi Miles in Smith Center picked their town because they saw possibilities for warm relationships. But they are more likely to have been lifelong residents or to have come because of a job opportunity, to be near family, or because of who they married. When some say that what they like best about their town is the people, the statement bears multiple meanings. It is sometimes an admission that the town has little else to offer—few stores, low wages, bad weather— though it was more often an expression of feeling at home.

Feeling at home implies that one's neighbors are good people, like oneself. The evidence that they are in fact good can be expressed simply. It is unnecessary to lock one's house at night or to lock one's car when parked on Main Street— or as a woman in Kansas joked, it *was* necessary because friendly neighbors would otherwise fill your backseat with zucchini. The proof of local goodness lay also in the fact that neighbors helped one another. They came knocking if they thought a person might be sick. They kept tabs on one another's children. They brought casseroles when someone died. They served individually and voluntarily, but also through organized activities, such as Kiwanis, chambers of commerce, churches, and the various school and hospital support groups that were so common in places like Mayville and Smith Center.

What it meant to be good was reinforced in stories about outsiders who violated the accustomed patterns. For instance, an elderly woman recounted being in a city and pulling away from the curb, accidentally leaving her purchases behind. A stranger appeared from nowhere, she recalled, and instead of helping, helped himself to her forgotten articles. Madge Schmidt recounted how drug dealers had come to town a few years ago and run up so much credit at the grocery store that it was forced to close.

Respect accrued not just to those who committed random deeds of kindness but to residents who contributed routinely to the common good. That meant serving the community as a teacher or school superintendent, a health professional, or a store owner. These were the community leaders that residents looked up to. They were the caretakers, as one man put it, the people who wanted to see their community thrive. "They're people who take the time to help organize things and get things done for the community," another explained. Leaders earned respect, too, by volunteering. It was important to be active in Kiwanis, Lions, and Rotary—perhaps all three—and to serve on the library committee, the school board, or on a committee at one's church.

Smaller communities necessarily had fewer voluntary associations than larger communities, but on a per capita basis, they had more. Across the Middle West, towns with fewer than 500 residents in 2005 averaged thirteen formally organized civic associations. In those towns, the average number of residents was approximately 200, meaning that there was one organization for every sixteen people. In towns with populations between 500 and 1,500, there were twenty organizations, or one for every forty-four residents. And in towns of 1,500 to 5,000 inhabitants, there were thirty-nine organizations, or one for every seventy residents. That compared with an average of ninety-one organizations in towns of 5,000 to 20,000, or one organization per 107 residents, and 137 organizations in towns of more than 20,000, or one organization for every 458 residents.[95]

Serving the common good also meant keeping one's own affairs in order. That involved little things, like keeping one's lawn mowed and not leaving junk around, but it mostly pertained to the use of money. A woman in her mid-fifties who had raised three children and worked in various service jobs in her community explained it well. Her life had been easier than that of her parents (who lived on her father's meager wages at a filling station) or of her husband's parents (who farmed in South Dakota), but she took pride in living simply. "There are people who just go out and buy whatever they want," she said. "And there are lots of days when I think I'm just going to stop at a restaurant and pick up food on the way home, but I don't. You go home and cook because it's cheaper. You don't go to the movies every weekend. I have girlfriends who get their nails done every week. I'm not a fancy person. I don't need those things. I'm frugal."[96]

This woman knew families in her community whose incomes were much lower than hers, and it bothered her when people looked down on these families because they were poor. What mattered to her was that poor families have jobs and that they live within their means. The key was discipline. When that was lacking, people got into trouble. As a woman in another town explained, "People can't afford things, and they put it on the credit card hoping something will come along. Better jobs aren't the answer because they'll probably just spend more. They aren't disciplining themselves." For both these women, residing in a small town and living frugally were nearly synonymous. Each implied a kind of sacrifice, a commitment to simplicity.[97]

Expectations about pitching in and living responsibly, behaving not only as a good citizen but also as a vigilant neighbor and loyal friend, required ways to excuse oneself at times from these obligations. The fact that "everyone knows your business," one man said, was both the best and worst aspect of living in his town. He was the school superintendent, which meant being especially visible and having to serve on several of the town's committees as well as attend all the school functions. He excused himself from further obligations by getting out of town with his family as often as he could. He preferred shopping in another town for the same reason. The town manager in another community said he went fishing by himself to get away from nosy neighbors. A farmer who lived on the edge of town noted that he interacted only with his immediate neighbors, happily avoiding others he feared would ask for his help. A woman who spent most of her waking hours volunteering for civic organizations moved to a farmstead outside of town to find some solitude. A woman in another town said candidly, "Other than a few church people that we're good friends with, I mean, the rest of the people I don't really care about. I know that sounds harsh, but they just don't affect my life."[98] Although they lamented the fact that people seemed not to socialize with one another as much as in the past, residents agreed that the changes in their communities were liberating. Online shopping was more efficient than having an extended conversation with a neighbor on Main Street. Seeing friends at a football game was easier than inviting them to dinner.

Not only was it true that townspeople excused themselves from neighborly obligations, there was also a penchant for personal independence that countered the popular image of small communities as beacons of neighborliness. It was the desire that farmers near Mayville expressed to prove one's self-sufficiency. Independence amounted to regional pride, born of living in a harsh climate, descending from hardy pioneers (real or imagined), taking "whatever is thrown at us, bouncing back, and gaining strength from it." There was a kind of freedom, residents said, that could not be found elsewhere. It was the ability to tinker, to live at a slow pace, freed of city traffic and the stress of working in a corporate environment. It was feeling that their children were safe or the satisfaction of living within a few blocks of their school. It was having a lake nearby and a recreational vehicle parked in the driveway. Some of the spirit that drove the towns' first inhabitants was still present. Small towns might now be declining, but living in one was still an adventure.

As residents in Clinton and Burns Flat awaited the maiden launch of a commercial vehicle from their spaceport, statistics painted a mixed picture of small communities in the Middle West. Nearly 3,000 towns in the region had fewer than 500 residents. In 2005, the average population in these towns was barely more than 200. Three-quarters were smaller than they had been in 1980. One-third had declined by at least 25 percent. Another 1,300 communities had populations averaging about 900. Sixty percent had become smaller. Demographers predicted that many of these communities would become ghost towns. Their passing would begin with a going-out-of-business sign, reporters wrote, perhaps in a shoe store window, at a florist's shop, or because "the railroad died, the hotel closed, jobs dried up, folks moved on."[99]

Other communities would likely fare better. There were more than 750 in the Middle West with populations between 1,500 and 5,000. Half of these grew between 1980 and 2005. Only 5 percent declined by a percent a year or more. Another 400 averaged about 10,000 residents in 2005. Seven in ten had grown. Only 2 percent had declined significantly. In these communities, it was more likely than it was in smaller towns that an ALCO or Walmart store would open. If they were located on an interstate or near a city, their chances of making it were especially good.

If three-quarters—or even half—of the Middle West's towns disappeared, the region's profile would be profoundly altered. Where there were once thriving communities, only prairie would exist, perhaps marked by crumbling foundations or a few remaining trees. Like so many of the towns that disappeared at the end of the nineteenth century, the last people to leave would have taken everything with them. Those were the images conjured by talk of the heartland's dying towns. But it was uncommon for a town to vanish completely. The smallest towns lost thirty-two people—or 13 percent of their population—on average during the 1980s, but only four people during the 1990s and five between 2000 and 2005. If the towns were dying, they were taking their time doing it. They were also adapting, serving more often as residences for people who worked in other towns, and depending less on their own Main Street's activity than on connections with stores, jobs, and services in neighboring communities.

To be sure, there were ghost towns and near ghost towns aplenty. Minnesota and Missouri each had twenty towns with fewer than fifty residents, Iowa and Oklahoma each had twenty-two, Kansas had twenty-three, Nebraska and South Dakota each had twenty-nine, and North Dakota had fifty-six. These towns lost about one-third of their meager populations in the 1980s but had not declined much after that. Frederick, Kansas, was one of the smallest. Had a tornado or fire struck again, there would not have been much to destroy. The brick school where the Masonic lodge met in the 1950s was in ruins. All that remained of the bank was a cement vault. The Baptists closed their church in 1978 and tore down the building. There was no mayor and no town council. But there was still some life in the town. The grain elevator was part of a regional cooperative association. There was a new weigh station for the large trucks that came during wheat harvest. Eleven people lived in Frederick. Five were retired or in poor health. The other six worked in white-collar jobs. They commuted to larger towns fifteen to twenty miles away. In these respects, Frederick was typical, although most of the smallest towns included a few families with children. About half the adult residents of these towns were employed, commuting twenty to thirty miles to work; about one-quarter were on public assistance. When elderly residents died, it was unlikely that any newcomers would take their place. The commuters might leave, too, if rising fuel prices elevated their driving costs or if jobs disappeared.

Larger towns might face similar dynamics, but they had more resources at their disposal. They still provided social support, roots, good homes, and basic necessities for the citizens who remained. In Mayville, there was guarded optimism that the worst decline in agriculture was over and that the town would adjust to being smaller. Although the number of farm proprietors statewide in North Dakota fell by 12 percent between 2000 and 2005 alone, the number in Traill County remained almost constant. Fuel costs were cutting into farm profits, but those were offset by record-high prices for corn and wheat. Mayville State University had a new president who seemed to be turning the institution's budget around. Stafford's future was less certain, but rising oil prices were bringing more oil drillers than the county had seen in thirty years. Clinton and Burns Flat were eager to reap the whirlwind of space tourism, but if that failed, as many thought it would, regional development plans and a more diversified economy held promise for the future.[100]

Throughout the region, residents of small communities did what they could to keep their towns as livable and attractive as possible. They knew that appearances mattered, and for that reason, in town after town, small efforts were made to beautify Main Street even as businesses became fewer. Flower baskets hung from lampposts. Beds of zinnias appeared in front of the post office. Instead of boarding up abandoned storefronts, owners rented empty buildings for next to nothing to anyone who would turn on the lights once in awhile. Youth who probably would have broken the large windows in these buildings had they been in cities somehow knew to resist that temptation. In other towns, community leaders condemned and tore down abandoned houses as quickly as possible to prevent squatters or low-income families from moving in. Other communities effectively appealed to government agencies for help in beautifying parks, fixing roads, and maintaining clinics.[101]

Some of the towns invested in plans they hoped would bring in new industries or at least attract tourists. Small historical museums emerged, celebrating a county's Indian heritage, its cattle trails, or its ethnic heritage. Racetracks and dirt-bike trails opened. Quilt shows and county fairs were advertised. Efforts were made to attract an ethanol plant, a feedlot, an organic-vegetable farm, or a telemarketing firm. There was an expectation that shrinking 401(k) portfolios would force urban retirees to seek cheaper housing in rural communities. Land was offered free or tax free to lure homesteaders. Farmers offered plots to newcomers interested in reclaiming a rural lifestyle, in having space for their children or to raise animals.[102]

In western Nebraska, Madge Schmidt was betting her town of two hundred residents would survive. It has become a bedroom community for people who work twenty or thirty miles away. She says the taxes are low, and people can find a house for one-tenth of what it would cost to live in a city. Several families have moved in from Denver and Omaha. Despite its declining enrollment, the school is in no danger of closing anytime soon. The women in town put on dinners at the Methodist church, and the men socialize at the filling station. One of the men says it would take a lot to get him to leave. He drives thirty miles to work but considers it an easy commute. "If you talk to people from big cities, thirty miles sounds like an ungodly amount, except here thirty miles is only thirty minutes. The location is just pretty nice."[103] When the heavy snow comes, volunteers with pickups and tractors plow the streets. Now that spring is on its way, the townspeople are pitching in to complete the new firehouse.

SIX

The Changing Face of Agribusiness

Juana was ten the year she started first grade in southwest Kansas. She could not read or write in any language. She spoke no English and had never been to school. Her family was from a small village in central Mexico. They came on temporary work permits that had to be renewed each year. Juana attended parochial school and during the summers went to classes for migrant workers' children. After five years, her family was eligible to apply for permanent residency.

"We had to go to Kansas City and fill out all kinds of forms and get pictures taken," Juana recalled. "They gave us a big old manila envelope and said, 'Don't open it, take it with you. You have to go back to Mexico and wait there until the Mexican Consulate calls on you. Then you can get your permanent residency and come back to America.' But we honestly did not believe we were coming back. We said goodbye to everybody, and the whole family was crying. We headed back to Mexico, and then we spent about a month on the border because my parents had purchased a little blue station wagon and the Mexican government wouldn't let them take it past a certain point. We didn't have much money, and my dad kept trying to work and do odd jobs. I helped sell oranges and things like that.

"After about six months, my parents were able to go to Mexico City to find out what was going on. 'Oh, you didn't have to wait for us to call you,' they were told, 'you could have just come in.' It took several weeks and a lot of red tape, but they got everything approved. We headed back to the United States still dreading being turned away, but they let us come across. Crossing the border was just an awesome feeling!"

Juana continued her schooling, attended the local community college, and eventually earned bachelor's and master's degrees in education with an emphasis on English as a second language. She became a citizen when she was twenty-five, took an active role in the community, and later served on the city commission, including a term as mayor. Her greatest sense of accomplishment comes from working with students whose parents are migrant laborers. "I tell them the opportunities are there. You just have to work hard and never give up."[1]

A local legend has it that Mrs. William D. Fulton was tending her garden one day when a stranger stopped to ask what the town was called. The railroad men were calling it Fulton, she replied, but she had decided that the permanent name should be something else. Well, the stranger said, eyeing her garden, why don't you call it Garden City? That was in 1878, nearly a century before Juana's family arrived and five years after the Atchison, Topeka and Santa Fe Railroad came through western Kansas. A few years earlier, the area had been the home of some three to four million buffalo. By 1875, nearly all the buffalo were gone. Settlers began planting wheat and made plans for a gristmill, but the operation never materialized. The region appeared too arid for crops. The sod would have to remain unbroken. Yet within a decade, the town was well on its way to becoming one of the prominent stopping points along the route from Kansas City to Colorado and New Mexico. In subsequent years, Garden City emerged as a community of innovative agricultural business ventures, including irrigation, sugar milling, alfalfa hay and seed production, and feedlots. By the end of the twentieth century, it was the home of the largest meat-processing plant in the country.[2]

Agribusiness transformed large sections of the Middle West during the last third of the twentieth century and was reshaped as it became part of a global food production and marketing system. The transformation was particularly evident in the region's increasing emphasis on packaged-food production, ranging from frozen dinners for wholesale and retail markets to boxed beef and poultry for fast-food franchises. Between the 1970s and late 1990s, food products from the nine Middle Western states rose in value from $3.6 billion annually to $20.9 billion. Relative to raw farm output, the value of processed food increased from 38 percent in the 1970s to 106 percent at the end of the century.[3] Commercial feedlots, animal-slaughtering facilities, and packaged-meat and poultry-processing plants appeared with increasing frequency in southwest Kansas, western Oklahoma, central and eastern Nebraska, western Iowa, parts of Minnesota and South Dakota, and northwestern Arkansas. The transformation brought new sources of employment and income to these regions. Much of the work involved low-wage employment in beef-, pork-, and poultry-processing plants. Many employees were recent immigrants from Mexico, Central America, and Vietnam. Communities formerly composed entirely of white European Americans became multiethnic and multicultural in little more than a few years. This was a different side of the Middle West than the one depicted by quiet cornfields, idyllic meadows, and somnolent towns.

The social patterns and modes of business organization were in many ways new in these previously farm-based communities. Longtime residents found themselves confronted with new neighbors whom they did not know and who sometimes did not speak their language. Leaders struggled with questions unheard of in the region's declining communities. How could new housing be provided quickly enough? Was population growth bringing in crime and straining social services? Could schools and hospitals keep up? Would established residents flee? Observers inevitably drew varying conclusions. It was necessary, some argued, for communities to grow by abandoning time-worn traditions and accommodating to the realities of multinational business. Others were certain the Middle West was bargaining with the devil. Workers were being exploited, and the environment was becoming toxic. Tainted, unhealthy food was the likely result. However you cut it, meat processing was a dirty business.

But there was a larger story easily missed in the debate about meat processing. Business enterprises on a scale radically different from the family farm and the small-town store had been part of the region's institutional DNA from the start. These were the grain elevator cooperatives, the farm machinery manufacturers, the beet growers' and cattlemen's associations, the hog slaughterers and poultry processors, the meat packers, and networks of commodities traders. They were the sinews that linked farms to markets, secured and organized capital, and connected communities in scattered places like Mayville, North Dakota, and Garden City, Kansas. They were a big part of the Middle West's economic strength at the start of the twenty-first century, creating new money through competitive business arrangements, but also generating a questionable record of labor relations.

The narrative that made sense of some of the facts attributed the changing economic and demographic landscape to the abrupt arrival of big business in small Middle Western communities. In this interpretation, ruthless meatpacking entrepreneurs capitalized on new butchering technology and transportation capacities by moving plants from Kansas City, Chicago, and other large cities to small towns like Garden City where wages were lower and unions were nonexistent. According to this interpretation, plants spread to other small communities as business expanded, more workers were needed, and even cheaper labor was found by recruiting new immigrants. The townspeople in these small communities were soon caught up in changes beyond their control as reluctant bystanders or as complicit participants. The disruptions to community life were often chaotic, but by then it was too late. Residents found themselves wrapped in a downward spiral of low wages, ethnic strife, and deteriorating social relations.

That narrative, however, lacked an adequate account of why small towns provided an attractive venue for large agriculture-related businesses in the first place. Although labor and transportation costs may have been low, it was unlikely that small towns could provide sufficient labor for new businesses needing thousands of workers, and it was even less likely that many towns would have an incentive to invite a large business into their midst. The standard narrative also failed to explain why the disruptions that analysts identified in some communities proved to be the exception more than the rule. To be sure, ethnic animosities surfaced, and service agencies were sometimes overwhelmed. But communities were surprisingly resilient in adapting to the changes they experienced. In emphasizing the power of large businesses, the standard narrative fell short, too, in describing how these organizations became part of an ever-widening circle of bankruptcies, mergers, and international acquisitions.

Bringing the missing pieces into focus requires starting earlier than the meat-processing revolution of the 1980s. Rural communities the size of Garden City had long been involved in commercial enterprises that required cooperation among farmers and townspeople and that extended well beyond their immediate locale. Many of these enterprises involved manufacturing, distribution, large-scale finance, and relations with government. Through these ventures, residents acquired experience in administration, developed organizations that could grow into larger ones, and created a pool of skilled and unskilled wage laborers. When larger businesses looked to relocate from cities to smaller towns, these resources were already in place. Communities adapted better than they otherwise would have because some of what was involved was familiar. That did not imply that the transition was easy. What was once manageable through informal community associations now required formal programs with regional, state, and federal cooperation. As producers and consumers, rural residents had always been affected by international markets, but now they were connected in new ways. It mattered not only that the demand for wheat in Russia or Egypt would affect prices in Kansas and North Dakota but that the meat plant in town was owned by a company in Brazil that slaughtered animals in Australia and distributed food in China.

If there was a single dynamic driving these changes, it was the effort by producers of agricultural goods to seize greater control over the markets in which they participated. Connecting more directly with meat-processing companies that could limit labor costs by locating in small towns was part of that dynamic, but only one among many. The first settlers in the Middle Western states controlled several important aspects of the agricultural production process in which they were engaged. Landownership was vital because it ensured the means with which to produce crops and livestock from year to year and encouraged capital improvements. Farms were small-scale household economies in which a share of the goods produced were also consumed, thus protecting families from having to participate in the market for these necessities. Otherwise, farm producers were largely at the mercy of forces beyond their control.

Not only did they face uncertain weather; they also depended on railroad companies to transport goods and received whatever grain dealers, livestock handlers, and other middlemen were willing to pay. Independent farmers had few alternatives. But they did have some, and over the decades, these became the basis for the agribusiness ventures that were so prominent at the end of the twentieth century.

As independent producers, farmers and ranchers had little ability to shape markets through monopoly practices, the way railroads did, or through unionized collective bargaining. But it is mistaken to think that these were the only ways of controlling markets. Producers largely manage their position in markets by controlling input costs and by stabilizing their own access to materials and supplies. Farm families did this by employing household labor and by hiring surplus laborers from neighboring farms and towns. In some instances, seasonal migrant labor was used, and machines increasingly replaced human labor. Materials and supplies—including seed, feed, animals, and fuel—were the second significant input that needed to be managed, and reliable transportation was the third.

Although household economies played an important role in the management of input costs, their limitations led producers of agricultural goods to develop forms of social organization that transcended the household. One was the corporate or commercial farm that operated for the benefit of investors and controlled production costs through economies of scale in land and labor. Outlawed in some Middle Western states and never popular in others, something resembling commercial farms nevertheless emerged through kin-related partnerships that brought larger landholdings under coordinated control. On a wider scale, farmers' cooperative associations served to provide information about farm practices and markets and as a means of obtaining discounted supplies. These associations sometimes enabled producers to influence markets through government regulations, tariffs, and price-support programs. Towns provided additional mechanisms of influence, serving as outlets for farm produce, as sources of supplies, as lenders, and as occasions for networking and cultivating trust. Vertical integration was the other method of achieving control, especially by bringing producers into closer relationships with suppliers of goods and services and by extending their reach into consumer markets.

Producers used these organizational mechanisms to increasing advantage during the last half of the twentieth century. Commercial feedlots and meat-processing plants grew in number and size. Cooperative associations included larger areas and became affiliated with federated cooperatives that provided a wider range of supplies and increasingly became involved in marketing farm products. Small towns continued to provide services and social interaction, while larger towns developed technical schools, floated bonds, and established utility companies. Vertical integration put feedlots and suppliers of grain and animals into contract agreements with packing companies, which in turn produced packaged food for shipment directly to supermarkets. In the process, producers whose role had once been limited to local communities became part of a profitable network of international businesses.

Yet the story was also replete with irony. As producers sought greater control of the markets in which they participated, they became increasingly involved in marketing directly to consumers and, in so doing, incurred greater exposure to the powerful organizations that shaped consumer preferences. These were the supermarket chains, wholesale food distributors, and discount retailers, whose scope and influence had also risen dramatically during the last decades of the twentieth century. Producers were stronger and better organized than ever before, and yet finding it increasingly necessary to engage in horizontal integration across product lines and having to develop foreign markets in order to compete. In small Middle Western towns, these dynamics were played out in complex relationships among agribusiness firms, workers, service providers, lawmakers, and consumers.

Garden City was an ideal location to view the long-term as well as recent developments in heartland agribusiness. Its economy was based in agriculture from the start, and like other county seats in Kansas, it benefited from serving as a market town for area farmers. In this respect, it was like Smith Center, which also fared better than surrounding towns because it was the county seat. But those were among the few similarities, and the contrasts were more instructive. While Smith Center's population declined during much of the twentieth century, Garden City's grew tenfold. At the turn of the twenty-first century, the diverging histories were abundantly evident. In Smith Center, the nearest McDonald's was sixty miles away, whereas in Garden City, two McDonald's competed with ten other fast-food restaurants. The Sears catalog store in Smith Center closed in 1993, but shoppers in Garden City could choose among Sears, Walmart, Home Depot, Target, and other stores along the extension of Kansas Avenue that joined with U.S. Highways 50, 83, and 400 on the east side. Smith Center's population was aging and ethnically homogeneous; Garden City's was younger and more diverse. Smith Center's transformation involved technological and social adaptations resulting in more highly productive family farms operated by fewer people. Garden City's typified communities at the forefront of the region's large-scale agribusiness developments.

In the 1870s, it seemed unlikely that Garden City would ever become a significantly larger community than Smith Center. Garden City was on the rail line and

Smith Center was not, but with hardly anyone living in Garden City, the train had no reason to stop. Mrs. Fulton sent letters by attaching them to a pole and holding them up for the conductor to snatch as the train roared by. While Smith County and towns in that part of the state attracted settlers quickly, Garden City did not. Freight rates to Kansas City were 25 percent higher to Garden City than to Smith Center. A railroad passenger in 1875 remarked favorably about the activity evident when passing through Wichita, Hutchinson, Great Bend, Larned, and Dodge City but described the settlements after that as "small and unimportant."[4] Skepticism about western Kansas had long been expressed by commentators who viewed it as part of the great American desert. "The country out there will not be settled for a long time, and is not of much particular value," remarked a delegate to the Kansas territorial legislature in the 1850s. It is "a miserable, uninhabited region," declared another, "not at all inviting."[5]

Settlers in Garden City and visitors who spent more time there agreed about its hardships and rarely expressed optimism about its opportunities. A visitor from eastern Kansas wrote, "Never have I been so impressed with the vastness of this western land. It was almost oppressive."[6] A letter to a boys and girls magazine from a girl in Garden City noted how dry it was. "I wish we could have some of the rain and snow you have East," she wrote.[7] An agricultural bulletin noted that "the hopes of the farmers were blasted" by the arid climate. "Many were compelled to sell or abandon their lands or claims and seek employment elsewhere."[8] A woman recalled, "There was nothing to do, nothing to see and nowhere to go, and should we have attempted to go anywhere we would only have become lost, for there were only a few dim trails leading to the claims of a few settlers." Conversations, she said, "always concerned the awfulness of living in such a desert, where the wind and the sun had full sweep."[9]

Over the years, those assessments of the region's climate continued, as residents commented on recurring forty-mile-an-hour winds, hot summers, frigid winters, and an endlessly flat landscape—"very tough living," one remarked; "sort of a Laura Ingalls Wilder existence," said another.[10] Yet there were more favorable assertions, too. The editor of one of the town's first newspapers gave a characteristically positive assessment emphasizing the area's "living verdure" and "great valleys watered and fertilized by the river."[11] A rancher testified in equally glowing terms that "the climate is mild and healthy," adding "I came to this section from Missouri and prefer the climate, the soil and the country here generally for all purposes."[12] "Ere long these plains, now so unattractive and lonesome," a clergyman predicted, "will be covered by vast populations."[13]

Garden City's growth in subsequent decades contrasted sharply with other towns' fates in western Kansas. With a population of 3,171 in 1910, it was already one of the largest towns in the western third of Kansas, and of the thirty-one county seats in that part of the state at the start of the twenty-first century, it was the largest. From 1910 to 1950, all of these towns had grown, and the majority did reasonably well for several more decades. By 1980, only six had lost population since 1950, and all but ten had grown by at least 10 percent. But after that it was a different story. During the quarter century after 1980, only eleven of the towns grew in population while twenty became smaller. The average county seat declined by 15 percent. Garden City grew by 50 percent. Its population in 2005 exceeded 27,000.[14]

The closest competitor in size and influence was Dodge City, fifty-two miles to the southeast. Dodge City's population, which exceeded a thousand by 1880, remained larger than Garden City's until 1970 and over the next three decades almost kept pace with it. The towns' rivalry, which would play a role in their efforts to develop agribusiness, was evident not only in competition for population but also in self-perception. From the start, Garden City defined itself as the more civilized of the two, leaving Dodge City to be known as the wickedest town in Kansas. Garden City took solace in not having been a military garrison in the 1860s or the destination of Texas cattle drovers in the 1870s. It prohibited saloons and whorehouses, had no need for celebrated lawmen like Wyatt Earp or Bat Masterson, and was not known for its boot hill.[15] In 1881, when the governor announced rewards of up to $500 for the arrest and conviction of liquor dealers, distillers, and uncooperative marshals in Dodge City, the drugstores in Garden City were quietly supplying liquor to their customers as a remedy for consumption while the sale of alcoholic beverages remained forbidden. In 1883, when martial law was declared in Dodge City because of a quarrel between two saloon operators who threatened that one or the other would "swallow blood" and "eat dust," a visitor described Garden City as a peaceful town of churchgoers who routinely voted down proposals to open a saloon.[16]

But Garden City's image was never quite as pristine as its residents wished. The national media that found Dodge City wonderfully colorful pictured Garden City as a site of western Kansas peculiarities. In 1889, the *New York Times* titillated readers with news that a gigantic ditch ninety-six miles long had been created near Garden City and that desperate farmers living in comfortless sod houses and dugouts had faith in this scheme for irrigation. A generation later, the *Chicago News* described Garden City residents racing around in automobiles on the open prairie at great speed in search of hapless coyotes. In 1922, the world learned that Garden City had somehow decided to construct the largest concrete swimming pool in the United States. In 1939, wire services announced the slaying of two bank robbers in a downtown melee reminiscent of the Wild West. In 1983 an amused writer noted that Garden City had passed a law against sauntering, spending time idly, or merely "hanging around" within the city limits. And in 1994, a reporter for the *Wichita Eagle* made headlines with news that workers at Garden City had extracted a giant hair ball weighing fifty-five pounds from a cow's belly.[17]

The most publicity the community ever received resulted from the gruesome killing of the Herbert Clutter family in 1959 just west of town near Holcomb. Initial reports portrayed the community merely as "one of the richest wheat areas" in the "fertile Arkansas river valley" and described the Clutters as successful farmers active in civic organizations. Over the next six years, New York writer Truman Capote worked on the book *In Cold Blood*, an instant best-seller that gave the murders much wider attention. In Capote's rendition, the Clutters represented a kind of naive innocence that modern readers in more cosmopolitan places could easily see through. The Clutters were overly rigid, pious, and complacent. Garden City was naive, isolated, filled with citizens too quick to judge and too vengeful to forgive. Subsequent writers described it less as a civilized community and more as a raw, lonely place. "Men, farm houses and windmills become specks against the vast sky," one wrote. "Tumbleweed rustles; Coca-Cola signs endlessly creak." The murders seemed to distill the essence of the place. "Spectacular violence seems appropriate to the empty stage of the plains, as though by such cosmic acts mankind must occasionally signal its presence."[18]

In Cold Blood attracted thousands of readers and moviegoers over the years, giving them an impression of Garden City as a lonesome area far away from any place they had been or could understand. "Garden City and 'In Cold Blood' are inseparable, no matter how much some would wish them not to be," a reporter wrote in 2005. Another reporter found residents reluctant to talk about it. One resident told her the memory was too painful. Another said the murders had left the community fearful and unwelcoming toward strangers. Especially in Holcomb, the reporter noticed that life seemed to have contracted since 1959. The orchard Herbert Clutter planted was gone. The congregation the Clutters attended was smaller. The riverbed near their home was dry.[19]

Although the tragic memory of the Clutters remained, Garden City and the surrounding countryside attracted increasing attention in the last decades of the twentieth century largely for different reasons. One was evident on clear days to airplane passengers flying cross-country at 30,000 feet. For fifteen miles in every direction, the fields inside the squares marked by country roads were round and green. They were inscribed by the huge center-pivot irrigation systems that pumped water up from the Ogallala aquifer. Another was more evident on the ground and was identified by smell more than by sight. These were the vast feeding lots to the north, west, and south of town in which thousands of cattle consumed the silage produced in the fields and awaited their destiny in the slaughterhouses. Yet another was evident in signs in front of the churches—Primera Iglesia Bautista, Iglesia Bautista Nueva Vida, and Mision Christiana, among others—and by the fact that Garden City was home to the only Buddhist temple between Wichita and Denver. When these developments began and how they remade Garden City were questions that illuminated the rising significance of agribusiness in the region.

The country's largest meat-processing plant locating there in 1980 made Garden City the place for scholars and journalists to seek understanding of what it could mean for a community to withstand the impact of phenomenal growth, to become multicultural overnight, and to live among the stench of massive feedlots and near the daily slaughter of thousands of animals. In the late 1980s, the Ford Foundation sent a team of social scientists to see if Garden City would erupt in ethnic violence as had neighborhoods in Los Angeles and Miami. In the early 1990s, journalists from the *New York Times* and the *Washington Post* filed stories about Garden City as the new face of immigrant America. The town's visibility continued a decade later when Eric Schlosser included it in his book *Fast Food Nation*, the best-selling chronicle of Americans' appetite for eating convenience foods and the meat industry that supplied it.[20]

The narrative that emerged from these academic and journalistic accounts emphasized the aftermath of the giant meat plant's opening. The transformation, writers argued, was nothing short of dramatic. Where once there had been a quiet country town, now there was a teeming populace of immigrant meat workers. Finney County, in which Garden City was located, was the fastest-growing county in the state, and it had the largest Hispanic population anywhere in the region. Schools were crowded, streets were jammed, and crime was rising. The intrigue was compounded by what was happening at the meat plant. This was no ordinary venture. It was an efficient killing operation run by Iowa Beef Processors (IBP), the company that had pioneered the transition from high-paying unionized jobs in Kansas City and Chicago to dirt-cheap wages in small towns. IBP's founder had been convicted on charges of conspiring with mob leaders to take over the meat business in New York City, and there were countless charges of worker injuries and abuse. Now Garden City was complicit in this scourge. Its residents had ushered viciousness into their midst and would surely suffer the consequences in rising crime, ethnic strife, and a lower standard of living.

Some of the expected trouble happened, but much did not, leaving writers with two unsolved mysteries. Why had Garden City's residents been so willing to invite IBP into the community in the first place, and having done that, how did they manage to adapt as well as they did? But it was impossible to answer either of these questions as long as the standard narrative began in 1980. With only passing references to the fact that a cattle lot was already present and a few Hispanics had come earlier, there was little with which to frame an account of how agribusiness had begun and what was already in place by the time IBP arrived. Without an understanding of these institutional precedents, it was equally impossible to see that Garden City's residents had more than goodwill to rely on for meeting the challenges of new growth and diversity. For examining the effects of new developments in agribusiness, Garden City provided, as it were, the perfect storm—largest plant, fastest growth, most diversity—and yet its uniqueness posed questions about what exactly could be learned there that applied to other towns or to the rest of the industry. To answer those additional questions, it was necessary to start much earlier than 1980.

In 1878, when Mrs. Fulton decided that it should be called Garden City, the town consisted of only four houses, a general store, and fifteen people. A rival town called Sherlock, six miles west, threatened to upstage it until the residents were able to secure an agreement with the railroad for a siding, station house, and telegraph in 1879. Within a year, forty buildings went up, including two lumberyards and two general stores. There was a blacksmith, a jeweler, a doctor, a lawyer, and a land agent. By 1883, the population stood at four hundred. Three years later, about half the residential lots closest to the business district had houses. The Opera Block on Main Street included the Windsor Hotel and Grand Central Hotel as well as several shops and the theater itself. Closer to the depot, there were five hotels in the first block and another across the street. The Garden City Lumber Company, Kansas Lumber Company, Chicago Lumber Company, and Prairie Lumber Company competed for newcomers' business. Methodist, Presbyterian, Congregational, Christian, and United Brethren churches vied for their attendance. Specialty shops included a cigar store, a billiard hall, and two Chinese laundries. The train trip from Kansas City took a mere eighteen hours. Local boosters arranged excursions promising participants a refund on their return ticket if they decided to stay.[21]

Presaging later developments, much of Finney County around Garden City in the 1880s was in the hands of large ranch companies. The W&R ranch occupied the northeast corner, Foy's and Martin's ranches were closer to Garden City, Bullard's ranch was just south of town, and Knause's was in the northwestern part of the county.[22] The register and receiver at the Garden City land office expressed concern that huge areas were passing into the hands of large cattle and land companies, often through fraudulent transactions.[23] Whether that was true or not, strips of land along the streams provided effective control of unwatered grazing areas much larger in size. "The profits of stock ranches well conducted," a visitor from Vermont wrote in 1882, "are simply immense."[24]

Small-scale crop farming proved more difficult. Although the 1878 season was encouraging for the region's first settlers, a drought in 1879 produced disappointing results. The lack of rainfall also prompted the first experiment with irrigation, a single ditch from the Arkansas River that flowed through town. The following February, an organization calling itself the Garden City Irrigating Company constructed a crude dam four miles west of Garden City and dug an irrigation ditch eight feet wide, two feet deep, and ten miles long at a cost of about $2,000. "The main point has been established," an observer reported to the Kansas Academy of Science that fall. "Water, in sufficient quantities for irrigation, and at moderate cost, can be taken from the Arkansas river by ditches, and carried to fields in the bottom lands in the valley of that river."[25] What the observer might also have noted was that the beginning of cooperative agribusiness ventures in the region had occurred. The following year the Kansas Irrigating Water Power and Manufacturing Company completed a second canal. A few years later, the main irrigation ditch of the Great Eastern Irrigating Company extended twenty-two miles. The Minnehaha Irrigation Company had one the same length. And three more were in operation. Approximately 60,000 acres stood ready for irrigation, and plans were taking shape to add 200,000 more. "There is something fascinating in the idea of every man being his own rain maker," a visitor exclaimed. "The 'windows of Heaven' are nothing to him: he runs the machine himself."[26]

Irrigation was indeed an exciting possibility, but putting it to use on any significant scale lay well in the future. During the 1880s and 1890s, the county's economy suffered a series of setbacks. The weather in 1886 was particularly harsh. A massive blizzard in January claimed the lives of a young mother and two small children ten miles northeast of Garden City. Crops and cattle were frozen. Two years later, drought caused the crops to fail again. "All that remained upon many homesteads to remind one that it had once known home life," a resident recalled, "were slight depressions or piles of sod marking the spots where the settlers' dugouts and shanties had stood." In 1889, only 10 percent of the land in Finney County was officially defined as farmland, and only one-third of that was improved. About 1 percent of the county's land was irrigated. Corn averaged only thirteen bushels an acre; wheat averaged eleven.[27]

Between 1890 and 1900, the total population of Finney County experienced a net increase of only 119 people, confirming the view that this was an unlikely region for farming to prosper.[28] The number of farms remained nearly constant. Farmers planted significantly less corn at the end of the decade than they had at the start and only slightly more wheat. A glowing report published in the *Rocky Mountain News* in 1894 speculated that wheat in Finney County would average twenty to thirty bushels per acre, but the crop came in at only six bushels per acre. Cattle were still the mainstay of the local economy, accounting for nearly four-fifths of total agricultural output. There were almost four times as many cattle in the county in 1899 as in 1889. The total value of livestock soared sevenfold.[29] Yet with high shipping costs to Kansas City or Denver, cattlemen faced increasing competition from ranchers in better locations, and by 1910, the number of cattle in Finney County was half what it was a decade earlier.[30]

In the decade after 1900, irrigation played an increasing role in the county's development. Unlike dryland farming and ranching, irrigation necessitated cooperation and was one of the surest signs that the area would become adept in organizing agribusiness ventures larger than the typical family farm. In 1902, the federal government provided support for irrigation projects through the New-lands Reclamation Act, and a year later, the United States Geological Survey conducted tests of underground water near the Arkansas River. In 1908, pumping stations and a power plant constructed by the Reclamation Service began supplying water to farms on the north side of the river.[31] By 1910, more than 17,000 acres were irrigated, still a far cry from the 260,000 projected a quarter century earlier, but nearly double the acreage in 1900. There were now thirty-two main irrigation ditches, totaling a hundred miles in length. In addition, more than 250 wells had been drilled. In a single decade, total investment in irrigation projects climbed from about $100,000 to more than $1 million, a staggering sum that would have been impossible to raise had it not been for farmers and investors initiating collaborative projects. About a quarter of the county's farmers were irrigating at least part of their land. Cattle accounted for a declining share of total agricultural output, and per-acre yields of wheat and corn were still low, but the number of acres planted rose more than tenfold. The most significant changes were in crops requiring irrigation. More than 3,000 acres were being planted in sugar beets, yielding more than eight tons per acre. Alfalfa hay was being mown and baled from more than 15,000 acres. Forage used to fatten cattle was sown on more than 26,000 acres. Smaller plots were yielding potatoes, sweet potatoes, and onions; and orchards produced in excess of 5,000 bushels of apples, peaches, and plums.[32]

For rural residents, life was more comfortable in 1910 than it had been in 1890, but many continued to face significant challenges. A study conducted in neighboring Ford County, which also straddled the Arkansas River, captured the difficulties. Dirt roads became impassable from drifting snow and heavy rain. "Next-door neighbors are often a mile or more apart," "'town' may be anywhere up to 20 miles away," and "from many places out on the plains there is hardly a dwelling in sight in any direction." On farms operated by tenants (a quarter in Finney County at the time) houses were "poorly built and in a wretched condition." Fewer than one family in five had running water in the house. Although medical care was generally available, and most births were attended by a physician, follow-up care for mothers and infants was rare. Hardly any of the women received help with daily chores before or after giving birth, and they often had one or two small children needing attention. Besides cooking for her own family, the typical farm wife prepared meals for a hired man at least half the year and for crews of half a dozen or more during the three weeks of harvest each summer. "Prosperity comes hard on the farmer's wife," the study concluded, "because prosperity here means practically always a larger farm and more wheat, and therefore more men to board for a longer time."[33]

The shifting patterns in agriculture, especially the growth of irrigation near the river, were reflected more clearly in Garden City itself. The town's population grew from 1,590 in 1900 to 3,171 in 1910. Additions during the 1890s included a bicycle repair shop, a bookstore, a Baptist church, an African Methodist Episcopal church, and an electric light plant run by a cooperative association. There was also a small community of Mexican-Americans who had come from Colorado, New Mexico, and Mexico to tend the irrigation ditches and do stoop labor in the fields. During the next decade, the electric light company expanded and added telephone service. An African Baptist church joined the other congregations, a People's Mission provided services to low-wage workers, and the Mexican Rooming House offered lodging to itinerant workers. The population included nearly 200 African-Americans and more than 100 Mexican-Americans. New specialty shops included a photography studio, a piano store, several gent's furnishings stores, and a motion picture theater. Outside of town was the United Well Works, which specialized in irrigation wells, pumps, and supplies. Another recent addition was the large United States Sugar and Land Company beet sugar factory, constructed in 1906 at a cost of $800,000. The plant, a magnificent five-story structure located along the Santa Fe tracks, employed 300 workers and was the true start of Garden City's involvement in agribusiness.[34]

The sugar plant was an early example of commercial agriculture and of vertical integration, bringing growers and manufacturing into a contractual relationship. It was an odd addition to the otherwise flat, sparsely populated, and largely barren landscape of western Kansas, but it prefigured many of the developments that would later give rise to the meat-processing industry. Water was one of the decisive factors. Sugar beet technology, developed in the 1890s by promoter George W. Swink in Rocky Ford, Colorado, an Arkansas River town 170 miles upstream from Garden City, required irrigation to supply water in exact amounts at the right times during the growing season. Locating a processing plant close to fields reduced transportation costs and spoilage, but a sufficient number of farmers had to contract with the company for a plant to be profitable. Swink also believed firmly in importing Asians and Mexicans to do the work that in his view was "pretty hard to get our American fellows to do." The feasibility of beet production was demonstrated in the 1890s at plants in Grand Island and Norfolk, Nebraska, and by the formation of the American Beet Sugar Company, which opened a factory in Rocky Ford in 1900. Besides water, a favorable political climate was also an important ingredient. In 1899, the Kansas legislature approved a measure authorizing towns to vote bonds for the construction of sugar factories, and a year later, the federal McKinley Act allocated a bounty of two cents a pound on domestic sugar and established protective tariffs against competition from imported cane sugar. The United States Sugar and Land Company was a syndicate of farmers and investors headed by Colorado mining tycoon Spencer Penrose. It controlled thirty thousand acres of irrigated land, including two of the five major canals, borrowed money from the town, oversaw the factory, and imported immigrants to work in the fields.[35]

From 1910 to 1930, irrigation, sugar, truck farming, dryland farming, and cattle facilitated continuing growth in Garden City. Population in the town doubled to more than 6,000 and in the county to more than 11,000. Both the number of farms and their average size increased. Overall acres devoted to farming doubled, as did the number of improved acres. The number of large farms with 500 acres or more tripled, and the value of machinery multiplied by a factor of ten. Mechanization was especially important in the production of grain. Corn rose by more than 250 percent from 1910 to 1925 and then tripled again by 1929. Wheat production increased even more rapidly, rising seventeenfold from 1910 to 1925 and another 250 percent by 1929. Another reason for better crops was more effective insect control as demonstrated in 1920 when, fearing a grasshopper invasion, the local Farm Bureau purchased fifteen tons of bran, fifteen barrels of syrup, $125 worth of lemons, and nearly a ton of arsenic and distributed them to farmers throughout the county.[36] The growing importance of irrigation was evident in acreage involved, which doubled, and in crops produced on irrigated land. Whereas 28,000 tons of sugar beets were produced in 1910, more than 45,000 tons were grown in 1925. As much alfalfa was grown in 1925 as in 1910 on about half as many acres. Irrigation also underwent a transformation as pumps increasingly took the place of canals.

The United States Sugar and Land Company expanded as acreage and tonnage of sugar beets in Finney County increased, but its independence from large conglomerates proved disadvantageous in the long run, just as would later be true for smaller companies in the poultry- and meat-processing industries. The plant at Rocky Ford was built by the Oxnard Construction Company, which was owned by Henry Oxnard, who also operated two plants in Nebraska and two in California. Under Oxnard's leadership, the American Beet Sugar Company constructed additional plants in California and in 1905 opened one in Lamar,

Colorado, only a hundred miles west of Garden City. At the Lamar plant and another one at Las Animas, which opened in 1907, Oxnard implemented vertical integration by purchasing large tracts of land, employing immigrant labor, and raising cattle and hogs as well as beets. About the same time, the Great Western Sugar Company built seventeen factories, including several in the richly irrigated area around Greeley and Longmont, north of Denver. Holly Sugar and Amalgamated Sugar each constructed multiple plants as well. Eventually, plants spread to other areas, including Iowa and Minnesota. By the late 1920s, farmers near Mayville, North Dakota, were growing beets for a factory at Grand Forks that would later be renovated and enlarged by the American Crystal Sugar Company. As long as the industry kept expanding, the Garden City facility remained competitive, but the market for beet sugar was gradually replaced by cane sugar, causing contraction and closings among the smaller plants. After being purchased by Holly Sugar, which acquired it for water rights and access to growers, the Garden City plant ceased operating in 1956, forcing the remaining growers to truck produce twenty miles to beet dumps at Ritchel and Lakin, but also creating an opening for the cattle industry.[37]

Prior to the Great Depression, Garden City had become involved in another effort by farm producers to compete more effectively in the expanding livestock and commodities markets. That was the cooperative movement. Although the electricity company and some of its irrigation projects were set up as cooperatives, the first general purpose cooperative in Garden City was the Garden City Cooperative Equity Exchange, chartered in 1920 to assist in marketing grain and securing supplies, following a failed attempt in 1901 to organize a cooperative grocery and feed store and a short-lived effort to form a farmers' exchange in 1915.[38] A national survey conducted by the United States Department of Agriculture in 1915 identified 5,424 cooperatives with 651,186 members and a total business volume of approximately $636 million. By 1929, the number of cooperatives nationwide more than doubled to 12,000, memberships exceeded 3.1 million, and gross sales reached $2.5 billion.[39] Upwards of 90 percent were marketing cooperatives that handled grain, livestock, and dairy products, benefiting producers by reducing shipping costs, distributing profits to members, and constructing elevators and other facilities. Cooperatives also ran milling operations that ground feed for livestock and, as tractors came into greater use, supplied gasoline and motor oil at discount prices.

Cooperatives were attractive because they permitted farmers and ranchers to benefit from economies of scale without compromising the integrity of individual ownership or entailing added financial risks. The rules were simple and conformed to federal laws regulating cooperatives. For a modest fee, farmers became members, and every member had a single vote no matter how large or small their landholdings might be. At an annual meeting, members voted for a board of directors and approved major business decisions. Profits were used for capital expansion, and remaining dividends were distributed to members in proportion to the amount of business they had conducted through the cooperative. Members purchased supplies at discounts made possible because the association bought from wholesalers in bulk, but members were also free to buy or sell to other firms. Cooperatives gave producers a way to compete more effectively with privately owned grain elevator and distribution chains, such as the Cargill conglomerate that began in the late 1870s in Minnesota and by the late 1880s controlled more than fifty elevators throughout western Minnesota, eastern South Dakota, and eastern North Dakota, including six near Mayville in Traill County.[40] Cooperatives gave producers greater bargaining power in negotiating contracts and shipping rates with railroads and after passage in 1921 of the Volstead-Capper Act, which exempted voluntary agricultural cooperative associations from antitrust laws, became the accepted alternative to corporate farming. Although most cooperatives were locally organized and served farmers in their immediate vicinity, they increasingly joined one another and became part of larger federations as well, which enabled them to purchase supplies in wider markets, develop their own products, and play a larger role in long-distance trade.[41]

In February 1929, the Garden City association, by then among the largest cooperatives in the state, became one of the first to sign an oil and gas contract with and purchase substantial stock in Union Oil, a new wholesale petroleum cooperative. Union Oil was the brainchild of Howard A. Cowden, a farmer's son and former schoolteacher who headed the Polk County Farmers Association in southwestern Missouri. Cowden pioneered the region's cooperative movement by pooling farm orders for supplies, selling eggs cooperatively in Kansas City at better prices, and establishing cold storage facilities for eggs and cream. Union Oil emerged as Cowden was able to secure the Missouri Farmers Association's contract for gasoline and oil previously held by Standard Oil. The cooperative purchased oil from Conoco and other suppliers and distributed it at discount prices to farmer-members. In 1935, it created the Consumers Cooperative Association and expanded its line to more than two hundred Co-op products, ranging from automotive accessories to paint and twine. In 1939, it launched a cooperative refinery at Phillipsburg, thirty miles west of Smith Center, in an attempt to stabilize its petroleum supplies through vertical integration.[42]

Although the Phillipsburg facility was at the northern edge of the region's most productive oil pools, the company purchased wells and leases in sufficient number to become a successful independent oil supplier by the end of

World War II. The refinery outlasted all but one of the other independents that formed in the 1930s. The remaining competitor was the Globe Oil refinery at McPherson, Kansas, which was purchased by five regional farm cooperatives in 1943 when wartime shortages made it difficult for farmers to acquire fuel. That refinery bought oil from leases in Rice, McPherson, and Stafford counties, built pipelines to Nebraska and Iowa, and was where Carl Swenson, the young man from central Kansas whose family farm was too small to earn a living, began working in the 1950s. It was eventually purchased by the same association that ran the refinery at Phillipsburg and supplied gasoline and oil to farmers and ranchers at Garden City.[43]

The connections cooperatives forged were seldom any deeper than attending an annual meeting and knowing that many in one's community were also members, and yet, what they lacked in intensity they made up for in scope. It was through these agricultural cooperatives that sugar beet farmers and cattle ranchers near Garden City had ties with fellow producers in eastern Colorado and Nebraska and with refinery workers in Phillipsburg and McPherson, who in turn were connected with oil well servicers in Stafford and Lyons and with egg producers in southwestern Missouri and wheat growers in North Dakota. The "Co-op" sign atop countless grain elevators was a symbol of both common participation and trust. It was also evidence of the growing interdependence that successful agricultural production required. Through layers of federated cooperative associations, producers created the organizational capacity on which subsequent agribusinesses would be built.

Like the rest of western Kansas, Finney County suffered during the 1930s from drought, dust storms, and poor crops. Rainfall that normally ranged from fifteen to twenty inches a year shrank to less than ten inches in 1934 and 1935 and again in 1937 and 1939. Population in the county and in Garden City ceased growing, and the number of farms declined. Wheat harvested in 1939 totaled less than one-fifth of the 1929 total. Corn declined from more than 500,000 bushels to about 2,000. Farmers planted 50 percent less sorghum and harvested only one-third as much. The number of cattle dropped from more than 25,000 to about 10,000. Declining prices for grain and livestock further reduced farm income. Total output in 1939 was valued at only 24 percent of the 1929 figure. Just south of Garden City, Haskell County was where research showed that farmers had prospered enough in the 1920s to build new schools, purchase automobiles, and drive into Garden City to shop and attend motion pictures. In the 1930s, a quarter of Haskell county's residents moved away, leaving farms untended or easily preyed upon by land speculators. Still, Garden City fared better than many of its neighbors. To the east, Ingalls lost a third of its population, and to the south Satanta declined even more. Garden City was three to five times larger than any of the surrounding county seats except Dodge City. In 1939, Garden City had twenty-seven filling stations, and there were nine more in the county. That compared with only seven in all of Haskell county. There were fourteen automobile dealerships, twelve clothing stores, and twenty eating establishments. The farmers cooperative had become the Garden City Consumers Cooperative in 1936. Santa Fe trains still provided daily passenger service, and Garden City's airfield was one of the regular stops for flights between Chicago and Los Angeles.[44]

Expectations that Garden City would become an important business center flourished after World War II. In 1948, officials announced plans for a new hospital that would serve a population of 25,000 by the end of the decade. A theater chain planned an office complex touted as the most ambitious commercial construction project in the town's history. This "dying dust bowl city," a reporter for the *New York Times* observed, was on the verge of becoming the "capital of a new industrial empire." Standard Oil of Indiana was reported to have chosen Garden City as the location for a revolutionary $80 million synthetic petroleum plant that would bring natural gas from the Hugoton field and combine it with oxygen and water to form gasoline.[45] But to the community's dismay, the plant never materialized. On April 19, 1948, Stanolind executives quietly announced that plans for a plant and housing development in Garden City were being shelved. Speculation continued that a plant might be built at Hugoton and a competitor named Carthage-Hydrocol did construct a plant at Brownsville, Texas, in 1950, where it began experimenting with what was known as the Fischer-Tropsch synthesis. But before the plant at Hugoton could be built, Carthage-Hydrocol determined that the process was a failure and ceased operations. The discovery of massive crude-oil fields in the Middle East in 1951 and a rise of natural gas prices in 1953 effectively ended all hope of a synthetic fuel plant being constructed at Garden City—at least for several decades.[46]

The chances of Garden City becoming a large agribusiness hub were rooted more firmly than anything else in the region's emerging livestock industry, which in turn reflected the county's agricultural and commercial developments of the preceding half century, including the difficulties of dryland crop farming, the cooperation involved in irrigation projects, and the lessons learned from sugar manufacturing. These developments demonstrated not only that profits could be made but also that an infrastructure of organizations other than the traditional family farm was necessary. By the time cattle feeding and meat processing became a significant part of the town's economy, Garden City was already well organized and well connected with producers and markets throughout the region through the Consumers Cooperative. It had experience with commercial agriculture through the United States Sugar and Land Company, and its farmers knew the necessity of working together to launch irrigation projects. It also understood that tariffs and government regulations could help or hinder and that it was sometimes necessary for the town itself to invest in business initiatives.

The path leading most directly to the location of the country's largest beef-processing plant in Garden City three decades later was the establishment of a commercial feedlot near town by entrepreneur Earl C. Brookover in 1951. Brookover grew up just north of Finney County near Scott City where he learned the cattle business from his father and then attended Kansas State University prior to settling in Garden City in 1947. During the 1950s, the Brookover operation grew quickly into one of the largest feedlots of its kind, benefiting at first from low grain prices and between 1952 and 1957 from drought that forced ranchers lacking sufficient pastureland to board cattle at the feedlot.[47] Brookover's operation was emphasized by nearly every writer who chronicled the rise of Garden City's packing industry. In that rendition, available livestock was the determining factor. But of course, there was more to it than that.

In 1950, almost twenty-six million cattle and calves were being raised in scattered locations across the nine heartland states. Iowa had 4.5 million, and Kansas and Nebraska each had 3.5 million. Counties with ample pastureland were generally the ones with more cattle, especially in Nebraska and Kansas. Finney County ranked twelfth among the state's 105 counties in total pastureland. But because of its arid climate and limited grazing capacity, the county ranked eighty-first in number of cattle and calves. Butler County near Wichita had four times as many, and Lyon County around Emporia had nearly three times as many. These were grassland counties in the Kansas Flint Hills, where ranchers had been successfully raising cattle for three-quarters of a century.[48]

In 1954, Finney County still ranked low (seventy-fifth) in number of cattle, but the emerging importance of feedlots was evident in the fact that it ranked fifteenth in value of cattle sold. By 1964, it rose to fourth, surpassing Butler and rivaling Lyon. Brookover was fattening several thousand cattle bought from ranchers in surrounding counties and in Oklahoma and fed with hay and grain grown on irrigated land. Other feeding operations included the Reeve Cattle Company southwest of Garden City, the Hitch feedyard across the state line in Oklahoma, Holly Cattle and Land Company to the west in Colorado, and Sublette Feeders where Paul Brown, the Stafford County oil-well servicer's son who settled in Haskell County after World War II, began feeding cattle in the 1950s and would build his "Cattle Empire" into one of the largest in the nation with a capacity of over 100,000 head.[49]

Brown attributed his success to irrigation, which provided the hay and grain his feedlot needed, and sugar beets, which he continued to raise after the plant in Garden City shut down and found profitable in years when cattle feeding was not. This was increasingly true throughout the region as center-pivot irrigation systems watered larger areas and as feedlots developed in their vicinity. Although there had been no statistical correlation between the two in the early 1950s, the value of cattle sold in Kansas and Nebraska counties with more than ten thousand acres under irrigation was about one-sixth greater in 1964 than in counties with less irrigation, and about 50 percent greater among counties in Oklahoma. What could be grown with irrigation was even more important. It made sense that hay was one of these, but sugar beets was too. Indeed, the strongest predictor of how much a county earned from selling cattle in the mid-1960s was the tonnage of hay and sugar beets it was already raising in the mid-1950s.[50]

The relationship among hay, sugar beets, irrigation, and cattle feeding was clearest in the area around Greeley, Colorado, where Warren Monfort and his son Kenneth pioneered an agribusiness arrangement that surpassed Brookover's in Garden City and eventually played a large role in shaping the meat industry, including in Garden City itself. Like Garden City but with even greater success, Greeley was a proving ground for irrigation almost as soon as it was settled. Located in the Platte Valley near the front range of the Rocky Mountains, its rainfall and water supply were significantly more abundant than in western Kansas. It enjoyed the further advantage of having been established as a colony of settlers who regarded themselves as a cooperative enterprise from the start.[51] By 1930, more than 82,000 acres in Weld County were in sugar beets, four times as much as in any other county in the state, and the Great Western Sugar Company plants at Greeley, Loveland, Longmont, and several smaller towns were processing more than a million tons of beets annually. Warren Monfort began feeding cattle that year, purchasing corn at Depression-era prices and using sugar beet by-products for roughage. By the early 1950s, Kenneth Monfort was trucking cattle to Greeley from ranches throughout western Nebraska, southern Wyoming, and eastern Colorado.[52]

Packing plants were attracted to Monfort's operation because its scale ensured a stable year-round supply of even-quality beef. But in 1960, when negotiations with a plant in Denver broke down, the Monfort company purchased a slaughterhouse in Greeley and within a few years was doing its own meat processing. Vertical integration reduced transportation and labor costs and enabled the company to grow significantly during the 1960s. As part of that expansion, Monfort bought into a feedlot in western Kansas in 1963, giving the company an additional source of cattle in that location. By the end of the decade, Monfort was one of the largest agribusiness firms in the Middle West, annually slaughtering more than 300,000 cattle and 600,000 lambs and earning revenue of $157.6 million. The Monfort operation demonstrated the advantages of locating where cooperative irrigation networks and sugar manufacturing provided an infrastructure for commercial agribusiness. It also showed that immigrant and itinerant farm laborers could be hired at relatively low cost.[53]

On a smaller scale, that was a lesson producers in Garden City were learning, as well. In 1963, a cooperative of 150 ranchers and feedlot owners formed the Producer Packing Company of Garden City, with a goal of processing approximately 50,000 cattle a year. This was not the first time meat processing had been attempted locally. Prior to World War II—when as many as twenty-five to thirty train cars loaded with cattle left Garden City every day for slaughter in Kansas City, Denver, or Chicago—Swift and Company operated a local egg and poultry plant in a three-story 40,000-square-foot building in Garden City, and the Walls Packing Company slaughtered beef for local markets. Both had gone out of business, though, by the early 1950s. The new Producer Packing Company was able to draw on a larger supply of feedlot cattle, work cooperatively with feedlot owners, and utilize workers from the declining sugar industry. Construction began in November 1964, and the plant opened in October 1965 with a payroll of 400. Its dedication ceremonies were sponsored by the Consumers Cooperative Association.[54]

But expansion of the meat-processing industry through vertical integration nearly came to a halt in the mid-1960s because of concern that these arrangements would reduce competition and lead to higher prices for consumers. Worries arose principally from developments in the poultry industry that analysts considered likely in beef and pork processing as well. In the early 1930s, a decade after Howard A. Cowden began helping egg producers in southwest Missouri secure better prices in Kansas City, a farm-bred truck driver named John Tyson was hauling chickens from northwest Arkansas to Kansas City and figuring out a different way to gain a stronger position in the market. Tyson not only began trucking more often and over longer distances to St. Louis and Chicago as well as Kansas City, but also purchased baby chicks and put his drivers to work on slow days grinding feed. By the late 1940s, Swift, Armour, and Swanson had located killing plants in northwest Arkansas, and Tyson was well positioned to provide live birds. In 1952, Tyson Feed and Hatchery was producing about 12,000 chickens a week. Five years later, the company had its own poultry-processing plant and feed mill, held contracts with numerous local growers and commercial hatcheries, and produced ten million broilers annually. Critics would later argue that mass production harmed poultry and yielded inferior meat, but consumers were unconcerned. They preferred a "consistent standard product," one farmer recalled, to something that "came out of an old henhouse" with "mites and manure" on it. With good reason, small producers and legislators feared that the poultry industry was rapidly being taken over by Tyson and a few other large companies that would control supplies and dictate prices.[55]

Through the consent decree of 1922, in which the largest packing firms responded to the Packers and Stockyards Act of 1921 by agreeing to divest holdings in stockyards, concentration of the meatpacking industry by the four largest firms—Swift, Armour, Wilson, and Cuddihy—gradually diminished from approximately two-thirds in 1925 to 41 percent in 1947 and then declined further to only 31 percent in 1963. In that year, the top twenty firms accounted for only 54 percent of total value added in the industry. The single most important factor in the rise of smaller independent companies was lower labor costs at nonunion plants. A study of slaughtering costs showed that two-thirds of the average cost was labor and that nonunion rates were approximately 20 percent lower than union rates. Additional savings of up to 25 percent were obtained in larger assembly-line plants that processed more head per hour. None of that suggested that meatpacking was again on the verge of becoming concentrated. The concern was rather that vertical integration of packing plants with feedyards would result in concentration, the way packers' control of stockyards had prior to 1922.[56]

Congressional hearings in 1957 and 1966 about possible revisions of the Packers and Stockyards Act illuminated the changing roles of cattle producers, feedyard owners, cooperative associations, packing firms, and wholesale food distributors. The 1957 hearings emphasized the government's rising difficulties in regulating the rapidly growing meatpacking industry—including its 2,300 packing firms, 2,000 livestock dealers, and 439 stockyards—but evoked nearly unanimous agreement from cattlemen's and livestock associations, Farm Bureau representatives, and the powerful American Meat Institute that the industry was in no danger of being monopolized by major packers and that current monitoring by the Department of Agriculture should remain unchanged and not be transferred to the Federal Trade Commission. The tenor of the 1966 hearings, held in Des Moines, Iowa, with Representative Graham Purcell of Texas presiding, was quite different. These hearings considered a bill introduced by the freshman Democratic Congressman Bert Bandstra from southern Iowa, with support from the Iowa Farmers Union, to prohibit packing companies from operating their own feedyards. The hearings were prompted by concerns from small livestock producers that the industry was becoming dominated once again by large firms that were vertically integrated through contract arrangements and direct ownership of large feedyards. The bill failed to pass, and Bandstra lost his seat in the House that fall, but the hearings drew widespread attention and revealed how the industry was changing.[57]

One of the witnesses testifying against the bill was Ken Monfort, who spoke not only as president of the Monfort Packing Company but also as a director of the Colorado Cattle Feeders Association, as a representative in the Colorado legislature, and on behalf of the Western States Meat Packers Association. It was clear, he told the subcommittee, that the legislation "would force us to either sell our packing plant to someone else or to shut the plant down," which would be devastating to its 450 employees and detrimental to Greeley's economy. Besides that, he argued, packer-feeding integration was beneficial to the industry—and ultimately to consumers—because it assured packers the steady supply of high-quality animals they needed and opened opportunities for independent feedyards in their vicinity, such as the ones that supplied 35 percent of the cattle Monfort slaughtered. Although he conceded that things might be different in Iowa, Monfort argued that feeder-packer integration in Colorado did not suppress cattle prices. "We have ten times as much money invested in inventory of cattle in our feedlot as we have invested in our packing business," which he said gave him a stake in a higher market.[58]

While Monfort's and other feeder-packers' opposition was predictable, the shifting position of farmers organizations and large cooperative associations had become ambiguous by the mid-1960s. Those who testified voiced concern that vertical integration reduced competition and lowered prices for farm producers, but they also expressed ambivalence about government intervention in the free markets they favored on principle and found it difficult to say where the line should be drawn between small and large producers. The latter was particularly vexing because farmers and farm cooperatives increasingly held stock in packing companies and would be banned from doing so if they also fed livestock. The influential Iowa Farm Bureau, which represented more than 113,000 farm families, exemplified the dilemma. On the one hand, it acknowledged the threat posed by large meat packers feeding their own livestock, but on the other hand, it opposed Bandstra's bill because many of its members had contracts with packers or with feeders owned by packers or with cooperatives engaged in packing. Faced with uncertain markets, farmers saw these contractual arrangements as a source of stable prices.

Estimates suggested that only 5 to 6 percent of the beef processed in 1966 came from feedlots owned by packing companies—which gave opponents further cause to argue that legislation was unnecessary. It might be sufficient, they suggested, to encourage packers and feeders to remain separate voluntarily. But Bandstra expressed doubts, likening the situation to prosecuting hog thieves when he was a country attorney. "I wished they wouldn't do it and that they would agree voluntarily to cut that out. I never got a contract whereby they agreed they would no longer make midnight raids on some of the unsuspecting hog lots down there. And I am afraid we are somewhat in the same position with the packers."[59] The packer that most concerned him was Iowa Beef Packers (IBP)—the emerging firm that would come to Garden City at the end of the next decade.

IBP was incorporated in 1960 by Currier Holman and A. D. Anderson, entrepreneurs with experience at Swift who saw the potential in new meatpacking technology and plant locations. A year later, near the small town of Denison (population 4,930) in western Iowa, they constructed a large one-story plant that lowered the cost and time involved in shifting beef carcasses up and down the traditional five-story plants in Chicago, St. Louis, and Kansas City. The location would later seem novel to writers who compared it with the big-city plants of earlier in the century, but Denison was a logical choice in many respects. It was the location of the Crawford County Packing Company, which Howard Cowden had purchased a year earlier for the Consumers Cooperative Association with plans to be used as a large hog-slaughtering facility. It also had good rail connections and was near Ida Grove, Iowa, where a new feed mill had recently been built. The plant's distinctiveness lay in its adoption of the principles of a Ford assembly line—though more appropriately termed a *dis*assembly line. Workers killed each animal as it entered the plant, then attached the carcass to a moving chain that passed other workers who separated meat from bones and by-products. The process, which took only thirty-two minutes from live animal to freezer, introduced economies of scale and enabled unskilled workers to perform tasks that were previously done by skilled meat cutters and butchers. The plant also benefited from being in nonunion territory.[60] In 1965 word spread that IBP planned to have its own feedlot at Irvington, Iowa, where it would feed 50,000 to 100,000 head of cattle. "What is going to happen," Congressman Bandstra asked, "as far as a free market is concerned?"[61]

What did happen was that IBP grew, other companies adopted its methods, and the packing industry became more concentrated as it expanded and brought agribusiness to new locations. In 1967, IBP opened a larger plant in Dakota City, Nebraska, near the Sioux City stockyards and over the next decade added plants at West Point, Nebraska; Emporia, Kansas; and locations in Texas, Idaho, and Washington state. These plants introduced what became known as the boxed-beef revolution, in which trimmed cuts of meat were vacuum-packed for direct shipment to supermarkets, thereby substantially reducing shipping costs. It was hard to deny that the IBP strategy was a good business plan on economic grounds, but analysts expressed concern about its effects on workers, communities, and competition. In 1969, an antitrust suit blocked IBP from acquiring additional plants, and labor disputes at the Dakota City facility a few months later resulted in a strike that included violence and extensive property damage. Contacts between IBP founder Holman and underworld figures in New York City during the same period led to the company and Holman being indicted on charges of bribery and conspiracy.[62] Meanwhile, concentration of boxed-beef production among the four largest firms increased, meat prices rose, and communities like Denison, Iowa, faced growing costs of providing social services for an expanding population.[63]

Packing plants had reason enough to locate near feedlots in small communities where labor was cheap and unions were weak, but it was less evident why some communities were eager to play host. One theory held that small Middle Western towns were in such desperate shape economically and demographically that they were ready to do almost anything to survive. That view was reinforced by evidence of population decline and by stories about communities offering companies lavish tax-relief packages. Another theory was that large companies picked the smallest, most economically depressed communities because it was easier to turn them into single-company towns where whatever the plant decided would carry the day. In reality, Garden City illustrated a more complex relationship.

The arrival in December 1980 of IBP, which by then stood for Iowa Beef Processors, did result in population growth and an immediate housing shortage. From a population of just over 23,000 in 1979, Finney County grew by 25 percent to nearly 29,000 in 1983 and surpassed 33,000 in 1990.[64] But it was untrue that Finney County had been experiencing a population slump before IBP arrived. Population had, in fact, risen every year since 1969, for a net increase of 24 percent during the decade prior to IBP's arrival. Arguments about towns needing agribusiness to prop up faltering economies did not apply, either. Average wage and salary disbursements in Finney County had risen steadily at a rate of approximately 2 percent annually from 1969 to 1979, as had per capita personal income.[65] To the extent that a slump was evident, it was within the beef industry itself, where prices remained lower in 1977 than in 1973 and fell in 1978 from $63 per hundredweight to $49 as a result of the Carter administration's easing of restrictions on imports, in which low output forced a temporary closing of the other Garden City plant just six months before the IBP plant opened.[66]

What did pertain in Garden City was the presence of a significant commercial infrastructure that could readily sustain the introduction of an additional meat-processing facility. By 1970, Finney County was home to nine commercial feedlots with more than 1,000 cattle each, five of which handled more than 10,000 cattle, and in total was sending 100,000 cattle to market annually. In the nine surrounding counties, there were twenty-seven feedlots with at least 1,000 cattle each. Two years later, the Ingalls Feed Yard east of Garden City increased its capacity from 30,000 to 40,000. By 1978, total sales of cattle and calves in Finney County exceeded 300,000. Meanwhile, the Sunflower Electric Cooperative completed a $16 million power plant, significantly expanding the capacity of electricity available for irrigation pumps, and Northern Natural Gas increased its production of natural gas. In 1972, American Crystal Sugar, the multistate conglomerate now operating the sugar plant at Rocky Ford, Colorado, closed its beet dumps at Ritchel and Lakin, effectively forcing beet growers to shift production into hay, grain, and silage. As population edged upward, Garden City merchants constructed a new shopping center that included a 50,000-square-foot ALCO store in place of the Duckwall's that had done business on Main Street since 1919. The Garden City Co-op was part of the Consumers Cooperative Association, which operated six grain elevators in the county, and the Producers Packing Company had merged with Farmland Industries. By the time IBP arrived, Finney County was home to 744 business establishments.[67]

The relevant infrastructure extended well beyond Garden City itself, giving IBP the ability to play one community against another in bargaining for incentives. The two nearest competitors were Garden City's longtime rival, Dodge City, to the east in Ford County, and Liberal, seventy miles to the south in Seward County. Dodge City, with a 1980 population of 18,000, was the home of the Hy-Plains Beef packing plant, and Liberal, with a population of almost 15,000, was the location of an independent packing plant established by the Jacobson family in 1968 and currently operated by National Beef. The plants' annual slaughter capacities were 250,000 and 400,000, respectively, and expansion at Dodge City was expected to give it a capacity of approximately one million within a few years. Both were surrounded by feedlots and had an ample supply of irrigated land, grain, cooperative grain elevators, and trucking companies. IBP could easily have opted for one of these locations.

The alternative that IBP officials considered most seriously was Lamar, Colorado, the town a hundred miles to the west that had pioneered irrigation from the Arkansas River and had developed a sugar beet industry similar to Garden City's. Lamar's distance from the three Kansas towns with packing plants made it a better location in this respect, giving it primary access to more than one million cattle in southeastern Colorado, western Kansas, and the Oklahoma panhandle. Like Garden City, Lamar had the further advantage of being near several large commercial feedlots, including the 50,000-capacity Colorado Beef Producers feedlot, the 40,000-capacity Lamar Feedyard, the 55,000-capacity Foxly feedlot, and more than twenty others with a total capacity of more than 250,000.[68] Small packers in the region were concerned that IBP would undercut their ability to purchase cattle in sufficient numbers to stay in business and lobbied strenuously against the plant. Had the supply of livestock been the only consideration, Lamar might well have secured the plant. But other factors favored Garden City. Colorado meat packers, having initiated strikes at the Monfort plant in 1970 and 1974, were successfully organized through the United Food and Commercial Workers union and at the time IBP was considering its new location were anticipating another strike, which went into effect a few months later and kept the Greeley plant shut for two years. The possibility of that happening at Lamar, coupled with IBP's contentious labor history in Nebraska, made southwest Kansas, where union organizing had been less effective, more attractive. Average employee costs for Colorado packers were $12 per hour, whereas IBP expected costs at its new plant to be no more than the rate at its Dakota City plant, which was less than $8 an hour.[69] A second consideration was that Garden City, with a population two and a half times the size of Lamar, had more of the supplemental organizations needed to support an additional labor force of 2,000 and their families. Garden City had twice as many business firms and three times as many manufacturing establishments as Lamar. A final consideration was the possibility of receiving more favorable tax incentives in Kansas than in Colorado.

Public hearings in 1979 to permit rezoning for the IBP plant led Garden City residents who knew the drawbacks of living near feedlots and meat-processing facilities to express concerns about odor, traffic congestion, and hikes in utility rates and taxes. Community leaders who saw possibilities for business expansion through population growth nevertheless voiced overwhelming approval.[70] To sweeten the deal, the city offered $3.5 million in tax relief and helped raise $100 million through industrial revenue bonds.[71] Construction began that fall on a 670-acre tract west of Garden City near Holcomb, and the plant opened a year later with an initial payroll of two hundred. As the plant increased to full capacity, employment grew steadily, reaching 2,500 in 1985. In 1982, the Farmland plant south of town reopened under the name of Kansas Beef with 400 employees and two years later, as a subsidiary of Val-Agri, expanded to 825 employees. Overall manufacturing in the county shot up from 1,800 employees in 1981 to 3,200 in 1983 and exceeded 4,100 in 1985. The two plants produced more than one billion pounds of beef that year.[72]

Garden City was among dozens of Middle Western towns that participated in the agribusiness expansion that occurred between the early 1960s and mid-1980s. These were the years in which IBP and other large firms reshaped the food-products industry through vertical integration, combining close contractual ties to commercial feedlots and poultry farms with low-wage plants in which animals were slaughtered and meat was processed into case-ready packages for shipment to wholesalers and supermarket chains. By 1985, more than six hundred meat- and poultry-processing plants were located in 314 (41 percent) of the counties in the nine Middle Western states. Missouri and Iowa each had more than one hundred, while Arkansas, Kansas, Minnesota, Nebraska, and Oklahoma each had more than fifty. Many of these plants were small facilities under independent management and operated with relatively few employees. One quarter had fewer than four employees and half had fewer than twenty. But there were forty-nine large plants, each with more than 500 employees, and twenty-one of these had more than 1,000 employees. The plants with more than 500 employees were located in or near forty-five towns. Sixteen of the large plants were in Arkansas, eleven were in Iowa, six were in Nebraska, six were in Kansas, five were in Minnesota, four were in Missouri, and one was in South Dakota.[73]

Towns with large meat-processing plants were certainly small compared with earlier locations in Kansas City and Chicago, but given the fact that three-quarters of Middle Western towns in 1980 had fewer than 1,500 residents, this was hardly surprising. By that standard, meat-processing towns were relatively large, averaging more than 15,000 residents in 1980. In this respect, larger towns like Garden City, Dodge City, and Liberal were more typical than smaller towns like Denison, Iowa, or West Point, Nebraska. Meat-processing towns were already larger than other towns before the arrival of meat plants, averaging 11,000 residents in 1950 and nearly 13,000 in 1960. They had also grown, though less rapidly than Garden City, averaging 11 percent increases in the 1960s and 8 percent increases in the 1970s. Like Garden City, they were in heavily agricultural counties, with farm products averaging more than $100 million in 1982, but they were also diversified, averaging sixty manufacturing establishments and approximately 4,000 manufacturing employees.[74] In short, they were towns with an established infrastructure of farms and businesses that could support the addition of a new plant.

At the county level, more than half of the plants were in locations similar to Finney, averaging 24,000 residents in 1985 and providing employment to an average of thirty-three manufacturing establishments. These were the counties in which most of the IBP plants were located, such as the ones at Denison and Storm Lake, Iowa; Emporia and Garden City, Kansas; Mapleton, Minnesota; and Dakota City, Nebraska. They included six of the Tyson poultry-processing plants in Arkansas and several Cargill plants in Iowa and Minnesota, as well as the beef-processing plants in Dodge City and Liberal. In 1960, these counties averaged 20,000 residents and, compared with many Middle West communities, were thriving. During the 1960s, before most of the plants opened, population grew in seventeen of the twenty-four counties and declined by more than 10 percent in only one. Median family income from 1959 to 1969 rose by 85 percent,

compared with an average of 80 percent across the region (unadjusted for inflation). In 1967, the twenty-four counties of approximately this size that would
become home to a large meat- or poultry-processing facility averaged 28 manufacturing establishments, 156 service establishments, and 268 retail establishments. On average, there were about 25 percent more business firms in these
counties than in other counties of similar size.[75] Only five of the counties with
large meat- or poultry-processing firms were small, averaging fewer than 10,000
residents in 1985, and four of these were within a hundred miles of a large city.
Sixteen of the counties were significantly larger than Finney, averaging 82,000
residents in 1985 and supporting an average of 116 manufacturing establishments.[76] While it was true that the meat- and poultry-processing industry had
moved into scattered rural locations, therefore, it was not concentrated in tiny
rural hamlets that belonged, as one writer claimed, in a Norman Rockwell painting.[77] A more accurate description would have emphasized the growth, innovation, and business activity that already characterized these communities.

In subsequent decades, the meat industry experienced a second wave of expansion. Commercial production of beef nationwide edged up from 24.2 billion
pounds in 1986 to 26.4 billion pounds in 2007, pork rose from 14.0 billion pounds
to 21.9 billion pounds over the same period, and broilers climbed from 19.7
billion pounds to 48.8 billion pounds.[78] In the nine Middle Western states, decennial census figures registered gains in total meat-industry employment from
68,280 in 1980 to 101,441 in 2000. Kansas experienced the largest percentage increase, with employment rising from 6,000 to more than 13,000. Employment in
Oklahoma, Nebraska, and Arkansas increased by more than 75 percent. At the
turn of the twenty-first century, the largest number of meat-industry workers
was in Arkansas, with more than 23,000 employees, followed by Iowa with
nearly 20,000, and Nebraska with nearly 15,000. Further change was evident
in the shifting composition of occupations within the industry. While nearly
half in 2000 were still employed as butchers and cutters, more than one-quarter
worked as packers and packagers, and nearly all of the remainder were machine operators and laborers. Indicative of increased machine processing and
packaging for supermarkets, growth was greatest among packagers and machine operators.[79]

From 1986 to 2006, the number of Middle Western meat- and poultry-processing
establishments employing at least 500 workers doubled from forty-nine to
ninety-nine. The largest increase occurred in Arkansas, where the number of
large plants grew from sixteen to twenty-seven, followed by Missouri, with an
increase from four to thirteen, and Nebraska, from six to fifteen. North Dakota
was the only Middle Western state with no large meat-processing firms. Iowa
had eighteen, Minnesota had nine, Kansas had eight, Oklahoma had seven, and

South Dakota had two. Overall, the number of Middle Western counties with at least one large plant increased from forty-five in 1986 to seventy-eight in 2006. Eighteen counties in Arkansas had at least one plant, and sixteen did in Iowa. Nebraska was next with eleven, followed by Missouri with ten. Seven counties in Kansas had large plants. That was the same number as in Minnesota and Oklahoma. Two counties in South Dakota had large plants.[80]

The earlier pattern of situating plants in larger communities with a more supportive commercial infrastructure continued. Of the seventy-eight counties with plants in 2006, twelve had populations of more than 100,000 in 1980, ten had between 50,000 and 100,000, and thirty-two had between 20,000 and 50,000. In all, two-thirds were in locations the size of Finney County or larger. Plants established after 1986 tended to be in larger counties than plants founded earlier, although there was considerable variation. Ten of the counties with newer plants had fewer than 15,000 residents in 1980, while an equal number had more than 100,000.[81]

As large meat and poultry plants spread across the Middle West, the issue that attracted increasing attention was their impact on host communities. Was agribusiness bringing growth and new prosperity, as optimists hoped, or was it a bargain with the devil? Garden City seemed the obvious place to find answers. For better or for worse, the new IBP plant seemed to be fulfilling community leaders' expectations of population growth. In 1981, net migration to Finney County exceeded 1,000, reached 1,100 the following year, and rose to more than 1,300 a year later. Overall, population growth averaged nearly 7 percent in 1981 and continued at that level in 1982 and 1983, compared with less than 2 percent during the three years before the plant opened. From 1980 to 1990, Holcomb was the fourth-fastest-growing town in the state, exceeded only by large suburbs near Kansas City and Wichita, and Garden City ranked fourteenth. Total employment in the county rose from fewer than 14,000 workers in 1979 to more than 19,000 in 1985. Nearly 700 new jobs emerged in the retail sector, and more than 1,000 did in services. Construction jobs quadrupled from 1,000 to more than 4,000.[82]

But it was less clear that Garden City's growth was uniquely associated with the new IBP plant. A fact that few observers noted was that population in Finney County had already risen by 18 percent in the 1960s and by 24 percent in the 1970s. Nor was it clear that the new plant would sustain longer-term growth. Following the relatively steep increase between 1980 and 1983, the county's population grew by only 2 percent annually during the remainder of the 1980s and 1990s, which was the same rate as during the early 1970s. Moreover, this growth was shaped as much by the community's changing demographic profile as by its ability to attract newcomers. Growth in the 1960s and 1970s meant a

population younger than in other towns, which in turn meant a higher proportion of subsequent growth from natural increase. During the 1980s, births in
Finney County exceeded deaths by a ratio of four to one. In consequence, more
than half of the county's growth in that decade was from natural increase.[83]

Among counties with large meat-processing facilities, Finney County's overall
growth was more the exception than the rule. In neighboring Ford County, where
a new 250,000-square-foot meat-processing facility opened in 1980, population
grew by only 3.7 percent in 1981, with half of that from natural increase, and
from then through 2006 averaged only 1 percent per year. To the south in Seward
County, home of the large National Beef plant in Liberal, growth averaged 1.1
percent during the same period. A similar pattern was evident in Lyon County,
where the IBP plant in Emporia sparked growth of almost 5 percent in 1977 but
fell to 1 percent the following year and over the next two decades averaged less
than 0.5 percent per year. Compared with counties that did not have large meat
plants, those that did grew more. But the notion that these communities typically became boomtowns was simply false. Only two of the seventy-eight Middle
Western counties with large meat plants experienced overall growth between
1980 and 2005 as high as Finney's. Median overall growth among these counties
during this twenty-five year period totaled a mere 1 percent.[84]

The most notable aspect of Garden City's population growth was its changing ethnic composition. Fourteen percent of the county's residents were Latino in 1980, up from 9 percent a decade earlier. That proportion rose to 25
percent in 1990, and then soared to 43 percent in 2000. Finney County was not
alone in this respect. Overall, Latinos accounted for 45 percent of meat-industry
employees in the nine Middle Western states by 2000, up from only 4 percent in
1980. Latinos made up 38 percent of the population in Ford County at the turn of
the century and 42 percent in Seward County. Other counties with large Latino
populations included Texas County, Oklahoma, the location of a large Seaboard
pork processing plant in Guymon, and Dawson County, Nebraska, where IBP
opened a plant near Lexington in 1990. Latinos were 30 percent and 25 percent
of these counties' populations, respectively. But if Finney was not alone, it was
nevertheless atypical. Although Latinos made up a large share of meat industry employees, most of the counties in which the meat industry was located
remained predominantly Anglo. In all, Latinos averaged only 8 percent of the
population in Middle Western counties with large meat or poultry plants—more
than in other counties (where the average was 3 percent) and yet far lower than
in Finney County. In half of the meat-processing counties the Latino population
was less than 5 percent.[85]

Garden City attracted Latinos in greater numbers than most other communities for several reasons, the most important of which were its location and

history. The Santa Fe Railroad employed Mexican workers from the start, also linking Garden City with large Mexican-American communities at La Junta and Trinidad, Colorado, and the U.S. Land and Sugar Company employed Mexican laborers in its sugar plant and beet fields. In 1906, for example, thirty-two-year-old Saladonis Negrete and his wife Anjela moved from Mexico to Garden City. A year later, twenty-year-old Nasario Ramirez, his wife Anna, and their baby daughter Merdides came and lived next door. Both men worked in the sugar beet fields. Neither spoke English. Like other families in the neighborhood, Nasario's migrated between jobs in Kansas and Colorado. Merdides neverthe-less went to school long enough to learn to read and write and, as a teenager, worked as a salesgirl at Dunn's dry goods store in Garden City.

By 1910, Finney County included 137 residents from Mexico. Eduardo Rod-riguez, a railroad section gang worker, came with his wife Florentina in 1907. Ra-phael Gonzales came in 1908 to work in the beet fields. His wife Francina joined him a year later, taking a job as a cook for the beet workers. In 1915, the number of residents of Mexican descent had grown to 217, and five years later to 300, of which seventy-three were children born in the United States. Nineteen of the adults worked for the Santa Fe Railroad, and seven were employed by the steam railroad used to transport sugar beets. Twenty-seven worked in the beet fields, seven for the Garden City sugar company, and twenty-five as farm laborers, mostly on ranches near Holcomb. One was a blacksmith, one was a barber, and one earned her living as a washerwoman.[86] By 1930, the number of residents of Mexican descent in Finney County exceeded 600, but the number declined over the next decade because of the Depression. During World War II, beet growers hired additional Mexican workers through the bracero program, and in the 1950s, Earl Brookover and other feedlot operators and farmers employed Mexican-Americans in increasing numbers. In the early 1960s, the Hispanic pop-ulation had grown to the point that the Catholic diocese began Spanish-language masses and aired a Spanish-language radio broadcast.[87] By the time IBP opened its plant, Finney County's population included more than 3,400 Latinos, the high-est number of any community in Kansas other than Kansas City and Wichita, and at least 4,000 Latinos lived in neighboring counties. As was true in metropolitan areas such as Miami, Houston, and Los Angeles, the presence of co-ethnics fa-cilitated the arrival of new immigrants who spoke the same language, shared the same heritage, and often came from the same hometowns.

Ethnic diversity posed challenges in Garden City, and yet the community's history assisted it in meeting these challenges. Unlike Kansas towns where resi-dents of white European descent made up nearly 100 percent of the population, Garden City had long been diverse enough that ethnic differences were tacitly acknowledged, resisted, periodically acclaimed, and sometimes embraced. In

1925, a three-day fiesta celebrated the 125th anniversary of Mexican Independence. In 1926, the National Association for the Advancement of Colored People held a banquet attended by 150 local residents. But in 1949, when more than three thousand people attended the annual Mexican Fiesta, Mexican Americans were still excluded from restaurants and required to sit in the balcony for motion pictures.[88] That year, members of the clergy representing nineteen of the town's churches launched an effort to integrate the city's swimming pool. In 1961, church leaders started a ministry to educate migrant workers' children, who previously spent days in fields with their parents. It was this school that Juana attended when she and her family arrived from central Mexico in the early 1970s. In 1973, the town elected its first Latino mayor. In 1975, refugees from Vietnam arrived, and by the end of the decade approximately 7,000 Vietnamese had made Garden City their home.[89]

The tensions that arose in conjunction with the community's rising ethnic diversity focused largely on immigration policies and education. Immigrants were subjected to periodic deportation efforts based on narrow interpretations of documentation for proof of citizenship and legal entry. In 1979, the Mexican American Council on Education (MACE) threatened to sue the school board unless a bilingual education program was offered. A few months later, MACE filed a class-action suit charging the board with misusing funds intended for Latino students and arbitrarily dismissing teachers sympathetic to bilingual programs. In the 1980s, as citizens passed three bond issues to build new elementary schools, tensions continued over immigration and school programs. Instances of discrimination and ethnic profiling were reported, including slurs, false arrests, and accusations that native-born citizens of Mexican descent were residing illegally in the community. Garden City nevertheless instituted a greatly enlarged English as a second language program, developed special programs for migrant children, and fared well enough in adapting to diversity that observers highlighted its accomplishments as much as its difficulties.[90]

In 1999, the political scientist Sheldon Hackney visited Garden City to see how it was handling its increasing ethnic diversity. The people who met with him one evening at the public library included Hispanics, Asians, and Anglos. They spoke enthusiastically about tolerance, pluralism, democracy, and equality. Hackney suspected they were putting their best foot forward for the stranger from an East Coast university. Inequality was evident enough, and ethnic tensions simmered just beneath the surface. However, Hackney sensed that people were adapting well to changes they found both troubling and reassuring. A Vietnamese man expressed the sentiments of others. Having risked everything to escape Vietnam, he worked hard to provide a good education for his two daughters. He was worried about them—what their values would be and how their identity was being transformed—but had no doubt that they would flourish.[91]

The principal concern about hosting a large meat-processing facility in a town was economic. Communities anticipated benefits from rising employment, but they stood to lose from added costs for roads, schools, and social services. Meat plants and feedlots dramatically increased heavy truck traffic on existing highways and required new construction. Tax incentives exempted plants such as IBP's $25 million Holcomb facility from having to pay local property taxes for up to ten years, and thus were of significant benefit in luring a prospective firm, but burdened existing property owners and frequently, as was the case in Finney County, necessitated securing additional revenue through a local sales tax.[92] Garden City not only constructed new schools but added special programs for children of transient families, hired staff skilled in multicultural education, built a juvenile detention center, and expanded technical training and language instruction at the local community college.[93] The $100 million in industrial revenue bonds that IBP received was part of a program in which the government of Kansas declared the entire state an economic opportunity zone and permitted corporations to secure revenue through tax-free bonds. The program permitted bonds to be issued by a sponsoring municipality, which held title to part of the company until the bonds were repaid, but incurred no liability for the company's debts and did not share in its profits. Other than a similar arrangement between Boeing and Wichita, IBP's $100 million was by far the largest of any industrial revenue bond offering in the state. Garden City's credit rating was unaffected, but the city's ownership exempted IBP from property taxes on that part of its capital investment. Overall, municipal and county budgets rose steadily during the 1980s and 1990s as Garden City's population increased, but expenses also climbed. Per capita personal income rose sharply in 1979, and again in 1981, but grew less rapidly over the next twenty-five years than in the 1970s.[94]

A study of the effects of growth in the meat-processing industry in Middle Western states by economists at Iowa State University using proprietary data from the Bureau of Labor Statistics showed results similar to those in Finney County. As the meatpacking industry's share of counties' total employment and wage bill increased during the 1990s, total employment grew. But employment in other sectors slowed, as did growth in local wages. There was some evidence that aggregate incomes grew less rapidly as well. The study also examined claims that growth in meatpacking resulted in disproportionate increases in crime but found no support for these claims, either in violent crime or property crime.[95]

The most contested aspect of the meat industry's expansion was its treatment of workers. On the one hand, meatprocessing plants provided employment in low-skill jobs for thousands of workers at regionally competitive wage rates. In 1980, annual incomes of wage workers in meatpacking in the nine Middle Western states averaged $10,245, compared with $8,726 among construction workers and $5,031 among farm laborers. Much of the difference stemmed from the fact that meat-industry employees were able to work an average of thirty-seven weeks per year, compared with thirty-two weeks among construction workers and twenty weeks among farm laborers. Across the region, meat-industry wages were 13 percent lower in small towns than in metropolitan areas, but rent was 26 percent lower and taxes and insurance were 32 percent lower. On the other hand, meat-industry employees fared less well relative to workers in other industries in subsequent decades as plants became larger and concentrated among fewer firms. By 2000, meat-industry workers in the Middle West were earning 20 percent less than construction workers, down from 17 percent more in 1980, and were earning only 15 percent more than farm laborers, compared with twice as much in 1980.[96]

Compounding the problem were rising concerns about human rights violations and workers' safety. In 2005, the international watchdog organization Human Rights Watch issued a comprehensive report describing meatpacking as the most dangerous factory job in America. Interviews and independent studies showed that injuries were exacerbated by the speed with which carcasses moved through processing plants and by the long shifts coupled with infrequent breaks. The report documented numerous instances in which firms failed to report injuries to regulatory agencies and denied workers access to medical treatment or appropriate compensation. The situation was especially grim for undocumented immigrants and for workers at nonunion facilities. The report called for stronger federal and state laws to reduce the line speed in meat and poultry plants and for strict enforcement of regulations governing workers' rights to organize and bargain collectively.[97]

Large firms held the upper hand in dealing with workers and yet found themselves in an ever-widening competitive spiral marked by vertical and horizontal integration, diversification, and mergers. Vertical integration shifted increasingly toward packaging and distribution. Horizontal integration brought beef, pork, and poultry processing together. Diversification linked meat processing with grain marketing, fuel production, agricultural lending, and finance. Mergers created larger and more geographically dispersed entities, including international commercial networks that sought to enhance food producers' position against the rising power of Walmart, wholesalers, and fast-food chains. By the first years of the twenty-first century, these changes brought the Middle West into a closer and more fully integrated complex of agribusiness relationships.

The packing plants in and around Garden City illustrated the wider transformation taking place. The Producer Packing Company that emerged as a local cooperative in 1963 became part of Farmland Foods in the early 1970s. Farmland Foods was launched in 1970 by Farmland Industries to market ham, bacon, and sausage. Farmland Industries, in turn, was the name adopted in 1966 by the Consumers Cooperative Association—the multistate cooperative founded by Howard Cowden and with which the Garden City Co-op had been affiliated since 1920. Consumers Cooperative had purchased the pork plant in Denison, Iowa, in 1959, launched its Farmbest pork products label the same year, and opened a second pork-processing plant in Iowa in 1963. By 1970, Farmland Industries was earning $200 million annually in gross revenue from its grain elevators and oil refineries and was increasingly engaged in pork, beef, and turkey processing and egg production. Its ties with farmer-members and producer-members in local communities remained strong, as did its efforts to maintain favorable employee relations and to raise capital through member investments. The Farmland Foods label was an effort at direct marketing to wholesalers and supermarkets. The Garden City plant expanded the firm's capacity in beef production.

Meanwhile, the other firms that would play a role in southwest Kansas were making similar moves. In 1969, IBP acquired Blue Ribbon Beef Pack, with plants at LeMars and Mason City, Iowa, and a year later changed its name to Iowa Beef Processors to better reflect its emphasis on case-ready production. That transition coincided with the National Beef plant opening in Liberal and the founding of Kansas Beef Industries in Wichita. Kansas Beef was a merger of Wichita's Kansas Packing Company and the Excel Packing Company, a firm that began in Chicago and moved to Wichita in 1936 when it was acquired by a new owner. In 1973, Kansas Beef changed its name to Excelcor, a year later became known as MBPXL (which stood for Missouri Beef Packing), and was soon the number-two beef packer in the country. In 1979 MBPXL, and other parts of Excel were acquired by Cargill, the privately held Minneapolis-based commodities and agricultural products company that had been operating in Minnesota and the Dakotas since the late nineteenth century. In 1980, with the infusion of capital from Cargill, Excel opened its new 250,000-square-foot packing facility in Dodge City. This followed an unsuccessful attempt in 1979 by ConAgra, the Omaha-based prepared-food and agribusiness conglomerate led by the former Pillsbury executive Charles Harper, to purchase MBPXL. Thus, nearly all of the important players—Farmland, Excel, Cargill, ConAgra, and IBP—either held or had sought to hold interests in southwest Kansas when IBP opened its Garden City plant in 1980.

Over the next five years, these firms engaged in head-to-head competition that led to further restructuring of the industry. In 1981, IBP was acquired by

Armand Hammer's Occidental Petroleum and, soon after, expanded its pork-processing operations as a hedge against stagnation and uncertainties in the beef industry. Farmland Industries had posted a record $3 billion in gross revenues in 1977 as a result of rapid diversification into insurance, regional grain cooperatives, and Co-op brand farm supplies, fertilizers, and pesticides. In 1979, Farmland Foods temporarily laid off all four hundred workers at its Garden City plant but determined to reopen despite the new competition in 1980 from IBP. Two years later, Farmland Industries' officials in Kansas City announced the first of what were to be a series of annual net losses. MBPXL suffered setbacks, too, causing it to re-merge with Excel and shift its workforce from Wichita to the new plant at Dodge City. Monfort's plant in Greeley remained closed due to the strike among its nine hundred workers, but in 1982, Monfort acquired and merged with the Swift Independent Packing Company, a spinoff from Swift that represented about 65 percent of its remaining business. One year later, a share of Swift Independent Packing came under ownership of Val-Agri, a firm in Wichita that also purchased the Farmland plant in Garden City.[98]

The last half of the 1980s and first years of the 1990s were marked by expansions and further acquisitions. ConAgra, which had grown from a Nebraska milling company founded in 1919 into a diversified international firm with large interests in poultry processing and packaged food, moved into the seafood business by purchasing the producer of the Taste O'Sea line and strengthened its position in the meat industry by acquiring a share of Armour in 1984. By 1986, Val-Agri in Wichita was experiencing financial difficulties, and ConAgra had entered the boxed-beef business by purchasing a company in Utah. In 1987, ConAgra bought out Val-Agri, purchased 50 percent of Swift Independent Packing, acquired the Farmland plant in Garden City, obtained a part interest in the Hyplains plant at Dodge City, and purchased Monfort for $365 million, making it the third-largest beef producer in the nation. These acquisitions followed a U.S. Supreme Court ruling that refused to block consolidation of the industry. In the meantime, Cargill expanded and diversified by initiating its Financial Markets Division, which benefited from the company's knowledge of trading in world markets, and by opening Excel plants in Canada, making it the top Canadian meat packer by 1992. IBP expanded as well, adding approximately eight thousand new employees and several new plants, including pork-processing plants at Perry, Iowa, in 1989; and Waterloo, Iowa, in 1990; and the beef plant at Lexington, Nebraska, also in 1990. Through a public stock offering in 1990, IBP ceased to be owned by Occidental Petroleum, and 14 percent of its stock was acquired by agribusiness giant Archer Daniels Midland. Farmland Industries, faced with increasing competition from these conglomerates, sustained periodic losses but retained a significant role in the beef industry by acquiring the

National Beefpacking plant at Liberal in 1992. Farmland further diversified by acquiring shares of the Land O'Lakes and Cenex Harvest States cooperatives and the Union Equity Cooperative Exchange of Enid, Oklahoma, which was one of the nation's largest grain marketers.

By 1995, it appeared that the meat-processing industry had stabilized under the leadership of the four largest conglomerates. IBP was strong in beef and pork processing, with plants in Iowa, Minnesota, South Dakota, Nebraska, Kansas, and Canada. Farmland Industries held stakes in the Dodge City and Liberal plants through mergers with National Beef, Hyplains Beef, and Supreme Feeders and was earning more than $5 billion annually in gross revenue. Expanding at a rate of about thirty-five acquisitions and joint ventures a year in the early 1990s, ConAgra had become the second-largest food company in the country, behind Philip Morris, and had launched ventures in China, Thailand, Australia, Denmark, Mexico, Japan, Canada, and Chile. Cargill was the number-three food company and operated in fifty-seven countries. The other firm of growing importance in the Middle West was Tyson Foods, which dominated poultry processing and operated plants primarily in northwestern Arkansas, Missouri, and Iowa. Together, these firms dominated nearly every aspect of the meat and poultry industry, from live animal slaughter to the marketing of such brands as Healthy Choice, Banquet, Holly Farms, Butterball, Tyson, Weaver, and Country Pride.

But the stability achieved in 1995 was short-lived. ConAgra and Cargill maintained their strength through increasing diversification into other industries, including investor services, petroleum, steel, fertilizer, pesticides, biofuels, and pet food, and by operating in markets in Europe, Latin America, and Asia. IBP acquired FoodBrands America in 1997 in an effort to expand its position in processed food, and in 1998 opened its first plant in China. Tyson purchased Hudson Foods, which had slaughter facilities in Kansas and Nebraska, and in 2001 acquired IBP for $2.7 billion in cash and stock, including the Garden City plant with 2,800 employees, giving itself 28 percent of the U.S. beef market and 18 percent of the pork market as well as 25 percent of the poultry market. By 1997, Farmland Industries was the largest farmer-owned cooperative in North America, with approximately half a million members. In 1998, it established a price floor to assist members engaged in hog production who faced growing competition from IBP; in 1999, it struck a favorable agreement with unionized workers at its pork-production plants. Declining profits nevertheless forced Farmland Industries to sell a minority interest in its Kansas packing plants to U.S. Premium Beef, and by 2000 the company suffered a substantial loss. Plant closings followed in Dubuque, Albert Lea, and Wichita. Farmland filed for bankruptcy in 2002 and went out of business a year later, selling its food division to Smithfield Foods of Virginia, which subsequently purchased ConAgra's branded-meats business as well. Farmland's twenty thousand bondholders received approximately fifty cents on the dollar for their investments. Between 2005 and 2008, Smithfield, the National Beef plants in Kansas, and the Swift-Monfort plant in Greeley were all acquired by JBS, a Brazilian company with sizable holdings in Latin America, Australia, Italy, Russia, and Africa.[99]

In Garden City, the story of agribusiness expansion was better summarized as one of transformation and uncertainty than of unanticipated costs or exceptional gains. On Christmas night in 2000, fire broke out at the ConAgra plant south of town, destroying enough of the 1.4-million-square-foot structure to force its closure. Twenty-three hundred employees lost their jobs, and consumers as far away as New York and New Jersey experienced a shortage of kosher meat.[100] The county commissioners periodically considered measures to encourage the plant's reopening but were unable to muster sufficient enthusiasm to provide persuasive incentives.[101] One of those expressing caution was Duane West, an outspoken retired attorney who had prosecuted the Clutter killers in the 1960s and now led efforts to protect the community against toxic emissions from the packing plant and runoff from the feedlots.[102] Despite local support, plans to add a second coal-fired power plant failed to survive a governor's veto, but the town's half-century-old hopes for synthetic fuel processing were partly realized with the opening of a fifty-five-million-gallon-capacity Bonanza BioEnergy ethanol plant. Tyson shut down its aging facility at Emporia and shifted more of its workforce to Garden City. The largest feedlot quadrupled its capacity. Ethnic diversity became more familiar, the schools expanded their bilingual programs, and residents colloquially termed the large discount store east of town "Wal-Mex," after its counterpart south of the border. Poverty remained acute in the mobile-home neighborhoods where most of the meat and feedlot workers lived. A mile from the abandoned ConAgra plant, another of Earl Brookover's dreams became a reality—a high-end golf course surrounded by five-bedroom houses with three-car garages.

Each of these developments underscored a larger point about the changing role of agribusiness in the community and region. Towns the size of Garden City with sufficient infrastructure to attract large meat-processing firms were also reasonably well equipped to withstand the loss of one. Between 2001 and 2007, Finney County's population declined by 5 percent. Unemployment rose temporarily, causing a related rise in demand for private and public social services. But the negative impact was softened by the fact that meat processing was an important part of the region, not just of the town, and by ConAgra's offer of jobs at its other plants to workers. While some 1,800 people left Finney County, population increased by a total of 1,600 in Ford and Seward counties as meat-industry workers found new jobs in those locations or at the Tyson plant near Holcomb. As important as meat processing and feedlots were to Garden City, the loss of ConAgra had little impact on many of the community's residents. The decline in population was insufficient to substantially affect their jobs in other industries, in the professions, or at the businesses and government offices that served surrounding towns.[103]

The county's inability to persuade ConAgra to reopen the plant illustrated how different agribusiness networks had become since 1980. At the earlier date, IBP officials had reason to believe that the efficient plant they planned to construct would be profitable despite stagnation and uncertainty in the beef market. The tax abatement and tax-exempt bonds provided an incentive to locate near Garden City. Two decades later, ConAgra had little reason to repair and reopen its plant. Capital was better spent diversifying into other product lines and could be raised more easily for ventures in other countries. Garden City's interests had also become more diversified. The county commissioners, who represented and sometimes met at the offices of feedlot owners, faced the increasing power of the town's board of commissioners, which represented its growing and more occupationally diverse population and gave a spokesperson like Duane West a platform from which to press quality-of-life issues. The county commissioners themselves had other options to promote, such as biofuels and the proposed power plant, which would bring revenue by selling electricity to Colorado. The proposal's failure to win gubernatorial support nevertheless reflected another change. The governor's base was in eastern Kansas, where population had grown even more rapidly than in Garden City, and the prospect of Kansas investing in a coal-fired plant at a time of mounting concern about global warming was politically disadvantageous compared with promoting ethanol and wind energy.[104]

Garden City's shifting economic and political climate was reflected in its responses to ethnic diversity as well. The income inequality separating residents of the mobile-home neighborhoods and residents of upscale neighborhoods remained acute and, as the Ford Foundation study concluded in the 1990s, kept Latinos, Southeast Asians, and white Anglos apart.[105] Yet it was widely recognized that Garden City's well-being depended on immigrants—"this would be a dreary little town if they hadn't chosen to come," one resident mused—and there were structures that brought the various groups together. The city's board of commissioners was especially important in this regard, because it represented residents ward by ward and was one of the principal venues in which concerns about bilingualism and immigration were expressed. It was through serving on the board that Tim Cruz, a third-generation Latino, became mayor, as was the case for Juana "Janie" Perkins. Ethnic identities were reinforced through new immigration and affirmed through the churches and civic programs, which also encouraged assimilation, provided language classes, and worked to support or serve as advocates for undocumented families as well as immigrant citizens. Leaders regularly took pride in describing the community's ethnic diversity, its inclusion of Cambodians and Somalians as well as Latinos and Vietnamese, its programs for students from more than twenty countries, and its efforts to meet with and represent the various groups. References to Wal-Mex were a form of code shifting that sometimes revealed resentment among Anglo residents but reflected the reality of transnational identities and signaled the rising importance of Walmart in the region's economy.[106]

Although the Garden City Co-op was no longer able to benefit from its association with Farmland Industries, it played a continuing role in the community. With four thousand members and annual gross revenue of $175 million, it was the largest locally owned establishment and was uniquely positioned to represent the community's changing relationships with agribusiness. Its financial strength following Farmland's collapse in 2002 came increasingly from its long-standing investment in petroleum and from providing fuel to a growing number of members and nonmembers. In 2006, three-quarters of the Co-op's net proceeds represented cash distributions from its participation in the petroleum refinery at McPherson, Kansas, and another refinery in Laurel, Montana. Through these, the Co-op marketed Cenex fuel and participated in Cenex Harvest States (CHS), which formed in 1998 as a merger between Cenex, Inc., and Harvest States Cooperatives, both headquartered in Minnesota. CHS was a Fortune 500 company specializing in food, grain, and energy products with annual gross sales of $17 billion. CHS acquired assets in 2003 from the closure of Farmland Industries, and over the next five years, it gained full or part ownership of firms in North Dakota, Texas, Mississippi, Brazil, Switzerland, and China. The Garden City Co-op also invested in multistate joint ventures specializing in grain, pesticides, and fertilizer and played a critical role in providing services and information about crop insurance, national crop production and commodities prices, and legislation through its newsletters, mobile Web site, and text-messaging service.[107]

Garden City's fortunes had always depended on its relations to the wider world—through its location on the railroad, the tariffs that protected its fledgling sugar industry, the Mexican laborers who worked its crops, and the Co-op's role in supplying fuel and marketing grain. The difference was that these relations were now intensified and more extensively organized. The packing plant was part of a vertically and horizontally integrated international food-processing network. Cattle came from Oklahoma, Texas, and Colorado and consumed far more than local farmers could supply. Trucking companies shipped in more than a thousand loads of grain a day from Iowa, Minnesota, and beyond for the feedlots that fattened the cattle being slaughtered in southwest Kansas.[108] Commodities brokers earned handsome livings selling grain futures to the feed-lot owners and farmers. The power plant that supplied energy to irrigate the fields and operate the disassembly line ran on coal brought in from Wyoming. Whether meat cutters and packagers would have work now depended on decisions at Tyson headquarters in Springdale, Arkansas, and on the financial climate in Brazil, imports from Canada, and consumers in China.

SEVEN

From Towns to Sprawling Suburbs

When Joyce Coker-Dreier and her husband moved to their Middle Western town in the early 1970s, the community had a population of about 20,000 and the feel of a small place where people still knew each other, shopped at the same stores, and congregated downtown on Saturday evenings. Three decades later, the population exceeded 100,000 and seemed to have fanned out in all directions. She recalls driving past a college located in the middle of a cornfield shortly after she arrived and wondering why it was so far from town. Today, it is in the middle of town, surrounded on all sides by housing developments and retail centers.

Joyce works for the chamber of commerce as senior vice president of community relations and technology. In this role, she emphasizes that her community has one of the best school systems in the country and one of the highest standards of living in terms of average family incomes. She says about ten new residents move in every day, drawn by safe neighborhoods and convenient transportation to one of the region's largest cities just twenty minutes away. The chamber is actively promoting additional growth through tax-abatement incentives and the construction of new roads and schools. "We've been really aggressive about going after commercial growth," she says. "We are out there pitching." Half the community's potential land area is still open for development, and plans are under way to fill it. Projections suggest a population of 300,000 by 2040. Growth is not only inevitable but undeniably positive, she believes. It is the single most important factor driving the local economy.

As wife, mother, and resident, Joyce emphasizes a rather different side of her community. She and her husband did not settle here because of the projected growth, availability of jobs, proximity to the city, or even the good schools. They came "following good friends from college who settled here." Because she grew up in a military family, this became "the only place I've ever had roots." She was smitten with wanderlust at first and expected to move on in a few years, but Joyce gradually settled in and made friends. Asked what she likes best about her community, she says having a lot of friends and living among friendly people where even strangers may roll down their car windows and chat with one another at a traffic light. It is not the bustle of a rapidly growing suburb that she likes but "the slower pace of life" and "the Midwestern sky." She loves her neighborhood because it was built on an area that was an old farm and still has a century-old wall that was part of the farm. There is a fishing lake nearby, a secluded woods, and a jogging path.[1]

The two impressions of Joyce's community are strikingly different and yet not that unusual or surprising. Aggressive expansion stands counterpoised against the desire for a slower pace of life. The bustle of accommodating newcomers, attracting businesses, and building high-end housing developments contrasts with the urge for good friends, quiet neighborhoods, conservative values, and some connection with the rustic life—however ephemeral or symbolic. These are tensions that run through the lives and sentiments of many Americans, perhaps especially in the Middle West.

One of the most dramatic changes taking place in the Middle West at the start of the twenty-first century was the continuing growth of sprawling suburbs and exurbs around the region's largest cities. Had someone been asked fifty years earlier to offer predictions, this may have seemed an unlikely outcome. Suburbs were characteristic of Chicago and Los Angeles and in rapidly growing Sunbelt cities like Atlanta and Phoenix, but not in the predominantly rural Middle West, at least not to the extent that they later appeared. It was not that suburbs somehow contradicted the region's ethos. Housing developments on the outskirts of Wichita, Omaha, St. Louis, and a few other cities became increasingly common during World War II and in the 1950s as the farm population declined. But it was harder to imagine that the region would continue to generate jobs in sufficient numbers in these bedroom communities to keep their populations multiplying over a long period. There was a limit to what an agricultural economy could sustain. The cities depended on income from the stockyards and flour mills. Some could expand as the U.S. War Department constructed air bases, and others could grow when oil was discovered. It was more difficult to think that vast numbers of people could support themselves in ways that depended so little on the region's natural resources. As the farm population dwindled, people fleeing the region entirely (as they had gone to California during the Dust Bowl) or gravitating to Dallas and Houston (where new jobs were more abundant) became a more likely scenario. Yet the region managed to remake itself culturally and economically and to retain sufficient numbers who otherwise may well have fled to other sections of the country. The great reshuffling involved not only the emptying of farms and small towns but also the rise of new centers of population, not in the cities but adjacent to them.

The writer Joel Garreau examined the phenomenon of suburban sprawl in his 1991 book *Edge City: The New Frontier*. Edge cities were dense agglomerations of shopping malls and housing developments on the periphery of large metropolitan areas and were principally identified, Garreau argued, by rapid population growth, massive commuting, and large-scale office complexes. Tysons Corner in northern Virginia on the outskirts of Washington, D.C., was the quintessential edge city. Its 1990 population of 15,809 had grown 50 percent since 1980, and it had more than five million square feet of office and retail space. Residents occupied upscale homes on large lots and clogged the Custis Memorial Parkway each morning commuting to work in the district. The other edge cities Garreau discussed were places near Los Angeles, such as Irvine and Anaheim, and near New York City, such as Stamford, Hauppauge, and Metropark. Edge cities were rising in growing numbers around Atlanta, Chicago, Houston, and Phoenix. The only edge cities Garreau mentioned in the Middle West were several listed in a brief appendix.[2]

In reality, edge cities have become an important feature of social life in the Middle West. Anyone who has driven the twenty miles of Interstate 94 from Minneapolis to Maple Grove or the forty miles of Interstate 70 from St. Louis to Wentzville knows the reality of edge cities. By 2005, there were twenty-four separately incorporated cities with populations in excess of 50,000 within twenty miles of the center of one of the region's eight largest metropolitan areas. There were six edge cities of this size near Kansas City, two on the Missouri side of St. Louis, two near Oklahoma City, and eleven near Minneapolis–St. Paul. One edge city of this size was located near Des Moines, one near Omaha, and one near Tulsa. In addition, there were twenty-five edge cities with 20,000 to 50,000 people and another forty-six with 10,000 to 20,000 residents. All told, about 3.4 million people lived in these edge cities—more than the number who lived within the city limits of the largest eight cities combined.

To the inhabitants of these edge cities, it made perfect sense that their communities were attractive and growing. Jobs were plentiful, neighborhoods were safe, schools were generally good, and the cost of living was lower than in many of the nation's largest metropolitan areas. Yet from a broader perspective, the rising popularity of these edge cities required closer investigation. After all, the Middle West was a region known for its farms and small towns, not for its bustling suburbs. It was not the Sunbelt, where millions of people flocked to escape the harsh prairie winters, and it was nowhere near the nation's east and west coasts, where international trade and immigration were swelling metropolitan areas like Miami, San Diego, Seattle, and San Francisco. If edge cities were the future of the Middle West, the sources of their growth needed to be better understood. Were they growing because the farms and small towns were dying? Were residents somehow too loyal to the region to move farther away? Were businesses locating there because of some special attraction to the region?

Like the settlers who crossed the Mississippi into the Middle West in the nineteenth century, the inhabitants of the region's rapidly growing edge cities were drawn by new opportunities. There were jobs and schools and chances of owning a home and earning a decent living. But like the first settlements, these new communities were less often the result of happenstance than of strategic planning. Land speculators and developers were at work in both instances. That much was evident to anyone watching the carefully planned housing communities, shopping malls, and warehouses being built. The government was centrally involved, too, though often less visibly. Like the surveyors, cavalry, and land offices representing the government during the region's initial settlement, town councils, zoning boards, and federal officials facilitated the growth of edge cities. It was not just that businesses were attracted by favorable tax-abatement plans and essential public infrastructure. It was also that federal policy dictated the location of regional government agencies and subsidized investment in science and technology. Edge cities may have appeared to be the location mainly of fast-food restaurant chains and shopping malls, but they were fundamentally the region's newest centers of innovation in avionics, finance, engineering, bioscience, and medical technology.

The fastest-growing edge city in the Kansas City metropolitan area was Olathe, Kansas, the suburban community where Joyce Coker-Dreier made her home in the 1970s. Between 1980 and 2005, Olathe's population mushroomed 300 percent from little more than 37,000 to nearly 115,000. It had become one of the largest cities in the state, and officials projected it becoming even larger. But Olathe was one of those fledgling prairie towns that had barely managed to get itself started at all. Its modest beginning was as a stopping point along the Santa Fe Trail. In 1857, when the town was incorporated, an enterprising group laid out a rival town they called Princeton just two miles away and opened several stores, a blacksmith shop, and a shoe shop in hopes of securing the status of county seat. Had it not been for a scheme to enfranchise the Shawnee Indians who favored Olathe, Princeton would likely have become the commercial center of Johnson County. A year later, Olathe's status was still sufficiently in doubt that it sought incorporation from the territorial legislature a second time. An early visitor said the town had little to offer besides a rough-hewn hotel measuring only twelve feet by fourteen feet that doubled as a grocery store and saloon. Four years later, the town had more than three hundred residents and seemed firmly established, but on September 6, 1862, the village was sacked by William Clarke Quantrill and 230 raiders from Missouri, who destroyed more than half its buildings.[3]

By 1870, Olathe's population had risen to 1,817, and the community included Presbyterian, Congregational, Methodist, Roman Catholic, and Baptist churches, as well as the Kansas Institute for the Deaf and Dumb, established in 1866, and plans were being made to open a college.[4] Olathe's principal asset was its location. In December 1868, the Kansas City, Fort Scott & Gulf Railroad which eventually served as the main artery to Galveston, Texas, reached Olathe. The Atchison, Topeka & Santa Fe Railroad, which followed the old Santa Fe Trail west, ran through Olathe soon after, and a third line connected the town to points east and north.[5] The community's proximity to Kansas City, Kansas, twenty miles northeast, provided opportunities for local farmers to supply milk, eggs, and produce and for farm youth to find employment. With business from the railroads and in its function as the county seat, Olathe's population grew to 3,451 by the end of the century, and promoters were already envisioning its future as an edge city. "It is the natural destiny of Olathe to become a splendid suburban home town as a suburb of Kansas City," the editor of the *Olathe Mirror* argued in 1899. Surely, he predicted, the growing middle class of Kansas City would aspire to live in a suburb with such "inviting salubrity."[6] Meanwhile, as was true across the Middle West, many of Olathe's neighboring towns—Aubry, Bonita, Chouteau, Clare, Craig, Frisbie, Holliday, Kenneth, Lackmans, Monticello, Morse, and Princeton—shriveled and died.

Over the next half century, Olathe's fortunes became increasingly linked with Kansas City's. By 1920, the combined population of Kansas City, Kansas, and Kansas City, Missouri, reached 324,410, making it the third-largest urban area in the nine Middle Western states, exceeded only by Minneapolis–St. Paul and St. Louis. On the Kansas side, population was spreading south from Wyandotte County into Johnson County, and on the Missouri side, east toward Independence and south across Jackson County. While Olathe's population remained unaffected, the community benefited economically from its proximity to Kansas City. In 1909, Johnson County farmers sold more than 1.2 million gallons of milk, surpassed only by Leavenworth County north of Kansas City and more than in Wyandotte County itself.[7] After 1906, commuting was facilitated by the Missouri and Kansas Interurban Railway, an electric streetcar line that ran along the high ground from Kansas City to Olathe. The line's promoter, William B. Strang, was also responsible for purchasing land and planning several suburban communities, including a six-hundred-acre tract that became the origins of Overland Park, one of the region's largest edge cities, and for building the area's first aviation park.[8] For those who could afford it, commuting to and from Kansas City by automobile became an attractive possibility. "For eighteen years I conducted my business in Kansas City and lived in Olathe," a resident wrote in 1913. "I did it because in Olathe I could have a home with a real yard around it, could rear my family in a wholesome small town atmosphere and could live cheaper than I could in Kansas City." Observed another, "Yes, a motor car may be beyond the dreams of avarice in the city, where there are so many other things to pay for, but it's a different proposition in the small town, where owning a car is only one step beyond owning a home."[9]

In later years, when historians enumerated the most notable developments in Olathe's history, a few signal events stood out: Quantrill's raid in 1862; George Washington Carver's brief residence there in 1879; the Hyer Boot factory's founding in 1880 and rise as one of the premier makers of cowboy boots; the lynching in 1916 of the convicted murderer Bert Dudley; and Ku Klux Klan members intimidating voters in 1922. Olathe was also known for its packing plant, its role in promoting the cooperative Grange movement among area farmers, and the W. G. Tainter chicken hatchery, a large establishment that may have served as inspiration for Don Tyson, who was born in Olathe in 1930. But observers' attention necessarily focused more on the community's growth than on its past. From fewer than 4,000 residents in 1940, Olathe's population rose to 5,593 in 1950, nearly doubled to 10,987 in 1960, climbed to 17,917 in 1970, and then shot up to 37,258 in 1980. The most common explanation was empty land: as Kansas City grew, people simply spilled into Johnson County because the area lay idle.

But of course that was untrue. In 1949, Johnson County was still a productive agricultural community. Farms made up approximately 242,000 acres, or 78 percent of the county's land. The county's 1,800 farmers harvested nearly 700,000 bushels of wheat and 1.3 million bushels of corn that year, and they produced more than four million gallons of milk. However, the transformation that was to accelerate in coming decades was already becoming evident. Milk production had fallen by two million gallons since 1940, and farms made up 21,000 fewer acres. During the 1950s, farms declined by another 20,000 acres, and that trend continued in the 1960s with a decrease of another 27,000 acres. By 1978, only 54 percent of Johnson County land was in farms, down from 96 percent in 1940.[10]

Johnson County farmers had good reason to sell land for housing developments and commercial use when opportunities arose. As early as 1906, farmers near the Strang line were said to be selling land for $1,000 an acre that otherwise would have gone for $100 an acre. By 1978, farmland in Johnson County was averaging $1,480 an acre, compared with $791 an acre in Miami County to the south and $507 in Linn County south of that. The price per acre in Johnson County rose almost tenfold in just twenty-eight years, whereas the value of crops and livestock produced increased only twofold. That meant a decline in gross return on investment from 22 percent in 1950 to 8 percent in 1978. It was part of the reason that the number of farms in Johnson County fell by almost two-thirds during those years and a factor in the additional loss of more than 30,000 acres of farmland over the next two decades. In 1950, there had been 158,000 acres of cropland in the county; in 1997, cropland totaled less than

88,000 acres. During the same period, wooded land fell from 20,000 acres to 6,400 acres.

Areas in northern Johnson County closest to Kansas City filled up first. By 1960, population density in Mission, Mission Hills, Mission Woods, Prairie Village, Roeland Park, Westwood, and Westwood Hills—all within ten miles of downtown Kansas City, Kansas—averaged 3,000 inhabitants per square mile. In comparison, there were only 359 people per square mile in Olathe. Over the next two decades, population density held steady among the closer towns but rose to 1,217 per square mile in Olathe and 1,855 in Overland Park. Between 1980 and 2000, Olathe annexed an additional twenty-four square miles and Overland Park added thirteen square miles, yet density in both grew significantly, reaching 1,715 per square mile in Olathe and 2,624 in Overland Park.

Across the state line, Kansas City, Missouri, expanded to encompass more than 199,000 acres by 1980, or nearly half of Jackson County, causing a decline in farmland of approximately 100,000 acres in the decades since World War II. Twelve miles south of downtown, Raytown's population grew from 17,000 in 1960 to nearly 32,000 in 1980 before leveling off at that size. Eight miles farther, Lee's Summit swelled from 8,000 in 1960 to nearly 29,000 in 1980 and then mushroomed to more than 80,000 in 2005. East of Kansas City, population spread further into Clay County, consuming approximately half of the county's 253,000 acres, engulfing Independence and extending along Interstate 70 to Blue Springs and Grain Valley.

Overall, the extent of suburban sprawl was most evident in comparisons between Kansas City proper and its surrounding counties. In 1950, the combined population of Kansas City, Kansas, and Kansas City, Missouri, was approximately 586,000. Another 228,000 lived in the four surrounding counties—Johnson and Wyandotte in Kansas and Jackson and Clay in Missouri. In 2005, population in the two parts of Kansas City was 588,000, or about the same as it had been fifty-five years earlier. But another 859,000 inhabited the four-county area—nearly four times as many as in 1950. The four counties included approximately one million acres of land. In 1950, less than one-quarter was used for nonagricultural purposes. By the end of the century that proportion had risen to nearly 60 percent. The greatest change was in Johnson County where the population grew from less than 63,000 residents in 1950 to approximately 500,000 in 2005 and where the number of housing units mushroomed from 20,000 to more than 200,000.

The story of suburban sprawl is usually a narrative about middle-class white people fleeing racially mixed inner-city neighborhoods for the comforts of larger homes with garages, swimming pools, and treed backyards. That was an important part of the story in Olathe. In 1950, only 1 percent of Johnson

County was black, compared with 18 percent in Wyandotte County and 10 percent in Jackson County. In 2000, the black population in Johnson County was only 4 percent, while that in Wyandotte County had risen to 28 percent and in Jackson County to 23 percent. Olathe's population was 3.7 percent black; Lee's Summit's, 3.5 percent; Overland Park's, 2.4 percent; Lenexa's, 3.2 percent; and Leawood's, 1.5 percent. Median household income in Kansas City, Kansas, was approximately $33,000, but ranged from $61,000 in Olathe and Lee's Summit to $102,000 in Leawood. But that was not all of the story.

Olathe's growth was ultimately a function of Kansas City's expanding industrial base, which in turn reflected developments in manufacturing technology, consumption, and the role of government. Until World War II, Kansas City's manufacturing sector depended on the city's centrality as a rail hub for stockyards and meat processing and increasingly as a production and distribution point for the region's consumer goods. By the 1920s, Kansas City's meat-packing business—dominated by Armour, Swift, and Cudahy and located near the junction of the Kansas and Missouri rivers—was second in size only to Chicago's. The stockyards covered more than two hundred acres and accommodated as many as 20,000 cattle at a time. Annually, more than 2.5 million cattle arrived by rail from all directions, and meat left the city for destinations as far away as New York and San Francisco. The trains that brought cattle also transported grain for processing at the General Mills, Monarch, Southard, and Southwestern milling companies and to be used at the Loose-Wiles Company, maker of Sunshine Biscuits and precursor of the Keebler label, and at the Corn Products Refining Company. Manufacturing flourished at the Kansas City Bolt & Nut steel plant, the Missouri Boiler Company, the Butler steel-fabricating plant, and the C. R. Cook Paint Company.

Kansas City was home to a threshing-machine company, an oil refinery, a denim-overalls manufacturer, two soap factories, and a foundry. Its larger establishments included the Consolidated Kansas City Smelter and Refining Company, Sheffield Steel, Procter & Gamble, the Victor Talking Machine Company, a recently enlarged 100,000-square-foot Ford Motor Company assembly plant, and a new Chevrolet plant. "I believe it is only a question of time when Kansas City will be the center for the manufacturing of motor cars, as well as for distributing them," one civic leader declared in 1913, adding, "Kansas City is as far west as raw material can be economically shipped for manufacture and as far east as the finished product can be economically obtained by one half of the United States."[11] The city's major manufacturing firms were concentrated near the central rail yards and along the Missouri River in locations appropriately called West Bottoms and East Bottoms or named for British industrial districts such as Sheffield and Leeds. The downtown airport, dedicated in 1927 by Charles Lindbergh, was constructed nearby to take advantage of air-rail connections and soon became a thriving hub for Transcontinental & Western Air. Across the river, Fairfax Airport, part of the Fairfax Industrial District initiated by the Union Pacific Railroad, provided additional facilities. Between 1928 and 1940, at least eight different companies manufactured airplanes in the Kansas City area, and small airfields emerged outside the urban core in Olathe, Overland Park, Leawood, Gardner, Raytown, Independence, and Mosby.

The war effort furthered the city's growth and facilitated expansion into the surrounding counties. The War Department strategically located munitions and military manufacturing sites in the Middle West where safety from attack was presumed to be greater and where output could be shipped to either front. Kansas City's rail yards and industrial plants made it an attractive location for military production. The Ford and General Motors plants turned out trucks and armored vehicles, Pratt & Whitney produced aircraft engines, and the Commonwealth Aircraft Company and North American Aviation became leading suppliers of aircraft. Space requirements dictated that some of these installations be built on the city's outskirts. Anticipating the need for additional aviation facilities, Kansas City acquired land and opened an auxiliary airport near Grandview, sixteen miles south of town in 1941. In 1943, the Navy erected a plant south of Kansas City to assemble engines for Navy fighter planes and contracted with Pratt & Whitney to operate the facility. Ten miles west of Olathe, the War Department purchased more than sixteen square miles of rural land, including the town of Prairie Center and approximately 150 farms, and turned the area into the massive Sunflower Ordnance Works with 12,000 employees and 5,000 buildings. The plant became the world's largest producer of powder and propellant. Four miles southwest of Olathe, the new $12 million Olathe Naval Air Station occupied more than 1,000 acres and trained more than 4,000 cadets.[12]

The government's role in the growth that eventually transformed Olathe into a populous edge city began early. In 1825, General William Clark, representing the federal government, negotiated a treaty with the Shawnee for land, including what became Johnson County. In 1838, the Methodist Episcopal pastor Thomas Johnson received a government grant of 2,400 acres to establish the Shawnee Mission manual labor school. A new treaty with the Shawnee in 1854 resulted in the purchase of thousands of acres in the Olathe area by speculators under favorable terms that the courts finally declared valid in 1879. In 1866, the Kansas School for the Deaf opened in a building constructed from an abandoned army barracks, after four years of wrangling in which Baldwin City and Topeka vied to keep the institution and a state senator succeeded in securing its permanent location in Olathe. In 1880, Charles Hyer began teaching boot making to students at the school, opened the Hyer Boot company a few years later, and, through contracts with the government for cavalry boots, built it into the largest handmade boot producer in the country, turning out some 15,000 boots a year during World War I.[13] In the 1930s, the Pendergast machine's ties to the Roosevelt administration succeeded in establishing more than a hundred federal offices in the greater Kansas City area under the New Deal and obtained numerous contracts from the Works Public Administration for roads, bridges, and public buildings. During World War II, the federal government spent almost $2 billion in the Kansas City area on major war-supply contracts and invested another $222 million in war facilities projects.

When the war ended, the facilities that had produced military supplies remained. General Motors purchased the North American Bomber Production Plant, where B-25 Mitchells had been manufactured, and turned it into an automobile assembly plant. In 1949, the Atomic Energy Commission took over the Pratt & Whitney facility south of Kansas City where Navy fighter engines had been assembled and contracted with the Bendix Corporation to produce nonnuclear components for nuclear weapons. The Sunflower Ordnance Works was reactivated in 1950 and continued to produce and store munitions during the Korean War. The Olathe Naval Air Station remained in operation, and the highway constructed to transport personnel and equipment to and from the station facilitated development between Olathe and neighboring cities. The Grandview Airport became an air force base in 1955.

Aviation was to have a profound impact on the subsequent development of Johnson County. The military lengthened the Olathe Naval Air Station's runways in 1951, and in 1959, the facility became part of the U.S. Army's Nike-Hercules Missile program. The station functioned until 1970 and became the Johnson County Industrial Airport in 1973. Its presence proved to be a major attraction for advanced technology industries locating at the New Century Business Park in the 1990s. Across the state line, the Richards-Gebaur Air Force Base at Grandview functioned until 1985, and an Air Force Reserve unit remained until 1994. In 1999, voters approved a proposal to build a rail-to-truck transfer facility at the airport on five hundred acres adjacent to the Kansas City Southern Railroad. The facility was expected to generate $36 million in annual revenue. In 1962, the Federal Aviation Administration established a regional air traffic control center in Olathe. The greatest impact, though, was from aviation technology.

In 1948, Ed King Jr., a 27-year-old electrical engineer from Dodge City with experience at RCA building radio equipment for the Navy, established the Communications Accessories Corporation to develop high performance multichannel aircraft components. During the Korean conflict, King built the firm to nearly 1,000 employees. In 1959, King left the company and formed the King Radio

Corporation at a farmhouse near Olathe. A year later, King Radio had thirty employees and was on its way to becoming one of the leading avionics firms in the area. The timing could not have been better. Flight hours in general aviation aircraft climbed from 8.2 million in 1952 to 12.9 million in 1959 and then grew to 36.8 million in 1981. Accidents were also rising and King's innovative technology offered more effective communication between pilots and control towers. The location was good too. King's assembly line was staffed by women with experience as solderers and assemblers at war production facilities and by farm wives supplementing their husbands' incomes. They included employees like Alma Fay Weber, who started as a shipbuilder in California during World War II and worked at King Radio until the 1980s; Dorothy Lawson, who worked at the Sunflower Ordnance plant before coming to King Radio; and LaVerne Lieberman, a Stafford native who worked as a seamstress in Wichita during the war prior to becoming a production-line assembler at King Radio. Another employee was Paul Wulfsberg, an avionics engineer with prior experience at Collins Radio who in 1970 founded his own company in Overland Park. As King Radio grew, King opened additional plants at Paola twenty miles south of Olathe and at Ottawa thirty-five miles southwest and by the early 1980s had 2,600 employees and gross sales of $100 million.[14]

Meanwhile, the Bendix-run Kansas City Plant fifteen miles east of Olathe completed a new manufacturing support building and expanded its work for the Atomic Energy Commission to include electronic circuit boards for the Talos missile, a long-range surface-to-air guided missile for the navy. In 1985, King Radio became a subsidiary of Bendix, which in turn was a subsidiary of Allied Chemical. By 1991, the company was operating under the name of Allied-Signal. The merger of King and Bendix made Allied-Signal one of the strongest manufacturers of aviation control and guidance systems and led to its merger with Minneapolis-based Honeywell in 1999.

Johnson County's growth was further affected in 1990 when Gary Burrell and Min Kao, two King Radio employees with expertise in developing combination navigation and communication equipment, recognized the commercial potential of global positioning system receivers and formed the Garmin Corporation to manufacture these units. A year later, the Olathe-based Garmin Ltd. produced its first product, and by 1995, net income on gross sales of $102 million reached $23 million. The next year, Garmin constructed a new 100,000-square-foot headquarters, and several years later, it expanded its plant to 240,000 square feet. In 2000, Garmin earned net income of more than $100 million on gross sales of nearly $350 million. That year, the U.S. Department of Defense, which operated the satellites from which global-positioning signals were received, discontinued its policy of degrading the accuracy of these signals for national security purposes, thereby allowing their accuracy for civilian purposes to increase ten-fold. Over the next seven years, Garmin manufactured and distributed more than thirty-one million GPS devices, including units installed in automobiles, on boats and aircraft, and in mobile phones. By 2007, the firm's Olathe headquarters served as the coordinating center for facilities in Taiwan and England, a holding company in the Cayman Islands, subsidiaries in Minnesota and Oregon, and distribution contract agreements with companies throughout Europe. Garmin invested more than $159 million in research and development that year alone, held more than three hundred U.S. patents, and increased its annual revenue to nearly $3.2 billion. Twenty-five hundred of its 9,000 employees worked in Olathe.[15]

While the evolution of King Radio, Bendix, and Garmin were associated with the area's history in aviation, another leader in the area's development emerged with virtually no indebtedness to the region's past other than its founder's affinity with eastern Kansas. That was Marion Laboratories, established in 1950 and incorporated in 1964 by Kansas City native Ewing Marion Kauffman, a Naval officer with sales experience at a pharmaceutical company in Decatur, Illinois. Marion Laboratories was located just across the state line from Johnson County, two miles from the Bendix plant and approximately twelve miles from Olathe. The company was poorly capitalized and in no position to compete with large chemical and pharmaceutical companies in developing products requiring expensive investments in research and development. Kauffman manufactured a simple calcium supplement from crushed oyster shells, kept overhead low, and relied heavily on aggressive sales outreach. The company grew by reformulating and developing existing products. It introduced the over-the-counter antacid Gaviscon in 1978 and the stomach-ulcer drug Carafate in 1982. In 1989, with gross revenue of $930 million, the company was acquired by Dow Chemical and took the name Marion Merrell Dow. By 1994, its revenue grew to $3.3 billion and its employees to nearly 10,000.[16]

The other company that became a significant factor in Johnson County's development was Sprint. Headquartered in Westwood, seventeen miles northeast of Olathe, GTE Sprint Communications emerged in 1983 from United Telecommunications, one of the region's largest telephone companies. Over the next five years, the company installed the nation's first complete fiber-optic long-distance network by utilizing easements along Southern Pacific and other railways to which it had access. In 1988, Sprint secured a contract to handle 40 percent of the federal government's long-distance business. By 1994, the company was the third-largest long-distance provider in the United States, with six million customers and an annual gross revenue of nearly $13 billion.[17]

From 1950 through 1970, Johnson County's population growth was largely attributable to residents commuting to Kansas City, but in subsequent years, the rise of suburban companies like Allied-Signal, Garmin, Marion Laboratories, and Sprint became increasingly important. One indication of the change was that retail space in the county prior to 1970 totaled 6.7 million square feet, or nearly as much as the 7.3 million devoted to industrial space, but during the 1970s, 14.3 million square feet of industrial space was added, or about twice as much as the 7.2 million of retail space that was constructed. During the 1960s, the number of manufacturing establishments in the county grew 117 percent, while total population increased 51 percent. That pattern accelerated during the 1970s, when the number of manufacturing establishments climbed 132 percent while population grew 24 percent. With more opportunities for employment in the suburbs, the overall effect was a decrease in commuting. In 1960, 62 percent of Johnson County's labor force worked outside the county, but that proportion dropped to 45 percent by 1980.

As growth spread in the suburbs, the federal government undertook projects to strengthen and revitalize downtown Kansas City. In 1965, the eighteen-story 1.2-million-square-foot Richard Bolling Federal Building occupying two full blocks in downtown Kansas City, Missouri, opened with 2,800 employees working in sixteen federal agencies, including the Social Security Administration, the Army Corps of Engineers, and the Department of Health and Human Services. In 2002, the building was renovated at a cost of $250 million. The Ilus W. Davis Civic Plaza near City Hall included the eleven-story Charles Evans Whitaker Federal Courthouse and the five-story regional office of the U.S. Department of Transportation. But government projects were increasingly located in the suburbs as well, furthering the growth of Olathe and neighboring communities. The Bendix plant thirteen miles south of downtown Kansas City was part of the Bannister Federal Complex, a 300-acre tract that included offices of the Department of Commerce, Department of Agriculture, National Archives, and Internal Revenue Service. By 2008, the General Services Administration was operating more than thirty leased properties in the greater Kansas City metropolitan area, and funds had been approved for a new government facility to be leased by Honeywell for 2,500 employees in Grandview near the Richards-Gebaur Airport. In 1981, only 1,673 residents of Johnson County were federal government employees. Over the next quarter century, that number rose to 6,157. During that period, federal grants and contracts in the county totaled $4.9 billion.

Sprawling suburbs like Olathe, Overland Park, and Lee's Summit generated increasing controversy as their numbers grew and the amount of land they occupied expanded. At first the questions focused on quality-of-life issues as psychologists and urban planners considered the consequences of massive housing developments. Studies of the new suburbs that sprang up around New

York City and Chicago after World War II examined whether residents were as neighborly as they had been in cities and small towns and whether mass conformity was being encouraged by the similarities in housing styles and consumer preferences. Neighborliness appeared to flourish, but the new communities tended to be ethnically and racially homogeneous and were catered to by chain stores and shopping malls that robbed downtowns of patronage and conviviality. Later on, the concerns focused more on environmental considerations, traffic, pollution, the energy costs of long commutes, expenditures for roads and bridges, and efforts to protect the land.

In 1966, Olathe was still a small town with fewer than 13,000 people and a distinct downtown area centered around Kansas Avenue and Santa Fe Street, where residents shopped at familiar landmarks like Miller's and Blake's, purchased gas at the Skelly station, watched movies at the Trail Theater, and visited franchise stores like Ben Franklin and Western Auto. But Interstate 35 cut through the eastern edge of town in 1959 and was soon complete from Ottawa to Kansas City. Homes and shops were locating farther from downtown. "It was almost as if the city exploded and a shopping and entertainment area grew up wherever a fragment landed," one resident observed.[18]

In hopes of bucking the fragmentation, community leaders secured a $3 million urban renewal grant from the federal government and used it to upgrade the downtown area. Over the next eight years, dozens of decaying structures were demolished, streets were realigned, an urban mall was created, and landscaping was added. The result was mainly that the downtown became more attractive for law offices and residents doing business at the courthouse and city hall. Routine shopping and pedestrian traffic diminished, and as the population climbed, homes and shops necessarily spread across a wider and wider area. Ken Roberts, a longtime resident and school administrator, remembers how quiet the downtown area became. "There was just nothing there. Nothing to draw people. Nobody there but lawyers and title agents."[19] In 1968, the hospital moved out near the interstate, where King Radio and the Hyer Boot Factory had already relocated, and the Nazarene church opened a college—the one Joyce Coker-Dreier saw in the cornfield—on the outskirts close to the Air Control facility the same year. By 1980, Olathe had annexed 440 acres north of town, and developers had constructed two new shopping malls.

At the start of the twenty-first century, after two decades of additional growth, Olathe's officials devised a strategic plan to anticipate future opportunities and needs. High on the list of anticipated challenges was traffic congestion. A survey of residents showed that only 27 percent were satisfied with current traffic flow and congestion management.[20] The survey showed overwhelming satisfaction with other aspects of community life, including parks, schools, and emergency services. But planners were concerned that the population was growing faster than budgets for the police and fire departments and other services such as waste removal. The number of cases being handled by the county court was escalating. More than a thousand miles of new streets had been constructed, but many more needed to be added or widened. Ten new schools had been built, and several more were being planned. Tax levies would likely increase but needed to be kept low to keep residents from opting to live in Missouri, and tax abatements seemed necessary to attract businesses. State and federal government had played such an important role in the past that community leaders looked there again for solutions, but they also believed that government would respond more favorably if the community could demonstrate that it was large and growing. As a member of the city council observed, "Size increases your influence with the state and federal governments. They listen to you better when you're bigger."[21]

Johnson County was in fact big enough to wield power in Topeka and Washington, and its promoters routinely publicized its rising prominence. More than one-third of commercial and residential real estate in the entire state was said to be located in Johnson County. Figures from the 2000 decennial census showed that there were twice as many people living in Johnson County alone as in thirty-eight of the state's western counties combined. Garden City's boosters could talk about growth in Finney County, but Johnson County's population had grown faster and was more than ten times as large. Hearing about eastern Kansas's influence seldom sat well in western Kansas, especially if it involved paying higher state income taxes or losing a coal-generated power plant that would bring revenue to their part of the state. Even in eastern Kansas, there were plenty of residents who worried that small-town values were being sacrificed on the altar of commercial progress.[22]

These challenges notwithstanding, Olathe continued to promote growth and to grow. What had once flowed in and out of Kansas City by rail now passed increasingly through Olathe and neighboring edge cities as freight carried by regional trucking companies, on fiber-optic cables, and as electronic financial transactions. Besides Sprint, Garmin, and Honeywell, Olathe's major companies included Farmer's Insurance with nearly 2,000 employees, TransAm Trucking with 1,000, and Sysco Foods with more than 700. John Deere located its regional sales and marketing center there, with more than 400 employees. Intermodal rail, air, and trucking capacity at the New Century and Richards-Gebaur sites attracted more than two million square feet of warehouse and distribution facilities with more than 1,000 employees. Large employers in surrounding communities brought new residents to Olathe, as well. Applebee's headquarters in Lenexa employed nearly 700. Black and Veatch, an engineering firm in Overland

Park, had 2,000. LabOne, a diagnostic medical and assaying service six miles from downtown Olathe in Lenexa, employed 3,000.

Growth of this kind forged new links between Kansas City's outer suburbs and the region's smaller towns. In 1989, Olathe housing developer Don Bell purchased one of Garden City's major banks, placed Olathe's mayor on its board of directors, and managed it until 2005 when loan losses necessitated its sale.[23] Another venture involving southwest Kansas was the Olathe defense contractor and avionics firm Butler National, which won a fifteen-year contract to build and manage an $88 million state-owned casino in Dodge City. In 1998, Smith Center resident Robert Orr established the national offices of his Brooke Corporation in Overland Park, just east of Olathe, and opened a branch office in Olathe a few years later. The Brooke Corporation was a franchise company Orr conceived while working as a bank manager in the Smith Center area. Its aim was to help struggling insurance and brokerage agents in small towns by providing them with information, business advice, and banking access. Orr maintained his residence in Smith Center and opened a processing and advertising center at a building vacated by KN Energy in nearby Phillipsburg, but he found it necessary to locate his headquarters in suburban Kansas City's financial nerve center. Over the next decade, Orr's company expanded to twenty-nine states, included more than five hundred local franchises, and became a public corporation valued at more than $100 million.[24]

Olathe's most aggressive efforts to position itself for further expansion focused on biotechnology. Building on the earlier successes of Marion Laboratories and the community's location midway between the University of Kansas twenty miles west in Lawrence and the KU Medical Center twenty miles northeast in Kansas City, Olathe's officials hoped the town could become the region's magnet for bioscience, as Silicon Valley had for the computer industry. There was good reason to believe this could happen. In 1995, Marion Merrell Dow was acquired by Hoechst of Germany for $7.1 billion and four years later became part of the multinational pharmaceutical company Sanofi-Aventis. These acquisitions expanded Marion's operations, involved it more directly in bioscience research, and connected it more closely with the growing lab-assaying business that included LabOne in Lenexa.[25] Other firms in the area with expertise in bioscience included Bayer, just north of Olathe in Shawnee; Bayer's animal health division in Merriam; and its agriculture division in Kansas City, Missouri. In addition, the area included the Cerner Corporation, a health-care information-technology firm in Kansas City, Missouri; and such stakeholders as the Stowers Institute for Medical Research and the Kansas City University of Medicine and Bioscience.[26] By 2006, some 200 biotech companies with more than 20,000 employees were said to be operating in the broader Kansas City metropolitan area.

Five of the firms were in Olathe, seven in Shawnee, twenty in Overland Park, and thirty-five in Lenexa. In 2007, Olathe became the location of a new ninety-two-acre Kansas Bioscience Park administered by the Kansas Bioscience Authority and anchored by the Kansas State University Olathe Innovation Campus. The plan, CEO Dr. Daniel Richardson explained, was a "testament to the core values of the Midwest"—its can-do attitude and its pioneering spirit. Long-term, the goal was not only to bring in more high-level jobs in animal health and food safety but also to provide training in bioscience that would draw young people into the field and encourage them to stay in Johnson County.[27]

To accommodate these commercial and research ventures, Kansas City's edge communities added hundreds of acres of land and built thousands of new homes. By 2004, Olathe had annexed more than 1,300 acres of additional land and over a four-year period approved more than 5,700 building lots. Between 2002 and 2007, it added nearly two million square feet of retail space and more than one million square feet of office space. Two new shopping malls opened and several new four-lane highways and interchanges eased the flow of east-west traffic and facilitated development in the northern part of the city. More than 5,000 new homes were built on lots averaging 14,000 square feet—up from 11,000 square feet in the 1990s—and the average cost soared from less than $130,000 to more than $280,000.

Similar growth occurred among Olathe's neighbors. In Overland Park, 4,000 new homes were built, with the average cost rising from $240,000 in 2002 to $371,000 in 2007. In neighboring Lenexa, 1,800 new homes appeared, rising in average cost from $208,000 to $302,000; and in Leawood, 1,000 homes went up, with the average cost climbing from $246,000 to $317,000. Home prices across the state line in Missouri were considerably cheaper, but in Jackson County, where more than 20,000 new homes were constructed between 2002 and 2007, prices increased 40 percent from an average of $127,000 to an average of $178,000. More than 5,000 new homes were constructed in Lee's Summit alone.

Whether they purchased new homes or old ones, it made sense to residents to become home owners. In Olathe, where three-quarters of homes were owner occupied, median home values rose 36 percent between 2000 and 2007 while median household incomes increased by only 13 percent. Owners might be stretched covering mortgage payments but generally anticipated a strong return on their investment. The only significant difficulty was the daily commute, which averaged twenty minutes and nearly always involved driving and thus became more of a burden on family budgets whenever gasoline prices rose. A study in Lee's Summit in 2007 showed that residents spent a total of $312 million during the year on car and truck purchases, gasoline and motor oil, and vehicle maintenance and repair. That was more than five times as much as residents spent on schooling for themselves and their children and was exceeded only by expenditures for food, which totaled $380 million.[28]

As Olathe celebrated its sesquicentennial, community leaders claimed with some satisfaction that it was one of the largest, fastest-growing, and most affluent cities in the region. It was home to more than fifteen office and industrial parks, seventeen large shopping centers, 220 restaurants, and approximately 3,300 companies. While many residents still commuted to jobs in Kansas City, Olathe had become a major commercial center in its own right. The costs of living were below the national average, and levels of education were above. Magazines and online rating services suggested it was a good place to live, and residents seemed to agree. A survey of 1,200 households in 2006 yielded a mean overall community satisfaction score of 117, up from 100 six years earlier and 20 percent above the Kansas City metropolitan area average. Residents were overwhelmingly satisfied with the quality of emergency services, parks and recreation, libraries, and schools. Eighty-one percent said they were satisfied with the quality of life in their neighborhood; 85 percent said they were satisfied with the overall quality of life in their city; 91 percent said Olathe was an excellent place to live.[29]

Mary Cochran was born in Olathe in 1923, went to school there, and after college returned to Olathe, where she and her husband raised their children and she worked as a school secretary. As a child she lived in Olathe when hardly anyone else did and when the dust storms were so bad that people wrapped handkerchiefs over their faces to walk across the street. She remembers her mother crying because the grasshoppers ate holes in the curtains and there was no money to replace them. She says the best thing about living in Olathe now is that it has "grown by leaps and bounds" and the worst thing is that "it's too big." She says this with no hint of the apparent irony. It is the same tension that Joyce Coker-Dreier expresses in emphasizing the community's tremendous expansion and its cozy small-town atmosphere. Mary Cochran believes the two are compatible. The small-town feel remains, she says, "because we've really worked at it." To her, that means pitching in as taxpaying citizens to keep the schools strong, having community leaders who bring in responsible companies, and trying to help people as she does through her church and family. Not everything goes well. As the city grows, traffic worsens, and people necessarily live more within their own circles of friends and neighbors. Her view is simply to be philosophical. "You've got to be flexible," she says. "You go with the flow."[30]

The growth that had taken place in Olathe and among Kansas City's other edge communities occurred on an even larger scale near Minneapolis and St. Paul. By 2005, when Kansas City included fourteen independently incorporated edge cities with populations of at least 10,000 within twenty miles of downtown, the Twin Cities had thirty-nine. In 1917, after eight years of study, the Minneapolis Civic Commission produced a detailed report predicting that the city, not counting St. Paul, would grow to 1.5 million by 1960 and that 150 square miles of land would be needed to accommodate this many people.[31] What the commission did not anticipate was that more than 700 square miles would be occupied by 1960 and that more people would be living in edge cities than in either Minneapolis or St. Paul. By 1980, the combined population of these edge cities was nearly one million. Twenty-five years later, their combined population totaled almost 1.4 million. They ranged in size from Mendota Heights, with fewer than 12,000 residents, to Bloomington, with more than 80,000. Plymouth, Brooklyn Park, Coon Rapids, Eagen, and Eden Prairie each had more than 60,000 residents. Maple Grove and Burnsville had almost that many. The fastest growing was Woodbury, which multiplied fivefold between 1980 and 2005 from a population of just over 10,000 to more than 52,000.

Woodbury is located approximately eight miles east of downtown St. Paul and is flanked on the north by Interstate 94, Oakdale, Landfall, and Lake Elmo; on the south by Cottage Grove; and on the east by Afton, which in turn borders Wisconsin. Interstate 494 cuts across its northwest corner, U.S. Highway 10 is a six-lane artery that follows the railway and the Mississippi River just to the west of Woodbury, and the community is bisected by Valley Creek Road and Bailey Road, which channel traffic east and west, and by Radio Drive and Woodbury Drive, which carry it north and south. Besides its highways and housing developments, Woodbury's terrain is defined by seven large lakes and numerous ponds. Woodbury was not only the fastest-growing suburb of Minneapolis and St. Paul during the quarter century after 1980 but boasted one of the region's highest levels of average household income and educational attainment.

In 1940, there were only 954 people living in Woodbury, which was still classified as a township rather than as a village or town, and 895 were listed as members of farm families. In all of Washington County, the population was 26,430, most of it rural. Oakdale had approximately 1,600 residents, Afton fewer than 800, and Lake Elmo fewer than 300. The largest community in the county was Stillwater, ten miles north along the St. Croix River, with 7,000. In 1950, Woodbury's population barely topped 1,000, but the community grew to just over 3,000 by 1960, leading to its incorporation as a city in 1967. Surpassing 10,000 in 1980, it reached 20,000 in 1990 and grew to more than 46,000 by the end of the century. Many of its residents held white-collar jobs in St. Paul or worked as insurance specialists for Hartford, as data analysts and financial advisers, or in government. As in many edge cities, Woodbury's largest employers were the school system and a hospital. Between 1991 and 2005, new commercial construction totaled more than six million square feet. With nearly a third of its land undeveloped, the community expected to add about 600 housing units each year, bringing its population to more than 70,000 by 2020.[32]

Amy Scoggins has served several terms on the Woodbury City Council. She and her husband moved here about a decade ago after having lived in Connecticut, North Carolina, and Illinois. Having grown up in the Midwest and gone to college in St. Paul, she was pleased to be living again near family and friends. Her husband commutes to Minneapolis, where he works as a sports writer for one of the newspapers, and she divides her time between raising their three children and attending meetings of the council and serving on school committees. Woodbury's growth is something she measures more through the comments of her acquaintances than from her own experiences. She remembers a college friend from Woodbury who gave her the impression it was a hick town in the boonies. Another acquaintance from Woodbury said they had to drive to St. Paul just to find a McDonald's hamburger. "When my husband and I moved back to Minnesota," Amy recalls, "the realtors wanted to show us some homes in Woodbury, and I thought, well, Woodbury's out in the middle of nowhere. They brought us out here, and we were just shocked at what a great place it had become." She thinks her views of Woodbury are shared by most of its residents. What she especially likes are the parks and trails, by which she means the bike paths that run all over town, including one right behind her house. After those, convenient shopping and safe neighborhoods are high on her list. It's great, too, she says, being close to Minneapolis and St. Paul. "You can get to a hockey game or go out for a good dinner. You just hop on the interstate and head right there."[33]

Like it has for Olatheans, growth has become a way of life for residents in Woodbury, and leaders like Amy Scoggins have had to be especially cognizant of how to channel this growth, perhaps even more than in Olathe since Woodbury has filled a larger percentage of its land and is situated where it cannot annex more. "We've had a lot more builders wanting to build homes here than we could reasonably allow," she says. It made no sense to have more homes than infrastructure to support them, so the council limited the number of new homes allowed. Retailers were also eager to locate in Woodbury. "We've had a ton of retail growth, and we'd like to let that slow down a bit and have more commercial growth so that people who live here can also work here and have good, high-quality, decent-paying jobs." She says the land could all be opened to retail development and would fill quickly, but that would not be good for the community in the long run. "We've got certain areas zoned for commercial development," she says. "We've put a lot of time and study into these plans about how we're going to be using our land in the future. We're really committed to sticking with those plans."

Woodbury currently makes no particular efforts to attract new residents because it does not have to, although it has a welcome wagon and tries to provide information through the schools and city offices for newcomers. Instead, its long-range plans focus on attracting businesses that will provide upscale jobs. The area around the Woodwinds Hospital, one of the largest employers, has been zoned as a medical district campus so that only firms in the medical field can locate there. Officials maintain close relations with 3M, where many of the residents work. From time to time, they also use tax increment financing, or TIF as they call it, to attract businesses or pay for infrastructure, such as a highway interchange a few years ago and an 800,000-square-foot open-air shopping area called Tamarack Village.[34]

Woodbury's growth was part of the Twin Cities' second wave of suburban development. The first, which created what became known as the inner ring and was later circumscribed largely within the I-694 arc to the north and east and the I-494 arc on the south and west, included communities that were well-established by the late 1940s. These communities experienced dramatic population surges during World War II and continuing growth through the 1950s. As soldiers returned and started families, housing in the Twin Cities was sufficiently scarce that officials set up Quonset huts in parks and builders scurried to develop open land in the suburbs. An outer ring followed suit a decade or so later and continued to grow through the end of the century.

The largest inner-ring city in 1950 was St. Louis Park, which was on a main rail artery coming into Minneapolis from the southwest and had been independently incorporated as an agricultural and manufacturing center since 1886. St. Louis Park grew from 7,700 residents to almost 23,000 during the 1940s and climbed to 43,000 a decade later. The second-largest edge city in 1950 was Richfield, just south of Minneapolis, which benefited from its proximity and from expanding business at the Wold-Chamberlain airport. Richfield grew from 3,700 residents to 17,000 during the 1940s and increased to nearly 43,000 by 1960. Several other communities experienced spectacular growth during these years. Just west of Richfield, for example, Edina, an older community established as an incorporated village in 1888, doubled in size during the 1940s to about 9,700 residents and then shot up to 28,000 during the 1950s. By 1960, fourteen inner-ring suburbs had populations of at least 10,000.[35]

The growth of these inner-ring communities resulted from dual economic trends during the 1940s. One was a dramatic statewide reduction in the number of farms and a related shift of farm population to cities and towns. Between 1940 and 1950, the number of farms in Minnesota declined from about 395,000 to 179,000, and the rural farm population dropped from 1.8 million to 740,000.[36] The other was an increase in manufacturing. Situated at the confluence of the

Mississippi, Minnesota, and St. Croix rivers, Minneapolis and St. Paul served as a rail, grain shipping, milling, and financial center and included firms reflecting the region's agricultural history. By 1905, more than 1,400 manufacturing establishments were located in the Twin Cities, including several major tractor, engine, threshing machine, and seed drill manufacturing companies. The Minnesota Beet Sugar Manufacturing Company operated in the area until it was acquired in 1925 by American Crystal Sugar, which dismantled the plant a decade later. The Cargill Elevator Company had headquarters there since 1890. Pillsbury, one of the nation's largest milling companies, had been located in Minneapolis since 1869, and by the end of the century, it and a dozen other companies were producing approximately fifteen million barrels of flour annually valued at $67.8 million—more than five times the output of any other city. Notable early-twentieth-century firms included General Mills, the North Star Woolen Mill Company, Minnesota Paints, Munsingwear, and the Minneapolis-Moline Power Implement Company. In 1940, the metropolitan area was the natural location for further growth in manufacturing and distribution.[37]

During World War II, the Twin Cities' manufacturing sector grew and spread into the suburbs as it focused on military and defense-related production. In Golden Valley, nine miles west of downtown Minneapolis, General Mills produced rations for the troops. The Minneapolis-Moline Power Implement Company manufactured army jeeps at its plant in Hopkins, southwest of Minneapolis. The Minnesota Mining & Manufacturing Company, which moved from Duluth to St. Paul in 1910, provided abrasive and adhesive compounds previously used in automobile production. The Northwestern Aeronautical Corporation, also in St. Paul, manufactured gliders. Minneapolis-Honeywell, a manufacturer of thermostats and burner control devices since 1927, became a major defense contractor with more than 3,000 employees specializing in turbo regulators, tank periscopes, and automatic release mechanisms for high-altitude precision bombing. The Northern Pump Company, which made hydraulic pumps for fire companies, moved from Minneapolis to a new plant in Fridley, nine miles north of downtown, after winning a $50 million contract from the navy to build gun turrets.[38] Northwest of Minneapolis, the Federal Cartridge Corporation, founded in 1922 in Anoka, where it manufactured bullets for hunters, received an $87 million contract from the War Department to produce munitions and operate the Twin Cities Ordnance Works near New Brighton, northeast of Minneapolis.[39] South of Minneapolis, the Gopher Ordnance Works, administered by DuPont on 11,000 acres of government-appropriated farmland near Rosemount in Dakota County, employed 3,000 workers producing gunpowder.[40]

By June 1945, the War Department had spent $1.4 billion in the Twin Cities area on combat equipment and war supplies and invested more than $300 million in industrial facilities.[41] Between 1940 and 1947, the number of manufacturing firms in the five counties in which Minneapolis and St. Paul were located or nearest increased from 1,804 to 2,154, and the number of production workers at these firms swelled from 50,887 to 96,359. Ninety-five percent of the firms and 89 percent of total manufacturing employment were in the two counties—Hennepin and Ramsey—where Minneapolis and St. Paul were located, but firms and their employees were increasingly moving to the suburbs. Between 1940 and 1950, the two cities' population rose by 53,000, but that of the two counties increased by a total of 153,000, the difference reflecting the growing numbers living in edge cities.

After World War II, several of the region's leading manufacturers underwent further expansion as defense contractors. Minneapolis-Honeywell's business with the Pentagon grew as the cold war escalated, and the company gained a greater role in the production of high-technology electronics for tanks, artillery, guided missiles, and spacecraft. Federal Cartridge continued to produce ammunition for the military as well as for civilian use and was eventually purchased by Alliant Techsystems, a spinoff from Minneapolis-Honeywell.[42] Northern Pump's subsidiary, Northern Ordnance, produced guided-missile launching systems and gun mounts until it was acquired by FMC Corporation in 1964, which continued production under defense contracts.[43] Northwestern Aeronautical went out of business but played a significant role in launching Engineering Research Associates, which won Navy contracts from 1946 to 1951 for high-speed computing devices and merged with Remington Rand in 1952.[44]

The inner-ring cities continued to expand rapidly during the 1950s. Twelve with at least 5,000 residents in 1950 grew from a total population of 122,000 to more than 266,000 in 1960. In addition, communities expanded near the edges of the inner ring and became formally incorporated as independent cities. With a 1950 population of almost 10,000, the township of Bloomington incorporated in 1953, became a city in 1958, and claimed a population of more than 50,000 in 1960. The completion of I-35W in 1956 made Bloomington a convenient bedroom community for residents commuting to downtown Minneapolis. Brooklyn Center, which had been incorporated since 1911, grew from approximately 4,200 residents in 1950 to more than 24,000 in 1960. To the northeast of St. Paul, Maplewood incorporated in 1957 and registered a population of more than 18,000 three years later.

It was in these communities that familiar features of suburban life, such as larger homes, an automobile culture, and shopping malls, made their debut. Sixty-two percent of families in Middle Western suburbs in 1960 lived in houses with three or more bedrooms, compared with 40 percent of families in central city areas and 47 percent in nonmetropolitan areas. Eighty-nine percent of these suburban households had an automobile; 32 percent had two.[45] The first drive-in movie theater in the Twin Cities area opened in Bloomington in 1947 to the dismay of traditional movie house owners and was instantly popular among residents. With young families eager to purchase homes, housing developers bought large flat tracts of open land and filled them with predesigned models. The Opus construction company built its first housing development in Richfield in 1953 and over the next half century completed more than 2,000 other projects, including residential developments in Bloomington and Minnetonka, commercial buildings in Minneapolis, and a corporate center in Olathe, Kansas.[46] In 1956, Southdale Center, the first indoor shopping mall in a Minneapolis suburb, opened in Edina. Southdale was owned by the Dayton-Hudson Company, a predecessor of Target Corporation. With incomes averaging significantly higher than in central cities or rural areas, suburban residents frequently described themselves as young middle-class families seeking comfortable homes, friendly neighbors, and good schools. In 1962, *Time* magazine noted that Bloomington had the youngest population of any city in the country.[47]

Suburban growth during the 1950s was facilitated by further expansion of the Twin Cities' manufacturing sector. Between 1947 and 1958, 280 additional firms emerged, and employment in manufacturing rose by nearly 39,000. The post–World War II baby boom led to further increases in population. In 1950, nearly one-quarter of all residents in Hennepin and Ramsey counties were children aged thirteen or younger. That was the same percentage as in 1920 and significantly higher than in 1940. During the 1950s, births exceeded deaths in the two counties by approximately 220,000. By 1960, the shift toward suburbs was clearly evident in the fact that only 63 percent of the population of Hennepin and Ramsey counties lived in Minneapolis or St. Paul, down from 81 percent in 1950 and 89 percent in 1940. Of approximately 1.5 million residents in the five-county area, only 54 percent lived in Minneapolis or St. Paul, compared with 72 percent a decade earlier and 81 percent in 1940.[48]

During the 1960s, the inner-ring cities continued to grow, collectively adding more than 175,000 residents and occupying more than 17,000 acres of agricultural or vacant land. In Bloomington, for example, where 500 new single-family homes and an equal number of multiunit residences were being built every year, population grew from 50,000 to more than 80,000.[49] Inner-ring commercial establishments grew, as well. The Dayton-Hudson Corporation opened its first Target stores in 1962 in Roseville and St. Louis Park and soon had stores in other locations. But as families aged and children left home, growth in these communities came almost to a standstill in the 1970s. Bloomington's population was about the same in 1980 as it had been a decade earlier. The same was true in North and West St. Paul. Brooklyn Center's population was smaller, as was Columbia Heights', Crystal's, Golden Valley's, Richfield's, Robbinsdale's,

St. Louis Park's, and South St. Paul's. Edina's had grown by only 5 percent and Maplewood's by 7 percent. Population density in the inner ring averaged more than 3,400 residents per square mile and remained at that level over the next two decades.

Growth shifted to the outer-ring suburbs, which expanded more rapidly during the 1960s than in the 1950s and continued to grow long after the inner-ring suburbs peaked. By 1970, more than 38,000 acres in the outer ring were occupied by housing and nearly 14,000 acres by commercial and industrial firms. Streets and alleys covered another 28,000 acres.[50] Expansion was particularly strong in the western and northern suburbs. Thirteen miles west of downtown Minneapolis, Plymouth became an incorporated village in 1955 and doubled in population from approximately 9,000 in 1960 to 18,000 in 1970. South of Plymouth, Minnetonka climbed from 25,000 to nearly 36,000. To the north of Plymouth, Brooklyn Park grew from 10,000 to 26,000 and Maple Grove edged up from 2,200 to 6,200. Each of these communities was located on the I-494/694 beltway, which was completed between 1960 and 1965 and followed the earlier Belt Line loop planned during World War II to facilitate the transport of war materials and serving after the war as a location for manufacturing firms, warehouses, and distribution centers. Growth to the north and east of the Twin Cities included Blaine, with a 1970 population of more than 20,000; Mounds View and Shoreview, each with more than 10,000; and White Bear Lake with 23,000.

By the end of the 1970s, edge cities were not only the area's centers of explosive population growth but also the location of an increasing share of its industrial and commercial strength. In 1977, more than 600 manufacturing firms with 22,000 employees were located on the outskirts of Minneapolis and St. Paul in Anoka, Dakota, and Washington counties. In 1980, the percentage of the labor force employed in manufacturing was higher in thirty of the thirty-nine edge cities than in Minneapolis or St. Paul. Companies opted for suburban sites, where land was cheaper and more abundant, to be closer to residential communities and in some instances to escape racial unrest in inner-city neighborhoods.

Control Data Systems, founded in Arden Hills in 1957 by former Navy contractor and Engineering Research Associates entrepreneur William C. Norris, was typical of firms expanding in these years through technological innovations. Norris built Control Data into the nation's fourth-largest supplier of computers for scientific research while also working on urban renewal programs, providing vocational training for prisoners, and experimenting with alternative energy projects.[51] Another edge-city business that expanded significantly during the 1960s was Toro, founded in Minneapolis in 1914 to produce engines for farm use and serving as a supplier of steam engines for merchant ships during World War I. After producing parts for tanks during World War II, Toro returned to developing the lawn mower business it had begun in the 1920s, relocated its headquarters to Bloomington in 1962, and expanded its sales to more than $350 million by 1979.[52] Yet another expanding company was Medtronic, founded in 1949 in a Minneapolis garage, which established itself by 1960 as a manufacturer of biomedical devices and over the next decade became the leading producer of implantable heart pacemakers, with eventual locations in Fridley, Brooklyn Park, and several other Minneapolis suburbs.[53]

Edge-city growth during the 1980s and 1990s was especially high in communities farthest from the urban core and with greater room to expand. Blaine's population grew to nearly 22,000 by 1980 and then climbed to almost 50,000 by 2005. Maple Grove's increased from 20,000 to 60,000 during the same period. While much of the growth extended north and west, the southern suburbs expanded as well. South of Bloomington, the population of which flattened at about 80,000 after 1970, Burnsville jumped from 25,000 in 1980 to 59,000 in 2005, and Apple Valley from 34,000 to 50,000. Other sizable southern suburbs included Eagan, with a 2005 population of 64,000; Eden Prairie, with 60,000; Savage, with nearly 27,000; and Rosemount, with 19,000.

In contrast to the inner ring, density in the outer ring averaged about 1,000 residents per square mile in 1980 and increased to fewer than 1,900 per square mile over the next twenty years. Densities were highest in the southern suburbs of Apple Valley, Burnsville, and Eagan, and the northwestern suburbs of Brooklyn Park, Champlin, Coon Rapids, and Mounds View. The fewest residents per square mile were in the northern suburb of Blaine, the southern suburbs of Inver Grove Heights and Rosemount, and the eastern suburb of Woodbury. At the start of the new millennium, there was room for further expansion, especially to the north of Mounds View in Anoka County, to the east and north of Woodbury in Washington County, and south of Apple Valley in Dakota County, but farmland in the five-county area had declined over the previous six decades by nearly 680,000 acres.

Besides available land for spacious homes on larger lots, outer-ring expansion reflected a further shift in the location of commerce and industry. Between 1960 and the end of the century, the number of manufacturing firms in Anoka County increased from 56 to 614, in Dakota County from 54 to 439, and in Washington County from 48 to 210. During that period, the number of employees working at manufacturing firms in these three counties grew from fewer than 18,000 to more than 35,000. By 2000, 28 percent of manufacturing firms and 28 percent of manufacturing employees in the five-county area were located in these three counties. In addition to locating plants in the suburbs, companies also purchased and held suburban tracts for possible future expansion. Honeywell, for example, bought a thirty-five-acre site in Eden Prairie in 1980 and held it undeveloped until 1999; United Health retained a similar undeveloped tract in Minnetonka.[54]

With growth pushing farther and farther in all directions, the Twin Cities' suburban expansion appeared indistinguishable from Kansas City's except that it was occurring on a larger scale. Yet there was an important difference. None of the edge cities around Minneapolis and St. Paul matched Olathe in size, and none were projected to grow to the astonishing proportions predicted for Olathe over the next quarter century. Bloomington—the largest Twin Cities suburb—was a third smaller than Olathe and Bloomington's population was declining, not rising. The Twin Cities' other large suburbs—Brooklyn Park, Eagen, Plymouth—were about half the size of Olathe. The difference was attributable to state laws governing townships. Kansas and Missouri, like Minnesota, historically organized schools according to township jurisdictions, but gave townships no other authority, instead centering local administrative and fiscal powers in county seats. Among other factors, this was one of the reasons Olathe's status as a county seat gave it early prominence in Johnson County while a dozen other towns went defunct. In contrast, the Minnesota legislature enacted a law on April 15, 1907, that granted townships "having therein a platted portion on which there resides 1,200 or more people" the same authority as villages. By easing the transition from township government to formal incorporation, the law proved useful to communities fearing the encroachment of neighboring cities. In 1911, for example, citizens in the township of Brooklyn, a garden farming area north of Minneapolis, organized a campaign that led to their incorporation as the village of Brooklyn Center, thus halting the northern expansion of Minneapolis and preserving the farm economy until the 1940s. Amended in 1953 to include townships within twenty miles of a large city (one with more than 200,000 people), the statute gave townships the authority to levy taxes, form duly elected governing bodies, and hold public meetings. Subsequent legislation enacted in 1959 further curbed municipalities' capacity to annex territory by granting freeholders within a mile of an existing municipality a formal procedure for initiating their own incorporation as a village and stipulating the manner in which petitions for annexation were to be approved. Most important, the legislation required annexation proposals to be approved by popular vote.[55]

As a result of Minnesota's legislation none of the edge cities near Minneapolis and St. Paul encompassed more than thirty-six square miles—the traditional six-by-six township defined by the Land Ordinance of 1785—and with Bloomington and Rosemount as the only exceptions, edge cities were composed of the same acreage as the townships from which they had been formed or less. The inner-ring cities averaged nine square miles while the outer-ring suburbs averaged twenty-three. Unlike Olathe, no municipality was able to grow larger and larger by annexing more and more territory, and unlike Kansas City, Missouri, where annexation of additional land occurred on several occasions, neither Minneapolis nor St. Paul enlarged the areas within their own city limits.[56]

The added consequence of Minnesota's statutes was noticeable diversity among the Twin Cities' suburbs. Although housing developments, thoroughfares, and shopping malls were common features, the suburbs acquired distinctive identities based on geographic features, kinds of housing, and residents' income and education levels. Woodbury, for example, was one of several upscale suburbs with high average household incomes and a large proportion of college-educated residents. Eden Prairie had a similar profile. Edina distinguished itself as an upscale community with older houses and an absence of growth. Columbia Heights and Blaine were known as working-class communities, although Blaine's recent growth was transforming its image. These distinctions were further evident in communities' plans and priorities. Whereas Woodbury, for example, sought to balance commercial and residential growth, Bloomington's absence of growth permitted it to focus on providing assisted-living facilities for senior citizens, maintaining an attractive balance of single-family and multiunit residences for different income levels, and meeting the needs of an ethnically and racially diverse population. Had the two communities been a single jurisdiction the size of Olathe, chances were greater that plans would have centered on growth and on achieving favorable amenities through additional expansion.

Yet the tension that Olatheans experienced between wanting a small down-home community with a rustic ambience and living in a populous edge city was one that Twin Cities area residents felt, too. Curt Larson is Blaine's economic development specialist. He hears both sides of the argument. On the one hand, Blaine's residents like the open space, the woods, and the wetlands. They enjoy watching the wildlife and sauntering along the trails. On the other hand, they wanted restaurants and shops, which, Curt says, they couldn't get "until we had the rooftops." The rooftops were built and amply supported the retail and service industries. More rooftops came. Soon office complexes and light manufacturing companies moved in, drawn by available land and hoping that employees would be attracted by not having to commute into Minneapolis. Then a big shopping mall opened, lured by a generous tax-abatement offer, and a Walgreen's, a Target, a movie theater, and an upscale grocery store soon followed. Nobody objected. The residents were getting the shopping they wanted and the landowners were making good money. Blaine's planners expect its population to reach 80,000 in a few years.[57]

Curt Larson grew up in a town of 1,800. The town is declining, and Curt rarely goes back. "It's just depressing," he says. He loves where he lives now. But he does not live in Blaine where people have to get in their cars and drive to a strip mall, where the developments are filled with "cookie cutter homes," where the houses are all tan and light blue. He calls that "suburban sprawl." He lives in Edina, which is one of the inner-ring suburbs that stopped growing in 1970. He likes it because he can walk to the store, get a cup of coffee, and sit by a lake. The houses are older and all different. They are close enough that people talk to their neighbors. People sit on the front porch together and drink beer. When he goes to the store, he sees people he knows. "Hey, how's it going?" he says. It has "kind of that small-town feel." A friend came to visit from Seattle. "What is this?" his friend asked. "Mayberry RFD?" "That's just the way it is," Curt replied. "People know each other." He wished it could happen in Blaine. He doubts that it will.

The Middle West's other large cities had their Blaines and their Olathes, their Overland Parks and their Bloomingtons. In suburban St. Louis, it was St. Charles and Florissant, Spanish Lake and Webster Groves, Kirkwood and sixteen other edge cities with a combined population in 2005 of nearly half a million. Near Omaha, it was Bellevue and Council Bluffs, La Vista and Papillion. There would have been more—including Beechwood, Dundee, Florence, and Elkhorn—but since 1915, Omaha had expanded by aggressively annexing surrounding towns and open land. Des Moines was surrounded by Altoona and Clive, Indianola and Urbandale. Oklahoma City, itself spreading nearly forty miles east and west and almost thirty miles north and south, radiated in the direction of Bethany and Del City, Edmond and Moore. Derby nestled near Wichita, which added more than a hundred square miles to its own territory during the half century after 1950. Broken Arrow and four other suburbs grew in Tulsa's vicinity.[58]

By the twenty-first century, the Middle West's edge cities included more than 1.3 million housing units, an increase of nearly half a million in just twenty years. That reinforced the view that these were bedroom communities for suburban residents. It was easy, too, to imagine that the principal businesses in these places were retail stores. An economic census conducted in 2002 identified more than 12,000 retail stores in these locations. Retail receipts that year totaled more than $51 billion. That was one-third more than retail receipts in the eight core cities combined.

But edge cities were not only communities of housing developments and shopping malls. As Olathe, Overland Park, and many of the towns near Minneapolis and St. Paul illustrated, edge cities were also the location of the region's growing industrial sector. Data released by the Census Bureau in 2002 for sixty-five Middle Western edge cities identified 3,904 manufacturing firms, and for ninety-one edge cities found 7,132 wholesale distributors. The manufacturing firms took in $36.8 billion that year and the wholesalers, $104.6 billion. Together, manufacturing and wholesale receipts were more than two and a half times larger than retail receipts in edge cities and exceeded total manufacturing and wholesale receipts in the region's core cities.[59]

Industry became increasingly important in edge cities for at least four reasons. First, there were independent towns that had been manufacturing centers from the start and only later became edge cities as a result of growth in neighboring core cities. Examples included St. Louis Park, Minnesota; Independence, Missouri; Council Bluffs, Iowa; and Sapulpa, Oklahoma. Industry continued to expand in all of these towns. Second, there were towns like Olathe, Richfield, and Fridley that experienced industrial growth during and after World War II because of airfields, munitions plants, and other defense-related facilities. Third, edge cities became attractive locations in the 1950s and 1960s for growing businesses that required more and cheaper land than was available in core cities. These included firms such as Honeywell, Marion Laboratories, Control Data, and Toro. Finally, edge cities continued to cultivate manufacturing and wholesale firms because an appropriate mix of industrial, commercial, and residential development was understood to be the key to favorable tax rates.[60] Industry not only contributed to communities' tax base but also boosted their credit ratings, which facilitated municipal borrowing.[61]

The coastal edge cities Joel Garreau visited in the 1980s persuaded him that something profoundly new was happening in these suburban places. "A brand-new future," he wrote, "the biggest change in a hundred years." He saw the creation of these new communities as a brave new experiment, and he came away hoping that the planners of these communities and the residents who lived in them would get it right. But he was worried, especially about the land—the sacred land, the environment.[62]

Middle Westerners say they view the land differently than a writer in the heart of New York City or Washington, D.C., does. Land is precious but it is also abundant, and if they own it, it is meant to be productive. It is not so built up that preserving a small plot is all that can be hoped for, and it has not been controlled by some financier or corporate conglomerate longer than anyone can remember. When a developer offers a good price, a farmer sells, and when residents call for a shopping center to be built, planners look for ways to make that happen.

Among the ninety-five edge cities circling the eight large core cities in the Middle West, the strongest factor in how populous they became was how much land they could occupy. The smaller suburbs with 10,000 to 20,000 residents averaged 7.6 square miles. Middle-sized suburbs with 20,000 to 50,000 residents averaged 12.5 square miles. And suburbs with more than 50,000 residents averaged 37.3 square miles. The smaller suburbs packed in nearly 3,000 people per square mile, while the larger ones housed only 2,000 in the same space.[63]

Because edge cities were known for spectacular growth, it was only to be expected that the most populous ones were closest to central cities, while the less populous ones were farther out and smaller because they were still growing. However, that was not the case. The smaller ones averaged 11.4 miles from the central city, while the larger ones averaged 15.7 miles. The inner suburbs, as was especially evident near Minneapolis and St. Paul, occupied less land, and after they were filled, population spread to the outer suburbs, where larger tracts were available.[64] It was in those larger outer suburbs that income levels were highest, providing families the means with which to purchase the larger, newer homes being built on more spacious lots.

Critics questioned the amount of land being eaten by sprawling suburbs and suggested that people would be wiser to stack themselves in high-rise townhouses and on smaller lots. The lots were indeed becoming larger, but the reason edge cities consumed as much land as they did was complicated. It was from interstate highways, streets, shopping malls, parking lots, government buildings, office complexes, and industrial parks using more of the available land. Home owners' lots accounted for no more than one-quarter of the land in many suburbs. There was also the desire of residents and planners to preserve open space or to fill it not only with stores and warehouses but also with parks and trees, golf courses and nature centers, ponds and hiking trails. Despite Johnson County's dramatic population increase, for example, there were tens of thousands more trees than in 1950, and residents prided themselves on having golf, hiking, fishing, and farms nearby. As densely populated as it was, Bloomington devoted a quarter of its available acreage to conservation areas and parks. Similar emphasis was evident in Woodbury and Blaine, where wetlands preservation was mandated by state law.

Yet it was true that maintaining the sanctity of the land was difficult. Johnson County residents planted trees and preserved open space, but traffic, paved-over land, and the county's proximity to Kansas City put the area in violation of Environmental Protection Agency standards for ozone levels on repeated occasions during the 1990s and lowered the water quality in built-up parts of the county.[65] The military installations and manufacturing centers that brought people to the suburbs a half century earlier were now attracting commercial and residential development, but not without environmental questions being raised. Between 1992 and 2002, federal health officials investigated concerns about hazardous waste at the Sunflower munitions plant and determined that the site contained miles of asbestos-covered steam pipes and possible groundwater contaminants that required consistent monitoring.[66] In 2006, the National Nuclear Security

Administration determined that cleanup of contamination at the Bannister Complex where Honeywell produced weapons components would cost taxpayers at least $287 million.[67] In the Twin Cities area, Blaine succeeded in attracting a "green" company that built a warehouse from recycled materials and utilized energy-efficient lighting, but concerns persisted about wetlands uses. Woodbury signed a climate-change reduction agreement and proposed a wind energy plant but faced zoning obstacles in getting one approved.[68]

If the environmental challenges were great, the quest for community was equally great. It was not that edge-city residents lacked friends and neighbors, but they did have to work harder at connecting with them. Instead of sitting together on front porches, they had to make friends by joining civic organizations or by driving across town to see them, and that took time. The political scientist Robert D. Putnam explored the effects of suburban sprawl in his widely discussed study of civic disengagement and concluded that urban and suburban residents nationally incurred a "sprawl civic penalty" of about 20 percent, compared with residents of small towns.[69] People in larger places, Putnam noted, had to drive farther to participate in meetings, perhaps lived in neighborhoods that did not encourage informal interaction, and may have felt less responsibility for their communities than would have been the case in small towns.

The Middle West probably did not differ from other parts of the country in these respects. However, a closer look at the available evidence suggests that edge-city residents were at least finding some ways to stay connected to one another, notwithstanding the difficulties involved. They and their counterparts in core cities were actually more likely, for instance, to say they had spent an evening visiting friends at least once a month in the past year than was true among residents in small towns. Two out of three edge-city residents in the one dataset that made comparisons possible said this. Edge-city residents were also just as likely as those in small towns to say they had spent an evening visiting relatives once a month or more in the past year. They were less likely than residents of small towns to have spent evenings with parents, but just as likely to have spent evenings with siblings. Where the sprawl penalty became evident was in visiting neighbors. Residents of edge cities and core cities were significantly less likely to have spent an evening visiting neighbors than their counterparts in small towns. In short, the data suggested that edge-city residents were reaching out selectively to be with other people. They may not have known their neighbors but were making an effort to keep in contact with friends and relatives.[70]

Selectivity was also evident in questions about memberships in voluntary organizations. Four out of five edge-city residents in the Middle West were members of at least one voluntary organization. That was higher than among core-city residents and just as high as among inhabitants of small towns. It was not surprising that most suburbanites belonged to some kind of organization. Information released by the Internal Revenue Service showed an average of 132 nonprofit associations in each of the ninety-five edge cities. Olathe, for instance, had 155; Woodbury, 129; Edina, 117; and Blaine, 58.[71] The survey data showed that edge-city residents participated in some organizations more than residents of small towns did—for example, sports clubs, professional societies, and labor unions—and were just as likely to say they belonged to school service organizations, youth groups, hobby clubs, and political clubs.[72]

Sara Vincent, a resident of Johnson County, illustrated the difficulties and successes edge-city residents experienced in seeking to feel involved in their communities. Her husband grew up in the Midwest, though not in Kansas, but she was raised in New England and found it hard making the transition. "I left claw marks" when they dragged me here, she recalled. Her family actually moved twice to Johnson County. The first time, they had barely gotten settled when her husband was transferred to another location; the second time came when he received a promotion. He is in management at Sprint, and she worked at Honeywell prior to becoming a mother full-time. Like many Johnson County homemakers, she spends much of her day driving. After she gets her oldest son off to high school on a typical morning (he drives himself), it's her turn in the car pool to take her middle son and a neighbor to the junior high. Upon returning home, she watches the *Today* show while completing a workout on the exercise machine and then drives the puppy to one of the town's shopping malls for his puppy shots. No sooner is she home than a friend pulls up in her minivan and off they go to see a house her friend is thinking of buying, stopping at the drive-up window of a fast-food place for Diet Cokes. Next she transports the lunch her son forgot over to the high school, then scurries to a shopping center across the state line to pick up a framed picture and to another store where a broken lamp is being repaired, phoning her junior high son on the way to say she will be fifteen minutes late picking him up from school to take him to his violin lesson. A quick dinner is a chicken dish she purchased at a place called Meal Smith as part of a fundraiser for the high school. A neighbor picks up her two younger boys for tennis lessons as dinner concludes, her oldest son leaves to see his girlfriend, who lives in another part of the county, and Sara heads to a committee meeting at one of the schools.[73]

Amidst this hectic routine, Sara has made Johnson County a home that includes friends and gives her a sense of being part of the community. The fast-food place has become enough of a regular stop that she knows the guy at the drive-by window by name, how many children he has, and what his wife does for a living. She chats with the veterinarian about where he went to college, and they exchange stories about their summer vacations. The friend in the minivan is a woman she met at church. The school committee put her in contact with other mothers, and the carpooling has been a godsend. People in Johnson County are genuinely nice, she says. At first it shocked her when total strangers said hello. "Oh my god, I don't even know you," she thought. But after awhile she got used to it. The community reinforces character and is a good place to raise children. "It is a simpler life here," she says. "A slower-paced life. People are valued."

Sara is also involved in Hope Center, an organization she learned about through a women's Bible study group a neighbor invited her to a few years ago. Hope Center is in a Kansas City neighborhood known for its crack houses, gangs, and drive-by shootings. The center is part of a housing and community development organization that provides activities for inner-city youth, offers lessons in conflict resolution and character development, sponsors a medical care program, and plans to initiate a charter school. Sara had been involved in charity work before, writing checks and doing fundraisers, but Hope Center eschews those as "Band-aid activities." It wants to address underlying community problems. For Sara, it has been eye-opening. "I live in a community of great privilege and have a wonderful family," she says. "But it is like a gilded cage. Residents in my community have no sense that literally seventeen minutes away there are people who are desperate and have nothing."

Driving west on Santa Fe Street from downtown Olathe, one passes old tree-lined side streets for about a dozen blocks and then travels for two miles between comfortable middle-class housing developments nestled in secure cul-de-sacs before arriving at the north edge of Olathe Lake. For the next seven miles until reaching the old Sunflower munitions facility, the land is occupied by pastures, cornfields, woods, and an occasional farmhouse. This area extending north almost to the Kansas River and south to the New Century Business Park at Gardner is one of Olathe's twelve designated growth corridors. It can easily accommodate more than 50,000 new homes on spacious half-acre lots. Add open land to the south toward Spring Hill and Stilwell and it is understandable that Olathe's officials anticipate having a population of 300,000 or more as part of a total population in Johnson County of nearly 750,000 by 2040. Growth on the same scale could not happen in Overland Park, Lenexa, Leawood, or Raytown, where nearly all available land is occupied, but it could occur across the state line in Lee's Summit and Grandview, to the east in Blue Springs, or further from Kansas City in towns like Liberty, Mosby, Raymore, and Pleasant Hill.

Officials are quick to point out that projections may be wrong, but they argue that there is little standing in the way of rapid growth other than a faltering economy. Further development seems to attract little organized resistance from farmers and land owners or from environmentally minded inhabitants. If the city decides to annex additional land, state law enables it to do so, and if farmers are reluctant to see property turned into developments, the city can require them to install sewers and drainage systems they cannot otherwise afford. Residents figure the way to reduce traffic congestion is to build more roads, and the only way to have more variety in restaurants and boutiques is to add more housing developments. The best estimate of future growth, officials say, is the recent past. Judging from that, building infrastructure is the surest way to attract a continuing stream of newcomers.

The social dynamics that draw people to suburban communities and keep them from leaving must be factored in as well, and these also point to sustained growth. People stay because they have friends and family in the area. In edge cities like Olathe where many residents are young and have families, births exceed deaths by a ratio of three to one, meaning simply that there are more children to grow up and potentially stay than in small rural communities composed of older residents. Major moves typically occur during and shortly after college for those who go to college. Places like Olathe with high-tech industries, near a major university, and with several colleges and research parks of their own are in good shape to attract recent grads.[74] In addition, college-educated residents working in professions and high-tech industries have spending capacity that drives markets for new retail stores and encourages new housing to be built as long as open land is available. Market-potential ratings that give small communities in the region low scores rate edge cities well above average. Scores are highest in the largest edge cities, which also happen to be the most affluent, and peg them as especially favorable markets for home and auto loans, appliances, furniture, computers, lawn and garden equipment, sporting events, and dining out.[75]

But the same factors suggest that future growth could occur less rapidly than leaders might anticipate. Preferences to live near friends and family and affinities for the region's ambience deter people from moving away but also discourage them from migrating into the region. Among all residents living in Middle Western edge cities when the 2000 decennial census was taken, two-thirds were natives of their state and of the remaining third, more than half had been born in the Midwest. Only 15 percent had been born in another region. Those figures suggest that residents of edge cities have roots in the area and are likely to stay, but they contradict impressions that these Middle Western cities are drawing huge numbers from other parts of the county. Only three percent of current residents had been born in the Northeast, 7 percent in the South, and 5 percent in the West. Measures of shorter-term movement underscore the strength of regional loyalties as well. Half lived in a different house in 2000 than in 1995, but few moved very far: 77 percent of edge city residents had lived in the same county, 88 percent in the same state, and 93 percent in the Middle West. Only 1 percent had lived in the Northeast, 3 percent in the South, and 2 percent in the West.[76]

Although its dramatic growth suggested that it had much to offer, Johnson County drew more heavily from the immediate region than from anywhere else. Fifty-four percent of its population in 2007 had been born in Kansas. That was true for 47 percent of Olatheans and 60 percent of Overland Park's residents. One reason was the county's relatively high ratio of births to deaths, allowing natural increase to account for 35 percent of its growth in the 1980s, 39 percent in the 1990s, and 43 percent from 2001 to 2007. A second reason was that the largest number of newcomers still came from Wyandotte County and that other important sources included Wichita and Topeka and the state's two largest college towns, Manhattan and Lawrence. Among migrants from other states, the largest numbers came from nearby Jackson and Clay counties in Missouri. Of the fifty counties sending the most people to Johnson County between 1995 and 2000, thirty were in Kansas, Missouri, Nebraska, Iowa, and Oklahoma. Smaller numbers trickled in from declining rural counties as well. During that half decade, for example, fifty-six people arrived from Smith County.

The point was not that Johnson County was unable to attract newcomers from other regions, only that selling a Kansas prairie town was not always easy. "Right about the time I was set to finish my sophomore year of high school, my father dropped a bombshell at the kitchen table," radio journalist Laura Lorson remembered. They were moving to Olathe. "Kansas? I asked. Dorothy? Wheat? Gateway to Nebraska? That Kansas?"[77] They did move, and she eventually made Kansas her home, but getting used to it was hard. Sara Vincent recalled the day her husband announced he was being transferred to Kansas. "I looked at him and I put my head down on the kitchen counter and I absolutely sobbed. 'What the hell are you doing wrong? I can't believe you're making me do this. What's in Kansas?' I just couldn't believe it."[78]

Moving to Johnson County was easier for people who lived in Kansas City or were escaping small towns in western Kansas or central Nebraska. Yet some of those residents found the bustling expansion unpleasant and relocated to quieter communities south or west of Johnson County, like Paola or Ottawa. Others found Olathe distressingly uninteresting, a place with shopping malls but no history and little diversity. The journalist Thomas Frank, who grew up near Olathe, said it was a cupcake land of look-alike McMansions.[79] The historian Randall J. Stephens, also from Olathe, found himself drawn to "gritty, dusty, frightening" topics unfamiliar in his hometown.[80] A Kansas Citian wrote that Johnson County had a "sterile feeling about it, too clean, too nice." Like a cupcake, it was "perfectly packaged, pretty and decorated and oh so sweet but empty of any substance."[81]

Residents of neighboring towns noted that Olathe had become too large and had too many four-lane highways and too many industrial parks. They preferred smaller communities with better-preserved downtowns and family businesses. Lee's Summit resident Nancy Burns, for example, said Johnson County had too many huge corporations, which created a "different attitude about life," whereas her community prided itself on small businesses and a historic downtown.[82] "We have a lot of chain restaurants and chain stores," Sara Vincent acknowledged, but little in the way of "mom-and-pop shops or a favorite dive where you want to go for pizza. It is very sterile that way. The communities are absolutely beautiful. Even the gas stations and car washes have flowerbeds. There is no wrong side of the track."

These were some of the possible deterrents to future edge-city growth. Another was that edge cities depended not only on their capacity to attract business and lure new residents but also on the commercial health of the larger metropolitan areas of which they were a part. Jordan Rappaport, a senior economist at the Federal Reserve Bank of Kansas City, examined this relationship in a national study of sixty-four metropolitan areas between 1970 and 2000. Overall, suburban growth and central-city growth were closely related. The areas with the highest growth were Phoenix, Tucson, Austin, and El Paso. Omaha, St. Louis, and Wichita had low city and suburban growth. Kansas City's population had declined, and its suburban growth was slower than would have been the case otherwise.[83] What Kansas City had in its favor was location. It was the largest metropolitan area between St. Louis and Denver and between Minneapolis–St. Paul and Dallas. So it was not unusual, as Robert J. Marcusse, president and CEO of the Kansas City Area Development Council, observed, "for a young man or woman to graduate from one of our regional universities and set their sights on the big city."[84] Kansas City attracted its share of college-educated young people, but at the same time, it felt the impact of competition from other cities and often struggled with its image of having little to offer those without families or not yet ready to settle in the suburbs. Then there were the uncertainties of jobs, fuel prices, and housing costs. Although housing was cheaper than in many locations, data collected among Olathe's 30,000 home owners in 2007 revealed that 85 percent held mortgages on their homes and that 25 percent were spending more than the recommended share of their monthly income on homeowner costs.[85] When joblessness rose and foreclosures took root, many found themselves in jeopardy.[86]

If the gilded cage was imperfect, its distinctiveness as a beacon of privilege nevertheless stood out. Median household incomes in Johnson County rose faster in every decade from 1950 to the end of the century than they did in Wyandotte County. The growing disparity was evident in the fact that Johnson

County incomes averaged only 20 percent more than Wyandotte County incomes in 1949, but that difference grew to 39 percent in 1959, 45 percent in 1969, 63 percent in 1979, 80 percent in 1989, and 102 percent in 2000. The difference between Johnson County and many of the state's rural counties was even greater. For instance, median household incomes in Smith County in 2000 were just 45 percent of those in Johnson County.[87]

Edge-city privilege made it harder for residents to see the other side. It was true, as Sara Vincent observed, that people in Kansas City's lower-income neighborhoods struggled with poverty and crime. They were seventeen minutes away and that was far enough to be out of sight and out of mind. Olatheans imagined how nice it would be to have a small-town atmosphere with a quaint downtown and mom-and-pop stores, but the reality of small Middle Western towns included vacant storefronts, decaying houses, and families who retreated there because they suffered misfortune or did not have the skills to function in Olathe's high-powered job market. Suburban residents valued diversity, but that sometimes referred to shopping options and dining opportunities.

Bobby Love moved to Olathe in 1981, raised by parents of modest means in the southwest Kansas meatpacking town of Liberal, where he expected to become a teacher some day. But during his senior year in college, Bobby started working for an oil company that transferred him from place to place until he landed in Olathe. A few years later, feeling a call to the ministry, he completed seminary and became a pastor. Reverend Bobby Love is passionate about Olathe. When he goes back home to Liberal, he says, he finds it depressing, but Olathe is "a land flowing with milk and honey." The city works hard to provide excellent schools, everything is new, parks and walking trails are everywhere, and when his parents—now in their eighties—come to visit, there is even a place nearby to go fishing. It's not the kind of community that's "affordable to the average Joe the plumber," he says.[88]

And that bothers him because the plumber who cannot afford to live in Olathe very often lives in Kansas City's lower-income tracts—or struggles to make ends meet in Johnson County—and is black or Hispanic. Reverend Love is the pastor of Olathe's oldest African American church, Second Baptist, organized in 1868 as the First Baptist Church of Olathe Colored. The congregation, nearly 100 percent of whom are African American, meets each Sunday in a white frame building constructed in 1882 on land its founders purchased near the center of town for $35. At that time, about two hundred African Americans lived in Olathe. Most lived in the northeast quadrant of town where the church was located, and their children attended an all-colored school four blocks from the church. In 1918, following a series of newspaper editorials warning that African Americans would likely be asking to send their children to one of the white schools if the dilapidated black school was not replaced, a new building was constructed. It remained segregated until 1957.[89] In 1981, when Bobby Love arrived, many of Olathe's African American residents remained in neighborhoods closest to the church. While only 11 percent of the total population lived in the census tract in which these neighborhoods were located, 47 percent of the town's African American population did.[90]

Over the next twenty years, as the city expanded, Olathe's African American population grew significantly and the earlier residential concentration diminished. When the 2000 decennial census was conducted, only 20 percent of the city's African Americans still lived in the neighborhoods closest to Second Baptist. Still, half of the black population lived in older sections of town where housing was least expensive, and African Americans accounted for less than 4 percent of the city's total population. In half the census tracts, there were fewer than a hundred African American residents; and in ten, there were fewer than fifty. Only twelve of Olathe's 1,300 schoolteachers were African American.[91]

That was better than in neighboring Leawood, where restrictive covenants had long been written to keep out African Americans and where an American Civil Liberties Union report alleged that racial profiling continued. But it was not the pattern Olathe's leaders advertised or hoped would continue. In 2004, the City Council's Strategic Planning Steering Committee summarized the results of a yearlong study of what the city's objectives should be. The report emphasized continuing vigilance in meeting rising demands for water, snow removal, waste disposal, transportation, and emergency services but noted the importance of being a "welcoming, diverse community that recognizes and celebrates the cultural richness that results from the respect of all people."[92] It was true that Olathe was becoming more diverse. During the 2007–2008 school year, more than 1,500 of the 26,000 students in Olathe's forty-three schools reported their race as African American. More than 1,100 were Hispanic and 2,400 said they were of mixed race. The district offered training in seven international languages, including Japanese and Chinese. Ten percent of the community's residents were foreign born. Like that of other relatively affluent edge cities, Olathe's population was also more diverse economically than casual appearances may have suggested. While 5 percent of families enjoyed incomes above $200,000, 13 percent earned less than $35,000. More than 1,500 families received food-stamp benefits or cash public assistance.[93]

Most of the members at Olathe's Second Baptist Church were middle class, but many had relatives in Kansas City and elsewhere who were not. Reverend Love routinely received requests for help from the homeless and from the county's NAACP director to assist needy families. The church did what it could to provide food and shelter, and Reverend Love often found himself on the forefront of racial and economic issues in the community. He headed Olathe's fair housing initiative, which investigated fair housing noncompliance cases, and worked through the city's Human Relations Commission on discrimination complaints and equal employment issues. He says it can be quite an adjustment for an African American family moving to Olathe. There were times when his son was the only black student in his class. Less than a handful of African Americans lived in Reverend Love's subdivision. As Olathe grows, he wishes it made more of an effort to encourage racial and economic diversity. "My pet peeve," he says, is wanting "a certain percentage of minority companies" and support for the disadvantaged "so that everybody is participating in the buildup of the community."

Edge cities like Olathe increasingly pride themselves on being more diverse and more accepting of diversity than they were in the past. Diversity sometimes means only that the percentage of African Americans is inching up slightly, that Hispanics are more numerous, and that there may be a new mosque somewhere in town or at least a greater variety of ethnic restaurants. The issue is not that anyone is opposed to having neighbors unlike themselves but that emphasizing good schools, high-paying jobs, and comfortable housing developments does not always lead to greater inclusion. Residents of edge cities say a person can do only so much. Even in the best of circumstances, pursuing the good life in suburbia has always juxtaposed the insistent longing for a serene tempo against the drumbeat of climbing expectations. Keeping one's affairs in order may be challenging enough without contemplating where the community is headed. People want what they want, Reverend Love says. "A big house. A new car. A house full of furniture. Everybody is overextended."

Afterword

Down the sanded country road, past an overgrown hedge row and an unused pasture, just beyond a small rise a quarter of a mile from where I grew up, stands an abandoned farmhouse owned by our closest neighbors, the Morgan-fields, before they retired in the late 1950s. The shabby frame house, nearly obscured by tall prairie grass and weeds, has turned a weathered gray. None of the windows are intact. Tenants made it their home for a few years, and squatters for a few more after that. A sagging shed that served well in its time as a chicken coop remains, but the grand red barn where fat roan cows once came to be milked has collapsed. A quarter mile to the south where the Bains, an enterprising young farm family, lived, nothing exists but a clump of trees and the outline of the house's and barn's foundations. After they quit farming, Mr. and Mrs. Bain lived in town for a few years and died one day when a truck careered into their car. A half mile beyond their former house is the remnant of the old Wilms place, which burned to the ground after being struck by lightning. A half mile to the north is where the Staffords lived, until a teenager stole his father's rifle one night and shot Mr. Stafford in the head through the kitchen window.

The farmhouse I grew up in fared a little better than any of its neighbors. Called Sunny Crest Farm by its original owners, it was solidly constructed in 1911, but after several subsequent families lived there, including one whose son committed suicide in the garage and another that lost everything during the Great Depression, it was in disrepair by the time my parents bought it in 1952. My mother sold it shortly after my father died in 1965. The new owners kept it for several years as a place to raise dogs and then sold it to a man who used it to salvage parts from wrecked vehicles that soon surrounded the house and decaying outbuildings.

The small farmhouse we occupied before that was three and a half miles away. My parents bought it in 1945 when my father came home from World War II. They invested their savings and poured their energy into fixing it up, installing indoor plumbing and electricity, planting hundreds of trees and a garden, and repairing the barn and shed. In 1951, the state condemned the property to build a highway. A year later, our house was gone. I visited the site a few years ago. In the ditch under a layer of dead weeds was a roll of barbed wire my father had used to put up a fence. No other sign of his work remained.

On that trip, I drove the two strikingly familiar miles into town where my parents bought groceries at Suchland's store and banked at the tall brick building on the corner and where I attended grade school. The grade school building was new in the late 1940s, and a large basketball gymnasium was added in 1958. In those years, more than a hundred children went to the school and about six hundred people lived in the town. Times were hard for us but even harder for the families of many people who had come as section hands for the railroad and to work in the oil fields or on the farms. My friend Jimmy lived with his family in a dugout cut into the side of a hill, surviving mostly on fifty-pound bags of peanuts during the long winter his father was laid up with a broken leg. Galen lived in a drafty, unpainted ramshackle house next to the railroad track with plastic nailed over the windows and practically no furniture. Diane carried deep scars from the night she was dragged out of the upstairs window of her burning house. By the end of the century, the school was boarded up and the town's population had dropped by two-thirds.

I grew up believing I would spend my life in the Middle West, probably farming the small plot of land my father owned and where I drove a tractor every summer until I was eighteen, and probably supplementing my income by teaching school, like my mother did, or doing bookkeeping and tax returns, which was one of the few professions available in a county seat of fewer than four thousand people. My father's death from a massive heart attack when I was a freshman in college altered those plans and eventually led me to graduate school and a very different life than the one I had imagined. Perhaps because I had expected to stay, and perhaps because I had known it as my home, I held a strong attachment to the Middle West even though I no longer lived there. But unlike writers who remain attached to their places of origin through family and friends, I had no such continuing connections. Nor did the heavy routine demands of work and family make it possible to return except on rare occasions. When I did return, there were the ghost memories of people who no longer existed and the strangeness of realities that had taken their place. Understanding how the Middle West had changed was the aim that impelled me to write this book.

The journey began with several lengthy road trips through the Middle West, driving thousands of miles along back roads and highways through small country towns and the region's larger cities. I talked to strangers at gas stations and restaurants, visited places I had heard about as a child, and looked up cousins I had not seen in years. I found the farm my German great-grandfather purchased in 1878 and his grave in the cemetery on land the railroad company gave to his neighbors. I located the farm my great-grandfather from West Virginia bought in 1870 and visited his unmarked grave at the state insane asylum where he spent the last twenty years of his life suffering from trauma inflicted by the Civil War. My travels took me onto an interstate built through the slum neighborhood where his widow ran a boardinghouse and through the cities where my grandmother worked as a stenographer and my mother taught school. I learned how little I knew about the region, despite having studied its history in school and having considered it home. But one lesson from my childhood was reaffirmed: if an outsider asked where you were from, you replied simply that you were from the Midwest, and if a Midwesterner asked, you probably said proudly that you were from Kansas or Nebraska or Iowa or Missouri; but your real identity was your hometown. Small or large, your home community was what you knew. It was Main Street, the streets and shops you knew, the school you attended, its mascot, its football field, the park, the favorite swimming hole, the doughnut shop where friends gathered, the church where funerals were held, the place where people knew your name.

I determined that whatever I might be able to learn about the Middle West as a region of the country, I had to be true to that realization about the importance of communities. I opted for what we sociologists call a multimethod research design. It would combine statistical data about individuals, towns, and counties with qualitative information about local histories, events, and perceptions drawn from interviews, observations, and publications. I also knew that I would have to write as an outsider. However much I might identify with the communities I studied, it was not possible to know them the way insiders did. And yet there is an advantage in approaching subject matter with which one is not intimately familiar. Had I never left the Middle West, it likely would not have occurred to me to write about it at all. My audience would be people like myself who did not live there, who may have had relatives who did, and who most likely regarded the Middle West as a large blank space between the excitement of the nation's coasts.

I had never been to Lebanon, Kansas, or Smith Center until one of my research trips took me there. They were enough like my home community that I felt it possible to understand them. They had the further good fortune of having been visited and written about enough by outsiders that impressions of their history could be pieced together. Putting their stories together with statistical evidence gave me a different picture of the rural Middle West in the 1950s than anything I had read in standard accounts. The story in those accounts was of hard times during the Dust Bowl of the 1930s, good times during World War II at least for those who stayed home, and even better times in the 1950s. That story fit some of what I grew up hearing my parents tell, but not all. I knew they had waited until the Depression was over to marry and that my father had worked as a farm laborer for a dollar a day in the 1930s. The part about later prosperity did not square with my parents' income of only a thousand dollars a year in the early 1950s or with the struggles of so many of our neighbors. The statistical evidence revealed that our experience was not unique. Recovery from the Great Depression lasted well into the 1950s. Farmers with luck enough to have purchased cheap land at the right time, to have struck oil, or to have had wealthy relatives did well. Tens of thousands of farmers did not. The decade after World War II was difficult for nearly everyone. Roads, electricity, telephone service, and machinery had all been put on hold by the Depression and the war. Marginal farmers were unable to make the transition. They did not have the capital to purchase additional land, to mechanize, or to invest in livestock. Ultimately, their failure nevertheless served the region and the nation. Farming became better capitalized and more efficient as a result.

A sociological truism is that in unsettled times, people tell stories to make sense of what they are experiencing. The trouble with this truism is that all times are, in their particular ways, unsettled. Certainly the Middle West was unsettled even in the nineteenth century when it was being, in a different sense of the word, settled. It was unsettled in the 1930s by the dust storms and in the 1940s by the war. Yet as I read stories of people growing up in the 1950s, pondered their accounts in interviews, and looked through old newspapers and magazines, I was struck that the Middle West was going through a transition that was as much cultural as economic or demographic. The old stories of cowboys and Indians, pioneers, and Dust Bowl survivors were being told, but with different meanings. The heartland was redefining itself, seeking to offset the country-bumpkin images still present in the mainstream press, and aiming to demonstrate that it was as modern as anywhere else while preserving some of its distinctive identity. A region's self-image is always in flux, but I believe the Middle West's emphasis on friendliness, hospitality, and native ingenuity owes much to the redefinition of its heritage that occurred in the 1950s and 1960s.

In seeking factors facilitating the Middle West's economic growth during the last half of the twentieth century, I was most surprised by the strength of its historic emphasis on education. I grew up believing that my parents valued education because my father's had stopped in eighth grade and my mother was in her fifties before she earned a college degree. By a truly unusual confluence of events, I wound up as an adult among people who traced their ancestry to graduates of elite colleges for five to ten generations and had little use for those who could not. But the Middle West was remarkably successful in bringing the cherished ideals of democratic education—of schooling for all—into reality. It became the education belt, with a strong system of primary and secondary education that prepared its children well for the challenges they faced on farms and in small towns, and it was on that basis that the region established the colleges and universities that became instrumental in its subsequent economic development.

My surprise in researching the decline of small communities was not that so many were losing population but that there was as much optimism and as robust a sense of community present in the ones that remained. This is not to suggest that things are going well in the region's smallest communities. In town after town, I was struck by the numerous houses that were in ill repair, by the families living in an abandoned schoolhouse they had fixed up as a home or in an aging trailer home, by the boarded-up stores and shops with no customers, by the churches no longer in use, and by the ancient pickup trucks and rusted automobiles. The smallest towns have become places where the elderly poor still reside and where younger families with meager incomes have sought refuge because it was all they could afford. The larger towns with even three thousand to five thousand residents, though, are doing better. The school very likely has fewer children than it did a few years ago, but it is probably the newest building in town and serves as a community center. A small manufacturing plant may keep some of the residents employed as others commute to larger towns twenty or thirty miles away. As long as fuel prices do not rise exorbitantly, these communities provide attractive locations for their residents.

The small communities were part of a regional network of railroads from almost the start, and they are more nearly woven together now than ever before by paved highways and trucking companies. Residents shop at Walmart for goods imported from China, order supplies online, and are connected in the remotest areas by cell phone. The agricultural cooperatives of the early twentieth century have expanded in geographic scope and product lines. Agribusiness has simply evolved to make better use of the decentralization that these modes of communication provide. The meat-processing industry is the part of agribusiness that has attracted the greatest attention, not only because of concerns about packaged meals in fast-food chains, but also because of questions about human-rights violations, immigrant labor, and ethnic tensions. Like other researchers, I was drawn to Garden City because of its prominence as a meat-processing center. But I came away impressed by the community's institutions as much as by the challenges it faced. Garden City was adapting to the growth, immigration, ethnic diversity, and economic uncertainties it experienced.

I saved the cities and suburbs until last, even though that is where the region's population is increasingly located, because the story of suburban growth is in many respects least characteristic of the Middle West. It is a story that researchers for many years have tracked near New York City, Los Angeles, Atlanta, Houston, Phoenix, and similar locations in the Sunbelt and on the coasts. Residents in the Middle West's edge cities informed me in no uncertain terms that it was not unusual at all to find populous suburbs in the region, and yet there is a history to these communities that residents who may have lived there only a few years do not always appreciate. Olathe and other communities in Johnson County, Kansas, are places where dramatic growth is a way of life and is expected to continue for decades to come. Olathe is also where one of my great grandfathers settled shortly after the Civil War, where my mother was born, near where she returned to teach school in the late 1930s, where my wife's father was a pastor in the 1940s, and near where my wife was born. Olathe's growth in the twenty-first century is continuous with its history in those earlier decades. It, like other edge cities, has taken the place of farms, but it has long depended on its adjacency to one of the region's largest urban centers and has developed not only as a bedroom community but also because of military installations, entrepreneurial manufacturing and distribution firms, and investments in education and technology.

The remaking of a region is evident in more ways than I have been able to describe here. Thirty miles from where I was raised, a massive wind farm has emerged with more than a hundred towering machines that produce energy free of ill effects to the environment. Nearby is a new ethanol plant that has weathered uncertain government policies and is bringing new jobs to the area. My hometown recently celebrated the construction of a new hospital that dramatically improves its medical capabilities. There is a small industrial park and a new community center. At the high school, where nearly 100 percent of the students used to be white Anglos, 30 percent are now Hispanic.

Sociologists sometimes pride themselves on studies that seize on one aspect of social life, such as class differences or the role of the state, and claim to explain everything else in relation to that aspect. I confess to never having found such studies appealing. Communities are too complex to be understood that way. The remaking of the Middle West has happened because of disparate developments in agriculture, culture, education, towns, and business. In popular accounts, a common thread in these developments is the region's emphasis on rugged individualism. Even now, many of the people I spoke to insisted that things would be better if they were simply left alone. They had little use for government intervention or regulation, especially if that meant the federal government. And yet the single theme that runs through so much of what I have described is the hand of government. Ordinary citizens may have chafed at government's role in subsidizing the railroads or commandeering land for munitions plants, but they were as often as not the beneficiaries of government planning as well.

That, though, is a lesson that probably speaks more to me than to anyone else. For I was the one who, as a five-year-old, protesting in my small way against government intrusion, committed my first act of civil disobedience by pulling up each of the orange-topped stakes the transportation department's surveyors placed on our property to mark where they planned to construct the highway through our home.

Appendix

Information about Middle Western communities and their residents was obtained through approximately 200 qualitative oral history and informant interviews. Each interview lasted about an hour and a half, with some ranging up to three hours, using semistructured interview guides that were tailored to different communities and included questions about personal life histories, community developments, perceptions, and values. The interviews were conducted in more than a hundred different communities, ranging in size from fewer than 100 people to more than 100,000. More than half were conducted in towns with fewer than 2,000. Respondents ranged in age from twenty-three to ninety-four and were currently or formerly employed in more than seventy different occupations, the most common of which were farmer, homemaker, pastor, school administrator, teacher, and town official. In addition to interviews with individuals, six focus groups were convened and their discussions tape-recorded. Interviews were conducted by Aislinn Addington, Brittany Hanstad, Bruce Carruthers, and Lori Wiebold-Lippisch, who were graduate students at the time in sociology at the University of Kansas; Cynthia Reynolds and Melissa Virts, an instructor and student, respectively, at Sterling College; Justin Farrell, a student from Nebraska at Princeton Theological Seminary; Sylvia Kundrats, Janice Derstine, and Stephen Myers of rural Pennsylvania; and Karen Myers, who also supervised the transcription of the interviews.

Archival materials were obtained from numerous collections at college and university libraries and at local and state historical societies through personal visits and interlibrary loan. I am especially grateful for assistance from Ben Primer at Princeton's Mudd Manuscript Library, Wangyal Shawa at Princeton's Geospatial Information Center, Thomas Whitehead in Special Collections at Temple University's Paley Library, Christine DiBella at the Historical Society of Pennsylvania, and Sharon M. Lake at the Iowa Women's Archives of the University of Iowa Libraries, as well as the staffs at the Kansas State Historical Society, Oklahoma Historical Society, State Historical Society of Wisconsin, Finney County Historical Museum, Finney County Register of Deeds Office, Stafford County Historical Society, Smith Center Public Library, Kansas State University Library, Pennsylvania State University Library, University of Minnesota Library, University of Wisconsin Library, North Dakota State Library, Vinton Public Library, Hagley Museum and Library, and Firestone and Stokes Libraries at Princeton University. Also of particular value were the electronic resources to which I had access through Princeton University, including America's Historical Newspapers, Ancestry Library Edition, Jstor, Lexis-Nexis Academic, Library of Congress Online Collections, Making of America Digital Books and Journals, Moody's, NewsBank, Proquest, and Securities and Exchange Commission Information.

Quantitative data were obtained as electronic datafiles from the Interuniversity Consortium for Political and Social Research at the University of Michigan and the

Missouri Census Data Center. These archives proved to be the best sources for data at the level of incorporated places, counties, zip codes, and census tracts. Individual-level census data were obtained from the Integrated Public Use Microdata Series produced by Steven Ruggles, Matthew Sobek, Trent Alexander, Catherine A. Fitch, Ronald Goeken, Patricia Kelly Hall, Miriam King, and Chad Ronnander at the University of Minnesota Population Center. Additional datafiles and hard-copy tabular information were obtained from the U.S. Census Bureau's online collections, the Internal Revenue Service, the Reference USA and ESRI corporations, the Middle West's state-level data centers, and departments of commerce, transportation, and education. Phillip Connor provided valuable assistance in assembling the various datafiles.

The tables in this appendix provide details supplementing what could reasonably be summarized in the text and in notes about many of the demographic and economic variables discussed. These tables include state-by-state comparisons of some of the material examined in the event that readers may be interested in those details. Several of the tables present the results of key binary logistic and ordinary least squares regression analyses. All of the data from which these tables and other analyses presented in the text were derived are in the public domain at the archives previously mentioned.

Table 1.

Population and Gross Domestic Product per Capita Relative to United States

	Population as Percentage of U.S. Population					
	1963	*1970*	*1980*	*1990*	*2000*	*2006*
Arkansas	0.99%	0.94%	1.01%	0.94%	0.95%	0.94%
Iowa	1.45%	1.38%	1.28%	1.11%	1.04%	0.99%
Kansas	1.17%	1.10%	1.04%	0.99%	0.95%	0.92%
Minnesota	1.87%	1.86%	1.79%	1.76%	1.75%	1.72%
Missouri	2.32%	2.28%	2.16%	2.05%	1.99%	1.95%
Nebraska	0.78%	0.73%	0.69%	0.63%	0.61%	0.59%
North Dakota	0.34%	0.30%	0.29%	0.25%	0.23%	0.21%
Oklahoma	1.29%	1.25%	1.34%	1.26%	1.22%	1.19%
South Dakota	0.37%	0.33%	0.30%	0.28%	0.27%	0.26%
Total	10.58%	10.17%	9.90%	9.28%	9.00%	8.78%

	Per Capita GDP as Percentage of U.S. per Capita GDP					
	1963	*1970*	*1980*	*1990*	*2000*	*2006*
Arkansas	62.9%	69.9%	73.5%	71.3%	72.2%	74.0%
Iowa	88.4%	91.4%	97.8%	88.6%	89.2%	94.7%
Kansas	86.5%	87.8%	99.9%	91.1%	89.1%	90.9%
Minnesota	94.8%	98.3%	101.9%	100.8%	108.7%	109.6%
Missouri	96.6%	96.2%	90.8%	89.5%	91.3%	88.4%
Nebraska	89.6%	93.7%	96.6%	94.1%	93.8%	96.8%
North Dakota	78.0%	74.7%	98.5%	79.4%	80.2%	91.5%
Oklahoma	78.1%	81.5%	104.2%	80.8%	75.3%	78.4%
South Dakota	70.9%	74.1%	83.1%	81.1%	88.5%	95.2%
Total	86.6%	89.3%	95.1%	88.4%	89.8%	91.5%

Source: U.S. Census Bureau; U.S. Bureau of Economic Analysis

Table 2.
Annual Change in U.S. Farm Population

Year	Farm Population (x 1,000)	To Farms (x 1,000)	From Farms (x 1,000)	Natural Increase (x 1,000)	Net Migration (x 1,000)
1936	31,737	825	1,624	375	−799
1937	31,266	719	1,553	363	−834
1938	30,980	872	1,533	375	−661
1939	30,840	823	1,368	405	−545
1940	30,547	819	1,522	410	−703
1941	30,273	696	1,329	359	−633
1942	29,234	822	2,246	385	−1,424
1943	26,618	824	3,799	422	−2,975
1944	25,495	1,095	2,658	377	−1,563
1945	25,295	916	1,480	364	−564
1946	26,483	2,585	1,721	324	864
1947	27,124	1,768	1,617	490	151
1948	25,903	1,016	2,702	465	−1,686
1949	25,954	1,171	1,542	422	−371
1950	25,058	995	2,309	418	−1,314
1951	24,160	597	1,899	404	−1,302
1952	24,283	643	914	394	−271
1953	22,679	528	2,524	392	−1,996
1954	22,099	674	1,636	382	−962
1955	22,438	547	572	364	−25
1956	22,362	504	939	359	−435
1957	21,606	461	1,595	378	−1,134
1958	21,388	475	1,051	358	−576
1959	21,172	440	988	332	−548

Source: U.S. Department of Agriculture

Table 3.
Mean Number of Children Born by State, Year, and Farm Status

	Farm Women Aged 45 and Older							
	1900	1910	1940	1950	1960	1970	1980	1990
Arkansas	6.3	6.2	4.1	4.2	3.9	3.4	3.1	3.2
Iowa	5.4	5.5	3.2	3.4	3.0	3.0	3.3	3.3
Kansas	5.7	5.7	3.4	3.3	3.0	2.7	3.0	3.3
Minnesota	5.9	6.2	3.8	3.9	3.5	3.4	3.7	3.7
Missouri	5.8	5.6	3.6	3.3	2.9	2.9	2.9	3.0
Nebraska	6.0	5.8	3.5	3.4	3.1	3.2	3.1	3.3
North Dakota	5.9	6.2	4.5	4.8	4.0	3.3	3.8	3.8
Oklahoma	6.0	6.3	3.9	3.8	3.5	2.9	3.0	2.8
South Dakota	5.6	6.2	4.1	3.3	3.6	3.1	3.5	3.7
Total	5.8	5.9	3.7	3.6	3.3	3.1	3.2	3.3

	Nonfarm Women Aged 45 and Older							
	1900	1910	1940	1950	1960	1970	1980	1990
Arkansas	5.1	5.0	3.3	3.3	3.3	3.0	2.9	2.9
Iowa	4.8	4.7	2.9	2.7	2.7	2.5	2.7	3.0
Kansas	4.7	4.8	2.9	3.0	2.7	2.4	2.6	2.9
Minnesota	4.6	4.8	2.9	2.9	2.8	2.5	2.9	3.4
Missouri	5.0	4.8	2.5	2.6	2.4	2.3	2.5	2.8
Nebraska	4.9	5.1	3.1	2.9	2.8	2.6	2.6	3.0
North Dakota	4.7	5.3	3.6	3.7	3.7	3.3	3.5	3.4
Oklahoma	4.7	5.3	3.6	3.3	3.1	2.7	2.7	3.0
South Dakota	4.5	4.9	3.4	3.2	3.3	3.0	3.1	3.4
Total	4.8	4.8	3.0	2.9	2.8	2.6	2.7	3.0

Source: U.S. Census, 1 Percent Public Use Microsamples

Table 4.
Sources of Decline in Agricultural Labor Force per County, 1950 to 1960

	Arkansas	Iowa	Kansas	Minnesota	Missouri	Nebraska	N Dakota	Oklahoma	S Dakota
Mechanization									
Farms with tractors 1950	-0.766	-0.768	-0.447	-0.976	-0.760	—	—	-0.743	—
Farms with tractors 1959	-0.511	-0.354	-0.387	-0.517	-0.662	—	—	-0.740	-0.296
Farms with trucks 1950	-0.606	-0.554	—	-0.427	0.469	—	—	-0.689	—
Farms with trucks 1959	-0.255	-0.429	—	-0.384	—	—	—	-0.677	—
Farms with telephones 1950	—	-0.723	—	-0.747	-0.573	—	—	-0.679	-0.735
Avg. farm electricity bill 1950	-0.396	-0.513	-0.289	-0.529	-0.610	—	—	-0.696	—
Magnet pull									
Avg. manufacturing wage 1947	—	—	-0.300	—	-0.511	—	—	-0.433	—
Avg. manufacturing wage 1958	—	—	—	—	-0.282	—	—	—	—
Percentage urban 1950	-0.337	—	—	-0.828	-0.707	—	—	-0.569	—
Marginality									
Median family income 1950	-0.500	-0.541	-0.497	-0.769	-0.960	—	—	-0.861	-0.358
Average farm value 1950	-0.630	-0.349	-0.497	-0.560	-0.613	—	—	-0.756	—
Value of farm products 1949	-0.572	-0.494	-0.242	-0.758	-0.739	—	—	-0.731	—
Value of crops sold 1949	-0.342	—	-0.253	-0.362	-0.231	0.260	—	-0.714	—
Value of livestock sold 1949	—	-0.330	—	-0.603	-0.576	-0.356	—	-0.391	—
Number of counties	75	99	105	87	115	93	53	77	68

Note: Standardized regression coefficients for percentage decline in agricultural labor force by each independent variable listed, controlling for total population, percentage agricultural labor force, and number of farms in 1950; coefficients shown significant at or beyond .05 probability

Table 5.
Sources of Decline in Farms per County, 1950 to 1960

	Arkansas	Iowa	Kansas	Minnesota	Missouri	Nebraska	N Dakota	Oklahoma	S Dakota
Mechanization									
Farms with tractors 1950	—	-0.848	-0.678	-0.946	-0.316	—	—	-0.678	—
Farms with tractors 1959	—	-0.431	-0.423	-0.618	-0.551	—	-0.374	-0.645	-0.456
Farms with trucks 1950	-0.901	-0.639	-0.379	-0.452	0.708	-0.356	—	-0.786	—
Farms with trucks 1959	-0.365	-0.397	-0.411	-0.300	0.258	-0.250	—	-0.728	—
Farms with telephones 1950	-0.567	—	—	-0.882	-0.699	—	—	-0.739	—
Avg. farm electricity bill 1950	-0.574	-0.427	-0.705	-0.444	-0.548	0.389	0.743	—	—
Magnet pull									
Avg. manufacturing wage 1947	0.397	—	-0.363	-0.295	-0.274	—	—	-0.422	—
Avg. manufacturing wage 1958	—	-0.280	—	-0.272	—	—	—	-0.394	—
Percentage urban 1950	—	—	—	-0.674	—	—	—	—	—
Marginality									
Median family income 1950	-0.739	-0.714	-0.552	-0.721	-0.857	-0.465	—	-0.795	-0.471
Average farm value 1950	—	-0.381	-0.770	-0.619	-0.312	-0.506	—	-0.740	-0.233
Value of farm products 1949	—	-0.681	-0.312	-0.798	-0.211	-0.438	—	-0.643	—
Value of crops sold 1949	0.404	—	-0.378	-0.313	0.319	-0.318	—	-0.576	—
Value of livestock sold 1949	-0.706	-0.527	—	-0.638	-0.490	—	—	-0.415	—
Number of counties	75	99	105	87	115	93	53	77	68

Note: Standardized regression coefficients for percentage decline in number of farms by each independent variable listed, controlling for total population, percentage agricultural labor force, and number of farms in 1950; coefficients shown significant at or beyond .05 probability

Table 6.
Educational Attainment in Middle Western States

	Percentage High School Graduate or More							
	1940	*1950*	*1960*	*1970*	*1980*	*1990*	*2000*	*2005*
Arkansas	15.0	23.3	28.8	39.9	54.9	66.3	81.7	81.4
Iowa	28.6	37.6	46.3	59.0	71.2	80.1	89.7	89.9
Kansas	28.2	39.2	48.2	59.9	72.3	81.3	88.1	91.4
Minnesota	24.8	34.6	43.9	57.6	72.4	82.4	90.8	92.7
Missouri	22.0	31.4	37.8	48.8	63.7	73.9	86.6	85.4
Nebraska	28.7	38.4	47.8	59.3	73.8	81.8	90.4	89.7
North Dakota	30.8	30.4	38.9	50.3	66.5	76.7	85.5	90.0
Oklahoma	26.4	33.0	40.5	51.6	65.7	74.6	86.1	85.2
South Dakota	24.6	31.4	42.2	53.3	68.5	77.1	91.8	88.5
United States	24.1	33.4	41.1	52.3	66.3	75.2	84.1	85.2

	Percentage with Four Years of College or More							
	1940	*1950*	*1960*	*1970*	*1980*	*1990*	*2000*	*2005*
Arkansas	2.3	5.2	4.8	3.6	9.7	13.3	18.4	17.5
Iowa	4.1	5.1	6.4	9.7	14.1	16.9	25.5	24.5
Kansas	4.6	6.0	8.1	11.3	15.7	21.1	27.3	30.4
Minnesota	4.2	5.6	7.5	11.1	16.7	21.8	31.2	34.3
Missouri	3.9	6.6	6.2	9.0	14.0	17.8	26.2	24.9
Nebraska	4.3	5.0	6.8	9.7	16.1	18.9	24.6	25.1
North Dakota	3.7	4.6	5.6	8.5	15.2	18.1	22.6	27.2
Oklahoma	4.7	6.2	7.8	10.0	15.7	17.8	22.5	24.0
South Dakota	3.8	5.0	5.8	8.6	14.2	17.2	25.7	25.1
United States	4.6	6.0	7.7	10.7	16.3	20.3	25.6	27.6

Source: U.S. Census; adults aged 25 and older

Table 7.

Literacy and Schooling in Six Middle West States in 1870

Literate (Age 25 and Over)	Odds Ratios from Binary Logistic Regression Models					
	Model 1	Model 2	Model 3	Model 4	Model 5	Model 6
Male	2.005	1.968	1.977			1.994
Age 25 to 40	1.509	1.453	1.406			1.435
Black	0.031	0.053	0.045		0.057	0.048
Northern birthplace		4.416	4.230		2.849	3.129
Foreign born		1.763	1.698			1.369
Foreign parents		1.009	0.902			0.858
Urban			1.693			1.687
Farm			0.897			0.867
Iowa				2.723	1.463	1.488
Kansas				1.786	1.372	1.355
Minnesota				1.948	1.281	1.225
Nebraska				4.368	2.631	2.454
Arkansas				0.342	0.593	0.700
Sig. (Wald statistic)	0.001	0.001	0.001	0.001	0.001	0.001
d.f.	3	6	8	5	7	13
Nagelkerke R square	0.234	0.282	0.288	0.098	0.263	0.294

In School (Age 5 to 13)	Model 1	Model 2	Model 3	Model 4	Model 5	Model 6
Male	1.100	1.100	1.107			1.112
Age 5 to 13	1.440	1.400	1.399			1.409
Black	0.177	0.230	0.223		0.268	0.238
Northern birthplace		1.754	1.791		1.388	1.097
Foreign born		0.760	0.797			0.534
Foreign parents		1.065	0.950			0.851
Urban			1.685			1.665
Farm			1.151			1.136
Iowa				2.118	1.540	1.961
Kansas				0.929	0.756	0.883
Minnesota				1.609	1.206	1.661
Nebraska				0.817	0.615	0.764
Arkansas				0.475	0.592	0.591
Sig. (Wald statistic)	0.001	0.001	0.001	0.001	0.001	0.001
d.f.	3	6	8	5	7	13
Nagelkerke R square	0.061	0.087	0.094	0.067	0.098	0.118

Source: 1870 U.S. Census, 1 Percent Public Use Microsample

Table 8.

Factors Predicting School Enrollment in the Middle West in 1870

Enrollment	Standardized Coefficients in OLS Regression Models					
	Model 1	Model 2	Model 3	Model 4	Model 5	Model 6
Percentage literate	0.421**	0.401**	0.275**		0.370**	0.368**
Percentage black	−0.164**	−0.183**	−0.262**		−0.259**	−0.253**
Percentage foreign born	−0.254**	−0.277**	−0.199**		−0.263**	−0.261**
Percentage urban		0.146**	−0.044			
Average farm value			0.397**		0.282**	0.268**
County tax per capita					0.049	
Local tax per capita						0.083*
Iowa				0.371**	0.272**	0.249**
Kansas				−0.057	0.020	0.021
Minnesota				−0.072	0.188**	0.183**
Nebraska				−0.114*	−0.041	−0.025
Arkansas				−0.179**	0.110*	0.118*
Adjusted R square	0.242	0.261	0.388	0.228	0.503	0.506
Standard error	0.227	0.224	0.191	0.229	0.164	0.163

Source: 1870 U.S. Census, County Data. Dependent variable = percent of population aged 5 to 18 enrolled in school in each county. ** .001 significance * .05 significance

Table 9.

Sources of County Variation in Secondary School Enrollment

	Percentage Illiterate 1910	Percentage Nonwhite 1950	Median Education 1950	Median Income 1950	Percentage Urban 1950	Percentage Clerical 1950	Adjusted R Square
Arkansas	−0.096	−0.299**	0.540**	0.373**	0.310**	0.343**	0.317**
Iowa	−0.337**	−0.039	0.278**	0.009	−0.072	0.039	0.190**
Kansas	−0.193*	−0.009	−0.090	0.033	−0.044	−0.105	0.025
Minnesota	−0.145	−0.135	0.201	0.431**	0.269*	0.306**	0.133*
Missouri	−0.702**	0.023	0.362**	0.259**	0.023	0.224*	0.512**
Nebraska	−0.037	−0.066	0.113	−0.010	−0.008	0.087	0.017
North Dakota	−0.445**	−0.024	0.382*	0.171	0.135	0.368**	0.134**
Oklahoma	−0.551**	−0.352**	0.303*	0.409**	0.012	0.090	0.284**
South Dakota	−0.169	−0.223	0.358**	0.458**	0.323*	0.373**	0.239*
Total	−0.385**	−0.090*	0.366**	0.395**	0.143**	0.268**	0.254**

Source: U.S. Census, County Data 1950, percentage of 14– through 17–year–olds enrolled in school in 1950; zero–order correlations and adjusted R squares. ** significant beyond .001 * significant beyond .01

Table 10.
Size of Middle Western Towns

		Percentage with Population in 1980 of:					
	Towns	Fewer than 250	250 to 499	500 to 1,499	1,500 to 4,999	5,000 to 19,999	20,000 or More
Arkansas	480	20.0	22.9	29.2	17.5	7.5	2.9
Iowa	948	28.4	21.0	30.1	13.5	5.1	2.0
Kansas	627	33.8	17.7	24.4	15.9	6.1	2.1
Minnesota	847	25.0	19.4	26.6	16.6	8.5	3.9
Missouri	904	27.1	20.8	23.3	17.0	8.8	2.9
Nebraska	531	36.9	23.0	25.6	8.5	4.5	1.5
North Dakota	359	50.4	18.9	18.9	7.5	3.1	1.1
Oklahoma	570	22.5	18.8	28.6	18.6	8.2	3.3
South Dakota	312	41.0	18.6	26.0	10.3	3.2	1.0
Total	5578	29.9	20.2	26.2	14.6	6.6	2.5

		Percentage with Population in 2005 of:					
	Towns	Fewer than 250	250 to 499	500 to 1,499	1,500 to 4,999	5,000 to 19,999	20,000 or More
Arkansas	496	24.4	20.6	24.8	19.2	6.7	4.4
Iowa	946	32.0	19.3	28.1	12.4	5.8	2.3
Kansas	626	36.4	17.1	23.5	13.7	6.2	3.0
Minnesota	851	28.1	14.9	24.2	16.5	10.6	5.8
Missouri	933	30.1	18.0	22.3	16.3	10.0	3.3
Nebraska	531	39.7	22.4	23.9	7.7	4.1	2.1
North Dakota	357	61.3	12.3	18.5	4.5	2.2	1.1
Oklahoma	584	27.9	17.6	26.7	15.4	8.9	3.4
South Dakota	308	44.8	17.2	25.0	8.4	3.2	1.3
Total	5632	33.8	17.9	24.4	13.5	7.1	3.2

Source: U.S. Census, 1980 and 2005, Incorporated Places

Table 11.
Average Town Size in Nine Middle West States, 1910 to 2005

						Mean Population of Towns in Each State					
	1910	1920	1930	1940	1950	1960	1970	1980	1990	2000	2005
Arkansas	1,420	1,557	1,641	1,704	2,149	2,340	2,559	2,878	2,973	3,292	3,485
Iowa	1,358	1,508	1,595	1,690	1,837	2,043	2,195	2,294	2,238	2,381	2,442
Kansas	1,681	1,761	1,944	1,827	2,056	2,525	2,804	2,964	3,143	3,450	3,580
Minnesota	1,375	1,646	1,868	2,062	2,332	2,884	3,337	3,682	4,042	4,547	4,844
Missouri	2,977	3,251	3,363	3,338	3,540	3,664	3,826	3,730	3,793	3,990	4,077
Nebraska	1,165	1,333	1,449	1,485	1,632	1,839	2,079	2,152	2,244	2,502	2,589
North Dakota	798	769	805	881	984	1,108	1,191	1,290	1,277	1,305	1,300
Oklahoma	1,497	1,886	237	2,393	2,695	3,291	3,663	4,063	4,071	3,890	4,618
South Dakota	616	783	875	954	1,103	1,274	1,328	1,452	1,476	1,545	1,689
Total	1,568	1,689	1,831	1,899	2,181	2,416	2,649	2,919	3,009	3,228	3,420

Mean Population of Towns, Excluding Cities of 150,000 or More in 1980

	1910	1920	1930	1940	1950	1960	1970	1980	1990	2000	2005
Arkansas	1,259	1,355	1,424	1,484	1,904	2,095	2,270	2,553	2,691	3,093	3,252
Iowa	1,254	1,368	1,438	1,518	1,646	1,821	1,983	2,095	2,039	2,183	2,243
Kansas	1,357	1,401	1,514	1,396	1,528	1,891	2,074	2,322	2,432	2,736	2,848
Minnesota	766	930	1,011	1,153	1,364	1,967	2,488	2,932	3,306	3,827	4,083
Missouri	1,381	1,410	1,500	1,601	1,810	2,185	2,532	2,739	2,876	3,168	3,264
Nebraska	787	844	894	902	970	1,029	1,147	1,241	1,252	1,354	1,366
North Dakota	798	769	805	881	984	1,108	1,191	1,290	1,310	1,343	1,313
Oklahoma	1,280	1,288	1,689	1,689	1,879	2,167	2,406	2,732	2,773	3,012	3,181
South Dakota	622	790	882	962	1,113	1,285	1,340	1,452	1,532	1,673	1,697
Total	1,074	1,149	1,273	1,330	1,507	1,805	2,055	2,287	2,392	2,656	2,764

Source: U.S. Census

Table 12.

Population Decline by Town Size in 1910 and 1950

	Percentage That Lost Population from 1910 to 1950						
Population in 1910	Fewer than 250	250 to 499	500 to 1,499	1,500 to 4,999	5,000 to 19,999	20,000 or More	All
Arkansas	27.4	37.7	27.2	11.5	0.0	0.0	25.6
Iowa	41.0	43.0	31.5	12.9	0.0	0.0	33.9
Kansas	56.4	67.5	49.0	26.5	19.0	0.0	51.2
Minnesota	9.0	15.1	9.3	19.1	19.1	0.0	11.3
Missouri	56.7	64.8	56.9	26.6	9.5	0.0	52.2
Nebraska	73.1	67.1	43.9	18.4	10.0	0.0	55.2
North Dakota	40.8	50.0	19.3	25.0	0.0	0.0	36.2
Oklahoma	48.6	53.9	39.1	15.9	9.1	0.0	39.6
South Dakota	21.2	48.1	34.6	15.4	16.7	0.0	31.0
Total	31.2	50.2	35.7	19.2	11.0	0.0	35.8

	Percentage That Lost Population from 1950 to 1980						
Population in 1910	Fewer than 250	250 to 499	500 to 1,499	1,500 to 4,999	5,000 to 19,999	20,000 or More	All
Arkansas	33.8	26.8	20.4	5.4	7.4	0.0	21.4
Iowa	57.0	47.9	30.4	23.5	27.0	21.4	41.3
Kansas	72.4	55.3	48.3	40.7	39.3	14.3	55.3
Minnesota	42.8	42.5	32.2	23.5	18.6	50.0	36.7
Missouri	48.7	45.1	24.9	15.1	24.4	38.5	35.2
Nebraska	63.3	54.8	49.2	30.8	13.3	0.0	52.3
North Dakota	87.6	82.8	53.5	40.9	0.0	0.0	73.2
Oklahoma	53.2	28.2	26.9	26.0	43.2	0.0	33.7
South Dakota	75.0	66.7	56.2	40.9	20.0	0.0	63.2
Total	58.1	48.4	35.5	24.6	24.8	20.0	43.6

Source: U.S. Census, 1910, 1950, and 1980, Incorporated Places

Table 13.
Population Decline 1980 to 2005

Population in 1980	Percentage That Lost Population from 1980 to 2005						
	Fewer than 250	250 to 499	500 to 1,499	1,500 to 4,999	5,000 to 19,999	20,000 or More	All
Arkansas	63.1	58.2	44.2	48.0	38.2	35.7	51.3
Iowa	80.8	75.9	65.5	57.5	43.8	52.6	69.6
Kansas	80.1	77.3	65.4	64.6	51.4	15.4	70.5
Minnesota	73.0	61.6	50.7	29.8	22.2	39.4	52.0
Missouri	64.1	58.8	49.8	44.1	44.9	52.4	54.2
Nebraska	67.4	75.5	74.3	60.0	39.1	12.5	68.3
North Dakota	90.4	88.2	91.2	92.3	77.8	0.0	89.0
Oklahoma	74.8	72.0	70.6	54.7	41.3	36.8	65.2
South Dakota	74.0	75.9	66.2	53.6	20.0	33.3	68.3
Total	74.8	69.7	61.5	50.8	39.9	37.3	63.6

Population in 1980	Percentage That Declined by One-Quarter or More						
	Fewer than 250	250 to 499	500 to 1,499	1,500 to 4,999	5,000 to 19,999	20,000 or More	All
Arkansas	32.6	20.0	14.4	10.4	2.9	7.1	17.7
Iowa	34.6	13.6	7.0	0.8	2.1	0.0	14.9
Kansas	37.4	28.2	11.1	12.1	2.7	0.0	22.5
Minnesota	35.6	14.6	5.8	5.0	2.8	0.0	14.3
Missouri	27.4	14.4	6.2	3.3	2.6	0.0	12.6
Nebraska	25.0	13.9	18.4	6.7	0.0	0.0	17.7
North Dakota	64.6	58.8	51.5	30.8	0.0	0.0	56.1
Oklahoma	40.6	29.0	25.0	13.2	4.4	0.0	24.4
South Dakota	42.5	29.3	12.5	21.4	0.0	0.0	28.4
Total	37.1	21.0	13.3	8.0	2.5	0.8	20.2

Source: U.S. Census, 1980, 2000, and 2005, Incorporated Places

Table 14.

Factors Associated with Towns' Population Decline

	1980 Town Size	Farms in 1980	Decline in Farms	College Town	Interstate in County	Urban Influence
Arkansas	0.734***	1.745**	3.212***	0.390	1.283	0.412***
Iowa	0.738***	1.344*	1.728***	0.423	0.565**	0.337***
Kansas	0.823*	1.082	3.246***	0.182**	0.574**	0.376***
Minnesota	0.678***	2.453***	2.248***	1.171	0.870	0.360***
Missouri	0.699***	1.713**	1.913***	1.593	0.989	0.416***
Nebraska	1.003	1.761**	0.768	0.092**	0.490*	0.179***
North Dakota	0.839	1.770*	1.098	0.677	0.286	0.052
Oklahoma	0.747***	0.654	3.231***	0.333	0.001	0.361***
South Dakota	0.817	1.862***	0.815	0.442	0.345***	0.937
Total	0.771***	1.536***	1.257***	0.486***	0.754***	0.381***

Source: U.S. Census, 1980 and 2005; U.S. Census County Databook, 1982, 2002; odds ratios from binary logistic regression; dependent variable = whether town's population was smaller in 2005 than in 1980. *** probability .001 ** probability .01 * probability .05

Table 15.

Population Trends by Towns' Characteristics

	Mean Population (Excluding Towns Larger than 20,000 in 1950)					
	1960	1970	1980	1990	2000	2005
Farm income 35% or more	616	599	623	569	570	546
Farm income 10–35%	1,063	1,117	1,204	1,155	1,200	1,202
Farm income below 10%	1,711	2,136	2,511	2,779	3,223	3,505
College town	8,645	11,405	12,981	14,217	16,063	16,972
Non–college town	1,150	1,302	1,533	1,601	1,783	1,880
Interstate in county	1,876	2,444	2,974	3,362	3,901	4,120
No interstate	1,095	1,163	1,309	1,283	1,369	1,407
Metro influence	1,738	2,219	2,656	2,951	3,436	3,745
No metro influence	1,053	1,095	1,203	1,159	1,192	1,179

Source: U.S. Census

Table 16.
Community Associations by Town Size and State

| | Average Number of Associations in Towns with Populations of: | | | | | |
	Fewer than 500	500 to 1,499	1,500 to 4,999	5,000 to 19,999	20,000 or More	All
Arkansas	16	20	26	60	97	25
Iowa	12	15	37	90	189	24
Kansas	8	16	35	88	132	22
Minnesota	15	23	42	108	132	38
Missouri	26	39	57	106	170	47
Nebraska	7	13	33	75	113	15
North Dakota	8	16	38	82	151	14
Oklahoma	13	13	27	60	98	22
South Dakota	8	17	35	133	166	18
Total	13	20	39	91	137	28
	Average Number of Residents per Association in Towns with Populations of:					
	Fewer than 500	500 to 1,499	1,500 to 4,999	5,000 to 19,999	20,000 or More	All
Arkansas	16	20	26	60	97	25
Arkansas	16	44	105	153	472	138
Iowa	19	60	72	93	289	100
Kansas	24	56	77	110	572	160
Minnesota	14	37	67	97	393	127
Missouri	8	22	49	95	409	87
Nebraska	29	66	77	108	739	167
North Dakota	17	56	58	153	386	92
Oklahoma	17	69	104	169	876	208
South Dakota	23	51	73	84	370	93
Total	16	44	70	107	458	122

Source: Internal Revenue Service, 2006

Table 17.
Value of Food Products

	Annual Value of Food Products ($ millions)			Ratio of Food Products to Farm Products		
	1963–1979	1980–1997	1997–2006	1963–1979	1980–1997	1997–2006
Arkansas	268	1,478	3,019	0.36	0.96	1.50
Iowa	750	2,558	4,299	0.35	0.72	1.12
Kansas	291	1,083	1,820	0.29	0.56	0.84
Minnesota	727	2,304	3,107	0.48	0.89	1.14
Missouri	864	3,047	4,819	0.87	2.03	2.85
Nebraska	393	1,248	1,979	0.36	0.47	0.68
North Dakota	45	184	366	0.06	0.17	0.30
Oklahoma	174	592	1,148	0.30	0.49	0.74
South Dakota	84	273	327	0.13	0.21	0.21
Total	3,597	12,767	20,883	0.38	0.74	1.06

Source: U.S. Bureau of Economic Analysis; SIC 1963–1997, NAICS 1997–2006

Table 18.
Meat Products Manufacturing Establishments

	Number of Establishments			Number of Large Establishments		
	1986	2006	Change	1986	2006	Change
Arkansas	72	86	14	16	27	11
Iowa	102	160	58	11	18	7
Kansas	61	80	19	6	8	2
Minnesota	72	120	48	5	9	4
Missouri	115	138	23	4	13	9
Nebraska	93	125	32	6	15	9
North Dakota	14	28	14	0	0	0
Oklahoma	65	78	13	0	7	7
South Dakota	19	41	22	1	2	1
Total	613	856	243	49	99	50

	Counties with Establishments			Counties with Large Establishments		
	1986	2006	Change	1986	2006	Change
Arkansas	32	35	3	13	18	5
Iowa	57	70	13	11	16	5
Kansas	33	48	15	5	7	2
Minnesota	38	55	17	5	7	2
Missouri	59	75	16	4	10	6
Nebraska	34	51	17	6	11	5
North Dakota	9	20	11	0	0	0
Oklahoma	39	42	3	0	7	7
South Dakota	13	29	16	1	2	1
Total	314	425	111	45	78	33

Source: U.S. Census Bureau, County Business Patterns, 1986 SIC code 2010 and 2006 NAICS code 3116; large establishments have 500 or more employees

Table 19.

Employment and Wages in Meat Industry Occupations

	Number of Employees			Annual Wages per Employee		
	1986	2006	Change	1986	2006	Change
State						
Arkansas	12,840	23,304	81%	4,510	13,954	209%
Iowa	17,020	19,867	17%	12,882	18,482	43%
Kansas	6,040	13,605	125%	9,742	17,695	82%
Minnesota	9,080	9,118	0%	8,989	17,217	92%
Missouri	6,920	9,673	40%	7,458	14,212	91%
Nebraska	8,200	14,828	81%	10,654	17,985	69%
North Dakota	400	342	−15%	7,149	8,913	25%
Oklahoma	4,040	7,933	96%	5,856	11,904	103%
South Dakota	3,740	2,771	−26%	12,088	18,237	51%
Total	68,280	101,441	49%	9,202	16,189	76%
Occupation						
Butchers and cutters	29,920	46,758	56%	10,612	16,029	51%
Packers and packagers	16,260	27,685	70%	7,145	15,987	124%
Inspectors	2,200	790	−64%	9,120	27,518	202%
Machine operators	5,780	13,608	135%	10,721	15,205	42%
Laborers	14,120	12,600	−11%	7,974	17,583	121%
Employment						
Full–year	33,860	56,931	68%	13,825	21,414	55%
Part–year	34,420	44,510	29%	4,654	9,507	104%
Location						
Metropolitan	19,340	30,666	59%	10,135	15,805	56%
Non–metropolitan	48,940	70,775	45%	8,833	16,356	85%
Gender						
Male	39,820	59,518	49%	11,972	17,754	48%
Female	28,460	41,923	47%	5,326	13,968	162%
Citizenship						
Citizen	66,620	64,752	−3%	9,229	16,558	79%
Non–citizen	1,660	36,689	2110%	8,122	15,539	91%
Etnicity						
Hispanic	2,900	45,390	1465%	9,368	15,927	70%
Black	5,520	9,357	70%	6,806	14,818	118%

Source: U.S. Census, 1980 and 2000, 5 Percent Public Use Microsamples

Table 20.
Comparison of Meat Workers and Construction Workers with Farm Workers

	Employees in 1980			Employees in 2000		
	Unstandardized Coefficients	Std. Error	Sig.	Unstandardized Coefficients	Std. Error	Sig.
Arkansas	−1083.17	35.79	0.000	−4069.77	126.14	0.000
Iowa	495.46	30.87	0.000	−1245.48	122.13	0.000
Kansas	295.97	37.13	0.000	−2473.48	129.85	0.000
Missouri	−288.65	32.96	0.000	−2883.20	118.05	0.000
Nebraska	301.69	36.48	0.000	−2629.23	132.63	0.000
North Dakota	675.30	48.35	0.000	876.55	197.61	0.000
Oklahoma	−957.12	38.20	0.000	−4187.90	129.94	0.000
South Dakota	−246.05	46.07	0.000	−3794.33	179.63	0.000
Weeks worked	1103.86	3.99	0.000	3010.51	14.22	0.000
Metropolitan area	927.90	24.04	0.000	1913.35	74.45	0.000
Male	4375.20	22.85	0.000	4597.61	89.16	0.000
Young	−3752.16	18.62	0.000	−8401.72	66.73	0.000
Black	−1380.52	42.88	0.000	−1070.10	145.47	0.000
Hispanic	−737.73	68.74	0.000	−2394.00	100.23	0.000
Construction	2747.32	22.99	0.000	3597.59	79.78	0.000
Meat worker	4748.71	27.24	0.000	1538.45	97.24	0.000
(Constant)	204.64	32.44	0.000	6997.34	130.13	0.000

Source: U.S. Census, 5 percent Public Use Microsamples; meat workers, construction, and farm laborers

Table 21.

Characteristics of Edge and Core Cities

	Small Edge Cities	Medium Edge Cities	Large Edge Cities	Urban Core Cities
Mean population				
1950	5,497	5,884	5,898	412,455
1960	8,680	13,435	17,160	436,206
1970	11,297	20,532	31,429	444,460
1980	13,659	22,331	40,396	406,527
1990	13,679	25,022	54,049	408,391
2000	14,958	27,850	66,107	429,717
2005	15,443	29,193	70,862	433,041
Annual population change				
1950 to 1960	5.8%	12.8%	19.1%	0.6%
1960 to 1970	3.0%	5.3%	8.3%	0.2%
1970 to 1980	2.1%	0.9%	2.9%	-0.9%
1980 to 1990	0.0%	1.2%	3.4%	0.0%
1990 to 2000	0.9%	1.1%	2.2%	0.5%
2000 to 2005	0.6%	1.0%	1.4%	0.2%
Location				
Miles from central city	11.4	13.3	15.7	—
Land area (square miles)	7.6	12.5	37.3	215.5
Population density per sq. mi. in 2000	2,947	2,731	1,999	1,994
Reduction in farm acreage since 1982	5,860	3,250	30,750	—
Percentage African American				
1980	1.8	3.2	1.5	18.2
2000	5.7	8.1	4.1	20.3
Married couples with children				
Percentage of households in 1980	32	35	39	22
Percentage of households in 2000	24	25	29	18
Percentage college grads (age 25 & over)				
1980	22	22	24	18
2000	32	33	36	25
Change	10	11	12	7
Median household income				
1980	$23,396	$23,193	$23,901	$15,604
2000	$53,821	$52,712	$57,988	$36,273
Increase	$30,425	$29,519	$34,087	$20,669
Percentage increase	130%	127%	143%	132%

Source: U.S. Census, Incorporated Places; edge cities are within twenty miles of core cities; smaller are 10,000 to fewer than 20,000 population in 2005; medium are 20,000 to fewer than 50,000; large are 50,000 ore more; core cities are Des Moines, Kansas City, Minneapolis–St. Paul, Omaha, Oklahoma City, St. Louis, Tulsa, and Wichita

Table 22.
Employment of Edge- and Core-City Residents

	Small Edge Cities	Medium Edge Cities	Large Edge Cities	Urban Core Cities
Occupations of employed males, 2000				
% in management and professions	37	38	40	31
% in service occupations	10	10	9	14
% in sales and office occupations	21	22	22	20
% in construction and extraction	14	13	13	15
% in production and transportation	17	17	15	20
Occupations of employed females, 2000				
% in management and professions	39	41	42	36
% in service occupations	16	15	14	18
% in sales and office occupations	39	39	39	37
% in construction and extraction	1	1	1	1
% in production and transportation	5	5	5	7
Percent working in county of residence				
1980	61	60	66	75
2000	67	64	72	77
Percent using public transportation				
1980	4	4	2	10
2000	2	2	2	5
Manufacturing Index				
1980	110	110	116	100
2000	102	105	108	100
Retail Index				
1980	108	110	111	100
2000	104	107	111	100

Source: U.S. Census, Incorporated Places; edge cities are within twenty miles of core cities; smaller are 10,000 to less than 20,000 population in 2005; medium are 20,000 to fewer than 50,000; large are 50,000 ore more; core cities are Des Moines, Kansas City, Minneapolis–St. Paul, Omaha, Oklahoma City, St. Louis, Tulsa, and Wichita; manufacturing and retail indexes are ratios of percent of total employment in each sector in edge cities to the percent in core cities

Table 23.
Effects of Distance and Land Area on Edge Cities' Population

	Zero-Order Effects		Controlling for Previous Pop. Level			
	Pearson Correlation	Sig.	Unstan- dardized Coefficient	Std. Error	Stan- dardized Coefficient	Sig.
Miles from center of core city						
Population in 1950	−0.347	0.001	−125.756	91.078	−0.061	0.172
Population in 1960	−0.279	0.007	−164.653	231.959	−0.053	0.480
Population in 1970	−0.135	0.196	477.922	214.770	0.112	0.029
Population in 1980	−0.035	0.733	493.544	160.668	0.127	0.003
Population in 1990	0.175	0.083	939.277	159.155	0.213	0.000
Population in 2000	0.270	0.007	573.897	144.595	0.108	0.000
Population in 2005	0.301	0.002	216.428	81.711	0.038	0.010
Land area in square miles in 1980						
Population in 1950	0.455	0.000	27.483	9.296	0.128	0.004
Population in 1960	0.433	0.000	31.863	26.782	0.093	0.238
Population in 1970	0.550	0.000	96.385	24.173	0.200	0.000
Population in 1980	0.646	0.000	91.108	20.319	0.208	0.000
Population in 1990	0.633	0.000	37.594	28.020	0.074	0.183
Population in 2000	0.593	0.000	−14.946	23.007	−0.024	0.518
Population in 2005	0.567	0.000	−20.861	11.539	−0.031	0.074
Land area in square miles in 2000						
Population in 1950	0.071	0.533	8.771	24.166	0.015	0.718
Population in 1960	0.117	0.280	36.854	61.587	0.042	0.551
Population in 1970	0.310	0.003	241.535	52.389	0.205	0.000
Population in 1980	0.525	0.000	301.183	35.747	0.282	0.000
Population in 1990	0.722	0.000	414.346	43.642	0.335	0.000
Population in 2000	0.805	0.000	346.297	50.985	0.233	0.000
Population in 2005	0.826	0.000	128.565	36.182	0.080	0.001

Source: U.S. Census, Incorporated Places, Middle West cities with 2005 population of at least 10,000 and located within twenty miles of one of the region's eight largest cities; number in 1950 = 80; in 1960 = 87, in 1970 = 89; in 1980 to 2005 = 95

Notes

CHAPTER ONE

1. Dr. Owen Carper, who grew up in Lebanon, kindly read and commented on a draft of this chapter. Susanne Perez Tobias, "A City Centered Lebanon Is Good at Being the Middle of America," *Wichita Eagle* (May 31, 1994); Catherine Watson, "Prairie Pilgrimage: Searching for Roots on the Sod-House Frontier," *Minneapolis Star Tribune* (May 30, 1993), 1G; Alan Attwood, "Greetings from Lebanon USA," *Age* (August 29, 1998), 1; Mark Baechtel, "Dead Center America," *Washington Post* (January 16, 2000), E1. Reports by other visitors include Alex Tizon, "Crossing America: Crisis a World Away from Kansas," *Seattle Times* (October 2, 2001); Carol Crupper, "Rural Kansas Gains National Spotlight," *Hays Daily News* (August 22, 2002); Rick Hampson, "War Intrudes on Heart of Heartland," *USA Today* (March 13, 2003), 8A; Laurent Belsie, "The Dwindling Heartland: America's New Frontier," *Christian Science Monitor* (February 11, 2003), 1; John G. Mitchell, "Great Plains," *National Geographic* (May 2004), online at magma.nationalgeographic.com; Tom Montag, "Notes from the Vagabond Journals: A Visit to Smith Center, Kansas," *Middlewesterner* (June 19, 2004), online at middlewesterner.blogspot.com; Cheryl Unruh, "From Cuba to Lebanon," *Emporia Gazette* (October 24, 2006); and Brooke Anderson, "Hollywood vs. Heartland," *CNN American Morning* (March 2, 2006), transcript.

2. E. G. Carey, "Oak Township Items," *Smith County Pioneer* (August 18, 1877), 1.

3. "Lebanon," *Atchison Daily Champion* (February 21, 1888), 3.

4. U.S. Census for years indicated; photos are in collections at Wichita State University and the National Weather Service; businesses according to Lebanon map, *Standard Atlas of Smith County, Kansas* (Chicago: George A. Ogle and Co., 1917), and Sanford Maps 1911.

5. Interview conducted January 17, 2008 (name withheld); field research notes, May 2007 and August 2009.

6. U.S. Census, housing vacancies are for 2005; Charles W. Holmes, "America's Vanishing Heart," *Palm Beach Post* (May 22, 2000), 1A. Interviews conducted July 3, 2008.

7. The most detailed account is found in Schoewe, "Geography of Kansas." A brief account is given in Schoewe, "Geographical Center." See also skyways.lib.ks.us/towns/Lebanon/history.html.

8. The creation and preservation of these myths and their place in perceptions of rural America are valuably examined in Burns, *Pastoral Inventions*; the Lake Wobegon reference is of course to Keillor, *Lake Wobegon Days*, and the numerous accounts on Keillor's *A Prairie Home Companion* radio program.

9. Egan, *Worst Hard Time*, 10, 310.

10. Among other discussions of the "farm problem" in the rural Midwest, see, for example, Harding, "On to the City, Farmer!" which emphasizes farm inefficiency;

Gordon, "Kansas Wheat Farm Culture," which concluded that educators faced major challenges in revising the attitudes of youth from farm backgrounds; and Gleason, "Attitude of the Business Community."

11. Examples of the social problems perspective are almost as abundant as the literature on rural America itself, but a good sampling can be found among the essays in Brown and Swanson, *Challenges for Rural America*, which offers information about such problems as commuting, globalization, fast food, land use, health, aging, the plight of immigrants and minority groups, gender relations, and a host of other topics.

12. Charlie LeDuff, "A Farmer Fears His Way of Life Has Dwindled Down to a Final Generation," *New York Times* (October 2, 2006), A10.

13. Blank, *End of Agriculture*; "Unsettled Plains," *New York Times* (June 3, 2001), 16.

14. A. L. Headley, "Smith County, Kansas" (unpublished manuscript, 1959); and *Smith County Pioneer* (January 27, 1876), republished April 16, 1903; cited in Pletcher, "History of Smith County," 13–14; the Headley account also indicates that the French trapper's story was confirmed by an Indian in the area who heard about the battle from Pawnee friends.

15. Greeley, *Overland Journey*, 83.

16. Ray Myers, "Historical Sketches of Lebanon and Oak Township," *Lebanon Times* (February 18, 1960), cited in Pletcher, "History of Smith County," 149.

17. Clipping files, Genealogical and Historical Collection, Smith Center Public Library. A photo of the Hyde elevator is included in Pletcher, "History of Smith County," 201; the Bible verses did not last long, as the Rock Island Railroad claimed they were in violation of an agreement between it and the grain elevator company.

18. Interview with Awilda Nelssen, conducted April 24, 2008; and events described in Pletcher, "History of Smith County."

19. Interview conducted January 18, 2008 (name withheld). Crop subsidy data are from the Environmental Working Group (EWG) Farm Bill Policy Analysis Database; online at farm.ewg.org; Sue Robinson, "Smith County Couple Honored," *K-State Research and Extension News* (March 2, 2007); John Russnogle, "High-Tech No-Till," *Soybean Digest* (April 2000); Roger Long, "No-Till for Profitability," *No-Till Newsletter* (2005); 2002 data for Smith County, in which Lebanon is located, from the National Agricultural Statistics Service of the U.S. Department of Agriculture showed that government subsidy payments averaged $6,562 per farm and that net cash farm income from operations averaged $14,519.

20. Interview conducted January 1, 2008 (name withheld).

21. Interview conducted January 19, 2008 (name withheld).

22. U.S. Census Bureau, American Community Survey, 2006; percentage of the population born in their current state of residence was 61.3 in Arkansas, 61.7 in Oklahoma, 59.1 in Kansas, 65.2 in South Dakota, 66.3 in Missouri, 65.5 in Nebraska, 71.0 in North Dakota, 69.1 in Minnesota, and 72.3 in Iowa; Massachusetts was 64.1, New York was 64.5, Michigan was 75.7, and Illinois was 66.9; the lowest figures were 23.1 in Nevada and 33.6 in Florida; Johnson County in Kansas and Benton County in Arkansas were low.

23. U.S. Census Bureau, population of cities in 2005; cities with 100,000 to 300,000 population were Little Rock, Cedar Rapids, Des Moines, Olathe, Overland Park,

Topeka, Independence, Springfield, Lincoln, Norman, and Sioux Falls; the larger cities were Minneapolis–St. Paul, Kansas City, Oklahoma City, Omaha, Tulsa, St. Louis, and Wichita.

24. U.S. Census Bureau, annual estimates for incorporated places, released June 21, 2007, SF1, Census 2000; obtained from Office of Social and Economic Trend Analysis, Iowa State University; for an illuminating analysis of trends in Nebraska, see David Drozd and Jerry Deichert, "2005 Nebraska Population Report," Center for Public Affairs Research Working Paper, University of Nebraska at Omaha (July 2006).

25. See table 1 in the appendix, which shows the population of each of the nine Middle West states as a percentage of U.S. population starting in 1963, the first year in which BEA economic data were available, for selected years through 2006. Collectively, the nine states accounted for 8.78 percent of U.S. population in 2006, compared with 10.58 percent in 1963, meaning that the 2006 figure was 17 percent smaller than the 1963 figure. For each of the nine states, the percentage in 2006 was smaller than the percentage in 1963. From 1960 through 2006, the annual rate of decline for the combined nine states as a percent of U.S. population was –.000493, compared with an annual rate of –.001127 from 1929 through 1959. In the earlier period, the sharpest declines occurred from 1940 through 1943 and in 1950; in the later period, from 1984 through 1989.

26. The data discussed are from the Bureau of Economic Analysis website (www .bea.gov), Regional Economic Accounts, Gross Domestic Product by State. The *ratio* of GDP per capita for the nine Middle Western states to GDP per capita for the country can be calculated starting in 1963 despite the change in industry classification definitions in 1997 from SIC to NAICS.

27. Ibid. In 1963, the ratio of GDP per capita in the nine Middle Western states to GDP per capita for the country was .866. In 2006, the ratio was .915. See table 1 in the appendix for further details. GDP per capita as a percentage of national GDP per capita rose in all nine states from 1963 until 1976, peaking in that year in Iowa and Kansas, a year later in Missouri, in 1978 for Arkansas and Nebraska, and in 1979 for Minnesota and South Dakota. The subsequent low point came in 1987 for Iowa, Nebraska, and Oklahoma, 1988 for North and South Dakota, 1989 for Kansas, and 1990 for Arkansas, Minnesota, and Missouri. After a decade of increasing percentages, all nine states declined in 1999, 2000, or 2001, and all but Missouri then rose to a higher level again by 2006.

28. See also Richard M. Beemiller and Clifford H. Woodruff III, "Gross State Product by Industry, 1977–98," *Survey of Current Business* (October 2000), 69–90.

29. Richard Kane, "Investigating Convergence of the U.S. Regions: A Time-Series Analysis," paper presented at the annual conference of the Mid-Continent Regional Science Association, Duluth, MN, June 2001.

30. G. Andrew Bernat Jr., "Convergence in State Per Capita Personal Income, 1950–99," *Survey of Current Business* (June 2001), 36–48.

31. Bettina H. Aten, "Report on Interarea Price Levels," Bureau of Economic Analysis Working Paper 2005-11 (November 30, 2005).

32. Bureau of Economic Analysis industry-specific figures, while subject to the 1997 reclassification (from SIC to NAICS), suggest that retail sales, wholesale sales, and construction were negatively affected by the region's decline in population

relative to the nation, as might be expected, but that farming, miscellaneous durable manufactured goods, oil and gas extraction, rail transportation and trucking, food products, insurance, federal military outlays, and expenditures for health, educational, and state and local government services were not (for these items, the ratio of the nine-state region's industry-specific contributions to figures for the nation remained nearly constant from 1963 through 2006 or 2007).

33. Bill Frey, "Three Americas: The Rising Significance of Regions," *Journal of the American Planning Association* (October 2002), online at MilkenInstitute.Org.

34. See Shortridge, *The Middle West*, especially the maps on pp. 85ff. The study was conducted in 1980 among almost 2,000 college students from thirty-two states. There was some indication that perceptions of the heartland's location were shifting from Iowa toward Kansas and Nebraska. The study asked students to say where they thought the "Middle West (Midwest)" was located, so it picked up some of the impressions shared by Easterners that the Midwest begins in Ohio. See also Shortridge, "Changing Usage"; and Shortridge, "Emergence of 'Middle West.'" A more recent study of commercial use of the term "heartland" found the highest concentration in Iowa, Kansas, Missouri, Nebraska, and North Dakota, with increasing usage in Oklahoma; see Rundstrom, "Heartland." On the relationship between geographic centrality and heartland imagery, an especially interesting discussion can be found in Bader, *Hayseeds, Moralizers, and Methodists*, 150–84.

35. Wherever possible, especially when drawing on census data and surveys, I have used the nine states mentioned in the text—Arkansas, Iowa, Kansas, Minnesota, Missouri, Nebraska, North Dakota, Oklahoma, and South Dakota—as the standard operational definition of the Middle West or heartland. These contiguous states share the common history of having been brought into the United States as territories acquired through the Louisiana Purchase in 1803 and benefiting from having been settled as the second wave of westward migration largely by immigrants from Ohio, Indiana, Pennsylvania, New York, and other northern states. For this reason, they bear similar governmental structures and educational institutions. Their economies were predominantly agricultural well into the twentieth century, and grain crops and livestock formed the basis of farming in all nine. Further similarities include the relative absence of large cities and the presence of small towns in large numbers, many of which have lost population in recent decades. Part of my reason for focusing on these nine states, however, is that they differ enough to provide interesting comparisons. For example, Arkansas, Missouri, and Oklahoma are more diverse racially than the other states, and the four states bordering the Mississippi have smaller farms than the five states to the west.

36. Andersen, *Portable Prairie*, ix.

CHAPTER TWO

1. Cutler, *History of the State of Kansas*; the quote is credited to "Prof. Hayden." "Northern Kansas: Smith County the Diadem in a Princely Heritage," *Atchison Daily Champion* (February 28, 1892), 5; greater detail than can be summarized here about the early settlement and lore of Smith Center can be found in Pletcher, "History of Smith County"; in 2005, the U.S. Census Bureau classified Smith County as a 9 on

a 1-to-9 urban-to-rural scale in which 9 designates a nonmetropolitan area with no town of 2,500 population and not adjacent to a metropolitan area; the topography was classified as open low hills. Among Kansas topographical regions, Smith County is variously classified as part of the Blue Hills Uplands or the High Plains; the lowest temperature on record in the state occurred in Smith County on February 13, 1905, at 40 degrees below zero; Self, *Environment and Man*, 56.

2. Kansas State Department of Transportation daily traffic reports for 2007 showed 1,120 vehicles entering or leaving Smith Center on U.S. Highway 281 South, 1,980 on U.S. Highway 36 East, and 1,780 on U.S. Highway 36 West; an average of 605 vehicles passed through Lebanon daily; approximately 10,000 vehicles a day traveled on Interstate 70 through Ellsworth and Russell counties to the south.

3. A distance of 82.5 feet separates the buildings on either side of Main Street; the standard width of traffic lanes is 11 or 12 feet; among other things, the width of most streets in early Kansas towns reduced the likelihood of fires spreading from one side to the other; many of the towns also adopted a standard layout provided by the railroad companies. The Quilted Four Patch is described in Stacie R. Sandall, "Quilted Passion," *Hays Daily News* (December 16, 2005).

4. Interview conducted January 11, 2008.

5. Loren C. Eiseley, "Evidences of a Pre-Ceramic Cultural Horizon in Smith County, Kansas," *Science* (March 10, 1939), 221; "High Plains," *Hays Daily News* (February 1, 1998); Stacie R. Sandall, "'Boneman' Donates Collection to Rolling Hills," *Hays Daily News* (November 3, 2004), refers to a collection of approximately 3,500 fossils from the Smith Center area; Rothenberger, *Weaving the Common Thread*, mentions that Lieutenant Zebulon Pike may have camped about thirty miles south of Smith Center in 1806 during his expedition to Colorado, although the consensus is that Pike's expedition came only into Republic County to the east; Barr, "Diary"; Josh Kirkendall, quoted in Alice Freed, "Biography of George Washington Kirkendall (1829–1907)," online at www.shivs.com; Mary Barr Norris, "The Official Story of 'Home on the Range,'" online at www.kansasheritage.org; see also Steve Lickteig, "Present at the Creation: Home on the Range," National Public Radio (April 29, 2002), online at www.npr.org.

6. Works Projects Administration, *Inventory*.

7. *Smith County Pioneer* (July 10, 1947). The county commissioners met in Cedarville on March 9, 1872, and Smith Center was selected as the county seat in an election in November of that year.

8. Travis Dennis and I. C. Steward, "Kansas Settlers Starving," *Daily Inter-Ocean* (November 24, 1874), 2; R. K. Smith, "Aid for Smith County, Kansas," *Daily Inter-Ocean* (November 24, 1874), 4; "The Diary of Virginia D. (Jones-Harlan) Barr" (May 22, 1940) (unpublished manuscript, Smith County Historical Society).

9. *Junction City Union* (October 25, 1876), quoted in Socolofsky, "Kansas in 1876," 1. Census figures as reported in *Kansas Board of Agriculture, Fourth Annual Report* (1875), which includes a map of land claimed in Smith County and the states from which immigrants came.

10. Will D. Jenkins, "Come to Kansas," *Smith County Pioneer* (December 28, 1876), 1.

11. Cameron, *Pioneer Days*, 6.

12. Cutler, *History of the State of Kansas*, chapter on Smith County, online at www.kancoll.org; 1880 U.S. Census of Agriculture, electronic datafile. Information

from electronic datafiles for agricultural censuses, and county-level decennial data are described in Gutmann, *Great Plains Population and Environment Data*; and Haines, *Historical, Demographic, Economic, and Social Data*; my analyses are for years and locations indicated using electronic datafiles downloadable to member institutions from the Inter-university Consortium for Political and Social Research.

13. Of the thirty-three prominent citizens of Smith County in 1882 whose biographies are included in Cutler's *History of the State of Kansas*, twenty-five had moved at least once before their move to Smith County and fourteen had moved three times or more. One had moved five times and another seven times. Movement of this extent was not uncommon. In his study of eastern Kansas, the historian James C. Malin found that only 26 percent of farmers could be found in the same township in 1860 and 1870, and only 44 percent between 1870 and 1880; Malin, "Turnover of Farm Population." A study of four townships in Iowa found persistence rates between 1860 and 1870 ranging from 37 to 56 percent; Bogue, *From Prairie to Corn Belt*. A more recent study of Kansas, Nebraska, and the Dakota Territory found 36 percent of inhabitants in 1870 living in the same township in 1880; Stewart, "Economic Opportunity or Hardship?" Also of interest is the broader discussion of turnover in Malin, "Kansas: Some Reflections."

14. Willa Cather, "Tommy, the Unsentimental," *Home Monthly* (August 1896), 6–7; reprinted in Faulkner, *Willa Cather's Collected Short Fiction*, 473–80.

15. Gates, *Fifty Million Acres*, 276, 287; see also "Northern Kansas," *Atchison Daily Champion* (February 28, 1892), for a contemporary view of these advantages.

16. U.S. Census, Smith County, Kansas, 1880, electronic datafile. Children aged fourteen or younger totaled 5,809; teens aged fifteen through nineteen, 1,343; adult women, 2,940; adult men, 3,795. The female-to-male ratio among adults was .77; 64 percent of the adult men and women were aged twenty through thirty-nine. Because it was not yet established as a county, a census was not taken in Smith County in 1870; the 1870 census in Jewell County to the east, which had just been settled, showed a ratio of men to women of more than three to one. School data are from Cutler, *History of the State of Kansas*. Plans for Gould College began in 1878, and the institution officially opened in 1881 with five faculty members and seventy-two students, six of whom were college level. Support from Gould did not occur and the United Brethren Church decided to close the college in 1888; Erik Paul Conrad, "Kansas' Closed Colleges," 72–74.

17. The price of butter, farm production, storage, and transportation are discussed in "The Marketing of Kansas Butter," *Agricultural Experiment Station Bulletin*, no. 216 (April 1917). Bateman, "'Marketable Surplus,'" 348, states that "butter and cheese, transportable over long distances, became to milk-producing farms what liquor was to many corn growers, a means of converting a product into a less quickly perishable and relatively higher-valued form." The Central Branch Railway built westward from Waterville in 1876 and provided service to Concordia in January 1878. The emerging mortgage market and perceptions of loan risks in Kansas are described in McFarlane, "British Investment"; and Bogue, "Land Mortgage Company." A letter from pension examiner Leslie Snow to his wife Susan Snow, from Osborne, Kansas, February 26, 1888, describes a trip from Osborne, directly south of Smith Center, to Logan in Phillips County, due west of Smith Center, in Barnes, "North Central Kansas."

18. Barr, "Diary"; Porter, "Northwest Kansas Claim," based on reminiscences from a homestead near Lenora, Kansas. Millbrook, "Mrs. Hattie E. Lee's Story," based on experiences near Wakeeney, Kansas. Ebbutt, *Emigrant Life*, a description of experiences near Junction City. Bivans, "Diary of Luna E. Warner," a teenager who lived in Osborne County.

19. U.S. Census of Agriculture for 1880 and 1890, electronic datafile; Bureau of Labor Statistics data indicate minimal inflation during this period for the nation as a whole, according to a consumer price index of 29 in 1880 and 27 in 1890 (with 1967 as base 100); U.S. Department of Labor, Bureau of Labor Statistics, *Handbook of Labor Statistics* (2007), online at www.minneapolisfed.org.

20. "Smith Center Jottings," *Atchison Daily Champion* (May 4, 1888), "Northern Kansas," *Atchison Daily Champion* (February 28, 1892); Smith Centre, *Smith County Directory* (McKenney, 1889).

21. U.S. Census for 1910 and 1920, electronic datafile; Smith Centre, *Smith County Directory*; Sanborn maps for 1892, 1899, 1904, and 1911; plat map for 1917; U.S. Census of Religious Bodies, 1916.

22. U.S. Census of Agriculture for 1910 and 1920. Plat maps of Smith County in 1917, especially Center and Washington townships; hopes continued for additional rail lines, see Miner, *Next Year Country*, 149–50.

23. U.S. Census of Agriculture for 1890, 1900, 1910, and 1920; the consumer price index held steady at around 28 or 29 from 1890 to 1920 (with 1967 as base 100); wheat prices from Kansas Department of Agriculture, *Kansas Wheat History* (Topeka: U.S. Department of Agriculture, Kansas Field Office, 2007). The average Smith County farm had equipment valued at $847 in 1920, compared with a value of $95 in 1890. A report that located Smith County as part of the state's "corn belt" showed total state, county, township, and school taxes increasing from $2,446 in 1910 to $6,072 in 1920; Harold Howe, "The Trend of Real Estate Taxation in Kansas, 1910 to 1935," *Agricultural Experiment Station Circular*, 192 (October 1938).

24. Sanborn map of Smith Center in 1925; U.S. Census for 1930.

25. Diary of Don Hartwell, quoted in Egan, *Worst Hard Time*, 244, 247; Hartwell lived on a farm about thirty miles north of Smith Center near Inavale, Nebraska.

26. Pletcher, "History of Smith County," 95.

27. Agricultural and business statistics for Smith County are from Kansas Board of Agriculture, *Annual Report, 1936* (Kansas State Historical Society); and U.S. Census of Agriculture, 1930, 1935, and 1950, electronic datafiles. Winton Slagle Sipe, *Memories of a Kansas Farm Boy* (undated), online at www.kancoll.org; Easterly, *Trend of Farm Population*, 22–69; Pletcher, "History of Smith County," 96–97, 240; a study of farm foreclosures that included data for three Midwestern states showed that foreclosures peaked in 1933 at approximately 6 percent of farms in North Dakota and Minnesota and 8 percent in South Dakota; Alston, "Farm Foreclosures."

28. U.S. Census of Agriculture conducted in 1934 and 1939 and U.S. Unemployment Census conducted in 1937; from electronic datafiles.

29. Fearon, "Regulation and Response"; U.S. Censuses for 1930 and 1940. Smith County population was 13,545 in 1930 and 10,582 in 1940. Smith Center population fell only slightly from 1,736 to 1,686. Population in Lebanon, Gaylord, Athol, and Cedar declined by about 10 percent and rose slightly in Kensington. The number of people in Smith County aged zero through nineteen dropped by 1,771 and aged

twenty to forty-four by 1,279, while the number aged forty-five and older rose by 92. The decline in the number of women aged fifteen to nineteen was 2.2 times greater than that of men of the same range, and among those aged twenty to twenty-four, the ratio of women to men was 1.66 to 1. In 1929, there were 153 retail stores in Smith County, one-third of them in Smith Center; a decade later, the total number of stores had risen slightly to 164, but total sales fell from $3.67 million in 1929 to $1.66 million in 1939. Partly offsetting this decrease was the fact that the consumer price index, which had risen from 30 to 52 during World War I and remained at that level until 1929, declined to 39 in 1933 and was at 42 in 1940. An additional offset was the fact that real estate taxes fell by one-third between 1930 and 1940. There were 2,299 farms in 1939, compared with 2,415 in 1929, with average acreage of 244, up from 226. The number of automobiles in Smith County rose from 2,978 in 1927 to 3,692 in 1930 and then fell to 2,773 in 1936. In the same years, homes with electricity rose from 1,250 to 1,298 to 1,524. In 1929, 9 percent of farms had tractors; 16 percent did in 1939.

30. U.S. Census Bureau, *Census of Agriculture: Kansas, Chapter A, Statistics for the State* (Washington, DC: Government Printing Office, 1950), figures for Smith County.

31. Wheat prices as listed by the U.S. Department of Agriculture and other information from U.S. Census for 1940 and 1950 and U.S. Census of Business for 1947, 1952, and 1957. Value of all farm products for Smith County was $1.548 million in 1939, $6.022 million in 1944, $6.296 million in 1949, and $9.258 million in 1954. The proportion from livestock was 57 and 58 percent, respectively, in 1939 and 1949; from crops, 28 and 30 percent, respectively; and from dairy and poultry sales, 15 and 12 percent. Farm tenancy declined from 48 percent of the total to 30 percent. Acres per farm increased from 285 to 364, and average farm value increased from $6342 to $14,293. The consumer price index rose from 42 to 72 (1967 as base 100). In 1954, retail sales, wholesale payroll, service trades receipts, and manufacturing revenue totaled approximately $7.186 million.

32. Interview with Roy and Cherry Brown, conducted January 18, 2007.

33. U.S. Department of Agriculture, Farm Production Indexes, 1947–90.

34. Disbursements of state highway funds for Kansas and other states from 1921 through 1959 are reported in U.S. Department of Commerce, Bureau of Public Roads, *Highway Statistics* (Washington, DC: Government Printing Office, 1960); details about roads in Smith and surrounding counties are from Kansas Department of Transportation maps for the years indicated.

35. U.S. Census, 1950 County Databook, electronic datafile; figures are for counties in Arkansas, Iowa, Kansas, Minnesota, Missouri, Nebraska, North Dakota, Oklahoma, and South Dakota.

36. Among U.S. farms nationally, only 46 percent had electricity in 1945 and only 32 percent had telephone service; U.S. Department of Agriculture, Rural Electrification Administration, *A Brief History of the Rural Electric and Telephone Programs* (Washington, DC: Government Printing Office, 1982).

37. U.S. Department of Commerce, Bureau of the Census, *Census of Housing*, vol. 6: *Rural Housing* (Washington, DC: Government Printing Office, 1960); more than one million farm dwellings were found to be deteriorating or dilapidated, and nearly 3 million rural nonfarm dwellings were placed in the same categories.

38. Hugh A. Fogarty, "Money Is Pouring In on Western Farmers," *New York Times* (September 28, 1947), E12.

39. "Golden Sky," *Time* (October 13, 1947).

40. "Plenty in the Smokehouse," *Time* (March 28, 1949).

41. Eugene Seibel, "Growing Up on the Seibel Family Farm" (unpublished manuscript, Fredonia, KS, 2004); income and average farm size figures for Wilson County are from the U.S. Census, 1950 County Databook, electronic datafile, my analysis.

42. Taylor, "Rural Life," 845.

43. Standardized coefficients from ordinary least squares regression for percentage of farms with electricity in 1950 for 772 counties in the nine-state region, with state included as a control variable, are –.260 for land area, .330 for number of farms, and .174 for percentage population growth from 1940 to 1950. The percentages lacking electricity in 1950 were 9 in Iowa, 16 in Minnesota, 22 in Nebraska, 26 in Kansas, 32 in Missouri and South Dakota, and 33 in North Dakota, Arkansas, and Oklahoma. Source: 1952 U.S. Census County Databook, electronic datafiles.

44. U.S. Census, 1950.

45. Margaret Pepperd Greene, "When the Wind Blows: A Kansas Dust Storm in the Dirty Thirties" (Tucson, AZ, 2007), online. Dust storms, though not of the same magnitude, continued month after month; see especially Pamela Riney-Kehrberg, *Waiting on the Bounty: The Dust Bowl Diary of Mary Knackstedt Dyck* (Iowa City: University of Iowa Press, 1999).

46. Interview with Russ and Mary Lou Stewart, conducted March 29, 2008.

47. Earl H. Bell, *Culture of a Contemporary Rural Community: Sublette, Kansas* (Washington, DC: U.S. Department of Agriculture, Bureau of Agricultural Economics, Rural Life Studies, 1942), 6, 113.

48. Wendel Ferrin, "Tornadoes in the Wilmore, Kansas Area" (November 11, 1987), online; "Twister Wrecks Wilmore Business District," *Wilmore News* (May 27, 1949), 1; Janet Schrock Hubbard, "Memories of Mrs. Ferrin and Maude" (April 1999), online.

49. Betty Jo Gigot, "Paul Brown," *CALF News* (June 1999): 16–17; annual rainfall as reported in Williams and Bloomquist, *From Dust Bowl to Green Circles*, 23; Haskell County is also included in the fine study of southwestern Kansas by Pamela Riney-Kehrberg, *Rooted in Dust*.

50. "Dust Storms Make Night Out of Day in Six States," *Chicago Daily Tribune* (February 20, 1954), 3.

51. "Return of the Dusters," *Time* (March 29, 1954).

52. Hall, *Journal of the Seasons*, 79.

53. Presidential Papers of Dwight David Eisenhower (January 1957), online; "Depressed by Drought," *Time* (January 28, 1957); "Text of Speech by President in Wichita," *New York Times* (January 16, 1957), 18.

54. *A Brief History of Farmers Home Administration* (Washington, DC: U.S. Department of Agriculture, 1989), 39, cumulative farm loans.

55. Powers, *Years of Struggle*, 42, 77.

56. A useful overview is given in Fearon, "Kansas History." Variation among counties was evident; see Fearon, "Regulation and Response"; and Fearon, *Kansas in the Great Depression*. See also Riney-Kehrberg, *Rooted in Dust*, 81, who observes that "'easy' government money, accepted when people forgot how to help themselves, fell outside the traditions of southwestern Kansas."

57. Letters from Edna Heim to Clarice Snoddy (1936 and 1938), Kansas State Historical Society, Kansas Memory Collection.

58. *Smith County Pioneer* (January 18, 1951).

59. The parity plan was part of the 1933 Agricultural Adjustment Act, passed when farmers' incomes were 43 percent less than the parity level; the goal of 90 percent parity was not reached, however, until 1941 as World War II started. Government payments were approximately 15 percent of realized net farm income in 1939 and 1940. In the 1950s, government payments averaged less than 2 percent of realized net farm income from 1950 through 1955 and rose to 4 percent in 1956, 8 percent in 1957 and 1958, and 6 percent in 1959; Grove, "State Variations"; on the origins and history of the parity program, see Danbom, *Born in the Country*.

60. U.S. Department of Agriculture, *Farm Population, Migration to and from Farms, 1920–1954* and *Farm Population, Estimates for 1950–59* (Washington, DC: Government Printing Office, 1959). See table 2 in the appendix. It is important to note that these figures include multiple moves by the same individuals to and from farms.

61. Ibid.

62. Pletcher, "History of Smith County," 3.

63. Schwieder, *Growing Up with the Town*, 122. As another example of high turnover, Schweider cites the study of North Dakota railroad towns between 1880 and 1920 conducted by Hudson, *Plains Country Towns*.

64. Mitchell County Historical Society, *Story of Mitchell County*, 78–79.

65. Gertrude Crowell, "Meroa, Iowa—1977" (transcribed by Deidre Badker), online.

66. Sanger, *Cedar County*, 49, 139.

67. Jeanne Van Kley, "A Family Together" (unpublished manuscript, Iowa Women's Archives, University of Iowa Libraries, Iowa City, 1987).

68. U.S. Census, County and City Databook, 1952; electronic datafile.

69. Interview conducted May 2, 2007.

70. Kollmorgen and Jenks, "Geographic Study," 452.

71. Kollmorgen and Jenks, "Suitcase Farming."

72. U.S. Census, 1950, 1 Percent Public Use Microsample, electronic datafile. This and all subsequent citations to 1 Percent Public Use Microsamples refer to the machine-readable Integrated Public Use Microdata Series: Version 4.0 (IPUMS-USA) database produced and distributed by Steven Ruggles, Matthew Sobek, Trent Alexander, Catherine A. Fitch, Ronald Goeken, Patricia Kelly Hall, Miriam King, and Chad Ronnander (Minneapolis: Minnesota Population Center, 2008).

73. Interview conducted March 23, 2007 (pseudonym used).

74. Raup and Johnson, *Minnesota Farm Real Estate Market*, report no. 512.

75. U.S. Census, 1900, 1910, 1940, 1950, 1960, 1970, 1980, and 1990, 1 Percent Public Use Microsamples, electronic datafile; my analysis of the mean number of children ever born per woman aged forty-five and older. The average for farm women in the nine-state region was 5.8 in 1900, 5.9 in 1910, 3.7 in 1940, 3.6 in 1950, 3.3 in 1960, 3.1 in 1970, 3.2 in 1980, and 3.3 in 1990. See table 3 in the appendix for further details and comparisons with nonfarm women.

76. Across the nine-state region, the mean number of children ever born to farm women aged fifteen through twenty-nine was 1.9 in 1900, 1.9 in 1910, 1.3 in 1940,

1.6 in 1950, 2.1 in 1960, 0.7 in 1970, 0.6 in 1980, and 0.6 in 1990; the pattern suggests postponement of fertility in the 1930s.

77. Among nonfarm women aged forty-five or older in the nine-state region, the mean number of children ever born was 4.8 in 1900, 4.8 in 1910, 3.0 in 1940, 2.9 in 1950, 2.8 in 1960, 2.6 in 1970, 2.7 in 1980, and 3.0 in 1990.

78. U.S. Census County Databooks, electronic datafiles; analysis of 772 counties in the nine-state region.

79. Tractors and combines were becoming more common but were by no means universal; for example, among farms in Kansas that primarily produced grain, 69 percent had combines; in North Dakota, 63 percent of the grain-producing farms had combines, and in South Dakota, 45 percent did. In the corn belt, 51 percent of farms in Iowa that specialized in grain had a corn picker, 45 percent did in Nebraska, and 38 percent did in Minnesota. Hay balers were just starting to be used. Fifteen percent of the farms in Oklahoma had a hay baler, the most of any state in the region, followed by 9 percent in Kansas and 8 percent in Iowa. Machines reduced the need for labor, but farmers still relied heavily on family members to do the work. In 1949, the percentage of farm operators who reported using unpaid family members for farm work ranged from 45 percent in Minnesota and Nebraska to 42 percent in South Dakota, 41 percent in Kansas and North Dakota, 40 percent in Iowa, 37 percent in Missouri and Oklahoma, and 30 percent in Arkansas. These were unpaid family members who worked fifteen or more hours a week doing farm work. They made up a considerable share of the rural labor force and were essential during harvest, at times of heavy field work, for daily chores, and when the farm operator was ill. Overall, there were approximately 1.1 million farm operators in the nine-state region, and their labor was supplemented by more than 750,000 unpaid family members. These data are from U.S. Census of Agriculture and U.S. Census County Databooks, electronic datafiles.

80. Other measures of mechanization and modernization showed similar results. These measures included the percentage of farms with tractors at the end of the period (1959), the percentage of farms with trucks at both the start and end, the percentage of farms with telephones in 1950, and the average monthly farm electricity bill in 1950.

81. See tables 4 and 5 in the appendix. Standardized ordinary least squares regression coefficients for percentage decline in agricultural labor force per county and percentage decline in number of farms per county between 1950 and 1960 for each measure of mechanization, magnet pull, and marginality, controlling for county population, percentage agricultural labor force, and number of farms in 1950; additional models in which counties in the Dakotas and Nebraska were combined and counties with total agricultural output valued at less than $1 million in 1950 were excluded show that farm labor decline was not associated with measures of mechanization, magnet pull, or marginality, but that decline in number of farms was associated with less mechanization, as measured by farms with tractors in 1950, and with marginality, as measured by median family income in 1950. On the costs of mechanization, see Vliet, "Increased Capital Requirements"; and Johnson, "Impact of Farm Machinery"; and for a discussion of variations by level of farm income and size, see Johnson, "Technological Changes."

82. U.S. Census 1 Percent Public Use Microsample data for 1960 for the nine-state region show that 45 percent lived in the same house as five years previously, 25 percent lived in the same county but in a different house, 9 percent lived in a different county in the same state, 8 percent lived in a different state, and 12 percent did not respond.

83. County-level comparisons are subject to the shortcoming that although less prosperous counties experienced greater decline in farms and farm workers, it might have been the more affluent farmers in those counties who left; that possibility, though, runs against the individual-level census results showing that it was actually lower-income families who left the farms. Other studies of rural out-migration in different areas and at different times show similar patterns of the better-off and those owning land staying and those with lower incomes leaving; see Hill, "Characteristics of the Farmers"; Guither, "Factors Influencing Farm Operators' Decisions"; Ducoff, "Trends and Characteristics"; Gregson, "Population Dynamics"; Gee, "Qualitative Study"; Riney-Kehrberg, *Rooted in Dust*, 194, which compares percentages of owners and nonowners who left between 1930 and 1940 in five southwestern Kansas townships; and Ruttan, "Farm and Non-Farm Employment Opportunities," which examines the plight of low-income farm families in Southeastern states.

84. These figures are from the Great Plains Census of Agriculture database, which does not include Arkansas or Missouri.

85. U.S. Census, *Census of Agriculture, 1950, Arkansas, Chapter B: Counties* (Washington, DC: Government Printing Office, 1950); U.S. Census County Databook, 1950 and 1960, electronic datafile; the U.S. Unemployment Census conducted in 1937 showed 818 residents registered as unemployed and 537 registered as partly unemployed; Billingsley, "Settlement Patterns"; and Newman, *Recollections*.

86. Wayne Leroy Ninemire, "I Should Not Talk So Much about Myself" (transcript written February 1998), online; Ninemire worked in transportation until his retirement in 1981, continuing his interests in farming through two small farms in Washington State on which he raised cattle and horses. Anthropologist Carl Withers, writing under the pseudonym James West in *Plainville, U.S.A.*, described the community in southwestern Missouri he studied in terms similar to Ninemire's account. Most of the farmers relied on kerosene for light and on wood-burning stoves for heat, only a third had telephone service, and a majority supplemented farm income with off-farm jobs.

87. "See It Now?" *Time* (February 6, 1956).

88. Roger Strickland, "Net Farm Income by State, 1949 to 2002," U.S. Department of Agriculture, Economic Research Service (March 14, 2003); and for a brief summary, "Who Is Hurting Most and Why?" *Farm Journal* (April 1956), 18. There were approximately 1.3 million farms in the nine-state heartland region in 1950 and 984,000 in 1959.

89. Randall and Masucci, "Farm and Nonfarm Income Comparisons"; U.S. Department of Agriculture, Economic Research Service, "Net and Gross Farm Income" (2003); U.S. Department of Agriculture, Economic Research Service, "Farm Output and Productivity Indexes, 1948–96" (2002).

90. U.S. Department of Commerce, Bureau of the Census, *Trends in the Income of Families and Persons in the United States: 1947 to 1960*, Technical Paper no. 8 (Washington, DC: Government Printing Office, 1963), 168; as reported for rural farm

families in the North Central region in 1959 constant dollars. National figures are discussed in Boyne, "Changes in the Income Distribution."

91. U.S. Census, Public Use Microsample for 1960, electronic datafile.

92. Roger Strickland, "Average Value per Acre of Farm Real Estate, 1950–1959," U.S. Department of Agriculture, Economic Research Service (January 29, 2002); adjusted for cost of living, farmland prices in 1959 compared with 1950 averaged 36 percent higher in Arkansas, 25 percent higher in Iowa, 20 percent higher in Kansas, 46 percent higher in Minnesota, 39 percent higher in Missouri, 20 percent higher in Nebraska, 42 percent higher in North Dakota, 27 percent in Oklahoma, and 33 percent higher in South Dakota.

93. In the nine-state region, counties in which 100 percent of the population was rural employed 120 people on average in manufacturing in 1958, up from 88 in 1947. Missouri averaged the most, with 247, followed by Arkansas with 218 and Minnesota with 196; U.S. Census, County Databooks for 1952 and 1962, electronic datafile.

94. U.S. Department of Agriculture, Economic Research Service Annual Reports on Average Value per Acre of Farm Real Estate; U.S. Census County Databooks, 1950 and 1960, electronic datafiles. Kennedy won Missouri by a large margin and Arkansas and Minnesota by narrow margins; Nixon won by large margins in Iowa, Kansas, Nebraska, North Dakota, Oklahoma, and South Dakota.

95. U.S. Census total population of Smith Center in 1960 was 2,379 and 1,931 in 2000; in Smith County, 7,776 and 4,536, respectively.

96. U.S. Census of Agriculture, electronic datafiles.

97. U.S. Census, County Business Patterns, electronic datafile.

98. U.S. Department of Agriculture reports for Smith County in 1959 and 1997, respectively, show total wheat production of 1.8 million bushels and 5.9 million bushels; corn, 0.6 million bushels and 1.3 million bushels; sorghum, 1.3 million bushels and 4.1 million bushels. The yields in 2006 were larger for all three crops than the 1997 yields.

99. Nalley, Barkley, and Chemley, *Agronomic and Economic Impacts*, wheat averaged 18.6 bushels per acre in Smith County in 1959 and 47.2 bushels in 1997. The 2006 crop averaged 44.6 bushels per acre. Corn increased from 26.7 bushels per acre in 1959 to 67.9 bushels per acre in 2006; sorghum increased from 25.7 bushels to 88.5 bushels.

100. Kent Stones, quoted in Roger Long, "No-Till for Profitability," *Leading Edge* (December 2001): 1–4.

101. U.S. Census County Databooks, 1960 and 2000, electronic datafiles for Smith County. In 1960 and 2000, respectively, the total labor force was 3165 and 2119; agriculture, 1540 and 363; wholesale/retail, 508 and 363; construction, 187 and 112; public administration, 135 and 395; education, 138 and 249; manufacturing, 109 and 176; transportation and utilities, 97 and 190; finance, 59 and 107; and other, 392 and 164.

CHAPTER THREE

1. Danbom, *Born in the Country*, 150–51; negative perceptions of rural life in Kansas are examined in detail in Bader, *Hayseeds, Moralizers, and Methodists*.

2. Whittier, *At Sundown*, 48.

3. Information about William F. Cody is from Yost, *Buffalo Bill*, which is based on extensive archival and firsthand accounts and corrects inaccuracies in previous biographies and in Cody's autobiography. Information about the Spence and Richardson families is from Spence, *Moving Out*. On efforts to organize other Wild West shows, see Hoig, *Cowtown Wichita*, especially chap. 15.

4. Spence, *Moving Out*, 101, describes a conversation indicating that the Richardsons and Brittons both hailed from Blair, Nebraska; however, according to "Early Settlers of Bethel Community," *Nebraska State Genealogical Society Journal* 20 (1997), 47, the Richardsons were from Lyons, Nebraska, north of Blair. The accounts are consistent in mentioning that the families journeyed by train to Valentine, Nebraska, on the Fremont, Elkhorn, and Missouri Valley Railroad (the railroad did not reach Fort Robinson until May 11, 1886, and the town of Crawford was platted at that time). Levi Richardson was the grandfather of Polly Spence's husband, Levi, and James Britton was the father of Jennie Britton, Polly Spence's mother-in-law.

5. Cutler, *History of the State of Nebraska*, chapter on Sioux County.

6. Details of the show are from a newspaper account included in full in Yost, *Buffalo Bill*, 134–36; and Deahl, "Nebraska's Unique Contribution," 194.

7. What became known as "Henry's ride" and the role of Fort Robinson soldiers before and after Wounded Knee are described in Buecker, *Fort Robinson*, 176–78.

8. Turner, "Significance of the Frontier."

9. Spence, *Moving Out*, 187, 192, 200.

10. Andersen, *Portable Prairie*, 83, 94.

11. Robert Pearman, "Kansas' Centennial Shifts into High Gear," *New York Times* (June 11, 1951).

12. Wilder, *Little House*.

13. Griswold and Wright, "Dynamic Endurance of Regionalism," in which the National Geographic Society survey is also discussed.

14. Hines, "Introduction," in *Laura Ingalls Wilder*, 1–2; another interesting discussion is given in Barbara Muhs Walker, "A Trail of History Refreshingly Free of Violence," *New York Times* (September 21, 1969), 15.

15. Wilder, *Little House*, 107, 109.

16. Miller, *Becoming Laura Ingalls Wilder*.

17. Laura Ingalls Wilder, "The Story of Rocky Ridge Farm" (July 22, 1911), in Hines, *Laura Ingalls Wilder*, 17–19, quotation is on page 19; editor Stephen Hines notes that the byline was A. J. Wilder (Laura's husband) but argues that the essay was more likely to have been written by Laura; "An Autumn Day" (October 20, 1916), in Hines, *Laura Ingalls Wilder*, 87–88, quotation is on page 87; "As a Farm Woman Thinks" (April 15, 1923), in Hines, *Laura Ingalls Wilder*, 287–88.

18. Rife, "Iowa's Rural Women Columnists," 123–43.

19. Cameron, *Pioneer Days*, 8.

20. On the earlier interpretations emphasizing manifest destiny, see especially Julie Wilson, "'Kansas Uber Alles?'"

21. Wilder, *Little House*, 330–31.

22. Wilder, "Favors the Small Farm Home" (February 18, 1911), in Hines, *Laura Ingalls Wilder, Farm Journalist*, 13–16, quotation is on page 16.

23. From an anonymous contributor to an Internet forum on the Dust Bowl at www.city-data.com (March 30, 2008).

24. Another contributor to the same forum (April 1, 2008).

25. Steinbeck, *Grapes of Wrath*; Shockley, "Reception of the Grapes of Wrath," discusses affirmations of regional pride; initial reactions in California are described in Tom Cameron, "'Grapes of Wrath' Author Guards Self from Threats at Moody Gulch," *Los Angeles Times* (July 9, 1939), A1; Keith Windschuttle, "Steinbeck's Myth of the Okies," *New Criterion* 20 (2002), online, summarizes the book's inaccuracies and its popularity; additional background is given in Steinbeck's *Working Days* and *Harvest Gypsies*.

26. Rogers, *L. Frank Baum*; Riley, *Oz and Beyond*.

27. The quote is from Frank S. Nugent, "The Screen Review," *New York Times* (August 18, 1939), 16; the debate about the film's relationship to prairie populism was initiated in Littlefield, "Wizard of Oz," and carried forward in Erisman, "L. Frank Baum"; Rockoff, "Monetary Allegory"; and Parker, "Rise and Fall."

28. Riney-Kehrberg, *Rooted in Dust*, 175.

29. Low, *Dust Bowl Diary*, 134.

30. Riney-Kehrberg, *Waiting on the Bounty*, 326.

31. Snyder, *Youngest Brother*, 105.

32. Powers, *Years of Struggle*, 70–74.

33. Spence, *Moving Out*, 161.

34. Faust, *Remember—No Electricity*, 6.

35. Andersen, *Portable Prairie*, 18.

36. Interview conducted June 21, 2007 (pseudonym used).

37. "Prof. Norton of Harvard Has Discovered the Rustic Loafer," *Milwaukee Sentinel* (August 24, 1897), 4.

38. "Chicago's Outposts," *Daily Inter Ocean* (September 21, 1890), 18.

39. "Wonders," *St. Paul Daily News* (September 24, 1892), 4.

40. Charles B. Cook, "The Scientific Man on the Farm," *Science* (October 6, 1893), 187–88.

41. Butterfield, "Social Problems." Bufferfield served as a member of the Country Life Commission.

42. Howard B. Woolston, "The Urban Habit of Mind," *American Journal of Sociology* 17 (1912), 602–14; quotation is on page 604.

43. McCarter, *Solomon Valley*.

44. Morris, *Home Place*, 6.

45. Danbom, *Born in the Country*, 169–80.

46. Ross, "Town-Country Conflict," 17. Ross does not give the date or author of the quoted publication.

47. Haggerty and Nash, "Mental Capacity of Children"; Collins, "Relation of Parental Occupation"; Klapp, "Fool as a Social Type."

48. Sewell and Ellenbogen, "Social Status"; the research demonstrated conclusively that children's intelligence test scores were a function of parents' educational attainment level rather than of urban or rural residence.

49. Taylor, "Rural Life."

50. Andersen, *Portable Prairie*, 12.

51. Bodensteiner, *Growing Up Country*.

52. U.S. Bureau of the Census, *Trends in the Income of Families and Persons in the United States: 1947 to 1960* (Washington, DC: Government Printing Office,

1963), 182. Family incomes for the North Central region (which included the nine states of the heartland region except for Oklahoma and Arkansas) averaged $3,148 in 1953 for rural farm families (in 1959 constant dollars), $4,566 for rural nonfarm (i.e., small-town) families, and $5,490 for urban families; 29 percent, 42 percent, and 57 percent, respectively, earned $5,000 or more; the Gini index of income inequality, respectively, was .443, .331, and .317. Across the region, farm equity in 1950 was $13,123, and 26 percent of farms held mortgages, averaging $4,344; U.S. Department of Agriculture, *Farm Mortgage Debt: Cooperative Report* (Washington, DC: Government Printing Office, 1952), 14.

53. Andersen, *Portable Prairie*, 86, 87.

54. U.S. Census Bureau, *Statistical Abstract* (Washington, DC: Government Printing Office, 1962), table 690, page 514; *U.S. Television Chronology, 1875 to 1970*, online.

55. U.S. Census County Databooks, electronic datafiles; for counties as the unit of analysis in the nine-state region and percent of farms with television in 1954 as the dependent variable, controlling for median family income in 1949 and total population in 1950, the standardized multiple regression coefficient for percent of farms with piped running water in 1954 is .501 and for percent urban in 1950 is .219, both significant at or beyond the .001 level of probability; 1960 data are from U.S. Census County Databooks, electronic datafiles, and for television stations, broadcast revenue, and expenditures on television sets, from U.S. Census, *Statistical Abstract* (Washington, DC: Government Printing Office, 1961), tables 692 and 693, page 515, and *Electronic Merchandising Week* (January 1961).

56. Johnson, "Camelot, Hooterville, or Watts?"

57. "Distorted Image," *Farm Journal* (April 1954), 104.

58. George McCall, "Sticks Nix Hick Pix," *Variety* (July 17, 1935), 1.

59. Marc and Thompson, *Prime Time*; Barnouw, *Tube of Plenty*.

60. A complete listing is available from *Ulrich's Periodicals Directory* (online); on Midwest prominence, see Brunn and Raitz, "Regional Patterns."

61. "Farmers Rely on Print Ads," *Advertising Age* (May 11, 1959); the study was conducted in Illinois by the Farm Research Institute.

62. A brief history of *Farm Journal* is given in Michael DeCourcy Hinds, "Philadelphia Journal: Farm Magazine Thrives in Fertile Asphalt Soil," *New York Times* (December 13, 1989). The Farm Journal Corporation was sold in 1997; information about the sale is included in Securities and Exchange Commission File 333-56563 (June 11, 1998).

63. Data on advertising revenue per client for 1961 are from the Farm Journal Archive held in the Special Collections Library at Temple University, Philadelphia.

64. "How to Be Queen" was produced by Carol Dee Legg, fashion editor of the "Farmer's Wife" section, herself a graduate of the journal's "School for Queens," and is available along with a summary of supermarket responses at the Temple University Farm Journal Archive.

65. John L. Gillis, Monsanto Vice President, as quoted in "'Average' Fails as Measure of Today's Farmer," *Rural Marketing* 14 (January 1959), 1; on file at the Temple University Farm Journal Archive.

66. "Letters," *Farm Journal* (January 1957), 90.

67. "Letters," *Farm Journal* (February 1956), 34.

68. "Letters," *Farm Journal* (March 1956), 159–60.

69. "Letters," *Farm Journal* (July 1956), 85.

70. "Letters," *Farm Journal* (January 1957), 90.

71. "Letters," *Farm Journal* (July 1956), 86.

72. Carroll P. Streeter, "Why It's Your Magazine," *Farm Journal* (April 1963), 4.

73. "Letters," *Farm Journal* (June 1956), 92.

74. "Quotes," *Farm Journal* (April 1963), 104.

75. Dale DeRuwe, excerpt reprinted in Longwell, *This Way of Life*, an anthology of 800 excerpts from letters submitted to *Farm Journal* between 1944 and 1971.

76. "Letters," *Farm Journal* (May 1957), 129.

77. Eva Allen, "Tie That Binds," *Farm Journal* (February 1956), 144.

78. Catherine Walker, "More Important Than Ever," *Farm Journal* (August 1951), 78.

79. "Letters," *Farm Journal* (February 1957), 137.

80. Quoted in Virginia Brown, "Is Your Club in a Rut?" *Farm Journal* (May 1957), 106.

81. Frances Ann Jones, "What's Your Treasure?" *Farm Journal* (June 1961), 94; "Letters," *Farm Journal* (July 1961), 70; "Letters," *Farm Journal* (August 1961), 65.

82. Frances McKenzie Ellis and Jeanne Schwartz, excerpts reprinted in Longwell, *This Way of Life*, 18–19.

83. Rife, "Iowa's Rural Women Columnists," 214–19; Gladys Rife, "Rural Reflections," *Iowa City Press-Citizen* (March 12, 1955), 4; Leah Jane Smith, "The Sunroom Window," *Rock Rapids Reporter* (1954), 37; Helen Attleson, "On the Lighter Side," *New Hampton Tribune* (1954), 32.

84. Carson, *Silent Spring*, 1.

85. Cather, *O Pioneers!*, 75.

86. Hall, *Journal of the Seasons*, 187.

87. Paula Wansa, excerpt reprinted in Longwell, *This Way of Life*, 257.

88. Durkheim, *Division of Labor*, 287.

89. Roland, "Do-It-Yourself."

90. Interview with Kathy Davis-Vrbas, conducted January 9, 2008.

91. Hamilton, *Deep River*, 155.

92. Interview conducted June 18, 2007 (name withheld).

93. Interviews conducted in 2007 and 2008.

94. Postings on moderated forums at www.city-data.com.

CHAPTER FOUR

1. Interviews conducted March 29, 2008, and May 10, 2008 (pseudonyms used and identifying details altered).

2. See table 6 in the appendix. Figures cited on educational attainment for the United States and for each state are from U.S. Census Bureau, *Statistical Abstracts* (Washington, DC: Government Printing Office, 1942–2008), and pertain to adults aged twenty-five and over; figures from decennial censuses 1940 through 2000 were cross-checked and rankings generated using 1 Percent Public Use Microsamples, electronic datafiles.

3. On education and earnings, Goldin and Katz, "Education and Income," is of particular interest because of its focus on Iowa; see also Goldin and Katz, *Education and Technology*.

4. The Land Ordinance of 1785 ("An Ordinance for Ascertaining the Mode of Disposing of Lands in the Western Territory," passed May 20, 1785) stated, "There shall be reserved the lot No. 16, of every township, for the maintenance of public schools, within the said township." Earlier wordings stated, "There shall be reserved the central Section of every Township, for the maintenance of public Schools" (*Journals of the Continental Congress* 28, April 26, 1785, 291–96). Article III of the Ordinance of 1787 ("An Ordinance for the Government of the Territory of the United States Northwest of the River Ohio") reaffirmed the commitment, stating, "Religion, morality, and knowledge, being necessary to good government and the happiness of mankind, schools and the means of education shall forever be encouraged." Details of the laws governing public lands for education are given in Treat, *National Land System*, 265–78.

5. Musick, *Stories of Missouri*.

6. The ninety-seven-year-old granddaughter of a woman who attended a one-room school in the 1850s recalled her grandmother telling of one teacher in particular known to the children as a "drunken fool." Interview with Aletta Edgar, conducted July 6, 2008.

7. W. H. Brinkerhoff, quote dated 1872 in Van Metre, *History of Black Hawk County*, 289.

8. U.S. Census, County Data, 1850, electronic datafile. St. Louis County had 54 academies with 3,715 pupils and 60 public schools with 3,607 pupils. Other counties in Missouri with a high proportion of private academies included Cape Girardeau, Chariton, Cooper, Gasconade, Greene, Harrison, Lafayette, McDonald, New Madrid, Ripley, Scott, and St. Genevieve; and in Arkansas, Benton, Clark, Crawford, Dallas, Hempstead, Hot Spring, Johnson, Ouachita, Phillips, Pulaski, and Union. Resistance to public education is discussed in Thomas, *Second Home*.

9. Cameron, *Pioneer Days*, 85.

10. U.S. Census, County Data, 1850, electronic datafile.

11. Aurner, *History of Education in Iowa*, 1:89. Aurner quotes sources in the 1850s and 1860s.

12. Ibid., 1:4–48; Alexander, *History of Iowa*.

13. *Report of the Secretary of the State Board of Education* (1859), 16; S. C. Hyde, *Historical Sketch of Lyon County* (1872), online; Floyd Hohman, "Larchwood's Schools" (undated), online.

14. Cutler, *History of the State of Nebraska*, part 13; Cutler, *History of the State of Kansas*, parts 19 and 20; Wagner, "First Decade."

15. Morse, "'Knowledge Is Power,'" 9; Power, "Crusade to Extend Yankee Culture."

16. U.S. Census, County Data, 1870, electronic datafile.

17. Ruth Gongwar Mumford, transcript included in McKenzie, *Her Own Story*, 88, courtesy of Vinton Public Library.

18. Occupations and states of origin in 1856 are from transcriptions of the Iowa state census by Sue Soden, online at iagenweb.com; Hill, *History of Benton County Iowa* population figures are from U.S. Census Bureau, electronic datafiles.

19. Information compiled by Lavonne Henkel, as reported in Steve Meyer, "Putting the Pieces Together: Vinton Woman Assembling History of Benton's County

Schools," *Cedar Rapids-Iowa City Gazette* (January 28, 2002), B2; Henkel's information included country schools Cedar No. 2, Homer No. 5, Kane No. 2, Eden No. 2, and Union No. 2 and town schools in Brandon, Elberon, Garrison, Keystone, Mount Auburn, Newhall, Shellsburg, and Urbana. The school official's quote appeared in *Iowa Instructor* 2 (1860), 58.

20. I. Van Metre, *Vinton Eagle* (1905), as quoted in Hill, *History of Benton County Iowa*, 47.

21. "Pioneering Journeys of the Ingalls Family," Herbert Hoover Presidential Library & Museum, online at www.hoover.archives.gov.

22. Aurner, *History of Education in Iowa*, 3:83–84.

23. U.S. Census of Agriculture, 1880, electronic datafile.

24. Hill, *History of Benton County Iowa*, 164–65; U.S. Census, Benton County, 1910, electronic datafile.

25. Hill, *History of Benton County Iowa*, 163; Nira Geiger, transcript in McKenzie, *Her Own Story*, 47.

26. U.S. Census, County Data, 1850, electronic datafile.

27. 1870 U.S. Census Public Use 1 Percent Microsample, electronic datafile. Aurner, *History of Education in Iowa*, 135, discusses the state's pride in its literacy rate but expresses skepticism that it demonstrates the state's school system's superiority.

28. 1870 U.S. Census Public Use 1 Percent Microsample, electronic datafile; included as northern states: Connecticut, Delaware, Illinois, Indiana, Iowa, Kansas, Maine, Massachusetts, Michigan, Minnesota, Nebraska, New Hampshire, New Jersey, New York, Ohio, Pennsylvania, Rhode Island, Vermont, and Wisconsin.

29. Ibid. Among adults aged twenty-five through forty-five, comparisons of literacy rates by birth state and state of current residence show the following: among those born in and still living in Ohio, 93 percent were literate, but this rate was 3 to 5 points higher among Ohioans currently living in Iowa, Kansas, Minnesota, or Nebraska; 97 percent of New Yorkers born and still living in New York were literate, but the percentages were 1 to 3 points higher among those having moved in Iowa, Kansas, Minnesota, or Nebraska; 93 percent of those born in and still living in Pennsylvania were literate, whereas the percentage was 97 for Pennsylvanians living in Iowa, 95 percent in Kansas, 100 percent in Minnesota, and 93 percent in Nebraska; among those born in and still living in Indiana, 89 percent were literate, whereas the rates were 2 to 11 points higher for those who had moved to the other states; in Illinois, 91 percent of those still living there were literate, and the rates were 1 to 9 points higher among those who had moved.

30. Ibid. Illustrative of the differences, among whites aged twenty-five through forty-five, 79 percent of native Virginians living in Virginia were literate, whereas 95 percent of Virginians in Kansas and 92 percent in Missouri were literate; among native Kentuckians, literacy was 79 percent in Kentucky, 88 percent in Kansas, and 85 percent in Nebraska; among black Kentuckians, the rates were 15 percent in Kentucky, 29 percent in Kansas, and 41 percent in Arkansas; among black Virginians, 9 percent in Virginia, 9 percent in Missouri, and 40 percent in Kansas.

31. Ibid.

32. These conclusions are drawn from the logistic regression analysis shown in appendix table 7. All coefficients shown are significant at or beyond the .001 level

of probability. Missouri is the excluded comparison variable in models with states included.

33. U.S. Census 1 Percent Public Use Microsample for 1870, electronic datafile. The percentages of children aged five through thirteen enrolled in school were: Iowa, 73; Minnesota, 67; Missouri, 55; Kansas, 53, Nebraska, 48; Arkansas 32. Results of logistic regression analysis for the six states are shown in appendix table 7.

34. U.S. Census, County Data, 1870; although data were available for some counties in Dakota Territory, these are incomplete and so are excluded. The results of ordinary least squares regression analysis are shown in appendix table 8. Percent literate refers to the percentage of the total population that could read, county and local tax rates are the respective tax amounts divided by males aged twenty-one and over as a proxy for taxpaying units; average farm value is total value of farmland and improvements divided by the number of farms and is more stable from year to year than data on farm output. Model 1 shows the effects of literacy, race, and foreign born. Model 2 includes percent urban, which has sometimes been considered a factor because of higher enrollments in towns; however, Model 3 shows that percent urban is insignificant when average farm value is included. Model 4 shows the raw effects of states, with Missouri as the excluded comparison variable, and indicates that Iowa scored significantly higher, Arkansas significantly lower, and Nebraska marginally lower. Models 5 and 6 introduce all variables simultaneously, showing that literacy, race, foreign born, and farm value continue to be significant, that county tax is not significant, but that local tax is significant. The inclusion of these variables reduces the overall effect of Iowa by only a third, elevates the net effect of Minnesota to significance, and shows that the deficit in Arkansas can be explained by these other factors. Two variables not shown that were tested and found to have no significant effects, either with the state variables included or absent, were manufacturing value per capita and state tax per capita.

35. Lensink, *"A Secret to Be Burried,"* 209, 250; Bunkers, *"All Will Yet Be Well."*

36. U.S. Census, *Statistical Abstract*, 1910, table 63, pp. 97–98, gives a total of 3.5 million enrolled for ages five through eighteen; U.S. Census Public Use 1 Percent Microsample, electronic datafile, yields the same number for that age range and 3.8 million with age unspecified. Compulsory school attendance laws were passed in Kansas in 1874, North and South Dakota in 1883, Minnesota in 1885, Nebraska in 1887, Iowa in 1902, Missouri in 1905, Oklahoma in 1907, and Arkansas in 1909. Studies of the timing and effects of these laws include Richardson, "Compulsory School Attendance Laws"; Lleras-Muney, "Child Labor Laws Effective?"; Landes and Solmon, "Compulsory Schooling Legislation."

37. Results are from ordinary least squares regression for counties in existence in Iowa, Kansas, Minnesota, Missouri, Nebraska, and Arkansas in 1870, with percentage of children aged six through seventeen enrolled in school in 1910 as the dependent variable, and percent literate in 1870, percent black in 1870, and percent foreign born in 1870 as independent variables, controlling for average farm value in 1870, and including states as variables. The standardized coefficient for literacy was .169; for percent black, −.298; and for percent foreign born, −.167; for Iowa, it was .145; for Kansas and Minnesota, .181; for Nebraska, .134; and for Arkansas, −.426.

38. U.S. Census Public Use 1 Percent Microsample, 1910. Deyoe, *Biennial Report*, 75–76. Foght, *Rural School System*; Barker and Muse, "One-Room Schools."

Samuelson, *One Room Country Schools*, 170. U.S. Department of the Interior, Bureau of Education, *Public Education in Oklahoma* (Washington, DC: Government Printing Office, 1922).

39. Edgar, "Iowa Farm Boy" (courtesy of Louise Edgar Copeland, Geneva College, Beaver Falls, Pennsylvania).

40. Ibid.

41. Samuelson, *One Room Country Schools*, 193; Fuller, *Old Country School*; John Coulter Hockenberry, "Rural School."

42. Freida Geiken, transcript in McKenzie, *Her Own Story*, 67–68. Bloomenshine, *Prairie Around Me*, 38. Mitchell County Historical Society, *Story of Mitchell County*, 62.

43. Ernest Wilder Fellows, "City School and Rural School Attendance"; Smiley, "Rural Schools and the Graded Town Schools"; Peirce, *Social Surveys*; Foght, *Rural School System*; Committee of the Graduate School of Education, *The Rural Teacher of Nebraska* (Washington, DC: Government Printing Office, 1919).

44. Foght, "The Country School," 150, 151. Implications of the Country Life Commission study are discussed in Carney, *Country Life*, 144.

45. Wilson, *Rural School Consolidation*; Kunkel and Charters, "Rural School Consolidation."

46. Stonecipher, " One-Teacher School"; Samuelson, *One Room Country Schools*, 170; Iowa closed 1,700 of 8,200 one-teacher schools between 1941 and 1946; "The Vanishing Red Schoolhouse," *Time* (August 26, 1946).

47. Enrollment figures are from U.S. Census Public Use 1 Percent Microsamples for 1910, 1920, 1930, 1940, and 1950, electronic datafiles; salaries are reported in U.S. Office of Education, *Biennial Survey of Education* (Washington, DC: Government Printing Office, 1942).

48. U.S. Census, *Statistical Abstracts*, 1950 through 1962.

49. Kenny and Schmidt, "Number of School Districts"; Reynolds, *There Goes the Neighborhood*; Edwards, "Compulsory Schooling Legislation." By 1954, Missouri's law raised compulsory attendance from age fourteen to age sixteen.

50. U.S. Census, *Statistical Abstracts*, 1920, 1930, 1940, 1950; percentages computed based on population aged fourteen through seventeen.

51. U.S. Census Public Use 1 Percent Microsamples for 1900, 1910, 1920, 1930, 1940, 1950, and 1960, electronic datafiles; in school and farm status were included in the data for each year; educational attainment was included in 1940, 1950, and 1960.

52. Butterworth, "High School Tuition."

53. Goldin and Katz, "Education and Income"; Goldin and Katz, "Human Capital and Social Capital."

54. Bell, "Changing Family Situations," 464.

55. Bell, "Contemporary Rural Community," 86.

56. U.S. Census for 1950, Public Use 1 Percent Microsample, electronic datafile. The percentages with four years of high school were: Nebraska, 74.7; Iowa, 71.9; Kansas, 71.6; Minnesota, 71.0; Oklahoma, 62.8, South Dakota, 62.1; Missouri, 59.3; North Dakota, 55.6; Arkansas, 42.9; the U.S. percentage was 57.8.

57. The cutoff used is less than or equal to 90 percent of the state average. The percentage of young people aged fourteen through seventeen enrolled in school in Mills County was 81 percent of the Iowa state average of 88 percent; Lyon and Boone

counties were 87 percent of the state average. Mills County, across the river from Omaha, had a large mobile population associated with Offutt Air Force Base; Lyon County, in the northwest corner, had a larger-than-average German and Norwegian population and few towns; and Boone County had a large Swedish population. The differences among states are also evident in standard deviations for the percentages of fourteen- through seventeen-year-olds enrolled in school in each county: Iowa, .041; Minnesota, .043; Nebraska, .052; Kansas, .054; Arkansas, Missouri, .062; Missouri, .075 (Oklahoma's variation was low, at .042, while South Dakota's and North Dakota's were high, at .068 and .984, respectively).

58. See table 9 in the appendix for comparisons of zero-order and multiple regression coefficients for U.S. Census county data in the nine Middle Western states, with percentage of fourteen- through seventeen-year-olds enrolled in school in each county in 1950 as the dependent variable and percent illiterate in 1910, percent nonwhite in 1950, median education of adults aged twenty-five and over in 1950, median family income, percent urban, and percent of labor force employed in clerical and sales jobs as independent variables. Comparisons of zero-order effects for variables in 1910 and 1950 showed that the race effect fell dramatically in Kansas and Missouri but remained strong in Arkansas; the effect of illiteracy in 1910 on school enrollment in 1950 remained especially strong in Missouri. Counties in Missouri with high levels of secondary enrollment included Caldwell, DeKalb, Gentry, and Holt in the northwest, Bates and Cass in the west, and Clark and Shelby in the northeast. Counties scoring low included New Madrid, Pemiscot, and Bollinger in the southeast and Ozark in the south. Arkansas counties with high scores included Pike, Sevier, Union, Howard, and Clark in the southwest and Cleveland, Jefferson, and Saline in the center; low-scoring counties included Poinsett, Lee, Crittendon, and Cross all in the east.

59. U.S. Census, County Data for 1850 and 1870, electronic datafiles. The Missouri counties were Callaway, Clay, Howard, Lafayette, New Madrid, and Saline; the Arkansas counties were Arkansas, Bradley, Chicot, Dallas, Desha, Hempstead, Jefferson, Lafayette, Ouachita, Phillips, Sevier, and Union.

60. U.S. Census Public Use 1 Percent Microsamples for 1880, 1910, 1940, 1950, and 1960, electronic datafiles; too few African Americans were resident in the other states throughout the period for comparisons.

61. Chicot, Crittenden, Lee, Little River, and Mississippi counties.

62. The text of the Kansas District Court ruling is included in Huxman, Mellott, and Hill, "Kansas Case Decision." On state laws and the incidence of school segregation, see "4 States Permit Separate Schools," *New York Times* (May 18, 1954), 23; and "40% of Public School Pupils in U.S. Are in Areas Where Laws Require Segregation," *New York Times* (May 18, 1954), 21. Contemporary reactions, including quotes, and the situation in Topeka are discussed in Dudziak, "Limits of Good Faith"; Fleming-Rife and Proffitt, "More Public School Reform Changes." Historical treatments of the Supreme Court case include Kluger, *Simple Justice*, and Patterson, *Brown v. Board of Education*.

63. On journalistic coverage, see Isaacs, "World Affairs."

64. Regional variations are examined in Pettigrew and Campbell, "Faubus and Segregation." Pettigrew and Campbell show especially strong support for Faubus in the delta counties in 1958. My comparison of delta and non-delta counties are from

the 1910 U.S. Census of Agriculture and the 1950, 1960, and 1970 U.S. Census County Databooks, electronic datafiles. In 1970, 37 percent of schoolchildren in delta counties were African American, compared with 11 percent in non-delta counties. In 1960, 20 percent of adults aged twenty-five and over had fewer than four years of schooling in delta counties, compared with 12 percent in non-delta counties.

65. Tack, *Iowa.*

66. National Center for Education Statistics, School District Survey, 1999, electronic datafile. The standard deviation relative to the mean was highest in North and South Dakota and lowest in Arkansas. Core expenditures per pupil, which averaged $3,702 per pupil across the nine states, were also highest in Minnesota, Nebraska, Iowa, and Kansas, and lowest in Arkansas and Oklahoma; within state standard deviation relative to means were slightly lower for core than total per pupil expenditures.

67. Interview with Karen Larson, conducted April 28, 2008; interview with Mike Timmermans, conducted June 27, 2008; interview with Mark Urlaub, conducted March 21, 2008; interview with Richard Farmer, conducted August 4, 2008; Vinton-Shellsburg Community School District, Financial Report Card, online at www.edinfo .state.ia.us; "AmeriCorps NCCC, North Central Region Campus, Vinton, Iowa," online at www.americorps.gov.

68. *U.S. Statistical Abstracts,* 1940 through 2008; in 1952, higher education enrollment figures reported for the nine states were 17,000 in Arkansas, 34,000 in Iowa, 29,000 in Kansas, 40,000 in Minnesota, 50,000 in Missouri, 19,000 in Nebraska, 7,000 in North Dakota, 36,000 in Oklahoma, and 6,000 in South Dakota.

69. Ibid.

70. Dana, "Western Colleges," 779.

71. Bryce, *American Commonwealth,* 2:552.

72. *U.S. Statistical Abstract,* 1932.

73. *U.S. Statistical Abstracts,* 1950 through 1971.

74. *Farm Journal* (March 1956), 28 (no author or title given).

75. "Do You Want to Go to College?" *Better Farming* (February 1955), 8–10.

76. Loren Donelson, "We'd Like to Hire More Farm Boys," *Farm Journal* (June 1957), 39–40.

77. "Do You Want to Go to College?" *Better Farming,* 8.

78. A total of 20,700 men were included in the 1962 Census Population Survey, electronic datafile. States of the respondents were not reported. The closest regional measure was for the North Central region, which included Ohio, Indiana, Illinois, Michigan, and Wisconsin as well as Minnesota, Iowa, Missouri, North Dakota, South Dakota, Nebraska, and Kansas, but did not include Arkansas and Oklahoma. There were too few cases to examine respondents only in their twenties for the North Central region. Among all respondents in the North Central region, 15 percent of fathers who were farmers had attended any high school and only 3 percent had attended any college. Among nonfarmer fathers, 29 percent had attended high school and 11 percent had attended college. Among the farmers' sons, 52 percent attended high school and 11 percent attended college. Among sons of nonfarmers, 69 percent attended high school and 21 percent attended college. These are the data examined in Blau and Duncan, *American Occupational Structure.* The results here are from my analysis of the data.

79. 1962 Census Population Survey.

80. Interview conducted June 28, 2007 (name withheld).

81. Interview conducted March 15, 2007 (pseudonym used).

82. General Social Surveys, 1973 through 1980, electronic datafile; for the nine Middle Western states, degree by sex for respondents whose residence at age sixteen was open country, farm, or town of 5,000 or less.

83. Haller, "Planning to Farm"; Sewell, "Community of Residence" Elder, "Achievement Orientations."

84. Interview conducted June 18, 2007 (pseudonym used).

85. Kirkpatrick, *Rural School from Within*, 27.

86. Tocqueville, *Democracy in America*, 303. Education, he wrote, meant that the United States "had no infancy, being born adult."

87. On leaving home as a cultural trope, see Bellah et al., *Habits of the Heart*, 56–62.

88. U.S. Census Public Use 1 Percent Microsample for 1940, electronic datafile.

89. U.S. Census Public Use 1 Percent Microsample for 1970, electronic datafile.

90. Rachel S. Franklin, "Migration of the Young, Single, and College Educated: 1995 to 2000," Census 2000 Special Reports, CENSR-12 (2003), online at www.census.gov.

91. National Center for Education Statistics, *Enrollment in Postsecondary Institutions, Fall 2006; Graduation Rates, 2000 & 2003 Cohorts; and Financial Statistics, Fiscal Year 2006* (Washington, DC: U.S. Department of Education, Institute of Education Sciences, 2006). Among students from each state who were attending college anywhere, the proportion who were attending in their home state was 87 percent in Arkansas and Iowa, 84 percent in Kansas and Missouri, 83 percent in Nebraska, 78 percent in Minnesota and South Dakota, 72 percent in North Dakota, and 90 percent in Oklahoma; nationwide, the lowest rates were in New Hampshire, Vermont, Connecticut, and New Jersey, and the highest was California. Net in-migration of students in 2006 was 897 in Arkansas, 8,568 in Iowa, 1,426 in Kansas, 2,335 in Missouri, 148 in Nebraska, 1,363 in North Dakota, 2,993 in Oklahoma, and 608 in South Dakota; Minnesota had net out-migration of 2,365.

92. Jeffrey Walser and John Anderlik, "Rural Depopulation: What Does It Mean for the Future Economic Health of Rural Areas and the Community Banks That Support Them?" *FDIC Banking Review* (2005), online.

93. U.S. Census Public Use 1 Percent Microsample for 2000, electronic datafile. Much of the difference between Kansas and Iowa resulted from Johnson County, near Kansas City, being a magnet for college-educated residents. For more on Johnson County, see chapter 7.

94. Les Christie, "Stopping the Great Plains Brain Drain," *CNN Money* (February 10, 2005), online; see also "Great Plains at Center of Mounting Brain Drain" *State Science & Technology Institute Newsletter* (February 21, 2008), online.

95. Teachers, staff, enrollment figures, and test scores for District 237 are posted at nces.ed.gov. Graduation rate and percentage going on to college in 1999 as reported in Griesel et al., *Situation and Trends*, 53–54.

96. Coach Roger Barta, quoted in Joe Drape, "A Football Power in a Small Kansas Town," *New York Times* (November 9, 2007), A1; Randy Gonzales, "Coach, Team Spend Time in Spotlight," *Hays Daily News* (December 15, 2007). Hubbard Stadium

is named in recognition of contributions from a Smith Center native, R. D. Hubbard, who earned a fortune in the glass-manufacturing business; Fred Mann, "$1.5 Million Gift Is Largest in College's History," *Wichita Eagle* (November 1, 2007), 1A.

97. Interview with Pam Barta, conducted January 21, 2008; NFL players included Mark Simoneau, Steve Tasker, and Nolan Cromwell; other notables included a Rhodes Scholar in physics, Ralph Simmons, as well as more than forty doctors, a dozen academic scientists, and numerous teachers, business leaders, and public officials.

CHAPTER FIVE

1. Interview conducted March 12, 2007 (pseudonym used and some identifying details altered).

2. See table 10 in the appendix for further details. These percentages are based on data from the 1980 U.S. decennial census for 5,578 incorporated places, including 480 in Arkansas, 948 in Iowa, 627 in Kansas, 847 in Minnesota, 904 in Missouri, 531 in Nebraska, 359 in North Dakota, 570 in Oklahoma, and 312 in South Dakota. The electronic datafile was obtained from the Missouri State Data Center in Jefferson City, Missouri. See also table 11 for the mean population of towns in each state from 1910 to 2005

3. Additional information about population decline from 1910 to 1950, 1950 to 1980, and 1980 to 2005 is shown in tables 12 and 13 in the appendix. The figures on percentages of towns with declining populations between 1980 and 2005 are based on a total of 5,517 cases, reflecting sixty-one communities for which population data were not available both in 1980 and 2005. These included thirty-two census-defined places (CDPs) that were not incorporated towns.

4. In the nine-state region, 1,644 towns had populations of fewer than 250 people in 1980, 1,125 had populations of 250 to 499, 1,456 had populations of 500 to 1,499, 801 were between 1,500 and 4,999, 357 were between 5,000 and 19,999, and 134 had 20,000 or more.

5. Interview conducted January 11, 2008.

6. Transcript tape recorded August 8, 2007.

7. A national survey conducted in October 2008 found that 26 percent of Americans lived in a small town and that 56 percent of those residents said they preferred to live in a small town. That percentage was significantly higher than the comparable proportion of city residents who said they preferred to live in a city. Unfortunately, the survey did not provide regional comparisons and based these conclusions on a subjective question asking residents what kind of place they lived in, which therefore gave no indication of how large or small these small towns may have been; "Community Satisfaction," *Pew Research Center* (October 2008), online at pewsocialtrends.org.

8. Transcript of tape recorded July 2, 2007.

9. Interview conducted January 15, 2008.

10. Interview conducted February 11, 2008 (name withheld).

11. Data on assets and annual income by town and name of organization are from the Internal Revenue Service as of 2006 at www.irs.gov.

12. Interview conducted January 21, 2008.

13. Interview conducted May 13, 2008.

14. Fitzgerald, *Ghost Towns of Kansas*. I counted towns in Kansas shown on 1890 county maps included in Prentis, *History of Kansas*, and came up with a total of 1,879, an average of eighteen per county.

15. The complete list of Nebraska towns current and historic, compiled by Ray Sterner from 1895 Rand McNally Atlas Maps, is available from the Nebraska Department of Economic Development at www.neded.org.

16. Of the 780 towns, 375 were in Iowa, 201 were in Kansas, 119 were in Nebraska, and 85 were in Arkansas. These data are from the U.S. decennial censuses for 1880 and 1890 as reported for incorporated places (towns). Electronic datafiles were constructed for these and subsequent years from spreadsheets and other tabulations provided by the various state data centers and supplemented with data available from the U.S. Census Bureau. The datafile for Minnesota was graciously provided by Steven Barker, Mankato State University. Although some towns incorporated with fewer than the required number of residents, the laws governing incorporation typically specified 250 as the minimum number. For example, an act of the Kansas legislature that took effect on April 3, 1871, specified these conditions for incorporation: "Whenever a petition, signed by a majority of the electors of any unincorporated town or village within the state, shall be presented to the judge of the district court of the county, setting forth the metes and bounds of their village and commons, and stating as near as may be, the number of the inhabitants of such town or village, and praying that such town or village may be incorporated as a city, with satisfactory proof that such petition has been published in full in some newspaper printed in said town or village, at least once in each week for three consecutive weeks, and such judge shall be satisfied that a majority of the taxable inhabitants of such town or village shall be in favor of such incorporation, and that the prayer of the petitioners is reasonable, and that the number of inhabitants of such town or village exceeds two hundred and fifty, and does not exceed two thousand, such judge may, by order (reciting the substance of such petition and the due publication thereof), declare such town or village incorporated as a city of the third class." Quoted in Dassler, *Compiled Laws of Kansas*, 187–88.

17. Population figures for 1,215 towns were available for both 1890 and 1900; 450 of the towns were in Iowa, 318 in Kansas, 241 in Nebraska, 116 in Arkansas, and 90 in South Dakota.

18. See appendix table 12. Data for a total of 4,265 incorporated places were available for 1910 and 1950. These included 254 towns in Arkansas, 822 in Iowa, 461 in Kansas, 577 in Minnesota, 843 in Missouri, 440 in Nebraska, 199 in North Dakota, 356 in Oklahoma, and 313 in South Dakota.

19. Fitzgerald, *Faded Dreams*, 164–65; accounts and photos of the 1914 tornado and the 1934 fire are at the Geneseo Museum, Geneseo, Kansas.

20. These percentages are for 4,265 towns with data available in 1910.

21. These conclusions are based on a comparison of 4,282 towns in the nine-state region, of which 722 were county seats in 1910. Among towns for which data were available, county seats grew on average from 2,240 residents in 1880 to 6,095 in 1910, while non–county seats grew from only 504 residents in 1880 to 600 in 1910.

22. Twenty-three county seats had fewer than 250 residents in 1910, but only one of these towns declined in population by 1950, compared with 32 percent of non–county seats of similar size. Among towns with 250 to 500 residents in 1910, 8 percent of county seats lost population, compared with 52 percent of non–county seats. Among larger towns with 5,000 to 20,000 residents in 1910, 9 percent of the county seats lost population, compared with 19 percent of the other towns. Ordinary least squares regression provides further evidence of the role of county seats (although the method is limited by high collinearity of population in 1950 with population in 1910; a standardized regression coefficient of .957). Taking account of population in 1910, population in 1950 was 2,148 higher in county seats than in non–county seats (significant at the .001 level). On the relationship between county seats and population change in subsequent decades, see Fuguitt, Brown, and Beale, *Rural and Small Town America*.

23. Quadrants for each state were determined by identifying the latitude and longitude of each center point and comparing the latitude and longitude of each town with that point. The highest rate of decline was in northwest Missouri (near Kansas City), where 68 percent of the 250 towns lost population between 1910 and 1950. The lowest rate was in southwest North Dakota, where only one of the eighteen towns lost population. In quadrants with more than 100 towns per quadrant, 37 percent of the towns declined, compared with 27 percent in quadrants with fewer than 100 towns.

24. The comparisons for cities represent towns that were within one degree latitude and longitude from each of the cities in the region with 150,000 population or more in 1950 (Des Moines, Kansas City, Wichita, Minneapolis–St. Paul, Tulsa, Oklahoma City, St. Louis, and Omaha) versus towns that were located elsewhere. Twenty-seven percent of towns in the region were within this distance to one of the eight cities. The exceptions were that towns nearest St. Louis and Minneapolis were no more likely to decline than other towns.

25. Across the region, 16 percent of towns were located in counties with no more than three towns, 29 percent were located in counties with four to six towns, and 55 percent were in counties with seven or more towns. The number of towns per county varied considerably from state to state; for example, 44 percent of towns in Arkansas were in counties with no more than three towns, while in Iowa and Minnesota less than 2 percent were.

26. The largest differences were in Kansas and Nebraska where 64 and 68 percent of the below-average towns, respectively, lost population, compared with 24 and 27 percent of the above-average towns. There were no differences in Minnesota. Differences in many of the states may have been due to towns established by railroads diminishing as railroads consolidated facilities in larger towns. Across the region, the differences between towns of above- and below-average size were also evident when towns within similar size ranges were compared.

27. Comparisons were drawn for 4,200 towns for which data were available by merging county-level agricultural data with place-level data.

28. Kansas provides an illustrative case. The difference between the two kinds of towns was in the changing value of farmland, buildings, and equipment, averaging about the same ($11,353 and $12,122 respectively) in 1910, and increasing by 139

percent to $29,018 in 1950 for farms in the counties surrounding towns that did not decline, but only 77 percent to $20,164 for towns that did decline.

29. These conclusions are drawn from logistic regression analysis of the odds of towns' population in 1950 being smaller than in 1910, with independent variables including whether a town's population in 1910 was between 250 and 500 or more than 5,000, whether the town was a county seat, whether it had no more than two competing towns in the county, whether its size was above the average size of towns in the county, whether the number of farms in the county declined by 25 percent or more, and whether the average value of farms in the county increased by less than 50 percent (controlling for state, with Missouri as the excluded reference state). All coefficients were significant at or beyond the .01 level of probability.

30. Cutler, *History of the State of Nebraska*, chapter on Clay County, produced by Diana Busing, online at www.kancoll.org/books/andreas_ne/clay. The person quoted is unnamed.

31. Ibid. The Nebraska legislature determined in 1880 that towns with populations below 1,500 would be designated as villages. On the Harvard Army Air Force Base, see www.harvardne.com/airbase.html. The history of the Blaine Naval Ammunition Depot is described at www.globalsecurity.org. The facility, located near Hastings to be equidistant from the Atlantic and Pacific oceans, included 2,200 buildings and employed more than 10,000 military and civilian workers at one point during World War II. Largely because of the facility, total farmland in Clay County was 6 percent smaller in 1950 than in 1910.

32. Further details are shown in table 12 in the appendix.

33. A brief history of Redbird can be found in William T. Janey, "Redbird," at www .ghosttowns.com.

34. From a comparison of towns in the nine-state region located in counties scoring highest on the U.S. Department of Agriculture's Amenity Scale (available at www.usda.gov).

35. See table 12 in the appendix.

36. Sixty-seven percent of the towns in northwestern Kansas lost population between 1950 and 1980, 62 percent did in northwestern Nebraska, and 45 percent did in northwestern South Dakota. Other regions with significantly higher rates of decline than in the earlier period included northwestern Iowa, southwestern Kansas, northeastern and northwestern Minnesota, southwestern Nebraska, northeastern and northwestern North Dakota, and southwest South Dakota.

37. Thirty percent of the towns in 1950 were located in counties where 50 percent or more of the labor force was employed in agriculture, 34 percent were in counties with 35 to 49 percent in agriculture, 17 percent in counties with 20 to 34 percent in agriculture, and 18 percent in counties with less than 20 percent in agriculture. The proportion of towns that lost population between 1950 and 1980 in counties that were 50 percent or more agricultural varied from 45 percent in Minnesota to 78 percent in North Dakota.

38. Declining towns were more often located in counties with struggling retail businesses. Between 1950 and 1982, the number of retail establishments per county increased by an average of 11 percent across the region. For towns that did not decline in population, this increase averaged 21 percent, but for towns that declined, the average fell by 13 percent. Over the same period, retail sales per county

multiplied approximately eightfold, not adjusting for inflation. Among towns with stable or growing populations, the figure was ninefold, but for declining towns, the average was sixfold. These differences were present among towns of all sizes.

39. Median family incomes, poverty, and vacancy rates are for incorporated places in 1980. Data on 1982 retail establishments, retail sales, and physicians per capita are from the 1988 U.S. Census County Databook, electronic datafile, merged with population figures for incorporated towns.

40. See table 13 in the appendix, which also shows the percentages of towns that declined by a quarter or more.

41. U.S. Census, 1880. U.S. Bureau of Land Management records show that 152 claims totaling 11,055 acres were filed in Traill County between 1875 and 1880; from 1881 through 1884, 1,326 claims were filed for 137,369 acres; and from 1885 through 1889, 784 claims were filed for 89,508 acres. Prior to 1890, 881 homestead claims were filed totaling 94,666 acres, 1,207 cash purchase claims were filed totaling 129,364 acres, and 176 military claims were filed totaling 14,221 acres. The population of Traill County increased from 4,123 in 1880 to 10,217 in 1890, making it the sixth-most-populated county in North Dakota.

42. Data on occupations, nativity, and family relationships for Mayville, the other communities in Traill County, and for the county as a whole are from the 1885 Dakota Territorial Census. There were 269 adults aged eighteen and older in Mayville in 1885. Of these, 181 listed occupations. There was also an opera house, two barbershops, three drugstores, a tailor, a wheelwright, a land office, a furniture store, and five dressmakers. Additional information about the first white traders in Traill County, its buffalo herds, and the role of competing railroad companies is included in Beal, *Centennial of Traill County* (courtesy North Dakota State University Library, Fargo).

43. Photograph of the Mayville and Portland I.O.O.F. anniversary parade, Institute for Regional Studies, North Dakota State University, Fargo; Beal, *Centennial of Trail County*, 27.

44. U.S. Decennial Census for dates indicated. *Traill County Tribune*, selected dates, 1945 to 1953, courtesy State Historical Society of North Dakota. The analysis of components of population change in Traill County was conducted by the Real Estate Center at Texas A&M University, College Station, Texas. That analysis showed net natural decrease of 361 and net decrease from migration of 1,023. More than 80 percent of net out-migration occurred in the 1980s during the farm crisis of those years.

45. *Traill County Tribune* (July 23, 1980).

46. Kollmorgen and Jenks, "Sidewalk Farming," 218–19.

47. U.S. Census of Agriculture for dates indicated, electronic datafile.

48. Timothy L. Mortensen, F. Larry Leistritz, Brenda L. Ekstrom, and Janet Wanzek, "Facing Economic Adversity: Experiences of Displaced Farm Families in North Dakota," North Dakota State University, Department of Agricultural Economics, *Agricultural Economics Report No. 252* (November 1989); Marilynn Wheeler, "North Dakotans Try Sunday Shopping," *Los Angeles Times* (February 17, 1991), 25; "Mayville School Crumbles as Bond Issues Fail," *Bismarck Tribune* (May 3, 1998), 9A; Michael K. Bradner, *North Dakota School District Profile Demographics, 2006–2007: May-Port CG Public School District #14* (Bismarck: North Dakota Department of Public Instruction, 2007); Ryan Bakken, "Mayville Pools Its Resources," *Grand*

Forks Herald (December 3, 2000), 1; Matt Cory, "Dealing with the Future, Rural Auto Sellers Feel Industry's Changes," *Grand Forks Herald* (June 27, 1998); U.S. Census Bureau, County Business Patterns, Zip Code Data for 1994 and 2005 by NAICS Classification, electronic datafile.

49. Annual net farm income figures for Traill County are from the U.S. Department of Commerce, Economics and Statistics Administration, Bureau of Economic Analysis, electronic datafile provided by the Missouri Data Center. Steve Schmidt, "It's Out with the Pianos and in with the Cessnas: Mayville State Ends Music, Art Programs," *Grand Forks Herald* (March 27, 1990), 1A; Marilynn Wheeler, "Two Schools Try to Make Fiscal Realities Work," *Bismarck Tribune* (February 3, 1994), 5C; Kyle Johnson, "The Mayville Question: Growing Deficits Could Spur More Debate about Closing Small Campuses," *Grand Forks Herald* (June 1, 2006); Mayville State University, *2003–2004 Annual Report*, Mayville, ND.

50. U.S. Department of Agriculture data on net farm incomes, as summarized by state in annual U.S. Census *Statistical Abstracts*. Of 225 year-to-year changes for the nine states between 1980 and 2005, 117 were declines.

51. U.S. Census, electronic datafiles, data for incorporated places 1980 and 2005, data for number of farms per county 1982 and 1997; among towns of 5,000 to 19,999, 47 percent lost population when located in counties where farms declined by 20 percent or more, compared with 30 percent in counties where farms did not decline. Among towns in counties where farm earnings in 1982 accounted for 35 percent of total earnings, 84 percent of towns declined, compared with 71 percent in counties where farm earnings were between 10 and 35 percent of total earnings, and only 49 percent in counties where farm earnings were less than 10 percent. Additional information is included in the appendix in table 14 which shows results of binary logistic regression models for towns' population having declined or not having declined between 1980 and 2005 and, as independent variables, town size in 1980 (six categories), farm earnings (three categories), decline in number of farms, presence of a four-year college or university, presence of an interstate highway in the county, and location within or adjacent to a metropolitan area. The results show that all variables are significant for the combined nine states and vary from state to state. The effects of college and interstate presence are stronger in models (not shown) in which urban influence is omitted. See also table 15 in the appendix for mean population of towns (excluding towns larger than 20,000 in 1950) by selected characteristics. See also Full, "Hinterland or Heartland."

52. Location of colleges, universities, and community colleges from www.univ source.com. Community colleges were concentrated in Arkansas, Kansas, and Minnesota in towns with populations larger than 5,000, and their presence or absence was unrelated to the likelihood of towns having gained or lost population. In both binary logistic and ordinary least squares models, the likelihood of a town's population being smaller in 1980 than in 2005 was significantly lower for towns with four-year colleges than for other towns, controlling for size of town in 1980 (six categories). From the logistic analysis, the odds of losing population were .48 as great among college towns as among noncollege towns.

53. These conclusions are based on comparisons of towns in counties differing on the U.S. Department of Agriculture's Rural-Urban Influence Scale, also known as the Beale index (available at www.usda.gov); comparisons of towns located within

one degree latitude and longitude of the region's largest cities and towns elsewhere yielded similar results.

54. For example, among towns with 500 to 1,500 residents in 1980, population averaged 689 and 777, respectively, for towns in counties with an Interstate and for towns in other counties and grew, respectively, to 823 and 799 in 1970, 890 and 873 in 1980, 892 and 820 in 1990, 1,025 and 872 in 2000, and 1,112 and 883 in 2005. In all, 1,830 towns (31 percent) in the nine-state region were in counties through which an interstate passed. The effect of interstate highway presence on population growth is consistent with data presented in Lichter and Fuguitt, "Demographic Response," which focuses more on the effects of highways on net migration and employment.

55. Daley and Broschat, *Labor Availability Study*.

56. Businesses and employee figures are from Reference USA 2006, electronic datafile (courtesy of Tsering Wangyal Shawa, Princeton University Geosciences and Map Library) and from U.S. Census, County Business Patterns, electronic datafile. Sales figures are from the North Dakota Office of the State Tax Commissioner, Bismarck, North Dakota.

57. Interview with Lindy Holt, conducted June 25, 2008.

58. Interview conducted June 30, 2008 (name withheld).

59. Interview conducted April 28, 2008 (name withheld).

60. Information provided by Levon Nelson, cofounder of Partners in Progress; interview conducted June 24, 2008; additional information given by Steve Hanson, interview conducted June 27, 2008.

61. A summary of George J. Miller's tour is given in Mitchell, "From Salina, Kansas."

62. A brief description of the family history of Bart and Mary Hartnett is given in *Stafford, Kansas, 1885–1985* (Shawnee Mission, KS: Kes-Print, 1985), courtesy of Sutra Library, San Francisco; details about the No. 1 Hartnett well are from the Kansas Geological Survey Oil and Gas Well Database, record no. 15-185-01482, which is also the source for production figures for the Zenith–Peace Creek field.

63. Interview with librarian and resident historian Dixie Osborn conducted July 28, 2008. Clippings files, Stafford County Historical Society Museum. References to the oil company agents and leases appear in *Stafford County, Kansas, 1870–1990* (Stafford, KS: Stafford County Historical and Genealogical Society, 1990), courtesy of Marbee Library, Washburn University, Topeka, Kansas.

64. Detailed accounts of the development of oil production in Kansas can be found in Nixon, "Petroleum Industry in Kansas"; and Beebe, "Application of Geological Principles."

65. The others, by ranking, were Rooks, Graham, Butler, Kingman, Morton, Ness, Cowley, and Greenwood.

66. Towns of 1,500 or more in 1960 in the top-ranking oil-producing counties were Arkansas City, Augusta, El Dorado, Ellinwood, Ellis, Eureka, Great Bend, Hays, Hoisington, Kingman, Lyons, Ness City, Plainville, Russell, St. John, Stafford, Sterling, Stockton, and Winfield; the comparison towns (excluding two large cities, Topeka and Kansas City) were Atchison, Baxter Springs, Belleville, Beloit, Bonner Springs, Clay Center, Columbus, Concordia, Galena, Lincoln Center, Marysville, Minneapolis, Smith Center, Wamego, and Washington.

67. Quoted in Berton Roueche, "Profiles: Wheat Country," *New Yorker* (January 3, 1983): 37–50 at 42; also quoted in Shortridge, *Cities on the Plains*, 198.

68. On Paul Brown, see chapter 2 in this book; see also Betty Jo Gigot, "Paul Brown—Building an Empire," *CALF News Cattle Feeder* (June 1999), 16–17.

69. Oil revenue in Stafford County rose again in 2003 as conflict in the Middle East and rising demand on the global market drove up oil prices.

70. County-level statistics for mineral industry establishments, employees, and value of shipments and receipts for 1958, 1967, and 1972 are from U.S. Census, County and City Data Books, 1962, 1972, and 1977, electronic datafiles. Additional data on Oklahoma are from the Oklahoma Geological Survey and the University of Oklahoma online at www.ogs.ou.edu.

71. Mitchell, "From Salina, Kansas."

72. U.S. Census of Population and Housing, County Business Patterns at the zip code level for 1994 and 2005; Reference USA 2006; Kansas Department of Education, School Enrollment, Yearly Totals, 1992 through 2008, electronic datafile.

73. Profile for Stafford City prepared by the Policy Research Institute, University of Kansas (www.ku.edu/pri) from U.S. Census 2000 Summary File 4, electronic datafile.

74. Interviews conducted April 3 and May 24, 2007 (pseudonyms used and some identifying details altered).

75. Interview with Kirsten Tretbar conducted August 9, 2008; Kirsten Tretbar, *Zenith* (Shawnee Mission, Kansas: Prairie Fire Films, 2001), information online at www.zeniththemovie.com.

76. Bishop and Leatherman, *Fiscal Conditions: Stafford County.*

77. Interview conducted November 10, 2008 (name withheld).

78. Interview conducted June 20, 2007 (name withheld).

79. Hurt, "Naval Air Stations"; "Public Health Assessment: Cornhusker Army Ammunition Plant, Grand Island, Hall County, Nebraska," Department of Health and Human Services, Agency for Toxic Substances & Disease Registry (September 30, 1992); "McAlester Army Ammunition Plant (MCAAP), Defense Ammunition Center, McAlester, Oklahoma," online description at www.globalsecurity.org.

80. Among towns of fewer than 20,000 residents located near active military bases, growth was more common than decline. Eighty percent grew between 1950 and 1980, and 57 percent were larger in 2005 than in 1980. On average, population in these towns grew from around 1,000 in 1950 to 2,500 in 1980 and exceeded 3,000 in 2005. In the aggregate, the effect of base closings was much less noticeable than was often anticipated by residents of the communities affected. Among towns with fewer than 20,000 people near bases that closed, 41 percent lost population between 1980 and 2005 and 59 percent gained. Among the larger towns, Blytheville was the only one that declined during these years.

81. "Clinton-Sherman, AFB," brief history online at www.globalsecurity.org; Revenstein, *Air Force Combat Wings.*

82. "Clinton," Vertical File, Research Division, Oklahoma Historical Society, Oklahoma City; *The History of Custer and Washita Counties, Oklahoma, 1883–1937* (Clinton, OK: Clinton Daily News, 1937); digital.library.okstate.edu/encyclopedia.

83. U.S. Census of Agriculture, 1930. electronic datafile; "History of Route 66," National Historic Route 66 Federation, online at www.national66.org; decennial census population figures from the Oklahoma Department of Commerce, online at www.okcommerce.gov; "Custer County" and "Burns Flat," Vertical File, Research

Division, Oklahoma Historical Society, Oklahoma City; *History of Custer and Washita Counties*.

84. U.S. Census, County Business Patterns, 1969 to 1979, electronic datafiles.

85. Interview conducted August 22, 2008 (name withheld).

86. Federal Defense Expenditures as reported by U.S. Census, Counties USA, online at www.census.gov; components of population change as tabulated by the Real Estate Center at Texas A&M University. Barrett Refining in Thomas, near Clinton, is mentioned in James Johnson, "Refinery Fueling Economy," *Daily Oklahoman* (Oklahoma City, March 29, 1987), and its closing in Jenna E. Ziman, "The Social and Environmental Costs of Oil Company Divestment from U.S. Refineries," *Multinational Monitor* 18 (May 1997), online at multinationalmonitor.org.

87. Data on establishments and employment from Reference USA 2006; U.S. Census County Business Patterns, 1994, 2000, and 2005, at the zip code level, electronic datafiles; additional information from Bob Doucette, "Tribe to Bring Gaming Format to Clinton," *Daily Oklahoman* (Oklahoma City, July 25, 2001), 5A; "Tronox Inc. Announces First Payout," *Daily Oklahoman* December 20, 2005), 4B.

88. Ron Jackson, "State Launches Mission to Land Shuttle Base," *Daily Oklahoman* (July 20, 1998), 1; Ron Jackson, "Burns Flat Farmer Doesn't Want to Lose Land for Spaceport," *Daily Oklahoman* (May 6, 2002), 7A; Tricia Temberton, "Burns Flat Countdown," *Daily Oklahoman* (February 5, 2004), 1B; Jeff Foust, "Little Spaceport on the Prairie," *Space Review* (June 7, 2004), 1–5; Frank Morris, "Companies Drop Cash on Dream to Fly into Space," *All Things Considered* (May 15, 2007), online at www.npr.org; Patrick G. Mahoney, "The Second Space Age," *Machine Design* (March 6, 2008): 58–64.

89. Interviews conducted August 22 and August 25, 2008 (names withheld).

90. G. Scott Thomas, "America's Dream Towns: Methodology," *Bizjournals* (August 7, 2006), online at www.bizjournals.com, based on census and business data for 2005, with several indicators reflecting trends from 1998 or 1999 to 2003 or 2004.

91. Interviews conducted August 8, 2007.

92. U.S. Census, business establishments reported at the zip code level for 1994 and 2005, electronic datafiles.

93. ESRI Professional Services, American Source Data, Spending Potential Indices, 2002, electronic datafile; additional information at www.esri.com.

94. Haury, "Come Back to the Five & Dime"; Duckwall and ALCO store locations from www.duckwall.com.

95. See table 16 in the appendix for details by state and town size. Numbers of civic organizations are from data collected by the Internal Revenue Service (online at www.irs.com) and include all organizations that submitted information to the IRS as required by law for nonprofit organizations. The data include organizations that handle money, such as donations and membership dues; include only a small percentage of churches, since churches are excempt from federal reporting statutes; and do not include informal gatherings, such as book discussion clubs.

96. Interview conducted July 19, 2007.

97. Interview conducted March 12, 2007.

98. Interview conducted July, 6, 2007.

99. Sharon Cohen and Tad Bartimus, "Life and Death of Rural America," *Associated Press* (August 6, 1989), A6.

100. As one community leader put it, folks in Clinton "don't ever like to talk about how good things are when they're good, and we don't talk too much about how things are if they're getting real bad." He said the national economic downturn was hurting business in Clinton, but western Oklahomans liked to think of themselves as recession proof because of the area's diversified role in energy production, agriculture, meat processing, and transportation; interview conducted January 21, 2009.

101. The "broken windows" syndrome as a symptom of neighborhood disorder in cities and as a source of crime has been widely discussed in conjunction with research conducted by sociologist Robert J. Sampson; see especially Sampson and Raudenbush, *Disorder in Urban Neighborhoods*, and Sampson and Raudenbush, "Seeing Disorder."

102. An interesting exploration of revival efforts in small communities in Kansas is presented in Richard Wood, *Survival of Rural America: Small Victories and Bitter Harvests* (Lawrence: University Press of Kansas, 2008); a useful guide that frankly discusses both the advantages and disadvantages for people considering relocating to small rural communities is included in Morgan Powell and Kerri Ebert, *Living in the Country* (Manhattan, Kansas: Kansas State University, Agricultural Experiment Station and Cooperative Extension Service, February 2008).

103. Interview conducted July 10, 2007.

CHAPTER SIX

1. Interview conducted October 22, 2007.

2. George W. Bolds, "Keeping Up with Chicago," *Railroad Magazine* (May 1947); Blanchard, *Conquest of Southwest Kansas*. Norman Lockyer, "Extermination of the American Bison," *Nature: A Weekly Illustrated Journal of Science* 42 (1890): 11–13. William E. Smythe, "Ways and Means in Arid America," *Century Illustrated* 51 (1896): 742–58

3. See table 17 in the appendix for the average annual value of food products produced in each of the nine Middle Western/ states from 1963 to 1979 and from 1980 to 1997 (SIC code) and from 1997 to 2006 (NAICS code). The table also shows increasing importance of processed food as a ratio of food products to farm products; for example, in Arkansas this ratio averaged .36 between 1963 and 1979, averaged .96 from 1980 to 1997, and averaged 1.50 from 1997 to 2006.

4. "Kansas: A Hasty Trip Through the Land of the Grasshopper," *InterOcean* (July 3, 1875), 7A.

5. James Blood and Solon O. Thacher, quoted in Morgan, *History of Wyandotte County*, 172.

6. Prentis, *South-Western Letters*, 29.

7. Dodge, *St. Nicholas*.

8. George Vasey, "Report of the Botanist," *First Report of the Secretary of Agriculture* (Washington, DC: Government Printing Office, 1889), 381.

9. Mrs. B. L. Stotts, who settled near Garden City in 1881, quoted in Blanchard, *Conquest of Southwest Kansas*, 67.

10. Interview with Richard Gerber, conducted July 7, 2007; interview with Betty Dague, conducted February 1, 2008.

11. L. D. Bailey, quoted in George E. Foster, *Se-Quo-Yah: The American Cadmus and Modern Moses* (Philadelphia: Indian Rights Association, 1885), xviii.

12. W. R. Hopkins, quoted in Charles Kendall Adams, *A Word in Behalf of Experiment Stations at Our Agricultural Colleges* (Ithaca, NY: Andrus and Church, 1896), 36.

13. S. E. Busser, "Report of the General Missionary for Southwestern Kansas," *Journal of Proceedings of the Thirty-Second Annual Convention of the Protestant Episcopal Church in the Diocese of Kansas, 1891* (Fort Scott, KS: Monitor Book and Printing Company, 1892), 73. Similarly, Methodists were encouraged enough by the town's possibilities to initiate a class meeting in 1882 and launch a building that was completed in 1884; Smith, *Centennial Saga*, 3–15.

14. The pattern among towns other than county seats was similar. Among these other towns, thirty-seven declined in population between 1980 and 2005 and fifteen grew. The average decline was 17 percent. Holcomb, near Garden City, was the only town to grow by more than 70 percent; U.S. Census, electronic datafiles.

15. Newton "N. J." Earp, Wyatt's half brother, served as constable in Garden City. Newton had a farm near Sterling, Kansas, in 1874, and Wyatt served briefly as sheriff in that county. Garden City's early promoters, including C. J. "Buffalo" Jones were from Sterling, approximately 175 miles to the east and located on the Santa Fe rail line.

16. "Rewards for the Conviction of Liquor Dealers," *Atchison Globe* (December 12, 1881); "Hard Men of Dodge City in a Desperate Quarrel," *Atchison Globe* (May 10, 1883). Cutler, *History of the State of Kansas*, chapters on Ford County and Unorganized Counties.

17. "Irrigation in Kansas," *New York Times* (August 26, 1889), 1; "Hunting in Motor Cars," reprinted from the *Chicago News* in the *New York Tribune* (January 9, 1910), B2; "Two Bank Robbers Slain," *Chicago Daily Tribune* (July 9, 1939); "Kansas Town Frowns on Mere Sauntering," *New York Times* (November 14, 1983), A14; Mike Berry, "No. 1 Hair Ball's Gross Weight: 55 Pounds," *Wichita Eagle* (March 13, 1994).

18. "Wealthy Farmer, 3 of Family Slain," *New York Times* (November 16, 1959), 39; "Find Farmer, Family Slain in Their Home," *Chicago Daily Tribune* (November 16, 1959), 1; Capote, *In Cold Blood*; Conrad Knickerbocker, "One Night on a Kansas Farm," *New York Times* (January 16, 1966), BR1.

19. Van Jensen, "The Book That Changed a Town," *Lawrence Journal-World & News* (April 3, 2005); Amber Brozek, "Beyond the Fame: Holcomb Has Changed Much from the Time Capote Wrote His Book," *Lawrence Journal-World & News* (April 6, 2005).

20. Bach, *Changing Relations: U.S. Communities*; Stull et al., *Changing Relations: Garden City*; Stull and Broadway, *Any Way You Cut It*; Stull and Broadway, *Slaughterhouse Blues*; Schlosser, *Fast Food Nation*.

21. "A Grand Opportunity," *Atchison Daily Champion* (June 4, 1887); Sanborn maps 1887; "Garden City Area History," online at www.gardencity.net/info/history; Kersey, *History of Finney County*.

22. *Kansas State Atlas* (New York: L. H. Everts and Co., 1887).

23. Hill, *Public Domain and Democracy*, 183.

24. Chase, *Editor's Run*, 38.

25. Adams, "Irrigation in Kansas," 78.

26. Prentis, *South-Western Letters*, 31; the locations of these canals are shown on 1887 maps of Finney county, *Kansas State Atlas*. More detail and an excellent summary of the primary literature is presented in Graves, "Garden City." The best history of irrigation in the region is Opie, *Ogallala*.

27. "Dead on the Plains," *Kansas City Star* (January 15, 1886); Blanchard, *Conquest of Southwest Kansas*, 38; U.S. Census of Agriculture, Finney County, 1890.

28. Births exceeded deaths by a ratio of approximately 3 to 1, meaning that net out-migration was necessary for population to remain stable.

29. George R. Caldwell, "A Garden Country: Agricultural Wealth of Finney County, Kansas," *Rocky Mountain News* (February 4, 1894), 9E; U.S. Census of Agriculture, 1890 and 1900.

30. U.S. Census of Agriculture, electronic datafile.

31. Graves, "Garden City," 78–79.

32. U.S. Census of Agriculture, 1900 and 1910.

33. Moore, *Maternity and Infant Care*. The study was conducted between 1914 and 1916; the name of the county is not disclosed, but its population, size, and other characteristics make it identifiable as Ford County.

34. Sanborn maps; "Progress of the Beet-Sugar Industry," *Report of the Secretary of Agriculture* (1905), 89–90.

35. Shortridge, *Cities on the Plains*, 202–3; details about the beet industry, costs, and the use of Mexican and Japanese laborers are given in the testimony of G. W. Swink on November 17, 1908 in *Tariff Hearings Before the Committee on Ways and Means of the House of Representatives, Sixtieth Congress, 1908–1909* (Washington, DC: Government Printing Office, 1909), 422.

36. Burr, *Rural Organization*, 43.

37. Interview with Patrick Coll, conducted June 18, 2007. American Crystal Sugar Company Records, 1883–1979, manuscript collection (Minneapolis: Minnesota Historical Society, 1979); Reeve, *Constant Frontier*, 161–67 (courtesy of the State Historical Society of Wisconsin, Madison).

38. Reeve, *Constant Frontier*, 26, 69.

39. *Farm Marketing, Supply and Service Cooperative Historical Statistics*, Cooperative Information Report 1, sec. 26 (Washington, DC: U.S. Department of Agriculture, 2004), 7; Brant, "Garden City Co-op."

40. Broehl, *Cargill: Trading the World's Grain*, 58–65.

41. Several valuable studies examine the organizational strengths and weaknesses of farmers cooperatives, including Torgerson, "Farmer Cooperatives"; Cook, "Future of U.S. Agricultural Cooperatives"; and Li Feng and George Hendrikse, "On the Nature of a Cooperative: A System of Attributes Perspective," unpublished paper, Erasmus Research Institute of Management, Erasmus University, Rotterdam.

42. Fite, *Beyond the Fence Rows*, 41.

43. National Cooperative Refinery Association, "The NCRA Story," online at www .ncrarefinery.com. Carl Swenson was one of the farm youths discussed in chapter 2.

44. U.S. Census of Business, 1940; Robert Wood, "Open Coast to Coast Air-Rail Route Tonight," *Chicago Daily Tribune* (June 14, 1929), 1; Garden City Consumers Cooperative Association, Kansas Secretary of State, Business ID Number, 1195320, formed April 28, 1936.

45. Peter Wyden, "Synthetic Gasoline Plant May Open New Era for Kansas," *New York Times* (March 13, 1948).

46. Burton H. Davis, "Fischer-Tropsch Synthesis: Overview of Reactor Development and Future Potentialities," *Topics in Catalysis* 32 (2005), 143–68; "Carthage Hydrocol, Inc., Brownsville Plant Operations Analysis of Synthesis Reactor Data," Chevron-Texaco, Engineering Development Group, Report No. 25 (March 29, 1952).

47. Commercial feedlots were exempt from state laws prohibiting corporate farming, and these exemptions were clarified and extended to commercial swine production facilities in a series of statutes enacted by the Kansas legislature between 1981 and 1998; see Kansas Legislature Statute 17-5904, Chapter 17 (Corporations), Article 59 (Agricultural Corporations), online at www.kslegislature.org. For an engaging first-person account of life in Garden City during the time Brookover's operation was expanding, see Holly Hope, *Garden City: Dreams in a Kansas Town* (Norman: University of Oklahoma Press, 1988).

48. U.S. Census of Agriculture, 1950; the zero-order Pearson correlation between pastureland acreage and number of cattle and calves was .352 for counties in Iowa, .665 for counties in Kansas, and .886 for counties in Nebraska.

49. Betty Jo Gigot, "Paul Brown: Building an Empire," *CALF News* (July 1999), 16–17.

50. U.S. Census of Agriculture, electronic datafile for Great Plains states. Zero-order Pearson correlation coefficient for 1,008 Great Plains counties, value of cattle sold in 1964 with acres of irrigated land in 1954 (.223, significant at the .001 level); standardized coefficients from ordinary least squares regression for value of cattle sold in 1964 as the dependent variable: acres of irrigated land (.048, significant at the .07 level), hay in tons (.327, significant at the .001 level), and sugar beets in tons (.427, significant at the .001 level).

51. Isabella L. Bird, the English traveler who visited the Greeley colony in 1873, wrote admiringly of its settlers: "They bought and fenced 50,000 acres of land, constructed an irrigating canal, which distributes its waters on reasonable terms, have already a population of 3,000, and are the most prosperous and rising colony in Colorado, being altogether free from either laziness or crime." Bird, *Lady's Life*, 31.

52. U.S. Census of Agriculture, 1930, electronic datafile; Monfort, Inc., Company History, online at fundinguniverse.com.

53. Monfort, Inc., Company History; the establishment of operations in Kansas on May 15, 1963, by Monfort Feed Lots, Inc., is listed as Business Entity ID Number 7012776 in the Kansas Secretary of State online business entity files, www.access kansas.org.

54. Finney County Historical Society Museum, Meat Packing Exhibit; Reeve, *Constant Frontier*, 178. The Swift egg and poultry plant opened in 1930 and closed in 1950 when its building was purchased by the Garden City Grain and Seed Company; the Walls Packing Company shut down in 1951.

55. Interview with Graff Williams, conducted June 16, 2008. Schwartz, *Tyson*, 1–12.

56. Richard J. Arnould, "Changing Patterns of Concentration in American Meat Packing, 1880–1963," *Business History Review* 45 (1971), 18–34.

57. *Jurisdiction of Packers and Stockyards Act*, Hearings before the House Committee on Agriculture on H.R. 7743 and H.R. 8536, 85th Cong., 1st Sess., July 9–12, 15, 31, and August 1, 1957 (Washington, DC: Government Printing Office, 1957); *Prohibit Feeding of Livestock by Certain Packers*, Hearings before the House Subcommittee on Livestock and Feed Grains of the Committee on Agriculture on H.R. 12115,

H.R. 12868, H.R. 13587, and H.R. 18172, 89th Congress, 2nd Sess., April 21, 22 and October 5, 6, 1966 (Washington, DC: Government Printing Office, 1966).

58. *Prohibit Feeding of Livestock*, 229–30; Walt Barnhart, "Packer Ownership: A Double-Edged Sword," *Drovers* (March 17, 2008), online at www.drovers.com; and Walt Barnhart, personal communication, September 4, 2008.

59. *Prohibit Feeding of Livestock*, 16.

60. IBP, Inc., Securities and Exchange Commission, Form 10-K (December 30, 2000), 6.

61. *Prohibit Feeding of Livestock*, 15.

62. IBP, Inc., Company History, online at www.answers.com.

63. General Accounting Office, *Beef Industry Packer Market Concentration and Cattle Prices* (Washington, DC: Government Printing Office, 1990).

64. The housing shortage is described in Hart, Rhodes, and Morgan, *Unknown World*, 96–103.

65. Average wage and salary disbursements were $5,133 in 1969 and $10,638 in 1979; per capita personal income in the respective years was $3,459 and $8,938.

66. Reeve, *Constant Frontier*, 211, 218; President Jimmy Carter, "Quantitative Limitation on the Importation of Certain Meat," Proclamation 4577 (July 4, 1978), online.

67. Reeve, *Constant Frontier*, 170, 187, 190, 193; Kansas Center for Community Economic Development, *Finney County, Kansas: KCCED County Profile* (Lawrence, KS: University of Kansas, Institute for Policy and Social Research, 2007), 16.

68. Barry Hobson and Forest E. Walters, "Market Share Analysis of Available Cattle Slaughter Supplies in Colorado and Surrounding Areas, 1979," Fort Collins, Colorado State University, Department of Economics, unpublished paper, April 1979.

69. *Small Business Problems in the Marketing of Meat and Other Commodities*, Part 3: *Concentration Trends in the Meat Industry*, Hearings before the House Subcommittee on SBA and SBIC Authority and General Small Business Problems of the Committee on Small Business, 96th Congress, 1st Session, May 1, 2, 14 and June 4, 1979 (Washington, DC: Government Printing Office, 1979), 50, 71–75.

70. Reeve, *Constant Frontier*, 213.

71. Stull, "On the Cutting Edge."

72. Reeve, *Constant Frontier*, 232.

73. The data are from U.S. Census, County Business Patterns, 1986, SIC code 2010, meat products manufacturing establishments; see also table 18 in the appendix.

74. U.S. Census, electronic datafiles for places and counties, 1950 through 1988.

75. U.S. Census, electronic datafiles for counties, 1960 and 1970.

76. These included packing plants near Fort Smith, Bentonville, and Springdale, Arkansas; Des Moines and Dubuque, Iowa; Albert Lea, Minnesota; and Sioux Falls, South Dakota.

77. The reference to small rural communities that seemed to belong in a Norman Rockwell painting is from Schlosser, *Fast Food Nation*, 8.

78. U.S. Department of Agriculture, National Agricultural Statistics Service, *Agricultural Statistics*, annually 1986 to 2008, online at www.nass.usda.gov/publications/ag_statistics.

79. See table 19 in the appendix.

80. See table 18 in the appendix.

81. U.S. Census, County Databooks, electronic datafiles.

82. U.S. Bureau of Labor Statistics, County Business Patterns, Finney County, 1969 to 2006, electronic datafile.

83. U.S. Census, Finney County, 1970 to 2007. Births in the 1980s totaled 6,714; deaths, 1,489; natural increase, 5,225; and total population change, 9,483. In 1980, the median age in Finney County was 26.2, compared with 30.1 for the state; in 2000, the median age was 28.1, compared with 35.2 for the state.

84. U.S. Census, County Databooks, electronic datafiles; overall population growth from 1980 to 2005 in Finney County was 63.6 percent; the two counties with higher growth rates were Dallas, Iowa, with 75.4 percent and Canadian, Oklahoma, with 74.8 percent. The unstandardized coefficient for presence of a meat-products establishment with at least 500 employees in multiple regression for percentage population growth from 1980 to 2005 was .134, controlling for population in 1980.

85. U.S. Census, 1980 and 2000, 5 percent Public Use Microsamples and County Databooks, electronic datafiles.

86. U.S. Census, 1920, Finney County, Kansas, transcribed by LeAnna Kennedy and proofread by Jerry Hembree. The transcriptions include year of immigration, age in 1920, occupation, language, and whether the person could read and write. The 1910 figure is from the Ancestry Library Edition, electronic database, courtesy of Firestone Library, Princeton University. In this database, the 1900 U.S. Census lists only two unnamed residents from Mexico living in Finney County. The 1910 census record lists Nasario's wife as Juana. The 1930 U.S. Census no longer includes Nasario Ramirez but shows his wife, listed as Anita, living in Garden City with seven children, two of whom were born in Colorado, and one of whom, nineteen-year-old Harry, is employed at the sugar factory. Finney County was not unique. In neighboring Ford County, where Dodge City was the location of a larger number of railroad workers, the number of residents of Mexican descent was approximately 50 percent greater than in Finney County.

87. Wenzl, *Legacy of Faith*; Henry J. Avila, "Mexican American Immigration in Kansas," *Brown Quarterly* 3 (1999), online at brownvboard.org. Another connection with Mexico by the early 1930s was that the ranchers in Garden City were buying and selling cattle in Mexico; Reeve, *Looking Back*, 31.

88. Interview with Dixie Baker, conducted January 24, 2008. Discrimination against Mexicans and Mexican-Americans elsewhere in Kansas is discussed in Oppenheimer, "Acculturation or Assimilation."

89. Reeve, *Constant Frontier*, 83, 147, 173, 205; interview with Vietnamese Association vice president Minh Duong, conducted March 1, 2008.

90. Bach, *Changing Relations*, 53; Deborah Sontag, "New Immigrants Test Nation's Heartland," *New York Times* (October 18, 1993). A hypothesis that circulated in some accounts suggested that ethnic tensions would have been greater had it not been for white flight. Schlosser, in *Fast Food Nation*, 165, for example, wrote of Lexington, Nebraska, where IBP opened a plant in 1990 that "the majority of Lexington's white inhabitants moved elsewhere." But if someone told Schlosser that, that person was simply mistaken. In 1990, Lexington's population included 6,471 white residents, and a decade later that number was 6,452. In all of Dawson County, where the white population was 19,145 in 1990, net white out-migration during the 1990s totaled 1,566, a rate of 8 percent, and the highest rate was among adults aged

twenty to twenty-four who very likely left to attend college. In Finney County, the net white out-migration rate was 16 percent and was also highest among college-age young adults. For all Middle Western counties, the correlation between the Hispanic net migration rate from 1990 to 2000 and the white net migration rate was –.023, not statistically significant at the .10 level of probability.

91. Hackney, *One America Indivisible*, 75–76.

92. Finney County Tax Appraisal Commercial Information for IBP plant, no. 028-251-02-0-00-001-00-0-01, 2007, appraised value of $24,861,370. Interview with Tim Cruz, conducted March 12, 2008.

93. Interview with Doris Ming, conducted January 8, 2008.

94. The annual rate of change in personal per capita income for Finney County was 24 percent in 1979, 4 percent in 1980, and 24 percent in 1981; from 1982 through 2006, the rate of change was 4 percent, compared with 14 percent from 1969 through 1979. Details on tax revenue and expenditures from 1997 through 2006 are included in Bishop and Leatherman, *Fiscal Conditions: Finney County*. On rules governing industrial revenue bonds, see *Steps to Success: A Resource Guide to Starting a Business in Kansas* (Topeka: Kansas Department of Commerce, 2008).

95. Georgeanne M. Artz, Peter F. Orazem, and Daniel M. Otto, "Meat Packing and Processing Facilities in the Non-Metropolitan Midwest: Blessing or Curse?" paper presented at the annual meeting of the American Agricultural Economics Association, Providence, Rhode Island, July 2005; Artz, Orazem, and Otto, "Measuring the Impact."

96. U.S. Census, 5 percent Public Use Microsamples, electronic datafiles; controlling for state, weeks worked, gender, metropolitan or nonmetropolitan location, race, age, and ethnicity, the ratio of wages in meatpacking to wages in construction decreased from 1.73 in 1980 to .43 in 2000; significant aspects of the change were the increasing number of younger workers and Hispanic workers in meatpacking. See table 20 in the appendix. A study by Warren, *Great Packing Machine*, estimates that when adjusted for the consumer price index, meatpacking employees' wages declined by an average of 49.7 percent in five Midwestern states (Iowa, Minnesota, South Dakota, Nebraska, and Kansas) between 1977 and 1997.

97. Human Rights Watch, *Blood, Sweat, and Fear: Workers' Rights in U.S. Meat and Poultry Plants* (Washington, DC: Human Rights Watch, 2005).

98. "Farmland Industries: Company History," online at www.fundinguniverse.com.

99. Broehl, *Cargill*; Kneen, *Invisible Giant*; Busch et al., *From Columbus to ConAgra*; "ConAgra, Inc.: Company History," online at www.fundinguniverse.com; "Tyson Foods and IBP Agree to Terms," *Associated Press* (June 28, 2001). In 2008, the U.S. Department of Justice filed an antitrust suit to block the JBS acquisition of National Beef.

100. Heather Hollingsworth, "Fire at ConAgra Could Mean Lost Jobs, Lower Cattle Prices," *Wichita Eagle* (December 28, 2000); Nancy Kletecka, "Spontaneous Combustion Caused Fire at ConAgra," *Southwest Daily Times* (Liberal, KS) (January 5, 2001); Roxana Hegeman, "Kosher Beef for Passover Has Its Price: December's Fire at the ConAgra Beef Plant in Garden City Destroyed the Largest Kosher Beef Producer in the Country," *Wichita Eagle* (April 7, 2001); Tim Vandenack, "Garden Still Recovering Six Years after Plant Fire," *Hutchinson News* (December 23, 2006).

101. Minutes of the regular meetings of the Board of Finney County Commissioners, January 3, 2000, through December 17, 2007. The closed ConAgra plant came

under ownership of JBS, which advertised it for sale shortly after the acquisition (Jon Ruhlen, "Brazilian Firm Buys Garden Plant: New Owners Could Sell Building," *Hutchinson News*, June 14, 2007).

102. Duane West served as Garden City mayor from 1978 to 1981, ran unsuccessfully against Republican Congressman Pat Roberts, and headed Garden City's Quality of Life Committee; the impression he made on Harper Lee, who accompanied Truman Capote during his time in Garden City investigating the Clutter murders, is included in Shields, *Mockingbird*, 165.

103. An excellent discussion of the impact through 2004 of the ConAgra plant closing is given in Broadway and Stull, "Meat Processing and Garden City." Additional data for 2005 through 2007 are from the U.S. Bureau of Labor Statistics and the Kansas Department of Social and Rehabilitation Services for Finney, Ford, and Seward counties. The specific impact on demand for social services climbed steadily from 357 families receiving Temporary Assistance for Families in 2000 to 1,064 in 2006 before declining in 2007, compared to relatively stable patterns in Ford County (549 in 2000 and 576 in 2006) and an increase of 44 percent (from 301 to 434) in Seward County. The wider impact on the county's economy was not reflected in nonfarm proprietors employment, which grew in 2001, held steady the next two years and increased again, rising by 15 percent between 2000 and 2006. A similar pattern was evident in state and local government employment. The impact was also not reflected in per capita income, which was constant from 2000 to 2002 and then rose steadily from 2002 through 2007 and at approximately the same rate as in Ford and Seward counties. Although per capita income in Finney County grew less rapidly from 2001 through 2007 than for the state of Kansas, that comparison is misleading because much of the state's growth was in its eastern urban and suburban counties and the divergence between state and Finney patterns began in 1983, not 2001. Comparisons with other meat-processing counties are useful for putting unemployment benefit payments in perspective. Benefits in Finney County jumped almost fourfold from 2000 to 2001, but fell by 50 percent in 2002 and remained at that level through 2006, suggesting that displaced workers were relocating or finding jobs. Broader factors were also at work in meat-processing counties. For example, in Ford, Seward, and Lyon counties, benefits increased in these years as well. Indeed, that was true in every county with a large meat-processing firm operated by one of the major conglomerates. Among counties larger, smaller, and similar in size to Finney County, benefits rose sharply in 2001 and 2002 and remained high in 2003 but dropped dramatically in 2004 through 2006.

104. In October 2008, the Ford County Commission approved plans for a wind farm near Dodge City, and by the following summer, the project was in operation.

105. U.S. Census, 2000, tract level, electronic datafile; 62 percent of the Hispanic population lived in two census tracts (tract 9605, encompassing the southeastern part of Garden City south of Highway 156, and tract 9606, west of Highway 83 and South of Highway 50/400) that were, respectively, 60 percent and 66 percent Hispanic; in these tracts, 42 percent and 25 percent, respectively, lived in mobile homes; 35 and 37 percent, respectively, were foreign born; and median family incomes were 10 percent and 30 percent below the mean.

106. Interviews with Tim Cruz, conducted March 12, 2008; Juana Perkins, conducted October 22, 2007; the late Father Joseph Bahr, conducted June 20, 2007;

Richard Gerber, conducted July 7, 2007; Dennis Mesa, conducted March 17, 2008; Reverend Jon Becker, conducted May 7, 2007; Reverend Rick Durham, conducted May 21, 2007; and Sister Janice Thome, conducted October 19, 2007; on ethnic identities in Garden City, see also Jimenez, "Replenished Identities"; Jimenez, "Immigrant Replenishment"; and Jimenez, "Mexican-Immigrant Replenishment." Jimenez argues that immigrant replenishment reinforced ethnic identity in Garden City, but it also resulted in divisions within the Latino community. Although attitudes toward undocumented workers varied, Father Bahr's view of extending help when it was needed was typical: "We don't inquire into their illegality or legality because if they are hungry, they are hungry."

107. Brant, *Alternative Strategic Financial Plans for Garden City Co-op*; *CHS Annual Report* (2007), online at www.chsinc.com; *Western Farmer* (2008), online at www.gccoop.com.

108. Chunxiao Liu, *Analyzing Highway Damage Costs Attributed to Truck Traffic of Processed Meat and Related Industries in Southwest Kansas* (Lawrence: University of Kansas, master's thesis, 2008); Yong Bai, Patricia Oslund, Tom Mulinazzi, Shyamala Tamara, Chunxiao Liu, Michael M. Barnaby, and Christine E. Atkins, *Transportation Logistics and Economics of the Processed Meat and Related Industries in Southwest Kansas* (Topeka: Kansas Department of Transportation, 2007).

CHAPTER SEVEN

1. Interview conducted on November 20, 2008.

2. Garreau, *Edge City*, see especially the photographs of Tysons Corner, circa World War II and 1998, included before the title page.

3. Blair, *History of Johnson County*; the hotel is described on page 104 and the Princeton town company's efforts on page 120; an account of Quantrill's raid was published in "The War in Kansas: The Sacking of Olathe," *New York Times* (September 15, 1862), 8. Pronounced "oh-lay-tha," the town's name is understood to have been a Shawnee word for beauty. The Princeton that began in Johnson County is not to be confused with the Princeton that survived in Franklin County, founded in 1857 as Ohio City and renamed sometime prior to 1869.

4. The population figure given here is from the U.S. Census, although some sources indicate a figure of approximately 2,000 in 1870.

5. Blair, *History of Johnson County*, 111–14, provides information about the railroads, as does Bauer, *Trails, Rails, and Tales*, 124–29.

6. Quoted in "Olathe Has an Ambition," *Kansas City Star* (November 28, 1899).

7. U.S. Census of Agriculture, 1909, electronic datafile. Leavenworth County reported 1,461,913 gallons of milk sold; Johnson County, 1,203,195; Wyandotte County, 1,058,514; and Shawnee County, 776,288; the mean for Kansas counties was 93,820 gallons. The close proximity of Leavenworth, Johnson, and Wyandotte county farms to Kansas City was advantageous for overnight deliveries of fresh milk.

8. "The Strang Line into Olathe," *Kansas City Star* (October 21, 1906).

9. Quoted in "Olathe Would Be Host," *Kansas City Star* (February 17, 1913).

10. U.S. Census of Agriculture for years indicated, electronic datafiles.

11. George Forsee, "Biggest Year in Industry," *Kansas City Star* (November 4, 1913).

12. "World War II," online excerpt from Mindi C. Love, *Johnson County, Kansas: A Pictorial History 1825–2005* (Olathe: Johnson County Museum, 2006), at www.jocohistory.net.

13. Bauer, *Trails, Rails, and Tales*, 89–92, 178–80.

14. Ibid., 181–82; additional information about the company's history and employees is from www.king-radio.com. Wulfsberg worked at Collins Radio from 1940 to 1965 and at King Radio from 1965 to 1970 when he founded Wulfsberg Electronics. The company was sold to Sundstrand Corporation in 1984, became part of Allied Signal in 1994 and Chelton Avionics in 1997.

15. Garmin Ltd., Form 10-K, United States Securities and Exchange Commission for fiscal year ended December 29, 2007. Interview conducted with Garmin media relations pecialist Jessica Myers, November 17, 2008.

16. Marion Merrell Dow, Inc., online at www.fundinguniverse.com.

17. Sprint Corporation, online at www.fundinguniverse.com.

18. Bauer, *Trails, Rails, and Tales*, 54.

19. Interview conducted on November 12, 2007.

20. *Departments and Strategic Plan Implementation Groups: Five-Year Business Plans, 2006–2010*, Olathe, Kansas, 2006.

21. Jim Randall, quoted in Bauer, *Trails, Rails, and Tales*, 67.

22. Such sentiments were often expressed by rural residents at hearings involving land annexation; for example, see Andy Hyland, "County Dwellers Blast Olathe's Annexation Plans," *Kansas City Star* (September 20, 2008).

23. *Solid Ground: The Story of Security Savings Bank*, promotional brochure online at www.securitysb.com; David Martin, "Don Bell Believed that God Smiled on His Bank," *Pitch* (Kansas City), October 14, 2008.

24. Ron Wilson, "Kansas Profile—Now, That's Rural: Brooke Corporation," *K-State Research and Extension News* (July 26, 2006); Joy Leiker, "Home-Grown Company Added to American Stock Exchange," *Hays Daily News* (May 29, 2003); Judy Sherard, "Brooke Corp.: Phillipsburg Fits Its Expansion Plans," *Hays Daily News* (November 21, 2005); Kevin Anderson, "It Takes an Entire Community to Lure Businesses to Area," *Hays Daily News* (July 1, 1996); besides national headquarters in Overland Park, Brooke Corporation offices as of 2008 included locations in Olathe, Shawnee Mission, Kansas City, Independence, and Raytown. Orr's previous banking experience was at Farmers State Bank in Phillipsburg, Brooke State Bank in Jewell, and First National Bank in Smith Center.

25. Marion Laboratories had begun to invest more heavily in bioscience research during the 1980s with its purchase of the American Biomaterials Corporation in 1988 and a minority interest in U.S. Bioscience in 1989. LabOne, headquartered in Lenexa, was incorporated in 1972, and as of 1995, 82 percent of its stock was held by the Kansas City holding company Seafield Capital Corporation. In 1997, LabOne acquired Gib Laboratories, a subsidiary of Prudential Insurance and became the exclusive provider of risk-assessment testing services for Prudential; LabOne, Securities and Exchange Commission File 0-15975 (December 31, 1995); "News Digest," *Kansas City Business Journal* (February 7, 1997).

26. Cerner had sales in excess of $2 billion in 2007; the Stowers Institute had a $2 billion endowment established by James Stowers, founder of American Century Mutual Funds; interview with Robert J. Marcusse conducted December 9, 2008.

27. "Biosciences," *Think KC*, online at www.thinkkc.com; K-State Olathe Innovation Campus, online at kstateoic.ksu.edu. Interview with Dr. Gary Morsch, conducted December 18, 2008; interview with Dr. Daniel Richardson, conducted January 13, 2009.

28. *The Lee's Summit Advantage*, Lee's Summit Economic Development Council, 2007; online at www.leessummit.org.

29. *Environmental Scan 2007* (Olathe: Chamber of Commerce, 2007); *City of Olathe: 2006 Direction Finder Survey Results* (Olathe: ETC Institute, 2006).

30. Interview conducted on February 6, 2008.

31. Edward H. Bennett, *Plan of Minneapolis Prepared under the Direction of the Civic Commission* (Minneapolis: Civic Commission, 1917).

32. Kevin Giles, "The Forecast for Woodbury: More of Everything," *Minneapolis Star Tribune* (June 10, 2008); Washington County Commissioners, *2008 Assessment Report*; Woodbury Economic Development Authority, *Commercial Development, 2008*, www.ci.woodbury.mn.us/econdev.

33. Interview conducted November 11, 2008.

34. Tax increment financing typically involves using the revenues from bond sales to subsidize a development project and then repaying the bonds through taxes on the property.

35. For present purposes, inner-ring cities include Bloomington, Brooklyn Center, Columbia Heights, Crystal, Edina, Fridley, Golden Valley, Hopkins, Maplewood, Mendota Heights, New Brighton, New Hope, North St. Paul, Oakdale, Richfield, Robbinsdale, Roseville, South St. Paul, St. Louis Park, and West St. Paul; outer-ring cities include Apple Valley, Blaine, Brooklyn Park, Burnsville, Champlin, Coon Rapids, Eagan, Eden Prairie, Inver Grove Heights, Maple Grove, Minnetonka, Mounds View, Plymouth, Rosemount, Savage, Shoreview, Vadnais Heights, White Bear Lake, and Woodbury. The distinction is based on distance from downtown Minneapolis or St. Paul and on an analysis of when rapid population expansion occurred. It differs in some instances from popular usage but is employed consistently in this chapter. See also *Land-Use Trends in the Twin Cities Metropolitan Area, 1960–1975* (St. Paul: Metropolitan Council, 1978), courtesy of Weyerhaeuser Library, Macalester College, St. Paul; inner-ring towns in this report correspond to my usage, as do "developing" suburbs with outer-ring cities, with the exception that I include Bloomington, Columbia Heights, Oakdale, and Robbinsdale in the inner ring.

36. U.S. Census of Agriculture, 1940 and 1950, electronic datafiles.

37. Hudson, *Half Century of Minneapolis*, 330–35, 386–93.

38. Kenney, *Minnesota Goes to War*, 112–14.

39. Robert C. Vogel, Deborah L. Crown, and Duane E. Peter, "The World War II Ordnance Department's Government-Owned Contractor-Operated (GOCO) Industrial Facilities: Twin Cities Ordnance Plant Historic Investigation," *Defense Technical Information Center Reports* (December 1995).

40. Dooley, "Gopher Ordnance Works." Like the Sunflower Ordnance Works near Olathe, the Gopher plant near Rosemount involved evicting scores of farmers and creating new facilities that drew employees to a location outside the central city that would later develop as a suburban commercial center. By 1946, the War Department established 216 of these facilities around the country and its landholdings increased to forty-six million acres.

41. U.S. Census, 1947 County Databook, electronic datafile; figures are for Anoka, Dakota, Hennepin, Ramsey, and Washington counties; except for $162.5 million for the Gopher Ordnance Works in Dakota County, nearly all of the expenditures were in Hennepin and Ramsey counties.

42. "Alliant Techsystems," *International Directory of Company Histories* (2000), online at fundinguniverse.com.

43. Agency for Toxic Substances and Disease Registry, *Public Health Assessment: Naval Industrial Reserve Ordnance Plant, Fridley, Anoka County, Minnesota* (September 26, 1999).

44. Engineering Research Associates Records Collection, Hagley Museum and Library, Wilmington, DE.

45. U.S. Census, Public Use 1 Percent Microsample, 1960, electronic datafile, household weight, using census designations for "metropolitan area, outside central city," "metropolitan area, central city," and "non-metropolitan." Average house value in the three areas, respectively, was $12,481, $9,104, and $4,033.

46. Interview with Opus Northwest real estate development director Bret Sheffield, conducted December 17, 2008.

47. "The Most and the Least," *Time* (November 9, 1962). Bloomington's drive-in theater is described in Kenney, *Twin Cities Picture Show*, 141. In the 1960 U.S. Census 1 Percent Public Use Microsample data among employed men aged twenty-five and over living in the nine Middle Western states, metropolitan residents outside central cities enjoyed an income advantage of $1,189 compared with residents of central cities, controlling for age and educational attainment. Differential family size was evident among women aged twenty-five and older, controlling for age and education, for whom the average number of children in the suburbs was .43 larger than in central cities.

48. U. S. Census, County Databooks, 1940, 1952, and 1960, electronic datafiles; underscoring the relationship between children and suburban relocation, analysis of data from the 1970 U.S. Census Public Use 1 Percent Microsample for Metropolitan Areas showed that 81 percent of married couples who moved into their residence in the past year had at least one child, compared with 69 percent in Hennepin County and 66 percent in Ramsey County.

49. *Comprehensive Plan 2000* (Bloomington, MN: Bloomington City Council, 2000); a total of 5,009 single-unit and 4,887 multiunit housing structures were constructed during the 1960s.

50. *Land-Use Trends* (see n. 35 above), 26.

51. Worthy, *William C. Norris*.

52. James, *Toro*; Melrose, *Making the Grass Greener*.

53. Medtronic History, online at www.medtronic.com.

54. Shannon Hahn, "Opus in Line for Honeywell Land," *City Business–Minneapolis* (December 31, 1999).

55. Minnesota Legislature, General Laws of the State of Minnesota, Chapter 193–H. F. No. 1193, April 15, 1907; Chapter 462–S. F. No. 1116, April 18, 1953; Chapter 686–S. F. No. 414, April 24, 1959. Details of current policies are presented in *Annexation Criteria: Report to the Legislature* (St. Paul: Minnesota Planning, 1995).

56. Land area in square miles as reported in the 2000 U.S. Census; comparisons with townships drawn from *Minnesota Atlas* (Chicago: Rand McNally, 1911).

57. Interview with Curt Larson, conducted November 6, 2008.

58. The edge cities of St. Louis and their combined population mentioned here refer only to those in Missouri.

59. Information from the 2002 U.S. Economic Census, available at www.census .gov. Because the Census Bureau withholds information that could reveal the identity of specific firms, data were available for the number of manufacturing firms for only sixty-five Middle Western edge cities, receipts of manufacturing firms for fifty-seven edge cities, number of wholesale firms for ninety-one, receipts of wholesale firms for seventy-four, and number of retail firms and retail receipts for ninety-one edge cities. Complete data were available for the eight core cities (combining Minneapolis and St. Paul and the two Kansas Cities). Partial data for edge-city manufacturing and wholesale firms means that their true contribution to overall receipts compared with retail receipts and core-city receipts is underestimated.

60. As an economic development official in Olathe explained, "Olathe woke up years ago and said, you know, we're overweighted by residential versus commercial, which creates a burden on the tax base. A residential acre costs a lot more to maintain in public services than a commercial acre does and is worth less. They purposefully made an effort to increase commercial and industrial development. Interview conducted December 17, 2008.

61. The relationship between industrial receipts and municipal credit ratings is drawn from an analysis of Moody's bond ratings for municipalities' general obligations incurred in 2008 or the most recent prior year available. The five Middle Western edge cities with Aaa ratings averaged $133,000 per capita in manufacturing and wholesale revenue, using the most recent 2002 U.S. Economic Census figures; the twenty-five edge cities with bond ratings of Aa1 or Aa2 averaged $58,000 per capita in manufacturing and wholesale revenue; and the forty-one edge cities with lower ratings (Aa3 to Baa1) averaged only $26,000 per capita in manufacturing and wholesale revenue.

62. Garreau, *Edge City*, xx–xxi.

63. Further comparisons among small, medium, and large suburbs and urban core cities in the Middle West are shown in the appendix in tables 21 and 22.

64. The data analysis summarized in table 23 in the appendix suggest several interesting conclusions. In 1950, incorporated suburbs were larger if they were closer to the center city and smaller if they were farther away. But the negative correlation between population and distance from center city became weaker in each successive decade, was statistically insignificant by 1970, and then reversed, becoming positive in 1990 and become stronger in 2000 and again in 2005. Population growth (in multiple regression equations with population as the dependent variable and controlling for the previous population level) showed similar relationships with distance from center cities, but the coefficients weakened between 1990 and 2005, possibly suggesting that geographic sprawl was diminishing. The zero-order correlations between population and land area (as of 1980) were strong and consistent from 1950 through 2005. However, the coefficients for population growth with land area were strongest in 1970 and 1980. The effect of annexation is reflected in the different patterns evident when land area in 2000 is considered as the independent variable. The zero-order correlations are insignificant in 1950 and 1960 and become consistently stronger between1970 and 2006. The coefficients for population change become stronger through 1990 and diminish in 2000 and 2005.

65. Bureau of Air and Radiation, *Kansas Air Quality Report, 2005–2006* (Topeka: Kansas Department of Health and Environment, 2006), 17. Barry C. Poulton, Teresa J. Rasmussen, and Casey J. Lee, "Biological Conditions in Streams of Johnson County, Kansas, and Nearby Missouri, 2003 and 2004," *USGS Fact Sheet* (July 2007), No. 2007-3044, provides evidence of the impact in urban parts of the county on water quality and aquatic life.

66. Agency for Toxic Substances and Disease Registry, *Public Health Assessment: Sunflower Army Ammunition Plant, Desoto, Johnson County, Kansas* (March 4, 2002).

67. "Clean Up, Don't Build Up the Kansas City Nuclear Weapons Plant," *Physicians for Social Responsibility Nuclear Watch* (October 13, 2008); "Suit Challenges Legality of Proposed Kansas City Nuclear Weapons Plant," *Natural Resources Defense Council News* (October 9, 2008). The environmental cost of suburban weapons plants was also evident in Arden Hills where the government spent between $150 and $300 million cleaning up the Twin Cities munitions facility.

68. Interview with Curt Larson, conducted November 6, 2008; and Amy Scoggins, conducted November 11, 2008; Maria Elena Baca, "Aveda Shares the Beauty of Being Green," *Minneapolis Star Tribune* (October 14, 2008); "Woodbury Striving to Be a Sustainable City," *Woodbury Green Times* (April 2008).

69. Putnam, *Bowling Alone*, 204–14; see also Oliver, "Civil Society in Suburbia."

70. These conclusions are drawn from data collected in the General Social Survey (GSS), conducted by the National Opinion Research Center at the University of Chicago between 1973 and 2006. The GSS staff generously provided me with a special version of the dataset that permitted residents of the Middle West (the nine states I have defined as the Middle West) to be distinguished from residents in other regions. The closest approximation of a variable for distinguishing edge-city residents was one identifying respondents living in suburbs of cities with populations of 250,000 or more. In the cumulative datafile, 771 respondents lived in these suburbs and 649 lived in the large cities of that size themselves. For the comparison with small towns, I selected respondents living in towns of 2,500 to 9,999 (there were 441 respondents) and those living in towns of fewer than 2,500 residents (557 respondents). The mean population size of locations in which core-city respondents lived was 410,650; suburban respondents, 29,610; and respondents in the two categories of small towns, 5,230 and 730, respectively. The questions about visiting friends, relatives, and neighbors were asked of a total of 356 city residents, 481 suburban residents, and 556 small-town residents. The percentages of each, respectively, who visited friends once a month or more in the past year were 69, 69, and 57; relatives, 66, 72, and 68; and neighbors, 47, 46, and 58. Logistic regression models in which age, income, education, race, marital status, size of household, and year were controlled and small-town residence was used as the comparison variable showed that suburban and urban residence were negatively associated with spending evenings visiting neighbors once a month or more (odds ratios of .647 and .547 respectively) and that the coefficients for these relationships with spending time visiting friends and relatives were statistically insignificant. Arguments about the decline of social capital would suggest that the percentages in recent years would be smaller than in the cumulative datafile; however, none of the coefficients for year in the regression models were statistically significant. Inspection of the data for respondents not living in the Middle West suggested similar patterns.

71. Internal Revenue Service, online at www.irs.gov; data for all nonprofit associations for which a Form 990 had been filed in 2006. The data were categorized by zip code and then reorganized to correspond with incorporated places, weighted by population whenever zip codes spanned more than one place. The data do not include most religious organizations, which are not required to file with the IRS.

72. General Social Survey Cumulative Data, electronic datafile. Using the same measures of residence as for visiting friends, relatives, and neighbors, 64 percent of city residents belonged to at least one voluntary association, 78 percent of suburban residents did, and 75 percent of small-town residents did. The respective percentages who belonged to two or more were 41, 53, and 56. Logistic regression models with the same controls as for the variables about visiting showed that suburban residence was insignificantly associated with belonging to at least one voluntary association and that urban residence was negatively associated (.665) at a marginal level of statistical probability (.098).

73. Interview conducted November 7, 2007; pseudonym used, some identifying details altered.

74. U.S. Census, 2000; of in-migrants to Johnson County between 1995 and 2000, the modal age groups were twenty-five to twenty-nine years and thirty to thirty-four years, the modal education level was bachelor's degree, and the modal household type was married couple with children.

75. ESRI Market Potential Data, 2005, electronic datafile. Market potential scores for eighteen categories averaged 119.6 for Middle West edge cities with 10,000 to 20,000 residents, 119.8 for edge cities with 20,000 to 50,000 residents, 124.9 for edge cities with more than 50,000 residents, and 84.1 for residents of core cities.

76. U.S. Census, County Databook 2002, electronic datafile. Reference to the "Midwest" in this paragraph is to the wider Midwest region as defined by the U.S. Census, the variable available in the data. The paucity of migrants to the Kansas City area from the West Coast contradicts the impression given by the anecdotes reported in Motoko Rich and David Leonhardt, "Saying Goodbye California Sun, Hello Midwest," *New York Times* (November 7, 2005).

77. Laura Lorson, "Commentary: Kansas Is a Good Place to Live," *All Things Considered* (September 1, 2004).

78. A national survey of 2,260 adults conducted in October 2008 asked respondents if they would like to live in each of thirty metropolitan areas; Kansas City ranked twenty-seventh, Minneapolis was twenty-sixth, and St. Louis was twenty-fourth. The difficulties Middle Western cities and suburbs faced in attracting new residents were underscored by the survey's finding that young adults preferred large coastal cities like New York and Los Angeles while older adults preferred Sunbelt locations like San Diego, Orlando, and Phoenix. Only 15 percent of the respondents said they would like to live in the Kansas City area, 16 percent did for Minneapolis, and 18 percent did for St. Louis; "Community Satisfaction," *Pew Research Center* (October 2008), online at pewsocialtrends.org.

79. Frank, *What's the Matter with Kansas*, 286.

80. Randall J. Stephens, autobiographical material posted at hnn.us/roundup.

81. "Adventures in Cupcake Land," blog posted February 1, 2006, at donaldopato.blogspot.com.

82. Interview conducted November 25, 2008.

83. Jordan Rappaport, "The Shared Fortunes of Cities and Suburbs," *Economic Review* (2005), 33–60.

84. Interview with Robert J. Marcusse, conducted December 9, 2008.

85. *ACS Demographic and Housing Estimates: 2007*, Kansas State Data Center, online at kslib.info.

86. Partial data on foreclosures in Johnson County showed an average of 63 per month during the first six months of 2004, rising to 150 per month during the same period in 2008; "Johnson County, Kansas, Foreclosures," Office of the Sheriff, Johnson County, Kansas, July 2008.

87. U.S. Census, County Databooks, 1952 through 2002, electronic datafiles. Tract-level comparisons of income disparities in the Kansas City metropolitan area between 1990 and 2000 are discussed in Frank Lenk, *Metro Outlook Live: 2007* (Kansas City, MO: Mid-America Regional Council, 2007), 26–67; and county-level estimates of household income, personal income per capita, and poverty rates are included in *Kansas Statistical Abstract 2007* (Lawrence: University of Kansas, Institute for Policy and Social Research, 2008), 335–49.

88. Interview conducted November 15, 2008.

89. *A Separate Society: Olathe's African-American Community, 1870–1920* (Olathe, KS: Johnson County Museum, 1999), no author indicated, online document at www.jocomuseum.org.

90. U.S. Census, 1980, tract-level data, electronic datafile, tract 528 in which 445 of Olathe's 947 black residents lived.

91. U.S. Census, 2000, tract-level data, electronic datafile; U.S. Survey of School Districts, 1999, National Center for Education Statistics, electronic datafile.

92. *Strategic Planning Report* (Olathe, KS: City Council, 2004), 2. Leawood's restrictive covenants were mentioned in several interviews with Leawood residents and discussed in "Leawood: The Security Zone," *Kansas City Star* (November 18, 2005).

93. U.S. Census, American Community Survey, 2007, electronic datafile. In Johnson County, the numbers officially below the poverty level grew slightly as the population increased but would have grown more had it not been for selective out-migration. Between 1995 and 2000, for example, the county experienced a net loss of nearly 2,000 people below the poverty line—the only category in which out-migration exceeded in-migration.

Selected Bibliography

Adams, F. G. "Irrigation in Kansas." *Transactions of the Kansas Academy of Science* 7 (1879–1880): 77–83.

Alexander, W. E. *History of Iowa*. Sioux City: Western Publishing Company, 1882.

Alston, Lee J. "Farm Foreclosures in the United States during the Interwar Period." *Journal of Economic History* 43 (1983): 885–903.

Andersen, M. J. *Portable Prairie: Confessions of an Unsettled Midwesterner*. New York: St. Martin's Press, 2005.

Arnould, Richard J. "Changing Patterns of Concentration in American Meat Packing, 1880–1963." *Business History Review* 45 (1971): 18–34.

Artz, Georgeanne M., Peter F. Orazem, and Daniel M. Otto. "Measuring the Impact of Meat Packing and Processing Facilities in Nonmetropolitan Counties: A Difference-in-Differences Approach." *American Journal of Agricultural Economics* 89 (2007): 557–70.

Aurner, Clarence Ray. *History of Education in Iowa*. 5 vols. Iowa City: State Historical Society of Iowa, 1914–1920.

Bach, Robert. *Changing Relations: Newcomers and Established Residents in US Communities, A Report to the Ford Foundation by the National Board of the Changing Relations Project*. New York: Ford Foundation, 1993.

Bader, Robert Smith. *Hayseeds, Moralizers, and Methodists: The Twentieth-Century Image of Kansas*. Lawrence: University Press of Kansas, 1988.

Barker, Bruce, and Ivan Muse. "One-Room Schools of Nebraska, Montana, South Dakota, California, and Wyoming." *Research in Rural Education* 3 (1986): 127–30.

Barnes, Lela. "North Central Kansas in 1887–1889." *Kansas Historical Quarterly* 39 (1963): 267–323.

Barnouw, Erik. *Tube of Plenty: The Evolution of American Television*. New York: Oxford University Press, 1990.

Barr, Virginia D. "The Diary of Virginia D. (Jones-Harlan) Barr" (1940). Smith County Historical Society, Smith Center, KS.

Bateman, Fred. "The 'Marketable Surplus' in Northern Dairy Farming: New Evidence by Size of Farm in 1860." *Agricultural History* 52 (1978): 345–63.

Bauer, George R. *Trails, Rails, and Tales: Olathe's First 150 Years*. Kansas City, MO: Kansas City Star Books, 2004.

Beal, Leonard. *Centennial of Traill County, 1875–1975*. Hillsboro, ND: Northwestern Bank of Hillsboro, 1975. Courtesy of North Dakota State University Library, Fargo.

Beebe, B. W. "Application of Geological Principles to Exploration for Oil and Gas in Kansas." *Transactions of the Kansas Academy of Science* 67 (1964): 256–80.

Bell, Earl H. "Changing Family Situations in a Small Community." *Scientific Monthly* 35 (1932): 462–65.

———. *Culture of a Contemporary Rural Community: Sublette, Kansas*. Washington, DC: U.S. Department of Agriculture, Bureau of Agricultural Economics, Rural Life Studies, 1942.

Bellah, Robert N., Richard Madsen, William M. Sullivan, Ann Swidler, and Steven M. Tipton. *Habits of the Heart: Individualism and Commitment in American Life*. Berkeley and Los Angeles: University of California Press, 1985.

Bennett, Edward H. *Plan of Minneapolis Prepared under the Direction of the Civic Commission*. Minneapolis: Civic Commission, 1917.

Billingsley, Carolyn Earle. "Settlement Patterns in Saline County, Arkansas." *Arkansas Historical Quarterly* 52 (1993): 107–28.

Bird, Isabella L. *A Lady's Life in the Rocky Mountains*, edited by Daniel J. Boorstin. Norman: University of Oklahoma Press, 1960.

Bishop, Rebecca, and John Leatherman, *Fiscal Conditions and Trends: Finney County 2007*. Manhattan: Kansas State University Research and Extension, 2007.

———. *Fiscal Conditions and Trends: Stafford County, 2008*. Manhattan: Kansas State University Research and Extension, 2008.

Bivans, Venola Lewis. "The Diary of Luna E. Warner." *Kansas Historical Quarterly* 35 (1969): 276–311.

Blair, Ed. *History of Johnson County, Kansas*. Lawrence: Standard Publishing Company, 1915.

Blanchard, Leola Howard. *Conquest of Southwest Kansas*. Wichita, KS: Wichita Eagle Press, 1931.

Blank, Steven C. *The End of Agriculture in the American Portfolio*. Westport, CT: Quorum Books, 1998.

Blau, Peter M., and Otis D. Duncan. *The American Occupational Structure*. New York: John Wiley and Sons, 1967.

Bloomenshine, L. L. *Prairie around Me: Childhood Memories*. San Diego: Raphael Publications, 1972.

Bodensteiner, Carol. *Growing Up Country: Memories of an Iowa Farm Girl*. Des Moines: Rising Sun Press, 2008.

Bogue, Allan G. *From Prairie to Corn Belt: Farming on the Illinois and Iowa Prairies in the Nineteenth Century*. Chicago: University of Chicago Press, 1963.

———. "The Land Mortgage Company in the Early Plains States." *Agricultural History* 25 (1951): 20–33.

Boyne, David H. "Changes in the Income Distribution in Agriculture." *Journal of Farm Economics* 47 (1965): 1213–24.

Brant, Barry. "Alternative Strategic Financial Plans for Garden City Co-op." MAB thesis, Kansas State University, 2008.

Broadway, Michael J., and Donald D. Stull. "Meat Processing and Garden City, KS: Boom and Bust." *Journal of Rural Studies* 22 (2006): 55–66.

Broehl, Wayne G., Jr. *Cargill: From Commodities to Customers*. Hanover, NH: University Press of New England, 2008.

———. *Cargill: Trading the World's Grain*. Hanover, NH: University Press of New England, 1992.

Brown, David L., and Louis E. Swanson, eds. *Challenges for Rural America in the Twenty-First Century*. University Park: Pennsylvania State University Press, 2003.

Brunn, Stanley D., and Karl B. Raitz. "Regional Patterns of Farm Magazine Publication." *Economic Geography* 54 (1978): 277–90.

Bryce, James. *American Commonwealth*. London: Macmillan, 1888.

Buecker, Thomas R. *Fort Robinson and the American West, 1874–1899*. Lincoln: Nebraska State Historical Society, 1999.

Bunkers, Suzanne L. *"All Will Yet Be Well": The Diary of Sarah Gillespie Huftalen, 1873–1952*. Iowa City: University of Iowa Press, 1993.

Burns, Sarah. *Pastoral Inventions: Rural Life in Nineteenth-Century American Art and Culture*. Philadelphia: Temple University Press, 1989.

Burr, Walter. *Rural Organization*. New York: Macmillan, 1921.

Busch, Lawrence, William H. Friedland, Lourdes Gouveia, and Enzo Mingione. *From Columbus to ConAgra: The Globalization of Agriculture and Food*. Lawrence: University Press of Kansas, 1994.

Butterfield, Kenyon L. "The Social Problems of American Farmers." *American Journal of Sociology* 10 (1905): 606–22.

Butterworth, Julian E. "An Evaluation of Methods of Providing Free High School Tuition." *School Review* 23 (1915): 85–96.

Cameron, Roderick. *Pioneer Days in Kansas: A Homesteader's Narrative of Early Settlement and Farm Development on the High Plains Country of Northwest Kansas*. Belleville, KS: Cameron Book Company, 1951.

Capote, Truman. *In Cold Blood: A True Account of a Multiple Murder and Its Consequences*. New York: Random House, 1966.

Carney, Mabel. *Country Life and the Country School: A Study of the Agencies of Rural Progress and of the Social Relationship of the School to the Country Community*. Chicago: Row, Peterson and Company, 1912.

Carson, Rachel. *Silent Spring*. Boston: Houghton Mifflin, 1962.

Cather, Willa. *O Pioneers!* Boston: Houghton Mifflin, 1913.

Chase, C. M. *The Editor's Run in New Mexico and Colorado*. Montpelier, VT: Argus and Patriot Steam Book and Job Printing House, 1883.

Collins, J. E. "Relation of Parental Occupation to Intelligence of Children." *Journal of Educational Research* 17 (1928): 157–69.

Conrad, Erik Paul. "A History of Kansas' Closed Colleges." PhD diss., University of Oklahoma, 1970.

Cook, Michael L. "The Future of U.S. Agricultural Cooperatives: A Neo-Institutional Approach." *American Journal of Agricultural Economics* 77 (1995): 1153–59.

Cutler, William G. *History of the State of Kansas*. Chicago: A. T. Andreas, 1883.

———. *History of the State of Nebraska*. Chicago: A. T. Andreas 1882.

Daley, Maren L., and Duane Broschat. *Labor Availability Study: Traill County and the Surrounding Area.* Bismarck: North Dakota Department of Commerce, 2004.

Dana, M.M.G. "Western Colleges: Their Claims and Necessities." *New Englander and Yale Review* 39 (1880): 774–93.

Danbom, David B. *Born in the Country: A History of Rural America.* 2nd ed. Baltimore: Johns Hopkins University Press, 2006.

Dassler, Charles Frederick William. *Compiled Laws of Kansas.* Topeka: Geo. W. Crane & Co., 1885.

Deahl, William E., Jr. "Nebraska's Unique Contribution to the Entertainment World." *Nebraska History* (1968): 194.

Deyoe, Albert M. *Biennial Report of the Iowa Department of Public Instruction.* Des Moines: State Printer, 1912.

Dodge, Mary Mapes. *St. Nicholas: An Illustrated Magazine for Young Folks.* New York: Century Company, 1890.

Dooley, Patricia L. "Gopher Ordnance Works: Condemnation, Construction, and Community Response." *Minnesota History* 49 (1985): 214–28.

Ducoff, Louis J. "Trends and Characteristics of Farm Population in Low-Income Farming Areas." *Journal of Farm Economics* 37 (1955): 1399–407.

Dudziak, Mary L. "The Limits of Good Faith: Desegregation in Topeka, Kansas, 1950–1956." *Law and History Review* 5 (1987): 351–91.

Durkheim, Emile. *The Division of Labor in Society.* New York: Free Press, 1933.

Dyck, Mary Knackstedt. *Waiting on the Bounty: The Dust Bowl Diary of Mary Knackstedt Dyck.* Iowa City: University of Iowa Press, 1999.

Easterly, Charles C. "The Trend of Farm Population and Land Ownership in Smith County, Kansas, 1900–1940." MS thesis, Hays State College, 1941.

Ebbutt, Percy G. *Emigrant Life in Kansas.* London: S. Sonnenschein and Co., 1886.

Edgar, John O. "Great Years in the Life of an Iowa Farm Boy." Unpublished manuscript, Beaver Falls, PA, 1980.

Edwards, Linda Nasif. "An Empirical Analysis of Compulsory Schooling Legislation, 1940–1960." *Journal of Law and Economics* 21 (1978): 203–22.

Egan, Timothy. *The Worst Hard Time.* New York: Mariner Books, 2006.

Elder, Glen H., Jr. "Achievement Orientations and Career Patterns of Rural Youth." *Sociology of Education* 37 (1963): 30–58.

Erisman, Fred. "L. Frank Baum and the Progressive Dilemma." *American Quarterly* 20 (1968): 616–23.

Faulkner, Virginia, ed. *Willa Cather's Collected Short Fiction, 1892–1912.* Lincoln: University of Nebraska Press, 1970.

Faust, Maurice. *Remember—No Electricity! A Reminiscence.* Brainerd, MN: Marvin Books, 1998.

Fearon, Peter. "Kansas History and the New Deal Era." *Kansas History* 30 (2007): 192–223.

———. *Kansas in the Great Depression: Work Relief, the Dole, and Rehabilitation.* Columbia: University of Missouri Press, 2007.

―――. "Regulation and Response: Kansas Wheat Farmers and the New Deal." *Rural History* 18 (2007): 245–64.

Fellows, Ernest Wilder. "A Comparative Study of City School and Rural School Attendance." *Studies in Education* 1 (1912): 3–28.

Fite, Gilbert C. *Beyond the Fence Rows: A History of Farmland Industries, Inc., 1929–1978*. Columbia and London: University of Missouri Press, 1978.

Fitzgerald, Daniel C. *Faded Dreams: More Ghost Towns of Kansas*. Lawrence: University Press of Kansas, 1994.

―――. *Ghost Towns of Kansas*. Lawrence: University Press of Kansas, 1988.

Fleming-Rife, Anita, and Jennifer M. Proffitt. "The More Public School Reform Changes, the More It Stays the Same: A Framing Analysis of the Newspaper Coverage of Brown v. Board of Education." *Journal of Negro Education* 73 (2004): 239–54.

Foght, Harold W. "The Country School." *Annals of the American Academy of Political and Social Science* 40 (1912): 149–57.

―――. *The Rural School System of Minnesota: A Study in School Efficiency*. U.S. Bureau of Education Bulletin No. 20. Washington, DC: Government Printing Office, 1915.

Frank, Thomas. *What's the Matter with Kansas? How Conservatives Won the Heart of America*. New York: Henry Holt, 2004.

Fuguitt, Glenn V., David L. Brown, and Calvin L. Beale. *Rural and Small Town America*. New York: Russell Sage Foundation, 1989.

Full, Jan R. Olive. "Hinterland or Heartland: The Survival of Small-Town Lake Mills, Iowa, 1850–1950." PhD diss., Loyola University Chicago, 2006.

Fuller, Wayne E. *The Old Country School*. Chicago: University of Chicago Press, 1982.

Garreau, Joel. *Edge City: Life on the New Frontier*. New York: Random House, 1991.

Gates, Paul Wallace. *Fifty Million Acres: Conflicts over Kansas Land Policy, 1854–1890*. Norman: University of Oklahoma Press, 1997. Originally published 1954 by Cornell University Press.

Gee, Wilson. "A Qualitative Study of Rural Depopulation in a Single Township, 1900–1930." *American Journal of Sociology* 39 (1933): 210–21.

Gleason, John Philip. "The Attitude of the Business Community toward Agriculture during the McNary-Haugen Period." *Agricultural History* 32 (1958): 127–38.

Goldin, Claudia, and Lawrence Katz. "Education and Income in the Early 20th Century: Evidence from the Prairies." *Journal of Economic History* 60 (2000): 782–818.

―――. "Human Capital and Social Capital: The Rise of Secondary Schooling in America, 1910–1940." *Journal of Interdisciplinary History* 29 (1999): 683–723.

―――. *The Race between Education and Technology*. Cambridge, MA: Harvard University Press, 2008.

Gordon, Ira J. "The Kansas Wheat Farm Culture, and Implications for Guidance at the Kansas State College." *Transactions of the Kansas Academy of Science* 55 (1952): 54–61.

Graves, Russell. "Garden City: The Development of an Agricultural Community on the Great Plains." PhD diss., University of Wisconsin, 2004.

Greeley, Horace. *An Overland Journey from New York to San Francisco in the Summer of 1859*. New York: C. M. Saxton, Barker & Co., 1860.

Gregson, Mary Eschelbach. "Population Dynamics in Rural Missouri, 1860–1880." *Social Science History* 21 (1997): 85–110.

Griesel, Janet L., John C. Leatherman, Sarah Grant, and Rebecca Bishop. *Situation and Trends, Smith County*. Manhattan, KS: K-State Research and Extension, 2002.

Griswold, Wendy, and Nathan Wright. "Cowbirds, Locals, and the Dynamic Endurance of Regionalism." *American Journal of Sociology* 109 (2004): 1411–51.

Grove, Ernest W. "State Variations in Farm Program Payments." *Journal of Farm Economics* 47 (1965): 222–33.

Guither, Harold D. "Factors Influencing Farm Operators' Decisions to Leave Farming." *Journal of Farm Economics* 45 (1963): 567–76.

Gutmann, Myron P. *Great Plains Population and Environment Data: Agricultural Data and Social Data, 1870–1997*. Ann Arbor: University of Michigan, Inter-university Consortium for Political and Social Research, 2000.

Hackney, Sheldon. *One America Indivisible: A National Conversation on American Pluralism and Identity*. Washington, DC: National Endowment for the Humanities, 1999.

Haggerty, Melvin E., and H. B. Nash. "Mental Capacity of Children and Parental Occupation." *Journal of Educational Psychology* 15 (1924): 559–72.

Haines, Richael R. *Historical, Demographic, Economic, and Social Data: The United States, 1790–2000*. Ann Arbor: University of Michigan, Inter-university Consortium for Political and Social Research, 2002.

Hall, Leonard. *A Journal of the Seasons on an Ozark Farm*. 1957. Reprint, Columbia: University of Missouri Press, 1980.

Haller, A. O. "Planning to Farm: A Social Psychological Interpretation." *Social Forces* 37 (1959): 263–68.

Hamilton, David. *Deep River: A Memoir of a Missouri Farm*. Columbia: University of Missouri Press, 2001.

Harding, T. Swann. "On to the City, Farmer!" *Scientific Monthly* 30 (1930): 149–55.

Hart, John Fraser, Michalle J. Rhodes, and John T. Morgan. *The Unknown World of the Mobile Home*. Baltimore: Johns Hopkins University Press, 2002.

Haury, David A. "Come Back to the Five & Dime." *Kansas Heritage* 12 (2004): 17–22.

Hill, Lowell D. "Characteristics of the Farmers Leaving Agriculture in an Iowa County." *Journal of Farm Economics* 44 (1962): 419–26.

Hill, Luther B. *History of Benton County Iowa*. Chicago: Lewis Publishing Company, 1910.

Hill, Robert Tudor. *The Public Domain and Democracy: A Study of Social, Economic and Political Problems in the United States in Relation to Western Development*. New York: Columbia University Press, 1910.

Hines, Stephen W. *Laura Ingalls Wilder, Farm Journalist: Writings from the Ozarks*. Columbia: University of Missouri Press, 2007.

Hockenberry, John Coulter. "The Rural School in the United States." PhD diss., University of Pennsylvania, 1908.

Hoig, Stan. *Cowtown Wichita and the Wild, Wicked West*. Albuquerque: University of New Mexico Press, 2007.

Hope, Holly. *Garden City: Dreams in a Kansas Town*. Norman: University of Oklahoma Press, 1988.

Hudson, Horace B. *A Half Century of Minneapolis*. Minneapolis: Hudson Publishing Company, 1908.

Hudson, John C. *Plains Country Towns*. Minneapolis: University of Minnesota Press, 1985.

Hurt, Douglas. "Naval Air Stations in Kansas during World War II." *Kansas Historical Quarterly* 43 (1977): 351–62.

Huxman, Walter A., Arthur J. Mellott, and Delman C. Hill. "The Topeka, Kansas Case Decision." *Journal of Negro Education* 21 (1952): 522–27.

Isaacs, Harold R. "World Affairs and U.S. Race Relations: A Note on Little Rock." *Public Opinion Quarterly* 22 (1958): 364–70.

James, Trace. *Toro: A Diamond History*. Bloomington, MN: Toro, 1989.

Jimenez, Tomas Roberto. "Immigrant Replenishment and the Continuing Significance of Ethnicity and Race: The Case of the Mexican-Origin Population." Working Paper 130, University of California at San Diego, Department of Sociology, December 2005.

———. "Mexican-Immigrant Replenishment and the Continuing Significance of Ethnicity and Race." *American Journal of Sociology* 113 (2008): 1527–67.

———. "Replenished Identities: Mexican Americans, Mexican Immigrants and Ethnic Identity." PhD diss., Harvard University, 2004.

Johnson, A. N. "The Impact of Farm Machinery on the Farm Economy." *Agricultural History* 24 (1950): 58–62.

Johnson, Sherman E. "Technological Changes and the Future of Rural Life." *Journal of Farm Economics* 32 (1950): 225–39.

Johnson, Victoria E. "Camelot, Hooterville, or Watts? American Network Television and the Struggle for National Identity, 1946–1974." PhD diss., University of Southern California, 1997.

Keillor, Garrison. *Lake Wobegon Days*. New York: Penguin, 1990.

Kenney, Dave. *Minnesota Goes to War: The Home Front during World War II*. Minneapolis: Minnesota Historical Society Press, 2004.

———. *Twin Cities Picture Show: A Century of Moviegoing*. Minneapolis: Minnesota Historical Society Press, 2007.

Kenny, Lawrence W., and Amy B. Schmidt. "The Decline in the Number of School Districts in the U.S.: 1950–1980." *Public Choice* 79 (1994): 1–18.

Kersey, Ralph. *History of Finney County, Kansas*, vol. 1. Garden City, KS: Finney County Historical Society, 1950.

Kirkpatrick, Marion G. *The Rural School from Within*. Philadelphia: J. B. Lippincott, 1917.

Klapp, Orrin E. "The Fool as a Social Type." *American Journal of Sociology* 55 (1949): 147–62.

Kluger, Richard. *Simple Justice: The History of Brown v. Board of Education and Black America's Struggle for Equality*. New York: Vintage, 1975.

Kneen, Brewster. *Invisible Giant: Cargill and Its Transnational Strategies*. 2nd ed. New York: Pluto Press, 2002.

Kollmorgen, Walter M., and George F. Jenks. "A Geographic Study of Population and Settlement Changes in Sherman County, Kansas: Part I, Rural." *Transactions of the Kansas Academy of Science* 54 (1951): 449–94.

———. "Sidewalk Farming in Toole County, Montana, and Traill County, North Dakota," *Annals of the Association of American Geographers* 48 (1958), 209–31.

———. "Suitcase Farming in Sully County, South Dakota." *Annals of the Association of American Geographers* 48 (1958): 27–40.

Kunkel, O. L., and W. W. Charters. "Rural School Consolidation in Missouri." *University of Missouri Bulletin* 1 (1911): 1–36.

Landes, William M., and Lewis C. Solmon. "Compulsory Schooling Legislation: An Economic Analysis of Law and Social Change in the Nineteenth Century." *Journal of Economic History* 32 (1972): 54–91.

Lensink, Judy Nolte. *"A Secret to Be Burried": The Diary and Life of Emily Hawley Gillespie, 1858–1888*. Iowa City: University of Iowa Press, 1989.

Lichter, Daniel T., and Glenn V. Fuguitt. "Demographic Response to Transportation Innovation: The Case of the Interstate Highway." *Social Forces* 59 (1980): 492–512.

Littlefield, Henry M. "The Wizard of Oz: Parable on Populism." *American Quarterly* 16 (1964): 47–58.

Lleras-Muney, Adriana. "Were Compulsory Attendance and Child Labor Laws Effective? An Analysis from 1915 to 1930." *Journal of Law and Economics* 45 (2002): 401–35.

Lockyer, Norman. "The Extermination of the American Bison." *Nature: A Weekly Illustrated Journal of Science* 42 (1890): 11–13.

Longwell, Maude. *This Way of Life*. Philadelphia: Farm Journal, 1971.

Low, Ann Marie. *Dust Bowl Diary*. Lincoln: University of Nebraska Press, 1984.

Malin, James C. "Kansas: Some Reflections on Culture Inheritance and Originality." *Journal of the Mid-Continent American Studies Association* 2 (1961): 1–19.

———. "The Turnover of Farm Population in Kansas." In *History and Ecology*, edited by Robert P. Swierenga, 269–99. Lincoln: University of Nebraska Press, 1984; originally published in *Kansas Historical Quarterly* 4 (1935), 339–72.

Marc, David, and Robert J. Thompson. *Prime Time, Prime Movers*. Syracuse, NY: Syracuse University Press, 1995.

McCarter, Margaret Hill. *The Peace of the Solomon Valley*. Chicago: A. C. McClurg, 1911.

McFarlane, Larry. "British Investment in Midwestern Farm Mortgages and Land, 1875–1900: A Comparison of Iowa and Kansas." *Agricultural History* 48 (1974): 179–98.

McKenzie, Bettie, ed. *Her Own Story: Ten Benton County Women.* Red Oak, IA: Vinton Branch American Association of University Women, 1992.

Melrose, Ken. *Making the Grass Greener on Your Side: A CEO's Journey to Leading by Serving.* San Francisco: Berrett-Koehler, 1995.

Millbrook, Mrs. Raymond. "Mrs. Hattie E. Lee's Story of Her Life in Western Kansas." *Kansas Historical Quarterly* 22 (1956): 114–37.

Miller, John E. *Becoming Laura Ingalls Wilder.* Columbia: University of Missouri Press, 1998.

Miner, Craig. *Next Year Country: Dust to Dust in Western Kansas, 1890–1940.* Lawrence: University Press of Kansas, 2006.

Mitchell, Martin D. "From Salina, Kansas to Taos, New Mexico." *Focus on Geography* 46 (2001): 21–28.

Mitchell County Historical Society. *The Story of Mitchell County, 1851–1973.* Mason City, IA: Klipto Printing Co., 1973.

Moore, Elizabeth. *Maternity and Infant Care in a Rural County in Kansas.* Washington, DC: U.S. Department of Labor, Children's Bureau, 1917.

Morgan, Perl W. *History of Wyandotte County Kansas and Its People.* Chicago: Lewis Publishing Company, 1911.

Morris, Wright. *The Home Place.* 1948. Reprint, Lincoln: University of Nebraska Press, 1999.

Morse, Scott N. "'Knowledge Is Power': The Reverend Grosvenor Clarke Morse's Thoughts on Free Schools and the Republic during the Civil War." *Kansas History* 31 (2008): 2–13.

Musick, John R. *Stories of Missouri.* New York: American Book Company, 1897.

Nalley, Lawton Lanier, Andrew Barkley, and Forrest G. Chemley. *The Agronomic and Economic Impacts of the Kansas Agricultural Experiment Station Wheat Breeding Program, 1977–2005.* U.S. Census of Agriculture Report 06-333-S. Manhattan: Kansas Agricultural Experiment Station, 2006.

Newman, Marvin. *Recollections of Saline County.* Marceline, MO: D-Books Publishing, 1997.

Nixon, Earl K. "The Petroleum Industry in Kansas." *Transactions of the Kansas Academy of Science* 51 (1948): 369–424.

Oliver, John Eric. "Civil Society in Suburbia: The Effects of Metropolitan Social Contexts on Participation in Voluntary Organizations." PhD diss., University of California–Berkeley, 1997.

Opie, John. *Ogallala: Water for a Dry Land.* 2nd ed. Lincoln: University of Nebraska Press, 2000.

Oppenheimer, Robert. "Acculturation or Assimilation: Mexican Immigrants in Kansas, 1900 to World War II." *Western Historical Quarterly* 16 (1985): 429–48.

Parker, David B. "The Rise and Fall of *the Wonderful Wizard of Oz* as a 'Parable on Populism.'" *Journal of the Georgia Association of Historians* 15 (1994): 49–63.

Patterson, James T. *Brown v. Board of Education: A Civil Rights Milestone and Its Troubled Legacy*. New York: Oxford University Press, 2001.

Peirce, Paul S. *Social Surveys of Three Rural Townships in Iowa*. Iowa City: University of Iowa Monographs, Studies in the Social Sciences, 1917.

Pettigrew, Thomas F., and Ernest Q. Campbell. "Faubus and Segregation: An Analysis of Arkansas Voting." *Public Opinion Quarterly* 24 (1960): 436–47.

Pletcher, Vera Edith Crosby. "A History of Smith County, Kansas to 1960." Kansas State University, 1960.

Porter, Catherine Wiggins. "'Holding Down' a Northwest Kansas Claim, 1885–1888," edited by Kenneth Wiggins Porter. *Kansas Historical Quarterly* 22 (1956): 220–35.

Powell, Morgan, and Kerri Ebert. *Living in the Country*. Manhattan, KS: Kansas State University, Agricultural Experiment Station and Cooperative Extension Service, February 2008.

Power, Richard Lyle. "A Crusade to Extend Yankee Culture, 1820–1865." *New England Quarterly* 13 (1940): 638–53.

Powers, Elmer G. *Years of Struggle: The Farm Diary of Elmer G. Powers, 1931–1936*. Ames: Iowa State University Press, 1976.

Prentis, Noble. *History of Kansas*. Winfield, KS: E. P. Greer, 1899.

———. *South-Western Letters*. Topeka: Kansas Publishing House, 1882.

Putnam, Robert D. *Bowling Alone: The Collapse and Revival of American Community*. New York: Simon & Schuster, 2000.

Randall, C. Kyle, and Robert H. Masucci. "Farm and Nonfarm Income Comparisons." *Journal of Farm Economics* 45 (1963): 359–66.

Raup, Philip M., and Johnson Jerome E. *The Minnesota Farm Real Estate Market in 1957*. St. Paul: University of Minnesota, Department of Agricultural Economics, Institute of Agriculture, 1958.

Reeve, Agnesa. *Constant Frontier: The Continuing History of Finney County, Kansas*. Garden City, KS: Finney County Historical Society, 1996.

Reeve, Marshall P. *Looking Back: A Cattleman on the High Plains*. Garden City, KS: B. J. Publishing, 2005.

Revenstein, Charles A. *Air Force Combat Wings: Lineage and Honors Histories, 1947–1977*. Washington, DC: Office of Air Force History, 1984.

Reynolds, David B. *There Goes the Neighborhood: Rural School Consolidation at the Grass Roots in Early Twentieth-Century Iowa*. Iowa City: University of Iowa Press, 1999.

Richardson, John G. "Variation in Date of Enactment of Compulsory School Attendance Laws: An Empirical Inquiry." *Sociology of Education* 53 (1980): 153–63.

Rife, Gladys Talcott. "Iowa's Rural Women Columnists, Especially of the Fifties: Their Cultural and Historical Import in a Comparative Context." PhD diss., University of Iowa, 1988.

Riley, Michael O. *Oz and Beyond: The Fantasy World of L. Frank Baum.* Lawrence: University of Kansas Press, 1997.

Riney-Kehrberg, Pamela. *Rooted in Dust: Surviving Drought and Depression in Southwestern Kansas.* Lawrence: University Press of Kansas, 1994.

———. *Waiting on the Bounty: The Dust Bowl Diary of Mary Knackstedt Dyck.* Iowa City: University of Iowa Press, 1999.

Rockoff, Hugh. "The 'Wizard of Oz' as a Monetary Allegory." *Journal of Political Economy* 98 (1990): 739–51.

Rogers, Katherine M. *L. Frank Baum: Creator of Oz.* New York: St. Martin's Press, 2002.

Roland, Albert. "Do-It-Yourself: A Walden for the Millions?" *American Quarterly* 10 (1958): 154–64.

Ross, E. A. "The Allaying of Town-Country Conflict." *Journal of Social Forces* 3 (1924): 15–21.

Rothenberger, Von. *Weaving the Common Threads of the Solomon Valley Fabric.* Woodston, KS: Western Books, 2002.

Rundstrom, Robert. "Heartland." In *The American Midwest: An Interpretive Encyclopedia,* edited by Richard Sisson, Christian Zacher and Andrew Cayton, 71–73. Bloomington: Indiana University Press, 2007.

Ruttan, Vernon W. "Farm and Non-Farm Employment Opportunities for Low Income Farm Families." *Phylon* 20 (1959): 248–55.

Sampson, Robert J., and Stephen W. Raudenbush. *Disorder in Urban Neighborhoods: Does It Lead to Crime?* Washington, DC: U.S. Department of Justice, National Institute of Justice, 2001.

———. "Seeing Disorder: Neighborhood Stigma and the Social Construction of 'Broken Windows.'" *Social Psychology Quarterly* 67 (2004): 319–42.

Samuelson, Bill. *One Room Country Schools of Kansas.* Emporia, KS: Chester Press, 1995.

Sanger, Steve. *Cedar County: A Memoir of Iowa.* New York: Writers Club Press, 2003.

Schlosser, Eric. *Fast Food Nation: The Dark Side of the All-American Meal.* New York: Houghton Mifflin, 2004.

Schoewe, Walter H. "The Geographical Center of the United States." *Transactions of the Kansas Academy of Science* 43 (1940): 305–6.

———. "The Geography of Kansas: Part I: Political Geography." *Transactions of the Kansas Academy of Science* 51 (1948): 253–88.

Schwartz, Marvin. *Tyson: From Farm to Market.* Fayetteville: University of Arkansas Press, 1991.

Schwieder, Dorothy Hubbard. *Growing Up with the Town.* Iowa City: University of Iowa Press, 2002.

Self, Huber. *Environment and Man in Kansas: A Geographical Analysis.* Lawrence: Regents Press of Kansas, 1978.

Sewell, William H. "Community of Residence and College Plans." *American Socio-logical Review* 29 (1964): 24–38.

Sewell, William H., and Bertram L. Ellenbogen. "Social Status and the Measured Intelligence of Small City and Rural Children." *American Sociological Review* 17 (1952): 612–16.

Shields, Charles J. *Mockingbird: A Portrait of Harper Lee.* New York: Macmillan, 2007.

Shockley, Martin Staples. "The Reception of the Grapes of Wrath in Oklahoma." *American Literature* 15 (1944): 351–61.

Shortridge, James R. "Changing Usage of Four American Regional Labels." *Annals of the Association of American Geographers* 77 (1987): 325–36.

——. *Cities on the Plains: The Evolution of Urban Kansas.* Lawrence: University Press of Kansas, 2004.

——. "The Emergence of 'Middle West' as an American Regional Label." *Annals of the Association of American Geographers* 75 (1984): 209–20.

——. *The Middle West: Its Meaning in American Culture.* Lawrence: University of Kansas Press, 1989.

Smiley, W. S. "A Comparative Study of the Results Obtained in Instruction in the 'Single Teacher' Rural Schools and the Graded Town Schools." *Elementary School Teacher* 11 (1911): 249–65.

Smith, Patricia Douglass. *Centennial Saga of First United Methodist Church, Garden City, Kansas, 1882–1982: A History of the Church and Its First Records.* Garden City, KS: First United Methodist Church, History Committee, 1982.

Smythe, William E. "Ways and Means in Arid America." *Century Illustrated* 51 (1896): 742–58.

Snyder, C. Hugh. *The Youngest Brother: On a Kansas Wheat Farm during the Roaring Twenties and the Great Depression.* Lincoln, NE: iUniverse, 2005.

Socolofsky, Homer E. "Kansas in 1876." *Kansas Historical Quarterly* 43 (1977): 1–43.

Spence, Polly. *Moving Out: A Nebraska Woman's Life,* edited by Karl Spence Richardson. Lincoln: University of Nebraska Press, 2002.

Steinbeck, John. *The Grapes of Wrath.* New York: Viking, 1939.

——. *The Harvest Gypsies: On the Road to the Grapes of Wrath.* San Francisco: Heyday Books, 2002.

——. *Working Days: The Journals of the Grapes of Wrath.* New York: Penguin, 1990.

Stewart, James I. "Economic Opportunity or Hardship? The Causes of Geographic Mobility on the Agricultural Frontier, 1860–1880." Unpublished paper, Department of History, Northwestern University, 2008.

Stonecipher, E. E. "A Brief History of the One-Teacher School." *Peabody Journal of Education* 25 (1947): 130–38.

Stull, Donald D. "On the Cutting Edge." In *A Place Called Home: Writings on the Midwestern Small Town,* edited by Richard O. Davies, Joseph A. Amato and David R. Pichaske, 390–400. Minneapolis: University of Minnesota Press, 2003.

Stull, Donald D., and Michael J. Broadway. *Any Way You Cut It: Meat Processing and Small-Town America*. Lawrence: University of Kansas Press, 1995.

———. *Slaughterhouse Blues: The Meat and Poultry Industry in North America*. San Francisco: Wadsworth, 2003.

Stull, Donald D., Janet E. Benson, Michael J. Broadway, Arthur L. Campa, Ken C. Erickson, and Mark A. Grey. *Changing Relations: Newcomers and Established Residents in Garden City, Kansas*. Lawrence: University of Kansas, Institute for Public Policy and Business Research, 1990.

Tack, Leland. *Iowa*. Iowa City: Iowa Department of Education, 1999.

Taylor, Carl C. "Rural Life." *American Journal of Sociology* 47 (1942): 841–53.

Thomas, Sue. *A Second Home: Missouri's Early Schools*. Columbia: University of Missouri Press, 2006.

Tocqueville, Alexis de. *Democracy in America*. 1835. Reprint, New York: Harper & Row, 1966.

Torgerson, Randall E. "Farmer Cooperatives." *Annals of the American Academy of Political and Social Science* 429 (1977): 91–102.

Treat, Payson Jackson. *The National Land System*. New York: E. B. Treat & Company, 1910.

Tretbar, Kirsten. *Zenith*. Shawnee Mission, KS: Prairie Fire Films, 2001.

Turner, Frederick Jackson. "The Significance of the Frontier in History." Paper presented at annual meeting of the American Historical Association, Chicago (July 12, 1893). First published in *Proceedings of the State Historical Society of Wisconsin* (December 14, 1893).

Van Metre, Isaiah. *History of Black Hawk County, Iowa, and Representative Citizens*. Chicago: Biographical Publishing Company, 1904.

Vliet, H. Van. "Increased Capital Requirements and the Problem of Getting Started in Farming." *Journal of Farm Economics* 40 (1958): 1613–22.

Wagner, Janelle L. "The First Decade of Educational Governance in Kansas, 1855–1865." *Kansas History* 24 (2001): 36–53.

Warren, Wilson J. *Tied to the Great Packing Machine: The Midwest and Meatpacking*. Iowa City: University of Iowa Press, 2007.

Wenzl, Timothy. *A Legacy of Faith: The History of the Diocese of Dodge City*. Dodge City, KS: Diocese of Dodge City, 2001.

West, James [Carl Withers]. *Plainville, U.S.A.* New York: Columbia University Press, 1945.

Whittier, John Greenleaf. *At Sundown*. Boston: Houghton Mifflin, 1893.

Wilder, Laura Ingalls. *Little House on the Prairie*. 1935. Reprint, New York: Harper & Row, 1953.

Williams, Duane D., and Leonard E. Bloomquist. *From Dust Bowl to Green Circles: A Case Study of Haskell County, Kansas*. Manhattan: Kansas State University Agricultural Experiment Station, Bulletin 662, 1996.

Wilson, Julie. "'Kansas Uber Alles?': The Geography and Ideology of Conquest, 1870–1900." *Western Historical Quarterly* 27 (1996): 170–87.

Wilson, R. H. *Rural School Consolidation*. Oklahoma City: Oklahoma State Board of Education, Committee on Rural Schools, 1911.

Wood, Richard. *Survival of Rural America: Small Victories and Bitter Harvests*. Lawrence: University Press of Kansas, 2008.

Woolston, Howard B. "The Urban Habit of Mind." *American Journal of Sociology* 17 (1912): 602–14.

Works Progress Administration. *Inventory of the County Archives of Kansas: Smith County*. Topeka: Kansas Historical Records Survey, 1941.

Worthy, James C. *William C. Norris: Portrait of a Maverick*. New York: Ballinger, 1987.

Yost, Nellie Snyder. *Buffalo Bill: His Family, Friends, Fame, Failures, and Fortunes*. Chicago: Swallow Books, 1979.

Index

accommodation, *xi*, 16

adaptability, 2, 12, 127; community resilience and, 174; institutional arrangements as context for, 6, 18–19, 22–23 (*See also* cooperatives, agricultural); manufacturing innovation and, 238–39; weather and agricultural, 31

African-Americans, 61, 98, 137, 184, 251–53; education and, 102–4, 105, 110–13, 251–52

agribusiness, *x*; cooperatives as institutional precursors for, 173–75; corporate farming, 10–11, 12, 187; criticisms of, 192–93; and decline of family farms, 10; ethnic diversity and, *xi*, 181; government regulation of, 193–94; immigrant labor and, 171; incentives offered to, 173–74, 197, 198, 210, 211; as market outlet for agricultural products, 141; population growth linked to, 5; and standardized product, 192–93. *See also* meat producing industry; *specific companies*

agriculture: acreage devoted to, 219; climate and weather as factor in, 1, 27, 39–41; cooperative ventures (*See* cooperatives, agricultural); crop diversification, 13, 55, 183; crop insurance, 55; employment compared to meat production industry and construction, 206; farm crisis of 1980s, 17, 18; federal government and, 12, 22, 36, 41, 42, 53; field crops as product, 142; irrigation and, 172, 178, 179, 182–86, 189–92, 197; land as resource for, *xi–xii*, 23; mechanization of, 31, 35; number of farms, 219; packaged foods and, 13, 172, 176, 208, 221, *278*; small towns as dependent on, 134–35, 136, 140–42, 144, *276*; subsistence agriculture by pioneers, 27–29; tenant farmers or sharecroppers and, 31, 34, 37, 53. *See also* agribusiness; economics, agricultural; farming; meat producing industry

Agriculture Conservation Program, 34

ALCO stores, 130, 146, 163–64, 197

Allied-Signal, 224

Ambrose, North Dakota, 137

Anderle, Craig, 153

Andersen, M. J., 64, 72, 75

Anderson, A. D., 195

anti-Semitism, 72

Arapaho Indians, 157

Asians, 184–85, 204–5, 211

associations, community, *277*

Atkinson, Wilmer, 78

Augusta, Kansas, 149, 150

automobiles, 31, 34, 37, 53, 75, 110, 188–89, 218, 236, 258

aviation, infrastructure for, 23, 34, 157, 221–23; avionics, 223–24; Strategic Air Command airfields, 156

avionics, 6, 217, 223–24, 229

Bahr, Joseph, Fr.: as interview source, 211–12, 325n106

Baker, Dixie: as interview source, 204

Bandstra, Bert, 193–95

Barta, Pam, 130; as interview source, 125

Baum, L. Frank, 70–71

BEA economic data, 16–18

beets, 6, 183, 185, 186, 203; as cattle fodder, 190–91, 197; sugar factories, 172, 184–86, 203, 235

Bell, Don, 229

Bell, Earl H., 39–40

bioscience industry, 16, 124, 239, 327n25

biotechnology, 228–30

Bird, Isabella L., 321n51

birth rates, 18, 47–48, 110, 133, 159, 237, *265*, 294n76

Blanchard, Iowa, 137

Bodensteiner, Carol, 75

Born in the Country (Danbom), 57

"brain drain" (out-migration of educated youth), 4, 95, 120–24

Brown, Paul and Evelyn, 40, 150–51

Brown, Roy, 35

Brown v. Board of Education, 111–12

Bryce, James, 116

buffalo, 11, 25, 63, 172